THE AMERICAN ENVIRONMENT:

*Readings in
The History of Conservation*

SECOND EDITION

Edited by
RODERICK NASH
University of California, Santa Barbara

ALFRED · A · KNOPF NEW YORK

For Sandy

THEMES AND SOCIAL FORCES IN AMERICAN HISTORY SERIES
Under the editorship of Robin W. Winks

Purpose: To explore major influences on the development of American society and character.

Second Edition

9876543

Copyright © 1968, 1976 by Newbery Award Records, Inc.

ISBN: 0-394-34922-9

Manufactured in the United States of America

Preface to the Revised Edition

Since the manuscript for the first edition of this book left my hands in 1967, the substance and the intensity of the American conservation movement has changed significantly. The new Part Five documents this development. Additions to the chronology (p. xix) and the bibliography (p. 362) are also intended to extend the usefulness of this book to students, scholars, and professionals in environmentally oriented fields.

For editorial and research assistance in the preparation of the revised edition I am indebted to Merry Tuten, an Environmental Studies major at the University of California, Santa Barbara.

Santa Barbara, California   R.N.
June, 1975

Preface to the First Edition

This book is offered to meet the need for an inexpensive collection of readings illustrating the development of the American conservation movement in theory and practice. This, in turn, forms part of the larger story of the impact of civilization on the American environment. I have not attempted to cover systematically every period and each natural resource. The emphasis is rather on the representative statements of the leading figures in conservation and the major milestones in its progress. In making the selections that follow I have extended the definition of "conservation" beyond its usual limits to include concern with historical sites, roads, even cities—in short, with the total environment. The organization of the parts and the introductory notes, along with the secondary selections, are intended to suggest an interpretative framework for the primary material. While directed to the needs of students and career conservation workers, this book also invites the general reader to sense the excitement of one of America's most important reform crusades.

I am grateful to Robin W. Winks for inspiring the beginning of this book. Donald C. Swain and Clarence A. Schoenfeld made several important suggestions in regard to content and interpretation. The dedication speaks in small part to the debt I owe my wife.

Santa Barbara, California   R. N.
March, 1968

Contents

v

The Potential of Conservation History

Look out the nearest window (if there isn't one, that too is revealing about attitude toward the environment) and consider the face of the land. What you see is a human creation. The tree or shrub or patch of grass is there, in other words, either because men put it there or because they allowed it to remain. Is the vegetation beyond your window carefully manicured, farmed, or growing wild? If the last, is it from choice or neglect? Such questions probe deeply into public tastes, values, and ambitions. Perhaps your glance meets only concrete and asphalt; this exclusion of nature tells something else about a people's preferences. And what of the buildings, utility installations, and other accouterments of civilization? Are they constructed with aesthetic considerations in mind, related to each other, to the landscape, and to human needs, or erected haphazardly?

The point is that any landscape is an artifact—an object made by man. Its condition, rightly seen, reveals a society's culture and traditions as directly as does a novel or a newspaper or a Fourth of July oration because today's environment, the "natural" part included, is synthetic. Especially since the advent of modern technology, man has shaped the face of the earth. He has, in fact, been the primary agent of change. In an hour a bulldozer performs the equivalent of thousands of years of erosion—perhaps more. And the choice *not* to alter the earth, in most regions, now also involves a conscious exercise of human will. The landscape, as a result, either developed or wild, is an historical document. The bulldozer (or its absence), as well as the pen, makes a record that the historian would do well to study. And the realization is growing in regard to the environment that today's choices will in large part determine tomorrow's experiences. So the land, in the last analysis, is not only a document revealing past thought and action but also a slate upon which the present outlines the kind of life it bequeaths to the future.

When consideration of the environment is broadened to include what people have *thought* about it as well as its actual condition, the potential of conservation history is increased. Indeed a new interdisciplinary field concerned with man's understanding of the environment seems imminent. Geographers, psychologists, anthropologists, and ecologists are combining with intellectual and cultural historians and students of literature and speech to investigate the many levels of man's relation to the land. We are only beginning to learn how and why men react to the outdoors. Often such knowledge is buried beneath intertwined layers of custom, symbol, and myth extending back to prehistory. Untangling the meaning of concepts such as garden and wilderness or determining the significance of the color green have astonishing possibilities.

It follows that conservation history may be studied as something more than past politics or economics or the record of resource management. Inextricably involved are ideas about national identity and purpose as well as a society's aesthetic, religious, and ethical convictions. The history of American conservation, in particular, can be made to bear on some of the basic issues in American life. Natural resource policy, for example, is one of the best places to examine the tension between individual freedom and social purpose. Enlightened use of the land demands a limitation on the action of a landowner because the easiest, or most lucrative, method of exploiting a resource is seldom in the best long-term interests of the nation as a whole. But in a society that covets individualism and free enterprise, especially as it concerns the land, how can conservation principles be instituted? The profit motive will not suffice although the payment of bonuses and extension of tax advantages to those who practice conservation has been tried. And, public lands aside, legal coercion is difficult since it means interfering with a man's relationship to his property. Telling an individual, or a corporation, how to manage his land is close enough to telling him how to furnish his house as to make most Americans uneasy. Consequently, conservationists have argued that some kinds of property are less private than others: specifically, those which everyone shares—in the environment. What one does inside one's home is truly private, but when individual action affects rivers and soil and scenery that other people use and see, individual rights must be redefined. Yet the assumption that the land I purchase is "mine" has proven hard to shake.

Faced with this problem, conservation leaders have endeavored to secure the voluntary cooperation of landowners and the sympathy of the citizenry. This explains the frequent justification of conservation in terms of patriotism, prosperity, national strength or greatness, democracy, and efficiency. Such ends, it is argued, are worth the extra cost and effort of intelligent custodianship of the land and its resources. But this line of reasoning evades the idea that land health and beauty are desirable ends in themselves. The relatively small, but increasing, number of American conservationists who have taken this position believe that land has rights which men should respect as part of their ethical code. The same restraints that, in theory, prevent a man from killing his neighbors, they assert, should prevent him from exterminating a species or destroying a forest. To be sure, such advocates of a land ethic as Aldo Leopold (20) * and Stewart Udall (36) were under no illusions about the difficulty of its acceptance. Yet they insisted that such a fundamental shift in values was a prerequisite for the success of conservation. Securing the public's cooperation was as big a problem as devising the techniques for managing the land.

Framed another way, this issue involves the relationship between the expert and the people. Frequently planners and scientists know what to do to further conservation, but persuading the people to apply this knowledge is a different matter. It is the horse-and-water problem in classic form; communication is the key. How does the expert, whose understanding of a situation is often built on years of technical research, convince the nonspecialist and secure his approval for instituting a program of land reform? In a totalitarian state, this is relatively easy: appropriate use of resources is simply decreed. The king's forest will *not* be clear-cut. But the democratic assumptions and institutions of American civilization as well as its pervasive anti-intellectualism (especially in regard to land, common sense is difficult to displace as the source of authority) complicate the matter. Policy decisions concerning the environment must be hacked out of a thicket of contending, often directly contradictory, interests. And once a course of action is set, there is no assurance, given the vagaries of public favor, that it will be continued. This is particularly unfortunate in the case of resources since the land responds slowly to treatment. Political leadership changes much more quickly than the environment.

---

* Throughout the book, numbers in parentheses will be used to refer to the correspondingly numbered selections.

The record of conservation in the United States has direct relevance to assessing the significance of the concepts of the frontier and of abundance in the national experience. A number of scholars have followed Frederick Jackson Turner in suggesting that if we have a national character, it is due to these formative influences. Conservation may be interpreted as an effort to extend both the frontier and abundance beyond the point at which they might otherwise have ended. Clearly, the desire for an easy way to a full stomach is not the only relevant factor here. At stake, many believe, is the perpetuation of American traits and ideals: democracy, individualism, independence, and even the nation's youth and confidence are being "conserved" along with resources. Nor can we discount as a factor in the American conservation movement the vague feeling that there is something special about the New World environment worth preserving —a certain freshness, a chance for a new start and for progress that inspired the transplanted Europeans with messianic expectations. The national sense of pride and identity, in sum, are closely connected to the history of conservation.

Another way conservation serves the study of basic issues in the American experience is in its ability to focus the chronic controversy between utilitarian and aesthetic interests. Obviously a particular natural object, such as a tree, can be claimed by both interests—as lumber or as scenery. The same is true of a canyon that could be dammed for use as a reservoir or preserved as wilderness. The fact that neither tree nor canyon can satisfy both demands simultaneously has given rise to violent alterations. In the context of allocating resources Americans have been confronted with basic questions of value and ultimately with choices about the nature of their civilization. Frequently the issue reduces to the question of whether the nation, with its well-known material abilities and appetites, also possesses an aesthetic and spiritual sense.

Conservation history is important for the way it illuminates the advantages and limitations of our custodianship of the land. Anyone professionally concerned with resource policy or involved in a citizens' crusade can benefit from knowing how his predecessors formulated ideas, secured the public approval necessary for their institutionalization, and evaluated their results. In attempting to "sell" conservation policies today, it is especially important to know something of the national taste in environment. Such information is perhaps best derived from an examination of how this task was formed.

Two pitfalls are commonly encountered in the teaching and writing of the history of resource management. The first is to speak of "conservation" as if it denoted a single school of thought. In fact, as some of the statements in this volume will reveal, conflicts among conservationists are as frequent and bitter as those between them and the parties they seek to restrain and reform. Pronounced differences in ends separate those who would preserve the environment for recreation from those who would develop its resources, albeit wisely, in the public's economic interest. Yet both factions (best represented today by the dam-building Bureau of Reclamation and the wilderness-minded Sierra Club) vigorously insist that they are conservationists. Even those in closely related fields often find themselves at odds: the optimum conditions for ducks are not the most conducive for the propagation of fish, and "outdoor recreation" ranges from wilderness backpacking to roadside picnicing. Yet in spite of evidence to the contrary, politicians, journalists, scholars, and the public at large usually refer to "conservation" as a unified interest. Part of the difficulty stems from the fact that nobody today is really against conservation any more than they are against peace or freedom. But when more specific definitions are demanded, the rhetorical similarity disappears.

The second common mistake is to approach the history of the environment with a manichean orientation. It is easy, in writing about the landscape, to fall into the rhetoric of moralism—the "good guys" versus the "bad guys." Most accounts of American conservation contain at some point an elegiac description of the "unspoiled" continent: once the country was beautiful and rich in resources, but then came the "greedy exploiters" who "raped" the "virgin" land. Such a representation unjustly uses the emotions of the present to describe the actions of the past. It fails to employ historical sympathy, to understand the past in its own terms. Neither the pioneers nor most subsequent resource developers considered themselves unthinking spoilers or were regarded as such by their contemporaries. Instead, they acted in a manner consistent with their environmental circumstances and intellectual heritage. When the forest seemed limitless, cut-out-and-get-out was an appropriate response. Certainly early Americans made mistakes in using the land, but they became such only in the opinion of later generations. Rather than shaking moralistic fingers, conservation historians would do well to attempt to understand why men acted as they did toward the environment.

The selections presented in this text not only concern natural resources; they also reflect distinctive traits of the American character. Almost uniquely among modern peoples, the emigrants who settled the New World had the opportunity and the responsibility to make their own environment. Nothing was inherited in this respect but wilderness. Asians or Europeans of the same era, on the contrary, had no alternative but to live in a physical setting shaped by thousands of years of occupancy. Except in a limited way, the landscape could not express their preferences. North Americans, on the contrary, had, and to some extent still have, the chance to make fundamental choices about the character of their environment. Attitudes toward the past, contemporary tastes, and ideals for the future combine to influence such decisions. There are, in sum, few richer lodes than conservation history from which to mine an understanding of American culture.

A Chronology of Important Events

1626 — Plymouth Colony passes ordinances regulating the cutting and sale of timber on colony lands.

1639 — Newport, Rhode Island, prohibits deer hunting for six months of the year.

1681 — William Penn, proprietor of Pennsylvania, decrees that for every five acres of land cleared, one must be left forested.

1691 — British colonial policy provides for reserving large trees, suitable for masts, in New England by marking them with a "broad arrow."

1828 — First experiment in federal forest management with live oaks
1831 — on Santa Rosa Peninsula, Florida.

1832 — George Catlin proposes a national park.

1849 — U.S. Department of the Interior established.

1858 — Mount Vernon purchased as an historical site.

1864 — Yosemite Valley, California, reserved as a state park.

1864 — George Perkins Marsh publishes *Man and Nature*.

1869 — John Wesley Powell descends the Colorado River through the Grand Canyon.

1871 — U.S. Fish Commission created.

1872 — Arbor Day designated as April 10 as a result of the efforts of J. Sterling Morton.

1872 — Yellowstone National Park established.

1875 — American Forestry Association organized.

1876 — Appalachian Mountain Club organized.

1879 — U.S. Geological Survey established.

1881 — Division of Forestry created in the Department of Agriculture as a fact-finding agency.

1882 — American Forestry Congress organized.

1885 — New York, in cooperation with Ontario, creates the Niagara Reservation, protecting the Falls.

1885 — New York establishes the Adirondack Forest Preserve (later Adirondack State Park).

1885 — Predecessor of the U.S. Biological Survey created in the Department of Agriculture as the Division of Economic Ornithology and Mammalogy.

1885 — Boone and Crockett Club founded.

1886 — New York Audubon Society organized.

1886 — Bernhard E. Fernow assumes direction of an expanded Division of Forestry.

1891 — Forest Reserve Act permits the President to establish forest reserves (later National Forests) on the public domain.

1891 — Yosemite National Park established.

1891 — National Irrigation Congress organized.

1892 — Sierra Club founded.

1895 — American Scenic and Hisoric Preservation Society founded.

1897 — Forest Management Act defines purpose of the forest reserves.

1898 — First college-level work in forestry offered at Cornell.

1898 — Gifford Pinchot named head of the Division of Forestry.

1900 — Society of American Foresters founded.

1900 — Lacey Act makes interstate shipment of game killed in violation of state laws a federal offense.

1902 — Reclamation (Newlands) Act establishes Bureau of Reclamation in the Department of the Interior and launches a federal reclamation program.

1905 — National Audubon Society formed.

1905 — Forest reserves transferred from the Department of the Interior to the Forest Service within Department of Agriculture.

1906 — Antiquities Act permits reservation of areas of scientific or historical interest on federal land as national monuments.

1907 — Inland Waterways Commission established.

1908 — Grand Canyon of the Colorado made a National Monument.

1908 — Theodore Roosevelt hosts a conference of Governors at the White House on the subject of conservation.

1908 — National Conservation Commission appointed to inventory resources.

1909 ⎱
1910 ⎰ — The Ballinger-Pinchot controversy disrupts the conservation movement.

1909 — North American Conservation Conference held in Washington.

1909 — National Conservation Association organized as a private group to replace the National Conservation Commission.

1910 — The Forest Products Laboratory established by the Forest Service in Madison, Wisconsin.

1911 — American Game Protective and Propagation Association founded.

1911 — Weeks Act, permitting purchase of forested land at headwaters of navigable streams for inclusion in the National Forest system, makes possible the establishment of National Forests in the East.

1913 — Hetch Hetchy Valley in Yosemite National Park granted to San Francisco for a reservoir after prolonged controversy.

1916 — National Park Service Act.

1918 — Migratory Bird Treaty Act implements 1916 treaty with Canada to restrict hunting of migratory species.

1918 — Save-the-Redwoods-League founded.

1920 — Mineral Leasing Act regulates mining on federal lands.

1920 — Federal Water Power Act gives the Federal Power Commission authority to issue licenses for hydropower development on public lands.

1922 — Izaak Walton League organized.

1924 — Teapot Dome scandal.

1924 — The Forest Service designates first extensive wilderness area in the Gila National Forest, New Mexico.

1924 — The first National Conference on Outdoor Recreation held in Washington, D.C.

1924 — Clarke-McNary Act extends federal ability to buy lands for inclusion in the National Forest system and provides for private, state, and federal cooperation in forest management.

1926 — Restoration of Williamsburg, Virginia, begun.

1928 — Boulder Canyon Project (Hoover Dam) authorized.

1928 — McSweeney-McNary Act authorizes a broad program of federal forestry research.

1933 — Civilian Conservation Corps established.

1933 — Tennessee Valley Authority created.

1933 — Franklin D. Roosevelt creates the Soil Erosion Service as an emergency measure.

1934 — Taylor Grazing Act provides for federal regulation of use of unreserved public domain.

1935 — Soil Conservation Act extends federal involvement in erosion control and establishes the Soil Conservation Service in the Department of Agriculture.

1935 — Wilderness Society founded.

1936 — Omnibus Flood Control Act establishes a national flood prevention policy under the U.S. Army Corps of Engineers and the Department of Agriculture.

1937 — Pittman-Robertson Act makes federal funds available to states for wildlife protection and propagation.

1939 — Forest Service "U" regulations extend the policy of wilderness preservation in the National Forests.

1940 — The creation of the U.S. Fish and Wildlife Service consolidates federal activities in this area.

1944 — Soil Conservation Society of America founded.

1946 — U.S. Bureau of Land Management established to consolidate the administration of the public domain.

1948 — Federal Water Pollution Control Law enacted to regulate waste disposal.

1949 — The first Sierra Club Biennial Wilderness Conference held.

1949 — Congress charters the National Trust for Historic Preservation.

1956 — Mission 66 launched as a ten-year improvement program for the National Parks.

1956 — Echo Park Dam scheduled for construction in Dinosaur National Monument deleted from the Upper Colorado River

Storage Project marking a major victory for wilderness preservation and the National Park system.

1958 — Congress appoints the Outdoor Recreation Resources Review Commission to study and report on the nation's future needs.

1959 — Canada and the United States complete the St. Lawrence Seaway.

1960 — The Multiple Use Act further defines the purpose of the National Forests.

1962 — John F. Kennedy hosts a White House Conference on Conservation.

1963 — Clean Air Act appropriates funds for a cooperative attack on air pollution.

1963 — The Bureau of Outdoor Recreation established within the Department of the Interior to coordinate federal efforts.

1964 — Land and Water Conservation Fund Act makes money available for local, state, and federal acquisition and development of park land and open space.

1964 — Wilderness Act establishes the National Wilderness Preservation System.

1965 — Lyndon B. Johnson hosts a White House Conference on Natural Beauty.

1966 — National Historic Preservation Act passed.

1968 — Paul Ehrlich publishes *The Population Bomb.*

1968 — National Wild and Scenic Rivers Act passed.

1969 — Santa Barbara, California oil spill.

1969 — Mankind's first contact with the moon dramatizes the idea of the earth as a spaceship.

1970 — National Environmental Policy Act of 1969 approved January 1.

1970 — First "Earth Day" celebrated April 22.

1970 — Clean Air Act.

1971 — Congress abandons support of the supersonic transport airplane.

1972 — United Nations Conference on the Human Environment held in Stockholm.

1972 — The Club of Rome's issuance of *The Limits to Growth* triggers worldwide debate.

1973 — Walt Disney interests abandon plans for a winter resort in Mineral King Valley, California.

1973 — Congress authorizes construction of an 800-mile oil pipeline across Alaska.

1974 — Oil shortages precipitate an "energy crisis" and retard environmental movement.

1975 — World Environment Day (June 5) marked by circulation of EARTHCARE petition.

Part One

The Conservation Impulse

Part One

The Conservation Impulse

From his beginnings in the early Pleistocene until only yesterday, geologically speaking, man directed his energies to conquering, not conserving, the environment. Such behavior was entirely appropriate for a people whose very survival depended on breaking nature to their will. With the sabretooth only a jump behind, conservation was inconceivable. In the first place, natural resources seemed inexhaustible—the problem was too many rather than too few trees. Moreover, the Judeo-Christian tradition taught that as the result of a gift from God the natural world belonged to man for his exploitation. Genesis 1:28 commanded the first couple to "be fruitful, and multiply, and replenish the earth, and subdue it: and have dominion over the fish of the sea, and over the fowl of the air, and over every living thing that moveth upon the earth." The environment, it followed, existed solely for the satisfaction of man's immediate desires.

The early Christian also sensed that concern about the natural environment was irrelevant since its destruction at the hands of a wrathful God appeared imminent. The Western religious focus was on preparation for another world, not concern for and enjoyment of the present one.

The first Americans stood squarely in this tradition. Their transatlantic migration to a wilderness stripped away centuries, recreating the fears and drives of primitive man. Later generations of frontiersmen continued the pattern. A massive assault was directed at the New World environment in the name of civilization and Christianity. Progress became synonymous with exploitation. Men slashed the earth in pursuit of raw materials. The strength of individualism and competitiveness in the American value system supported the pioneer's (and his descendant, the entrepreneur's) insistence that the land he owned could be used as he willed. The long term interest of society made little difference. Considerations of

3

immediate profit dictated the relationship with the land. A scarcity of natural resources? Absurd! Over the next ridge was a cornucopia of wood, water, soil, and game! Up to the late 19th century, in short, Americans experienced a population-to-land ratio unconducive to the conservation idea. But with the ratio reversed, with man in control and his needs pressing against the capacity of the earth to fulfill them, conservation made sense.

The attitude toward natural resources subsequently labeled "conservation" received its first major statement in the writings from which the following selections are taken. To be sure, there had been earlier pleas for caution with certain natural resources, but they were neither extended beyond local problems nor argued with much sophistication. The first American conservationists, here represented, had in common a willingness to challenge the dominant conception of the land's purpose and to expose inexhaustibility as a myth. They were also prepared to question the dogma of free enterprise which balked at the prospect of government regulation in society's interest. Finally, a few of the conservation pioneers made so bold as to suggest that growth and quantity were not the only possible criteria for progress and for happiness. The kind of the life lived amid abundance, they implied, also had its claims and sometimes, as in the case of parks, demanded that limits be set to civilization's expansion.

In considering the following statements it is important to bear in mind the long, pervasive, anticonservation tradition against which they were arrayed. Far from being considered heroes or prophets in nineteenth-century America, the authors of these documents were generally regarded as unprogressive cranks. But time was on their side. The conditions which prompted their concern were becoming increasingly obvious to larger numbers, and when the Progressive conservation crusade (Part Two) began, it was these harbingers who furnished inspiration and prescription.

1

An Artist Proposes a National Park
GEORGE CATLIN (1832)

George Catlin's frequent travels in the West for the purpose of studying and painting the American Indian gave him ample opportunity to observe the effects of an advancing civilization. In the spring of 1832, Catlin set out for the headwaters of the Missouri. In May he arrived at Fort Pierre, in present-day South Dakota, where he made these observations in his journal. They first appeared in print that winter in a New York newspaper and later as part of Catlin's North American Indians.

Catlin's plea is outstanding as the first recognition (by twenty-five years) of the fact that without formal preservation the remaining American wilderness would vanish. Although overshadowed in reputation by Henry David Thoreau (2) and John Muir (14), Catlin deserves credit for originating the national park idea. Fifty years after his journal entry Congress established a 2,000,000-acre reserve several hundred miles west of Fort Pierre, and Catlin had his "monument" in Yellowstone National Park.

When I first arrived at this place, on my way up the river, which was in the month of May, in 1832, and had taken up my lodgings in the Fur Company's Fort, . . . [I was told] that only a few days before I arrived (when an immense herd of buffaloes had showed themselves on the opposite side of the river, almost blackening the plains for a great distance), a party of five or six hundred Sioux Indians on horseback, forded the river about mid-day, and spending a few hours amongst them, recrossed the river at sun-down and came into the Fort with *fourteen hundred fresh buffalo tongues*, which were thrown down in a mass, and for which they required but a few gallons of whiskey, which was soon demolished, indulging them in a little, and harmless carouse.

This profligate waste of the lives of these noble and useful animals, when, from all that I could learn, not a skin or a pound of the

George Catlin, *North American Indians: Being Letters and Notes on their Manners, Customs, and Conditions, Written during Eight Years' Travel amongst the Wildest Tribes in North America, 1832–1839* (2 vols. London, 1880), I, 288–295. In this selection and elsewhere, I have silently changed obvious errors in spelling and punctuation. [Ed.]

meat (except the tongues), was brought in, fully supports me in the seemingly extravagant predictions that I have made as to their extinction, which I am certain is near at hand. . . .

From the above remarks it will be seen, that not only the red men, but red men and white, have aimed destruction at the race of these animals . . . .

Thus much I wrote of the buffaloes, and . . . of the fate that awaits them; and before I closed my book [i.e., diary or journal], I strolled out one day to the shade of a plum-tree, where I lay in the grass on a favourite bluff, and wrote thus:—

It is generally supposed, and familiarly said that a man 'falls' into a rêverie; but I seated myself in the shade a few minutes since, resolved to *force* myself into one; and for this purpose I laid open a small pocket-map of North America, and excluding my thoughts from every other object in the world, I soon succeeded in producing the desired illusion. This little chart, over which I bent, was seen in all its parts, as nothing but the green and vivid reality. I was lifted up upon an imaginary pair of wings, which easily raised and held me floating in the open air, from whence I could behold beneath me the Pacific and the Atlantic Oceans—the great cities of the East, and the mighty rivers. I could see the blue chain of the great lakes at the North—the Rocky Mountains, and beneath them and near their base, the vast, and almost boundless plains of grass, which were speckled with the bands of grazing buffaloes!

The world turned gently around, and I examined its surface; continent after continent passed under my eye, and yet amidst them all, I saw not the vast and vivid green, that is spread like a carpet over the Western wilds of my own country. I saw not elsewhere in the world, the myriad herds of buffaloes—my eyes scanned in vain for they were not. And when I turned again to the wilds of my native land, I beheld them all in motion! For the distance of several hundreds of miles from North to South, they were wheeling about in vast columns and herds—some were scattered, and ran with furious wildness—some lay dead, and others were pawing the earth for a hiding-place—some were were sinking down and dying, gushing out their life's blood in deep-drawn sighs—and others were contending in furious battle for the life they possessed, and the ground that they stood upon. They had long since assembled from the thickets, and secret haunts of the deep forest, into the midst of the treeless and bushless plains, as the place for their safety. I could see in an hundred places, amid the wheeling bands, and on their skirts and flanks, the leaping wild horse darting among them. I saw not the arrows, nor heard the twang of the sinewy bows that sent them; but I saw their victims fall!—on other steeds that rushed along their sides, I saw the glistening lances, which seemed to lay across them; their blades were blazing in the sun, till dipped in blood, and then I lost them! In other parts (and there were many), the vivid flash of *fire-arms* was seen—*their* victims fell too, and over their dead bodies hung suspended in air, little clouds of whitened smoke, from under which the flying horsemen had darted forward to mingle again with, and deal death to, the trampling throng.

. . . Hundreds and thousands were strewed upon the plains— they were flayed, and their reddened carcasses left; and about them bands of wolves, and dogs, and buzzards were seen devouring them. Contiguous, and in sight, were the distant and feeble smokes of wigwams and villages, where the skins were dragged, and dressed for white man's luxury! where they were all sold for *whiskey*, and the poor Indians lay drunk, and were crying. I cast my eyes into the towns and cities of the East, and there I beheld buffalo robes hanging at almost every door for traffic; and I saw also the curling smokes of a thousand *Stills* *—and I said, 'Oh insatiable man, is thy avarice such! wouldst thou tear the skin from the back of the last animal of this noble race, *and rob thy fellow-man of his meat, and for it give him poison!'*

Many are the rudenesses and wilds in Nature's works, which are destined to fall before the deadly axe and desolating hands of cultivating man; and so amongst her ranks of *living*, of beast and human, we often find noble stamps, or beautiful colours, to which our admiration clings; and even in the overwhelming march of civilised improvements and refinements do we love to cherish their existence, and lend our efforts to preserve them in their primitive rudeness. Such of Nature's works are always worthy of our preservation and protection; and the further we become separated (and the face of the country) from that pristine wildness and beauty, the more pleasure does the mind of enlightened man feel in recurring to those scenes, when he can have them preserved for his eyes and his mind to dwell upon.

Of such "rudenesses and wilds," Nature has nowhere presented more beautiful and lovely scenes, than those of the vast prairies of the

---

* Devices for making whiskey. [Ed.]

West; and of *man* and *beast,* no nobler specimens than those who inhabit them—the *Indian* and the *buffalo*—joint and original tenants of the soil, and fugitives together from the approach of civilised man; they have fled to the great plains of the West, and there, under an equal doom, they have taken up their *last abode,* where their race will expire, and their bones will bleach together.

It may be that *power* is *right,* and *voracity* a *virtue;* and that these people, and these noble animals, are *righteously* doomed to an issue that *will* not be averted. It can be easily proved—we have a civilised science that can easily do it, or anything else that may be required to cover the iniquities of civilised man in catering for his unholy appetites. It can be proved that the weak and ignorant have no *rights*—that there can be no virtue in darkness—that God's gifts have no meaning or merit until they are appropriated by civilised man—by him brought into the light, and converted to his use and luxury. . . .

Reader! Listen to the following calculations, and forget them not. The buffaloes (the quadrupeds from whose backs your beautiful robes were taken, and whose myriads were once spread over the whole country, from the Rocky Mountains to the Atlantic Ocean) have recently fled before the appalling appearance of civilised man, and taken up their abode and pasturage amid the almost boundless prairies of the West. An instinctive dread of their deadly foes, who made an easy prey of them whilst grazing in the forest, has led them to seek the midst of the vast and treeless plains of grass, as the spot where they would be least exposed to the assaults of their enemies; and it is exclusively in those desolate fields of silence (yet of beauty) that they are to be found—and over these vast steppes, or prairies, have they fled, like the Indian, towards the "setting sun;" until their bands have been crowded together, and their limits confined to a narrow strip of country on this side of the Rocky Mountains.

This strip of country, which extends from the province of Mexico to Lake Winnipeg on the North, is almost one entire plain of grass, which is, and ever must be, useless to cultivating man. It is here, and here chiefly, that the buffaloes dwell; and with, and hovering about them, live and flourish the tribes of Indians, whom God made for the enjoyment of that fair land and its luxuries.

It is a melancholy contemplation for one who has travelled as I have, through these realms, and seen this noble animal in all its pride and glory, to contemplate it so rapidly wasting from the world, drawing the irresistible conclusion too, which one must do, that its species is soon to be extinguished, and with it the peace and happiness (if not the actual existence) of the tribes of Indians who are joint tenants with them, in the occupancy of these vast and idle plains.

And what a splendid contemplation too, when one (who has travelled these realms, and can duly appreciate them) imagines them as they *might* in future be seen (by some great protecting policy of government) preserved in their pristine beauty and wildness, in a *magnificent park*, where the world could see for ages to come, the native Indian in his classic attire, galloping his wild horse, with sinewy bow, and shield and lance, amid the fleeting herds of elks and buffaloes. What a beautiful and thrilling specimen for America to preserve and hold up to the view of her refined citizens and the world, in future ages! A *nation's Park*, containing man and beast, in all the wild and freshness of their nature's beauty!

I would ask no other monument to my memory, nor any other enrolment of my name amongst the famous dead, than the reputation of having been the founder of such an institution. . . .

2

The Transcendental View
HENRY DAVID THOREAU (1851)

The ideas of Henry David Thoreau underlie many subsequent American interpretations of the significance of nature. A Transcendentalist, Thoreau believed that the natural world symbolized or reflected spiritual truth and moral law. And nature, especially in its wilder forms, possessed a fertilizing vitality that civilized men needed for strength and creativity. Thoreau personally found such nourishment near his Concord, Massachusetts, home and on occasional forays into northern Maine. His writings attempted to convince his contemporaries of their shortsightedness in prizing only the material potential of the environment. As early as 1858 he joined Catlin (1)

Henry David Thoreau, "Walking," in *Excursions, The Writings of Henry David Thoreau*, Riverside edition (11 vols. Boston, 1893) **IX**, 251, 258–260, 264–267, 275, 277–280, 292.

in calling specifically for the preservation of wilderness in national parks. But, like Catlin, Thoreau spoke a half-century before most Americans were prepared to listen sympathetically to his message. Nevertheless, his philosophy survived to become the intellectual foundation of an important part of the American conservation movement [see (13), (14), (23), and (33)].

Thoreau first composed "Walking," below, in 1851 as a lecture before the Concord Lyceum. It is crowded with ideas about the significance of the American environment for patriotism, character, and culture.

I wish to speak a word for Nature, for absolute freedom and wildness, as contrasted with a freedom and culture merely civil,—to regard man as an inhabitant, or a part and parcel of Nature, rather than a member of society. I wish to make an extreme statement, if so I may make an emphatic one, for there are enough champions of civilization: the minister and the school-committee and every one of you will take care of that. . . .

When we walk, we naturally go to the fields and woods: what would become of us, if we walked only in a garden or a mall? . . . Of course it is of no use to direct our steps to the woods, if they do not carry us thither. I am alarmed when it happens that I have walked a mile into the woods bodily, without getting there in spirit. In my afternoon walk I would fain forget all my morning occupations and my obligations to society. But it sometimes happens that I cannot easily shake off the village. . . .

Nowadays almost all man's improvements, so called, as the building of houses, and the cutting down of the forest and of all large trees, simply deform the landscape, and make it more and more tame and cheap. A people who would begin by burning the fences and let the forest stand! . . .

I can easily walk ten, fifteen, twenty, any number of miles, commencing at my own door, without going by any house, without crossing a road except where the fox and the mink do: first along by the river, and then the brook, and then the meadow and the woodside. There are square miles in my vicinity which have no inhabitant. From many a hill I can see civilization and the abodes of man afar. The farmers and their works are scarcely more obvious than woodchucks and their burrows. Man and his affairs, church and state and school, trade and commerce, and manufactures and agriculture, even politics, the most alarming of them all,—I am pleased to see how little space they occupy in the landscape. . . .

At present, in this vicinity, the best part of the land is not private property; the landscape is not owned, and the walker enjoys comparative freedom. But possibly the day will come when it will be partitioned off into so-called pleasure-grounds, in which a few will take a narrow and exclusive pleasure only,—when fences shall be multiplied, and man-traps and other engines invented to confine men to the *public* road, and walking over the surface of God's earth shall be construed to mean trespassing on some gentleman's grounds. . . .

What is it that makes it so hard sometimes to determine whither we will walk? I believe that there is a subtle magnetism in Nature, which, if we unconsciously yield to it, will direct us aright. It is not indifferent to us which way we walk. There is a right way; but we are very liable from heedlessness and stupidity to take the wrong one. We would fain take that walk, never yet taken by us through this actual world, which is perfectly symbolical of the path which we love to travel in the interior and ideal world; and sometimes, no doubt, we find it difficult to choose our direction, because it does not yet exist distinctly in our idea.

When I go out of the house for a walk, uncertain as yet whither I will bend my steps, and submit myself to my instinct to decide for me, I find, strange and whimsical as it may seem, that I finally and inevitably settle southwest, toward some particular wood or meadow or deserted pasture or hill in that direction. My needle is slow to settle,—varies a few degrees, and does not always point due southwest, it is true, and it has good authority for this variation, but it always settles between west and south-southwest. The future lies that way to me, and the earth seems more unexhausted and richer on that side. . . . Eastward I go only by force; but westward I go free. Thither no business leads me. It is hard for me to believe that I shall find fair landscapes or sufficient wildness and freedom behind the eastern horizon. I am not excited by the prospect of a walk thither; but I believe that the forest which I see in the western horizon stretches uninterruptedly toward the setting sun, and there are no towns nor cities in it of enough consequence to disturb me. Let me live where I will, on this side is the city, on that the wilderness, and ever I am leaving the city more and more, and withdrawing into the wilderness. I should not lay so much stress on this fact, if I did not believe that something like this is the prevailing tendency of my countrymen. I must walk toward Oregon, and not toward Europe. And that way the nation is moving, and I may say that mankind progress from east to west. . . .

We go eastward to realize history and study the works of art and literature, retracing the steps of the race; we go westward as into the future, with a spirit of enterprise and adventure. The Atlantic is a Lethean stream, in our passage over which we have had an opportunity to forget the Old World and its institutions. . . .

The West of which I speak is but another name for the Wild; and what I have been preparing to say is, that in Wildness is the preservation of the World. Every tree sends its fibres forth in search of the Wild. The cities import it at any price. Men plough and sail for it. From the forest and wilderness come the tonics and barks which brace mankind. Our ancestors were savages. The story of Romulus and Remus being suckled by a wolf is not a meaningless fable. The founders of every state which has risen to eminence have drawn their nourishment and vigor from a similar wild source. It was because the children of the Empire were not suckled by the wolf that they were conquered and displaced by the children of the northern forests who were.

I believe in the forest, and in the meadow, and in the night in which the corn grows. We require an infusion of hemlock-spruce or arbor vitæ in our tea. . . .

I would not have every man nor every part of a man cultivated, any more than I would have every acre of earth cultivated: part will be tillage, but the greater part will be meadow and forest, not only serving an immediate use, but preparing a mould against a distant future, by the annual decay of the vegetation which it supports. . . .

Ben Jonson exclaims,—

How near to good is what is fair!

So I would say,—

How near to good is what is wild!

Life consists with wildness. The most alive is the wildest. Not yet subdued to man, is presence refreshes him. One who pressed forward incessantly and never rested from his labors, who grew fast and made infinite demands on life, would always find himself in a new country or wilderness, and surrounded by the raw material of life. He would be climbing over the prostrate stems of primitive forest-trees.

Hope and the future for me are not in lawns and cultivated fields, not in towns and cities, but in the impervious and quaking swamps. . . . I derive more of my subsistence from the swamps which sur-

round my native town than from the cultivated gardens in the village. . . .
My spirits infallibly rise in proportion to the outward dreariness.
Give me the ocean, the desert, or the wilderness! . . . A town is saved,
not more by the righteous men in it than by the woods and swamps
that surround it. A township where one primitive forest waves above
while another primitive forest rots below,—such a town is fitted to
raise not only corn and potatoes, but poets and philosophers for the
coming ages. In such a soil grew Homer and Confucius and the rest,
and out of such a wilderness comes the Reformer eating locusts and
wild honey.

3

Man's Responsibility for the Land
GEORGE PERKINS MARSH (1864)

*For most of his history man simply accepted the environment into which he
was born as a fact of life—a given. George Perkins Marsh, a Vermonter
whose varied career included extensive travel in Europe and the Near
East, was one of the first Americans to understand that the condition of the
land was as much a product of man as of nature. In* Man and Nature; or,
Physical Geography as Modified by Human Action, *published in 1864,
Marsh contended that man's power to transform the natural world should
entail a commensurate sense of responsibility. That it did not, he warned,
constituted one of the gravest threats to the welfare, indeed the survival, of
civilization. Focusing most of his book on the disastrous consequences of
deforestation for water supply, Marsh pointed to empires whose declines
paralleled that of their woodlands. His examples were so dramatic and his
argument for remedial action so persuasive that* Man and Nature *exerted a
profound influence on the beginnings of American conservation. Marsh's
concept of "geographical regeneration," presented below, was a harbinger
of regional reclamation efforts such as that involving the Tennessee Valley
(25).*

George P. Marsh, *Man and Nature; or, Physical Georgraphy as Modified
by Human Action* (New York, Charles Scribner, 1864), [iii], 35–41, 45–47,
328–329. Marsh's footnotes have been omitted.

The object of the present volume is: to indicate the character and, approximately, the extent of the changes produced by human action in the physical conditions of the globe we inhabit; to point out the dangers of imprudence and the necessity of caution in all operations which, on a large scale, interfere with the spontaneous arrangements of the organic or the inorganic world; to suggest the possibility and the importance of the restoration of disturbed harmonies and the material improvement of waste and exhausted regions; and, incidentally, to illustrate the doctrine, that man is, in both kind and degree, a power of a higher order than any of the other forms of animated life, which, like him, are nourished at the table of bounteous nature. . . .

Man has too long forgotten that the earth was given to him for usufruct alone, not for consumption, still less for profligate waste. Nature has provided against the absolute destruction of any of her elementary matter, the raw material of her works; the thunderbolt and the tornado, the most convulsive throes of even the volcano and the earthquake, being only phenomena of decomposition and recomposition. But she has left it within the power of man irreparably to derange the combinations of inorganic matter and of organic life, which through the night of æons she had been proportioning and balancing, to prepare the earth for his habitation, when, in the fulness of time, his Creator should call him forth to enter into its possession.

. . . man is everywhere a disturbing agent. Wherever he plants his foot, the harmonies of nature are turned to discords. The proportions and accommodations which insured the stability of existing arrangements are overthrown. Indigenous vegetable and animal species are extirpated, and supplanted by others of foreign origin, spontaneous production is forbidden or restricted, and the face of the earth is either laid bare or covered with a new and reluctant growth of vegetable forms, and with alien tribes of animal life. These intentional changes and substitutions constitute, indeed, great revolutions; but vast as is their magnitude and importance, they are . . . insignificant in comparison with the contingent and unsought results which have flowed from them.

The fact that, of all organic beings, man alone is to be regarded as essentially a destructive power, and that he wields energies to resist which, nature—that nature whom all material life and all inorganic substance obey—is wholly impotent, tends to prove that, though living in physical nature, he is not of her, that he is of more exalted parentage, and belongs to a higher order of existences than those born of her womb and submissive to her dictates.

There are, indeed, brute destroyers, beasts and birds and insects of prey—all animal life feeds upon, and, of course, destroys other life,—but this destruction is balanced by compensations. It is, in fact, the very means by which the existence of one tribe of animals or of vegetables is secured against being smothered by the encroachments of another; and the reproductive powers of species, which serve as the food of others, are always proportioned to the demand they are destined to supply. Man pursues his victims with reckless destructiveness; and, while the sacrifice of life by the lower animals is limited by the cravings of appetite, he unsparingly persecutes, even to extirpation, thousands of organic forms which he cannot consume.

The earth was not, in its natural condition, completely adapted to the use of man, but only to the sustenance of wild animals and wild vegetation. . . .

[But men] . . . cannot subsist and rise to the full development of their higher properties, unless brute and unconscious nature be effectually combated, and, in a great degree, vanquished by human art. Hence, a certain measure of transformation of terrestrial surface, of suppression of natural, and stimulation of artificially modified productivity becomes necessary. This measure man has unfortunately exceeded. He has felled the forests whose network of fibrous roots bound the mould to the rocky skeleton of the earth; but had he allowed here and there a belt of woodland to reproduce itself by spontaneous propagation, most of the mischiefs which his reckless destruction of the natural protection of the soil has occasioned would have been averted. He has broken up the mountain reservoirs, the percolation of whose waters through unseen channels supplied the fountains that refreshed his cattle and fertilized his fields; but he has neglected to maintain the cisterns and the canals of irrigation which a wise antiquity had constructed to neutralize the consequences of its own imprudence. While he has torn the thin glebe [i.e., soil] which confined the light earth of extensive plains, and has destroyed the fringe of semi-aquatic plants which skirted the coast and checked the drifting of the sea sand, he has failed to prevent the spreading of the dunes by clothing them with artificially propogated vegetation. He has ruthlessly warred on all the tribes of animated nature whose spoil he could convert to his own uses, and he has not protected the birds which prey on the insects most destructive to his own harvests.

Purely untutored humanity, it is true, interferes comparatively little with the arrangements of nature, and the destructive agency of man becomes more and more energetic and unsparing as he advances in civilization, until the impoverishment, with which his exhaustion of the natural resources of the soil is threatening him, at last awakens him to the necessity of preserving what is left, if not of restoring what has been wantonly wasted. The wandering savage grows no cultivated vegetable, fells no forest, and extirpates no useful plant, no noxious weed. If his skill in the chase enables him to entrap numbers of the animals on which he feeds, he compensates this loss by destroying also the lion, the tiger, the wolf, the otter, the seal, and the eagle, thus indirectly protecting the feebler quadrupeds and fish and fowls, which would otherwise become the booty of beasts and birds of prey. But with stationary life, or rather with the pastoral state, man at once commences an almost indiscriminate warfare upon all the forms of animal and vegetable existence around him, and as he advances in civilization, he gradually eradicates or transforms every spontaneous product of the soil he occupies. . . .

It is, on the one hand, rash and unphilosophical to attempt to set limits to the ultimate power of man over inorganic nature, and it is unprofitable, on the other, to speculate on what may be accomplished by the discovery of now unknown and unimagined natural forces, or even by the invention of new arts and new processes. But since we have seen aerostation, the motive power of elastic vapors, the wonders of modern telegraphy, the destructive explosiveness of gunpowder, and even of a substance so harmless, unresisting, and inert as cotton, nothing in the way of mechanical achievement seems impossible, and it is hard to restrain the imagination from wandering forward a couple of generations to an epoch when our descendants shall have advanced as far beyond us in physical conquest, as we have marched beyond the trophies erected by our grandfathers.

I must therefore be understood to mean only, that no agencies now known to man and directed by him seem adequate to the reducing of great Alpine precipices to such slopes as would enable them to support a vegetable clothing, or to the covering of large extents of denuded rock with earth, and planting upon them a forest growth. But among the mysteries which science is yet to reveal, there may be still undiscovered methods of accomplishing even grander wonders than these. Mechanical philosophers have suggested the possibility of accumulating and treasuring up for human use some of the greater natural forces, which the action of the elements puts forth with such astonishing energy. Could we gather, and bind, and make subservient to our control, the power which a West Indian hurricane exerts through a small area in one continuous blast, or the momentum expended by the waves, in a tempestuous winter, upon the breakwater at Cherbourg [France], or the lifting power of the tide, for a month, at the head of the Bay of Fundy, or the pressure of a square mile of sea water at the depth of five thousand fathoms, or a moment of the might of an earthquake or a volcano, our age . . . might hope to scarp the rugged walls of the Alps and Pyrenees . . . , robe them once more in a vegetation as rich as that of their pristine woods, and turn their wasting torrents into refreshing streams.

Could this old world, which man has overthrown, be rebuilded, could human cunning rescue its wasted hillsides and its deserted plains from solitude or mere nomad occupation, from barrenness, from nakedness, and from insalubrity, and restore the ancient fertility and healthfulness . . . , the thronging millions of Europe might still find room on the Eastern continent, and the main current of emigration be turned toward the rising instead of the setting sun.

But changes like these must await great political and moral revolutions in the governments and peoples by whom those regions are now possessed, a command of pecuniary and of mechanical means not at present enjoyed by those nations, and a more advanced and generally diffused knowledge of the processes by which the amelioration of soil and climate is possible, than now anywhere exists. Until such circumstances shall conspire to favor the work of geographical regeneration, the countries I have mentioned . . . will continue to sink into yet deeper desolation . . . .

All human institutions, associate arrangements, modes of life, have their characteristic imperfections. The natural, perhaps the necessary defect of ours, is their instability, their want of fixedness, not in form only, but even in spirit. The face of physical nature in the United States shares this incessant fluctuation, and the landscape is as variable as the habits of the population. It is time for some abatement in the restless love of change which characterizes us, and makes us almost a nomad rather than a sedentary people. We have now felled forest enough everywhere, in many districts far too much. Let us restore this one element of material life to its normal proportions, and devise means for maintaining the permanence of its relations to the fields, the meadows, and the pastures, to the rain and the dews of heaven, to the springs and rivulets with which it waters the earth. The establishment of an approximately fixed ratio between the two most broadly characterized distinctions of rural surface—woodland and

plough land—would involve a certain persistence of character in all
the branches of industry, all the occupations and habits of life, which
depend upon or are immediately connected with either, without implying a rigidity that should exclude flexibility of accommodation to
the many changes of external circumstance which human wisdom can
neither prevent nor foresee, and would thus help us to become, more
emphatically, a well-ordered and stable commonwealth, and, not less
conspicuously, a people of progress.

4

The Value and Care of Parks

FREDERICK LAW OLMSTED (1865)

*As Frederick Law Olmsted realizes here, the preservation of natural scen-
ery in the form of public parks was an American innovation in keeping with
the best of the nation's ideals. Olmsted himself took a leading role in
formulating and instituting the park concept. The first professional landscape architect in the United States, Olmsted was primarily responsible for
translating the State of New York's 1853 authorization for a "public place"
in New York City into Central Park. In 1863 Olmsted interrupted his
distinguished career as a consultant on parks and city planning in the East
to spend three years in California. His acquaintance with Yosemite Valley
began with a visit in the summer of 1864. The following September
Olmsted received an appointment as a commissioner to manage the valley
which had been granted by Congress to the State of California the previous
June "for public use, resort, and recreation." Sensing at once the significance of the grant, Olmsted made the following report on August 8, 1865,
with the purpose of showing Yosemite's values and suggesting principles for
its management. So novel and altruistic were his ideas, however, that they
found little favor with California's politicians and entrepreneurs, and late in
1865 Olmsted returned to his career in the East. Yet he did not forget*

Frederick Law Olmsted, "The Yosemite Valley and the Mariposa Big Trees,"
Landscape Architecture, **XLIII** (1952), 17, 20–23. Reprinted by permission
of *Landscape Architecture.*

Yosemite; twenty-five years later another champion of the valley, John Muir (14), secured Olmsted's assistance in a successful campaign to establish Yosemite National Park.

It is the will of the nation as embodied in the act of Congress [of June 30, 1864, granting Yosemite Valley to California as a public park] that this scenery shall never be private property, but that like certain defensive points upon our coast it shall be held solely for public purposes.

Two classes of considerations may be assumed to have influenced the action of Congress. The first and less important is the direct and obvious pecuniary advantage which comes to a commonwealth from the fact that it possesses objects which cannot be taken out of its domain, that are attractive to travellers and the enjoyment of which is open to all.

To illustrate this it is simply necessary to refer to certain cantons of the Republic of Switzerland, a commonwealth of the most industrious and frugal people in Europe. The results of all the ingenuity and labor of this people applied to the resources of wealth which they hold in common with the people of other lands which have become of insignificant value compared with that which they derive from the price which travellers gladly pay for being allowed to share with them the enjoyment of the natural scenery of their mountains. These travellers alone have caused hundreds of the best inns in the world to be established and maintained among them, have given the farmers their best and almost the only market they have for their surplus products, have spread a network of railroads and superb carriage roads, steamboat routes and telegraphic lines over the country, have contributed directly and indirectly for many years the larger part of the state revenue and all this without the exportation or abstraction from the country of any thing of the slightest value to the people. . . .

A more important class of considerations, however, remains to be stated. There are considerations of a political duty of grave importance to which seldom if ever before has proper respect been paid by any government in the world but the grounds of which rest on the same eternal base of equity and benevolence with all other duties of republican government. It is the main duty of government, if it is not the sole duty of government, to provide means of protection for all its citizens in the pursuit of happiness against the obstacles, otherwise insurmountable, which the selfishness of individuals or combinations of individuals is liable to interpose to that pursuit.

It is a scientific fact that the occasional contemplation of natural scenes of an impressive character, particularly if this contemplation occurs in connection with relief from ordinary cares, change of air and change of habits, is favorable to the health and vigor of men and especially to the health and vigor of their intellect beyond any other conditions which can be offered them, that it not only gives pleasure for the time being but increases the subsequent capacity for happiness and the means of securing happiness. The want of such occasional recreation where men and women are habitually pressed by their business or household cares often results in a class of disorders the characteristic quality of which is mental disability, sometimes taking the severe forms of softening of the brain, paralysis, palsy, monomania, or insanity, but more frequently of mental and nervous excitability, moroseness, melancholy or irascibility, incapacitating the subject for the proper exercise of the intellectual and moral forces.

It is well established that where circumstances favor the use of such means of recreation as have been indicated, the reverse of this is true. For instance, it is a universal custom with the heads of the important departments of the British government to spend a certain period of every year on their parks and shooting grounds or in travelling among the Alps or other mountain regions. This custom is followed by the leading lawyers, bankers, merchants and the wealthy classes generally of the empire, among whom the average period of active business life is much greater than with the most nearly corresponding classes in our own or any other country where the same practice is not equally well established. . . .

If we analyze the operation of scenes of beauty upon the mind, and consider the intimate relation of the mind upon the nervous system and the whole physical economy, the action and reaction which constantly occur between bodily and mental conditions, the reinvigoration which results from such scenes is readily comprehended. Few persons can see such scenery as that of the Yosemite and not be impressed by it in some slight degree. All not alike, all not perhaps consciously, and amongst all who are consciously impressed by it, few can give the least expression to that of which they are conscious. But there can be no doubt that all have this susceptibility, though with some it is much more dull and confused than with others.

The power of scenery to affect men is, in a large way, proportionate to the degree of their civilization and the degree in which their taste has been cultivated. Among a thousand savages there will be a much smaller number who will show the least sign of being so affected than among a thousand persons taken from a civilized community. This is only one of the many channels in which a similar distinction between civilized and savage men is to be generally observed. The whole body of the susceptibilities of civilized men and with their susceptibilities their powers, are on the whole enlarged.

But as with the bodily powers, if one group of muscles is developed by exercise exclusively, and all others neglected, the result is general feebleness, so it is with the mental faculties. And men who exercise those faculties or susceptibilities of the mind which are called in play by beautiful scenery so little that they seem to be inert with them, are either in a diseased condition from excessive devotion of the mind to a limited range of interests, or their whole minds are in a savage state; that is, a state of low development. The latter class need to be drawn out generally; the former need relief from their habitual matters of interest and to be drawn out in those parts of their mental nature which have been habitually left idle and inert.

But there is a special reason why the reinvigoration of those parts which are stirred into conscious activity by natural scenery is more effective upon the general development and health than that of any other, which is this: The severe and excessive exercise of the mind which leads to the greatest fatigue and is the most wearing upon the whole constitution is almost entirely caused by application to the removal of something to be apprehended in the future, or to interests beyond those of the moment, or of the individual; to the laying up of wealth, to the preparation of something, to accomplishing something in the mind of another, and especially to small and petty details which are uninteresting in themselves and which engage the attention at all only because of the bearing they have on some general end of more importance which is seen ahead.

In the interest which natural scenery inspires there is the strongest contrast to this. It is for itself and at the moment it is enjoyed. The attention is aroused and the mind occupied without purpose, without a continuation of the common process of relating the present action, thought or perception to some future end. There is little else that has this quality so purely. There are few enjoyments with which regard for something outside and beyond the enjoyment of the moment can ordinarily be so little mixed. The pleasures of the table are irresistibly associated with the care of hunger and the repair of the bodily waste. In all social pleasures and all pleasures which are usually enjoyed in association with the social pleasures, the care for the opinion of others, or the good of others largely mingles. In the pleasures of literature, the laying up of ideas and self-improvement are purposes which cannot be kept out of view.

This, however, is in very slight degree, if at all, the case with the enjoyment of the emotions caused by natural scenery. It therefore results that the enjoyment of scenery employs the mind without fatigue and yet exercises it; tranquillizes it and yet enlivens it; and thus, through the influence of the mind over the body, gives the effect of refreshing rest and reinvigoration to the whole system.

Men who are rich enough and who are sufficiently free from anxiety with regard to their wealth can and do provide places of this needed recreation for themselves. They have done so from the earliest periods known in the history of the world, for the great men of the Babylonians, the Persians and the Hebrews, had their rural retreats, as large and as luxurious as those of the aristocracy of Europe at present. There are in the islands of Great Britain and Ireland more than one thousand private parks and notable grounds devoted to luxury and recreation. The value of these grounds amounts to many millions of dollars and the cost of their annual maintenance is greater than that of the national schools; their only advantage to the commonwealth is obtained through the recreation they afford their owners (except as these extend hospitality to others) and these owners with their families number less than one in six thousand of the whole population. The enjoyment of the choicest natural scenes in the country and the means of recreation connected with them is thus a monopoly, in a very peculiar manner, of a very few, very rich people. The great mass of society, including those to whom it would be of the greatest benefit, is excluded from it. In the nature of the case private parks can never be used by the mass of the people in any country nor by any considerable number even of the rich, except by the favor of a few, and in dependence on them.

Thus without means are taken by government to withhold them from the grasp of individuals, all places favorable in scenery to the recreation of the mind and body will be closed against the great body of the people. For the same reason that the water of rivers should be guarded against private appropriation and the use of it for the purpose of navigation and otherwise protected against obstruction, portions of natural scenery may therefore properly be guarded and cared for by government. To simply reserve them from monopoly by individuals, however, it will be obvious, is not all that is necessary. It is necessary that they should be laid open to the use of the body of the people.

The establishment by government of great public grounds for the free enjoyment of the people under certain circumstances, is thus justified and enforced as a political duty.

Such a provision, however, having regard to the whole people of a state, has never before been made and the reason it has not is evident. It has always been the conviction of the governing classes of the old world that it is necessary that the large mass of all human communities should spend their lives in almost constant labor and that the power of enjoying beauty either of nature or of art in any high degree, requires a cultivation of certain faculties, which is impossible to these humble toilers. Hence it is thought better, so far as the recreations of the masses of a nation receive attention from their rulers, to provide artificial pleasure for them, such as theatres, parades, and promenades where they will be amused by the equipages of the rich and the animation of crowds.

It is unquestionably true that excessive and persistent devotion to sordid interests cramps and distorts the power of appreciating natural beauty and destroys the love of it which the Almighty has implanted in every human being, and which is so intimately and mysteriously associated with the moral perceptions and intuition, but it is not true that exemption from toil, much leisure, much study, much wealth, are necessary to the exercise of the esthetic and contemplative faculties. It is the folly of laws which have permitted and favored the monopoly by privileged classes of many of the means supplied in nature for the gratification, exercise and education of the esthetic faculties that has caused the appearance of dullness and weakness and disease of these faculties in the mass of the subjects of kings. And it is against the limitation of the means of such education to the rich that the wise legislation of free governments must be directed. . . .

It was in accordance with these views of the destiny of the New World and the duty of the republican government that Congress enacted that the Yosemite should be held, guarded and managed for the free use of the whole body of the people forever. . . .

The main duty with which the Commissioners [appointed to manage Yosemite Valley as a park] should be charged should be to give every advantage practicable to the mass of the people to benefit by that which is peculiar to this ground and which has caused Congress to treat it differently from other parts of the public domain. This peculiarity consists wholly in its natural scenery.

The first point to be kept in mind then is the preservation and maintenance as exactly as is possible of the natural scenery; the restriction, that is to say, within the narrowest limits consistent with the necessary accommodation of visitors, of all artificial constructions and the prevention of all constructions markedly inharmonious with the scenery or which would unnecessarily obscure, distort or detract from the dignity of the scenery.

Second: it is important that it should be remembered that in permitting the sacrifice of anything that would be of the slightest value to future visitors to the convenience, bad taste, playfulness, carelessness, or wanton destructiveness of present visitors, we probably yield in each case the interest of uncounted millions to the selfishness of a few individuals. . . .

At some time, therefore, laws to prevent an unjust use by individuals, of that which is not individual but public property must be made and rigidly enforced. . . .

It should, then, be made the duty of the Commission to prevent a wanton or careless disregard on the part of anyone entering the Yosemite or the Grove, of the rights of posterity as well as of contemporary visitors, and the Commission should be clothed with proper authority and given the necessary means for this purpose.

This duty of preservation is the first which falls upon the state under the Act of Congress, because the millions who are hereafter to benefit by the Act have the largest interest in it, and the largest interest should be first and most strenuously guarded. . . .

5

The Beginnings of Federal Concern
CARL SCHURZ (1877)

Before 1890, Secretary of the Interior Carl Schurz stands as one of the few exceptions to the rule of federal indifference to forest conservation. A

Annual Report of the Secretary of the Interior on the Operations of the Department for the Fiscal Year Ended June 30, 1877 (Washington, D.C., Government Printing Office, 1877), [iii], xv–xx.

German immigrant, Schurz was familiar with the methods of scientific forestry then practiced in Europe. During his tenure as Secretary (1877–1881), he repeatedly called for the reservation and rational management of America's forests. At the time his pleas made little impression on a government dedicated to protecting the freedom of private enterprise, but Schurz persisted. The germ of the National Forest idea appears below in an excerpt from his annual report for 1877. Not until March 3, 1891, however, did Congress pass an act permitting the President to create "forest reserves" by withdrawing land from the public domain. Significantly, the prime mover behind the Forest Reserve Act was another German immigrant, and head of the federal Division of Forestry from 1886 to 1898, Bernhard E. Fernow.

Sir: I have the honor to submit the following summary of the operations of this department during the past year, together with such suggestions as seem to me worthy of consideration: . . .

The subject of the extensive depredations committed upon the timber on the public lands of the United States has largely engaged the attention of this department. That question presents itself in a twofold aspect: as a question of law and as a question of public economy. As to the first point, little need be said. That the law prohibits the taking of timber by unauthorized persons from the public lands of the United States, is a universally known fact. That the laws are made to be executed, ought to be a universally accepted doctrine. That the government is in duty bound to act upon that doctrine, needs no argument. There may be circumstances under which the rigorous execution of a law may be difficult or inconvenient, or obnoxious to public sentiment, or working particular hardship; in such cases it is the business of the legislative power to adapt the law to such circumstances. It is the business of the Executive to enforce the law as it stands.

As to the second point, the statements made by the Commissioner of the General Land Office, in his report, show the quantity of timber taken from the public lands without authority of law to have been of enormous extent. It probably far exceeds in reality any estimates made upon the data before us. It appears, from authentic information before this department, that in many instances the depredations have been carried on in the way of organized and systematic enterprise, not only to furnish timber, lumber, and fire-wood for the home market, but, on a large scale, for commercial exportation to foreign countries.

The rapidity with which this country is being stripped of its forests must alarm every thinking man. It has been estimated by good authority that, if we go on at the present rate, the supply of timber in the United States will, in less than twenty years, fall considerably short of our home necessities. How disastrously the destruction of the forests of a country affects the regularity of the water supply in its rivers necessary for navigation, increases the frequency of freshets and inundations, dries up springs, and transforms fertile agricultural districts into barren wastes, is a matter of universal experience the world over. It is the highest time that we should turn our earnest attention to this subject, which so seriously concerns our national prosperity.

The government cannot prevent the cutting of timber on land owned by private citizens. It is only to be hoped that private owners will grow more careful of their timber as it rises in value. But the government can do two things: 1. It can take determined and, as I think, effectual measures to arrest the stealing of timber from public lands on a large scale, which is always attended with the most reckless waste; and, 2. It can preserve the forests still in its possession by keeping them under its control, and by so regulating the cutting and sale of timber on its lands as to secure the renewal of the forest ·by natural growth and the careful preservation of the young timber. . . .

. . . I have reason to believe that the measures taken by the department have already stopped the depredations on the public lands to a very great extent, and that, if continued, they will entirely arrest the evil. A comparatively small number of watchful and energetic agents will suffice to prevent in future, not, indeed, the stealing of single trees here and there, but at least depredations on a large scale. To this end, however, it is necessary that Congress, by an appropriation for this purpose, to be immediately available, enable this department to keep the agents in the field, and also to provide a more speedy and effective system for the seizure and sale of logs, lumber, or turpentine, cut or manufactured from timber on the public lands, than is now provided by existing laws. . . .

. . . Nowhere is a wasteful destruction of the forests fraught with more dangerous results than in mountainous regions. The timber grows mostly on the mountain sides, and when these mountain sides are once stripped bare, the rain will soon wash all the earth necessary for the growth of trees from the slopes down into the valleys, and the renewal of the forests will be rendered impossible forever; the rivulets and water-courses, which flow with regularity while the forest stands, are dried up for the greater part of the year, and transformed into raging torrents by heavy rains and by the melting of the snow, inundating the valleys below, covering them with gravel and loose rock swept down form the mountain-sides, and gradually rendering them unfit for agriculture, and, finally, for the habitation of men. Proper measures for the preservation of the forest in the mountainous regions of the country appear, therefore, of especially imperative necessity. The experience of parts of Asia, and of some of the most civilized countries in Europe, is so terribly instructive in these respects that we have no excuse if we do not take timely warning.

To avert such evil results, I would suggest the following preventive and remedial measures: All timber-lands still belonging to the United States should be withdrawn from the operation of the pre-emption and homestead laws, as well as the location of the various kinds of scrip.

Timber-lands fit for agricultural purposes should be sold, if sold at all, only for cash, and so graded in price as to make the purchaser pay for the value of the timber on the land. This will be apt to make the settler careful and provident in the disposition he makes of the timber.

A sufficient number of government agents should be provided for to protect the timber on public lands from depredation, and to institute to this end the necessary proceedings against depredators by seizures and by criminal as well as civil action.

Such agents should also be authorized and instructed . . . to sell for the United States, in order to satisfy the current local demand, timber from the public lands under proper regulations, and in doing so especially to see to it that no large areas be entirely stripped of their timber, so as not to prevent the natural renewal of the forest. . . .

The extensive as well as wanton destruction of the timber upon the public lands by the willful or negligent and careless setting of fires calls for earnest attention. While in several, if not all, of the States such acts are made highly penal offenses by statute, yet no law of the United States provides specifically for their punishment when committed upon the public lands, nor for a recovery of the damages thereby sustained. I would therefore recommend the passage of a law prescribing a severe penalty for the willful, negligent, or careless setting of fires upon the public lands of the United States, principally valuable for the timber thereon, and also providing for the recovery of all damages thereby sustained.

While such measures might be provided for by law without

unnecessary delay, I would also suggest that the President be authorized to appoint a commission, composed of qualified persons, to study the laws and practices adopted in other countries for the preservation and cultivation of forests, and to report to Congress a plan for the same object applicable to our circumstances.

I am so deeply impressed with the importance of this subject, that I venture to predict, the Congress making efficient laws for the preservation of our forests will be ranked by future generations in this country among its greatest benefactors. . . .

6

The Reclamation Idea
JOHN WESLEY POWELL (1878)

John Wesley Powell's insights into the geography of the Far West laid the basis for federal involvement in reclamation. A one-armed veteran of the Civil War, Powell made the first descent of the Colorado River in 1869. Two years later he again took boats through the Grand Canyon. Powell continued to study the Great Basin between the Rocky Mountains and the Sierra and published his observations as a government document in 1878 under the title, Report on the Lands of the Arid Region of the United States. *His findings destroyed several American myths by revealing the Basin as neither agrarian paradise nor desert, but rather as a region adaptable to a limited amount of cultivation provided that the federal government supported extensive irrigation projects. Powell's comparative pessimism about the West's ability to support agriculture and his suggestion that the government take an active role in its economy did not find a warm reception in many circles. But his enthusiastic advocacy of irrigation from the position, after 1881, of Director of the United States Geological Survey inspired younger men like WJ McGee (8) and Frederick H. Newell (10) to press forward. In 1902, the year Powell died, Congress passed the*

John Wesley Powell, *Report on the Lands of the Arid Region of the United States,* U.S. House of Representatives, Executive Document 73, 45th Cong., 2d Sess. (April 3, 1878, Washington, D.C., Government Printing Office), viii, [1]–3, 5–10, 19–22.

Reclamation Act which institutionalized many of his recommendations and laid the basis for the Bureau of Reclamation.

The eastern portion of the United States is supplied with abundant rainfall for agricultural purposes, receiving the necessary amount from the evaporation of the Atlantic Ocean and the Gulf of Mexico; but westward the amount of aqueous precipitation diminishes in a general way until at last a region is reached where the climate is so arid that agriculture is not successful without irrigation. This Arid Region begins about midway in the Great Plains and extends across the Rocky Mountains to the Pacific Ocean. . . . Experience teaches that it is not wise to depend upon rainfall where the amount is less than 20 inches annually, if this amount is somewhat evenly distributed throughout the year; but if the rainfall is unevenly distributed, so that "rainy seasons" are produced, the question whether agriculture is possible without irrigation depends upon the time of the "rainy season" and the amount of its rainfall. Any unequal distribution of rain through the year, though the inequality be so slight as not to produce "rainy seasons," affects agriculture either favorably or unfavorably. If the spring and summer precipitation exceeds that of the fall and winter, a smaller amount of annual rain may be sufficient; but if the rainfall during the season of growing crops is less than the average of the same length of time during the remainder of the year, a greater amount of annual precipitation is necessary. In some localities in the western portion of the United States this unequal distribution of rainfall through the seasons affects agriculture favorably; and this is true immediately west of the northern portion of the line of 20 inches of rainfall, which extends along the plains from our northern to our southern boundary. . . .

The limit of successful agriculture without irrigation has been set at 20 inches, that the extent of the Arid Region should by no means be exaggerated; but at 20 inches agriculture will not be uniformly successful from season to season. Many droughts will occur; many seasons in a long series will be fruitless; and it may be doubted whether, on the whole, agriculture will prove remunerative. On this point it is impossible to speak with certainty. A larger experience than the history of agriculture in the western portion of the United States affords is necessary to a final determination of the question. . . .

The Arid Region is the great Rocky Mountain Region of the United States, and it embraces something more than four-tenths of the whole country excluding Alaska. . . .

Within the Arid Region only a small portion of the country is irrigable. These irrigable tracts are lowlands lying along the streams. On the mountains and high plateaus forests are found at elevations so great that frequent summer frosts forbid the cultivation of the soil. Here are the natural timber lands of the Arid Region—an upper region set apart by nature for the growth of timber necessary to the mining, manufacturing, and agricultural industries of the country. Between the low irrigable lands and the elevated forest lands there are valleys, mesas, hills, and mountain slopes bearing grasses of greater or less value for pasturage purposes.

Then, in discussing the lands of the Arid Region, three great classes are recognized—the irrigable lands below, the forest lands above, and the pasturage lands between. . . .

In Utah Territory agriculture is dependent upon irrigation. . . . In order to determine the amount of irrigable land in Utah it was necessary to determine the areas to which the larger streams can be taken by proper engineering skill, and the amount which the smaller streams can serve. In the latter case it was necessary to determine first the amount of land which a given amount or unit of water would supply, and then the volume of water running in the streams; the product of these factors giving the extent of the irrigable lands. A continuous flow of one cubic foot of water per second was taken as the unit, and after careful consideration it was assumed that this unit of water will serve from 80 to 100 acres of land. . . .

Having determined from the operations of irrigation that one cubic foot per second of water will irrigate from 80 to 100 acres of land when the greatest economy is used, and having determined the volume of water or number of cubic feet per second flowing in the several streams of Utah by the most thorough methods available under the circumstances, it appears that within the territory, excluding a small portion in the southeastern corner where the survey has not yet been completed, the amount of land which it is possible to redeem by this method is about 2,262 square miles, or 1,447,920 acres. . . . Excluding that small portion of the territory in the southeast corner not embraced in the map, Utah has an area of 80,000 square miles, of which 2,262 square miles are irrigable. That is, 2.8 per cent of the lands under consideration can be cultivated by utilizing all the available streams during the irrigating season. . . .

This statement of the facts relating to the irrigable lands of Utah will serve to give a clearer conception of the extent and condition of the irrigable lands throughout the Arid Region. Such as can be redeemed are scattered along the water courses, and are in general the lowest lands of the several districts to which they belong. In some of the states and territories the percentage of irrigable land is less than in Utah, in others greater, and it is probable that the percentage in the entire region is somewhat greater than in the territory which we have considered.

. . . [I]t will be interesting to consider certain questions relating to the economy and practicability of distributing the waters over the lands to be redeemed.

There are two considerations that make irrigation attractive to the agriculturist. Crops thus cultivated are not subject to the vicissitudes of rainfall; the farmer fears no droughts; his labors are seldom interrupted and his crops rarely injured by storms. This immunity from drought and storm renders agricultural operations much more certain than in regions of greater humidity. Again, the water comes down from the mountains and plateaus freighted with fertilizing materials derived from the decaying vegetation and soils of the upper regions, which are spread by the flowing water over the cultivated lands. It is probable that the benefits derived from this source alone will be full compensation for the cost of the process. Hitherto these benefits have not been fully realized, from the fact that the methods employed have been more or less crude. When the flow of water over the land is too great or too rapid the fertilizing elements borne in the waters are carried past the fields, and a washing is produced which deprives the lands irrigated of their most valuable elements, and little streams cut the fields with channels injurious in diverse ways. Experience corrects these errors, and the irrigator soon learns to flood his lands gently, evenly, and economically. It may be anticipated that all the lands redeemed by irrigation in the Arid Region will be highly cultivated and abundantly productive, and agriculture will be but slightly subject to the vicissitudes of scant and excessive rainfall.

A stranger entering this Arid Region is apt to conclude that the soils are sterile, because of their chemical composition, but experience demonstrates the fact that all the soils are suitable for agricultural purposes when properly supplied with water. It is true that some of the soils are overcharged with alkaline materials, but these can in time be "washed out." Altogether the fact suggests that far too much attention has heretofore been paid to the chemical constitution of soils and too little to those physical conditions by which moisture and air are supplied to the roots of the growing plants. . . .

The irrigable lands and timber lands constitute but a small fraction of the Arid Region. Between the lowlands on the one hand and the highlands on the other is found a great body of valley, mesa, hill, and low mountain lands. To what extent, and under what conditions can they be utilized? Usually they bear a scanty growth of grasses. These grasses are nutritious and valuable both for summer and winter pasturage. Their value depends upon peculiar climatic conditions; the grasses grow to a great extent in scattered bunches, and mature seeds in larger proportion perhaps than the grasses of the more humid regions. In general the winter aridity is so great that the grasses when touched by the frosts are not washed down by the rains and snows to decay on the moist soil, but stand firmly on the ground all winter long and "cure," forming a *quasi* uncut hay. Thus the grass lands are of value both in summer and winter. In a broad way, the greater or lesser abundance of the grasses is dependent on latitude and altitude; the higher the latitude the better are the grasses, and they improve as the altitude increases. In very low altitudes and latitudes the grasses are so scant as to be of no value; here the true deserts are found. These conditions obtain in southern California, southern Nevada, southern Arizona, and southern New Mexico, where broad reaches of land are naked of vegetation, but in ascending to the higher lands the grass steadily improves. Northward the deserts soon disappear, and the grass becomes more and more luxuriant to our northern boundary. In addition to the desert lands mentioned, other large deductions must be made from the area of the pasturage lands. There are many districts in which the "country rock" is composed of incoherent sands and clays; sometimes sediments of ancient Tertiary lakes; elsewhere sediments of more ancient Cretaceous seas. In these districts perennial or intermittent streams have carved deep waterways, and the steep hills are ever washed naked by fierce but infrequent storms, as the incoherent rocks are unable to withstand the beating of the rain. These districts are known as the *mauvaises terres* or bad lands of the Rocky Mountain Region. In other areas the streams have carved labyrinths of deep gorges and the waters flow at great depths below the general surface. The lands between the streams are beset with towering cliffs, and the landscape is an expanse of naked rock. . . .

After making all the deductions, there yet remain vast areas of valuable pasturage land bearing nutritious but scanty grass. The lands along the creeks and rivers have been relegated to that class which has been described as irrigable, hence the lands under consideration are away from the permanent streams. No rivers sweep over them and no creeks meander among their hills. . . .

The grass is so scanty that the herdsman must have a large area for the support of his stock. In general a quarter section of land alone is of no value to him; the pasturage it affords is entirely inadequate to the wants of a herd that the poorest man needs for his support.

Four square miles may be considered as the minimum amount necessary for a pasturage farm, and a still greater amount is necessary for the larger part of the lands; that is, pasturage farms, to be of any practicable value, must be of at least 2,560 acres, and in many districts they must be much larger. . . .

. . . [T]he arid lands, so far as they can be redeemed by irrigation, will perennially yield bountiful crops, as the means for their redemption involves their constant fertilization.

To a great extent, the redemption of all these lands will require extensive and comprehensive plans, for the execution of which aggregated capital or coöperative labor will be necessary. Here, individual farmers, being poor men, cannot undertake the task. For its accomplishment a wise prevision, embodied in carefully considered legislation, is necessary. . . .

Part Two

The Progressive Conservation Crusade

Part Two

The Progressive Conservation Crusade

The first major surge of the American conservation movement occurred during the Progressive period of the early twentieth century. Within the space of a few years the concept of conservation came to have wide public usage and was extended to subjects as diverse as the improvement of rural schools and the reform of the parcel post system. Even human health and lengthening of the life span were regarded as "conservation" problems. The literary remains of Progressive conservation are extensive. Hundreds of articles and pamphlets and dozens of books treated resource management. In politics, the conservation issue played a major role, contributing particularly to the schism of 1912 in the Republican party.

One way to understand the sudden emergence of Progressive conservation is in terms of its historical context. The idea of "ripeness" is useful: Americans were *ready* to be concerned about their environment. A national mood or temper existed that had been absent, with a few exceptions, a generation before. Its dominant characteristic was anxiety over change in the American environment. The change involved industrialization, urbanization, and a growing population, but it can be expressed most succinctly as the ending of the frontier. The Census of 1890 simply announced this fact. Three years later Frederick Jackson Turner wrote *The Significance of the Frontier in American History*. But few, Turner included, were willing to speak publicly about the prospects of a frontierless America. Yet a vague uneasiness over this situation was widespread. The frontier had been almost synonymous with the abundance, opportunity, and distinctiveness of the New World. For two and a half centuries its presence largely explained America's remarkable material growth as well as many characteristics of her people. Few, as a consequence, could regard its passing without regret.

One result was a general tendency to look favorably on conservation. It would "string out" the remaining abundance, deny the chilling implications of the Census pronouncement, and assuage anxiety over population growth and industrial expansion. Conservation, to be sure, was not the only beneficiary of American uneasiness. Imperialism and the movement for immigration restriction, for instance, also reflected turn-of-the-century anxieties. But conservation had special appeal because it directly attacked the problem, which was, at root, environmental. Conservation would *be*, in a sense, the new frontier, keeping the nation young, vigorous, prosperous, democratic, replete with opportunity for the individual, and, because of its relation to nature, wholesome and moral. These had once been the frontier's functions. For a civilization that had begun to notice its first gray hairs, conservation was welcome tonic, for the land as well as for the minds of its inhabitants.

There were several other factors that figured in the growth and character of conservation before World War I. One was the existence in the United States of a technological capacity capable of at least entertaining the large-scale ideas for environmental engineering that Progressive conservationists put forward. In addition, the national indignation, growing since the 1870's, at concentrated wealth conditioned some Americans to accept the ideology of conservation. And the movement would have taken a different, and probably a less potent, form had it not coincided with the widespread acceptance of the philosophy that the central government should be strong and willing to use its strength in the public interest. Along with the passing of the era of easy resources, such developments conditioned Americans to accept Progressive conservation.

7

The Birth of "Conservation"
GIFFORD PINCHOT (1947)

In the public estimation at least, the man most closely associated with the history of conservation in the United States is Gifford Pinchot. And while in the autobiographical account that follows, Pinchot may have exaggerated his personal role in originating the movement, no one did more to publicize it during the Progressive era. Graduating from Yale in 1889, Pinchot became the first American to choose forestry as a career. George Perkins Marsh's book [see (3)] admittedly influenced his decision as did a love of the outdoors, especially fishing, and a taste for innovation. Since professional training in forestry was unavailable in the United States and the Pinchot family had ample means, Gifford enrolled at the French Forest School in Nancy. Returning fired with enthusiasm for the idea of managing forests as a crop, Pinchot quickly capitalized on his virtually unique skills. Through Frederick Law Olmsted (4), he obtained an appointment as forester on George W. Vanderbilt's North Carolina estate, Biltmore. In 1898 Pinchot became chief of the federal Forestry Division (later renamed the United States Forest Service and given control of the National Forests). A personal friend of Theodore Roosevelt and a masterful publicist, Pinchot was the driving force behind the Progressive conservation movement, the origin of which he describes here. Pinchot's philosophy of resource management is represented in selection (11).

. . . [Early in 1905] there were three separate Government organizations which dealt with mineral resources, four or five concerned with streams, half a dozen with authority over forests, and a dozen or so with supervision over wild life, soils, soil erosion, and other questions of the land.

It was a mess, a mess which could be cured only by realizing that these unrelated and overlapping bureaus were all tied up together, like the people in a town. The one and only way to bring order out of this chaos was to supply a common ground on which each could take its proper place, and do its proper work, in co-operation with all the rest.

It had never occurred to us that we were all parts one of another. And the fact that the Federal Government had taken up the protection of the various natural resources individually and at intervals during more than half a century doubtless confirmed our bureaucratic nationalism. . . .

It was my great good luck that I had more to do with the work of more bureaus than any other man in Washington. This was partly because the Forest Service was dealing not only with trees but with public lands, mining, agriculture, irrigation, stream flow, soil erosion, fish, game, animal industry, and a host of other matters with which other bureaus also were concerned. The main reason, however, was that much of T.R.'s [Theodore Roosevelt's] business with the natural resources bureaus was conducted through me.

It was therefore the most natural thing in the world that the relations of forests, waters, lands, and minerals, each to each, should be brought strongly to my mind. But for a long time my mind stopped there. Then at last I woke up. And this is how it happened:

In the gathering gloom of an expiring day, in the moody month of February, . . . [1907] . . . a solitary horseman might have been observed pursuing his silent way above a precipitous gorge in the vicinity of the capital city of America. Or so an early Victorian three-volume novelist might have expressed it.

In plain words, a man by the name of Pinchot was riding a horse by the name of Jim on the Ridge Road in Rock Creek Park near Washington. And while he rode, he thought. He was a forester, and he was taking his problems with him, on that winter's day . . . when he meant to leave them behind.

The forest and its relation to streams and inland navigation, to water power and flood control; to the soil and its erosion; to coal and oil and other minerals; to fish and game; and many another possible use or waste of natural resources—these questions would not let him be. What had all these to do with Forestry? And what had Forestry to do with them?

Here were not isolated and separate problems. My work had brought me into touch with all of them. But what was the basic link between them?

Suddenly the idea flashed through my head that there was a unity in this complication—that the relation of one resource to another was not the end of the story. Here were no longer a lot of different, independent, and often antagonistic questions, each on its own separate little island, as we had been in the habit of thinking. In place of them, here was one single question with many parts. Seen in this new light, all these separate questions fitted into and made up the one great central problem of the use of the earth for the good of man.

To me it was a good deal like coming out of a dark tunnel. I had been seeing one spot of light ahead. Here, all of a sudden, was a whole landscape. Or it was like lifting the curtain on a great new stage.

There was too much of it for me to take it all in at once. As always, my mind worked slowly. From the first I thought I had stumbled on something really worth while, but that day in Rock Creek Park I was far from grasping the full reach and swing of the new idea.

It took time for me to appreciate that here were the makings of a new policy, not merely nationwide but world-wide in its scope—fundamentally important because it involved not only the welfare but the very existence of men on the earth. I did see, however, that something ought to be done about it. . . .

. . . It was [WJ] McGee * who grasped [the new idea] best. He sensed its full implication even more quickly than I had done, and saw its future more clearly.

McGee became the scientific brains of the new movement. With his wide general knowledge and highly original mind we developed, as I never could have done alone, the breadth and depth of meaning which lay in the new idea. McGee had constructive imagination.

It was McGee, for example, who defined the new policy as the use of the natural resources for the greatest good of the greatest number for the longest time. It was McGee who made me see, at long last and after much argument, that monopoly of natural resources was only less dangerous to the public welfare than their actual destruction.

Very soon after my own mind was clear enough to state my proposition with confidence, I took it to T.R. And T.R., as I expected, understood, accepted, and adopted it without the smallest hesitation. It was directly in line with everything he had been thinking and doing. It became the heart of his Administration.

Launching the Conservation movement was the most significant achievement of the T.R. Administration, as he himself believed. It seems altogether probable that it will also be the achievement for which he will be longest and most gratefully remembered.

---

* See (8).

Having just been born, the new arrival was still without a name. There had to be a name to call it by before we could even attempt to make it known, much less give it a permanent place in the public mind. What should we call it?

Both Overton [Price, an associate of Pinchot in the Forest Service] and I knew that large organized areas of Government forest lands in British India were named Conservancies, and for the foresters in charge of them Conservators. After many other suggestions and long discussions, either Price or I (I'm not sure which and it doesn't matter) proposed that we apply a new meaning to a word already in the dictionary, and christen the new policy Conservation.

During one of our rides I put that name up to T.R., and he approved it instantly. So the child was named, and that bridge was behind us.

Today [Pinchot was writing in 1945.], when it would be hard to find an intelligent man in the United States who hasn't at least some conception of what Conservation means, it seems incredible that the very word, in the sense in which we use it now, was unknown less than forty years ago. . . .

8

The Conservation Mentality
WJ McGEE (1910)

In the previous document Gifford Pinchot singled out the versatile, self-taught scientist William John (he insisted on "WJ," without punctuation) McGee as "the scientific brains" of the conservation movement. McGee's crusading zeal, exemplified in this selection, was typical of Progressive conservationists. His involvement in federal resource work began in 1878 when John Wesley Powell (6) invited him to join the United States Geological Survey. Powell's philosophy of scientifically studying and devel-

WJ McGee, "The Conservation of Natural Resources," *Proceedings of the Mississippi Valley Historical Association,* **III** (1909–10), 365–367, 371, 376–379.

oping resources captured McGee's imagination as did the democratic re-
form endeavors of Lester Frank Ward and Henry George. Late in 1906 at a
meeting of the Lakes-to-the-Gulf Deep Waterway Association, and several
months before Pinchot "discovered" conservation, McGee glimpsed the
possibility of comprehensive and systematic management of the environ-
ment in the public interest. He thereafter worked closely with Pinchot in
persuading President Theodore Roosevelt to appoint the Inland Waterways
Commission (March 14, 1907) which launched the national conservation
crusade.

. . . [America's Founding Fathers] saw Land as the sole natural
resource of the country, so the succeeding generations remained indifferent to the values residing in the minerals below and the forests
above . . . . Herein lay what now seems the most serious error in the
world's greatest Republic. Monarchs are accustomed to retaining royal
or imperial rights in the forests and minerals, and these eventually
inure to the benefit of their people; ecclesiastic institutions allied with
monarchial rule have commonly held rein over rarer resources until
they were reclaimed by the growing generations of men; but through
a lamentable lack of foresight our Republic hasted to give away,
under the guise of land to live on, values far greater than the land
itself—and this policy continued for generations. . . .

The policy of free giving grew into thoughtless habit, and this
into a craze which spread apace . . . . States and cities followed the
national lead, and all manner of franchises—rights of way, water
rights, and the rest—were given for long terms or in perpetuity to all
comers, generally without money and without price. In all the world's
history no other such saturnalia of squandering the sources of permanent prosperity was ever witnessed! In the material aspect, our individual liberty became collective license, and our legislative and administrative prodigality grew into national profligacy; the balance
between impulse and responsibility was lost, the future of the People
and Nation was forgotten, and the very name of posterity was made a
by-word by men in high places; and worst of all the very profligacies
came to be venerated as law and even crystallized foolishly in decisions or more questionably in enactments—and for long there were
none to stand in the way of the growing avalanche of extravagance.
The waste was always wildest in the West, for as settlement followed
the sun new resources were discovered or came into being through
natural growth . . . .

. . . [T]he free gift of these resources . . . opened the way to monopoly, and the resources passed under monopolistic control with a rapidity never before seen in all the world's history; and it is hardly too much to say that the Nation has become one of the Captains of Industry first, and one of the People and their chosen representatives only second. With the free gift, under the title of land, of resources far exceeding the land in value, the aspiration of the Fathers for a land of free families failed; for the mineral-bearing and wood-bearing lands were devoted to mining and milling and manufacturing instead of homes, and the People became in large measure industrial dependents rather than free citizens. . . .

Done in a few lines, the history of the country and its resources . . . [has been one of] wealth beyond the visions of avarice and power above the dreams of tyranny . . . [coming] to the few—at vast cost to the just patrimony of the multitude—while much of the substance of the Nation has been wasted and many of the People have passed under the domination of the beneficiaries of Privilege. Ample resources indeed remain—enough to insure the perpetuity of the People—but the question also remains whether these shall be held and used by the People, whose travail gave them value and whose rights therein are inalienable and indefeasible under the Declaration of Independence and the Constitution, or whether they shall go chiefly into the hands of the self-chosen and self-anointed few, largely to forge new shackles for the wrists and ankles of the many! This problem of history is not one of passion or for reckless action. The simple facts are that the inequities arose chiefly in the confusion of other resources with Land, and that the inequalities in opportunity due to this confusion have arisen so insidiously as to escape notice. Yet the question remains: How may American freemen proceed decently and in order to reclaim their own?

. . . [Gifford] Pinchot and [James R.] Garfield * especially, and [Theodore] Roosevelt in his turn, sought to counteract the tendency toward wholesale alienation of the public lands for the benefit of the corporation and the oppression or suppression of the settler; and in the end their efforts resulted in what is now known as the Conservation Movement . . . .

On its face the Conservation Movement is material—ultra-material. . . . Yet in truth there has never been in all human history a popular movement more firmly grounded in ethics, in the

---

* Secretary of the Interior from 1907 to 1909. [Ed.]

eternal equities, in the divinity of human rights! Whether we rise into the spiritual empyrean or cling more closely to the essence of humanity, we find our loftiest ideals made real in the Cult of Conservation. . . .

. . . What *right* has any citizen of a free country, whatever his foresight and shrewdness, to seize on sources of life for his own behoof that are the common heritage of all; what *right* has legislature or court to help in the seizure; and striking still more deeply, what *right* has any generation to wholly consume, much less to waste, those sources of life without which the children or the children's children must starve or freeze? These are among the questions arising among intelligent minds in every part of this country, and giving form to a national feeling which is gradually rising to a new plane of equity. The questions will not down. Nay, like Banquo's ghost they tarry, and haunt, and search! How shall they find answer? The ethical doctrine of Conservation answers: by a nobler patriotism, under which citizen-electors will cleave more strongly to their birthright of independence and strive more vigorously for purity of the ballot, for rightness in laws, for cleanness in courts, and for forthrightness in administration; by a higher honesty of purpose between man and man; by a warmer charity, under which the good of all will more fairly merge with the good of each; by a stronger family sense, tending toward a realization of the rights of the unborn; by deeper probity, maturing in the realizing sense that each holder of the sources of life is but a trustee for his nominal possessions, and is responsible to all men and for all time for making the best use of them in the common interest; and by a livelier humanity, in which each will feel that he lives not for himself alone but as a part of a common life for a common world and for the common good. . . .

Whatever its material manifestations, every revolution is first and foremost a revolution in thought and in spirit . . . . [The last of humanity's great revolutions] was inspired in the New World by the new realization that all men are equally entitled to life, liberty, and the pursuit of happiness . . . . Still the hope of the Fathers for a freehold citizenry joined in equitable and indissoluble Union is not fully attained. The American Revolution was fought for Liberty; the American Constitution was framed for Equality; yet that third of the trinity of human impulses without which Union is not made perfect—Fraternity—has not been established: full brotherhood among men and generations has not yet come. The duty of the Fathers was done well according to their lights; but some new light has come out of the West where their sons have striven against Nature's forces no less fiercely than the Fathers against foreign dominion. So it would seem to remain for Conservation to perfect the concept and the movement started among the Colonists one hundred and forty years ago—to round out the American Revolution by framing a clearer Bill of Rights. Whatever others there may be, surely these are inherent and indefeasible:—

1) The equal Rights of all men to opportunity.

2) The equal Rights of the People in and to resources rendered valuable by their own natural growth and orderly development.

3) The equal Rights of present and future generations in and to the resources of the country.

4) The equal Rights (and full responsibilities) of all citizens to provide for the perpetuity of families and States and the Union of States.

The keynote of all these is Fraternity. They look to the greatest good for the greatest number and for the longest time; they are essential to perfect union among men and States; and until they are secured to us we may hardly feel assured that government of the People, by the People, and for the People shall not perish from the earth.

9

Publicizing Conservation at the White House
THEODORE ROOSEVELT (1908)

The year 1908 marked the zenith of Progressive conservation. On February 26 the Inland Waterways Commission submitted its comprehensive plan for multipurpose river development. At President Theodore Roosevelt's invita-

Theodore Roosevelt, "Opening Address by the President," *Proceedings of a Conference of Governors in the White House,* ed. Newton C. Blanchard (Washington, D.C., Government Printing Office, 1909), 3, 5–10, 12.

*tion, a thousand national leaders, including the state governors, met from
May 13 to 15 for a conference on conservation. Gifford Pinchot organized
the dramatic gathering at the White House to publicize the new concept of
resource management and, with the assistance of WJ McGee, wrote most of
the proceedings. The speeches sparkled with enthusiasm and high ideals.
Words, however, were the principal result of the conference. The National
Conservation Commission, appointed by Roosevelt as a result of the conference, suffered from vagueness of purpose and foundered on the shoals of
Congressional parsimony. The Inland Waterways Commission also perished
from want of appropriations. And, after a North American Conservation
Conference in February 1909, the international movement bogged down
when President William Howard Taft scotched plans for a World Conference the following September. Still, Pinchot insisted, the 1908 conference
was "a turning point in human history." Roosevelt opened it as follows.*

Governors of the several States; and Gentlemen:

I welcome you to this Conference at the White House. You have
come hither at my request, so that we may join together to consider
the question of the conservation and use of the great fundamental
sources of wealth of this Nation.

So vital is this question, that for the first time in our history the
chief executive officers of the States separately, and of the States
together forming the Nation, have met to consider it. It is the chief
material question that confronts us, second only—and second always—to the great fundamental questions of morality. [Applause] *

With the governors come men from each State chosen for their
special acquaintance with the terms of the problem that is before us.
Among them are experts in natural resources and representatives of
national organizations concerned in the development and use of these
resources; the Senators and Representatives in Congress; the Supreme
Court, the Cabinet, and the Inland Waterways Commission have
likewise been invited to the Conference, which is therefore national in
a peculiar sense.

This Conference on the conservation of natural resources is in
effect a meeting of the representatives of all the people of the United
States called to consider the weightiest problem now before the Nation; and the occasion for the meeting lies in the fact that the natural

---

* This and subsequent indications of audience reaction were inserted by
WJ McGee, the recording secretary. [Ed.]

resources of our country are in danger of exhaustion if we permit the old wasteful methods of exploiting them longer to continue.

With the rise of peoples from savagery to civilization, and with the consequent growth in the extent and variety of the needs of the average man, there comes a steadily increasing growth of the amount demanded by this average man from the actual resources of the country. And yet, rather curiously, at the same time that there comes that increase in what the average man demands from the resources, he is apt to grow to lose the sense of his dependence upon nature. He lives in big cities. He deals in industries that do not bring him in close touch with nature. He does not realize the demands he is making upon nature. . . .

In [George] Washington's time anthracite coal was known only as a useless black stone; and the great fields of bituminous coal were undiscovered. As steam was unknown, the use of coal for power production was undreamed of. Water was practically the only source of power, save the labor of men and animals; and this power was used only in the most primitive fashion. But a few small iron deposits had been found in this country, and the use of iron by our countrymen was very small. Wood was practically the only fuel, and what lumber was sawed was consumed locally, while the forests were regarded chiefly as obstructions to settlement and cultivation. The man who cut down a tree was held to have conferred a service upon his fellows.

Such was the degree of progress to which civilized mankind had attained when this nation began its career. It is almost impossible for us in this day to realize how little our Revolutionary ancestors knew of the great store of natural resources whose discovery and use have been such vital factors in the growth and greatness of this Nation, and how little they required to take from this store in order to satisfy their needs.

Since then our knowledge and use of the resources of the present territory of the United States have increased a hundred-fold. Indeed, the growth of this Nation by leaps and bounds makes one of the most striking and important chapters in the history of the world. Its growth has been due to the rapid development, and alas that it should be said! to the rapid destruction, of our natural resources. Nature has supplied to us in the United States, and still supplies to us, more kinds of resources in a more lavish degree than has ever been the case at any other time or with any other people. Our position in the world has been attained by the extent and thoroughness of the control we have achieved over nature; but we are more, and not less, dependent upon what she furnishes than at any previous time of history since the days of primitive man. . . .

. . . The wise use of all of our natural resources, which are our national resources as well, is the great material question of today. I have asked you to come together now because the enormous consumption of these resources, and the threat of imminent exhaustion of some of them, due to reckless and wasteful use, . . . calls for common effort, common action.

We want to take action that will prevent the advent of a woodless age, and defer as long as possible the advent of an ironless age. [Applause] . . .

A great many of these things are truisms. Much of what I say is so familiar to us that it seems commonplace to repeat it; but familiar though it is, I do not think as a nation we understand what its real bearing is. It is so familiar that we disregard it. [Applause]

The steadily increasing drain on these natural resources has promoted to an extraordinary degree the complexity of our industrial and social life. Moreover, this unexampled development has had a determining effect upon the character and opinions of our people. The demand for efficiency in the great task has given us vigor, effectiveness, decision, and power, and a capacity for achievement which in its own lines has never yet been matched. [Applause] . . .

. . . [I]t is safe to say that the prosperity of our people depends directly on the energy and intelligence with which our natural resources are used. It is equally clear that these resources are the final basis of national power and perpetuity. Finally, it is ominously evident that these resources are in the course of rapid exhaustion.

This Nation began with the belief that its landed possessions were illimitable and capable of supporting all the people who might care to make our country their home; but already the limit of unsettled land is in sight, and indeed but little land fitted for agriculture now remains unoccupied save what can be reclaimed by irrigation and drainage—a subject with which this Conference is partly to deal. We began with an unapproached heritage of forests; more than half of the timber is gone. We began with coal fields more extensive than those of any other nation and with iron ores regarded as inexhaustible, and many experts now declare that the end of both iron and coal is in sight. . . .

. . . [W]e began with soils of unexampled fertility, and we have so impoverished them by injudicious use and by failing to check erosion that their crop-producing power is diminishing instead of increasing. In a word, we have thoughtlessly, and to a large degree unnecessarily, diminished the resources upon which not only our prosperity but the prosperity of our children and our children's children must always depend.

We have become great in a material sense because of the lavish use of our resources, and we have just reason to be proud of our growth. But the time has come to inquire seriously what will happen when our forests are gone, when the coal, the iron, the oil, and the gas are exhausted, when the soils shall have been still further impoverished and washed into the streams, polluting the rivers, denuding the fields, and obstructing navigation. These questions do not relate only to the next century or to the next generation. One distinguishing characteristic of really civilized men is foresight; we have to, as a nation, exercise foresight for this nation in the future; and if we do not exercise that foresight, dark will be the future! [Applause] We should exercise foresight now, as the ordinarily prudent man exercises foresight in conserving and wisely using the property which contains the assurance of well-being for himself and his children. We want to see a man own his farm rather than rent it, because we want to see it an object to him to transfer it in better order to his children. We want to see him exercise forethought for the next generation. We need to exercise it in some fashion ourselves as a nation for the next generation.

The natural resources I have enumerated can be divided into two sharply distinguished classes accordingly as they are or are not capable of renewal. Mines if used must necessarily be exhausted. The minerals do not and can not renew themselves. Therefore in dealing with the coal, the oil, the gas, the iron, the metals generally, all that we can do is to try to see that they are wisely used. The exhaustion is certain to come in time. We can trust that it will be deferred long enough to enable the extraordinarily inventive genius of our people to devise means and methods for more or less adequately replacing what is lost; but the exhaustion is sure to come.

The second class of resources consists of those which can not only be used in such manner as to leave them undiminished for our children, but can actually be improved by wise use. The soil, the forests, the waterways come in this category. Every one knows that a really good farmer leaves his farm more valuable at the end of his life than it was when he first took hold of it. So with the waterways. So with the forests. In dealing with mineral resources, man is able to improve on nature only by putting the resources to a beneficial use which in the end exhausts them; but in dealing with the soil and its products man can improve on nature by compelling the resources to renew and even reconstruct themselves in such manner as to serve increasingly beneficial uses—while the living waters can be so controlled as to multiply their benefits.

Neither the primitive man nor the pioneer was aware of any duty to posterity in dealing with the renewable resources. When the American settler felled the forests, he felt that there was plenty of forest left for the sons who came after him. When he exhausted the soil of his farm, he felt that his son could go West and take up another. The Kentuckian or the Ohioan felled the forest and expected his son to move west and fell other forests on the banks of the Mississippi; the Georgian exhausted his farm and moved into Alabama or to the mouth of the Yazoo to take another. So it was with his immediate successors. When the soil-wash from the farmer's field choked the neighboring river, the only thought was to use the railway rather than the boats to move produce and supplies. That was so up to the generation that preceded ours.

Now all this is changed. On the average the son of the farmer of today must make his living on his father's farm. There is no difficulty in doing this if the father will exercise wisdom. No wise use of a farm exhausts its fertility. So with the forests. We are over the verge of a timber famine in this country, and it is unpardonable for the Nation or the States to permit any further cutting of our timber save in accordance with a system which will provide that the next generation shall see the timber increased instead of diminished. [Applause]

Just let me interject one word as to a particular type of folly of which it ought not to be necessary to speak. We stop wasteful cutting of timber; that of course makes a slight shortage at the moment. To avoid that slight shortage at the moment, there are certain people so foolish that they will incur absolute shortage in the future, and they are willing to stop all attempts to conserve the forests, because of course by wastefully using them at the moment we can for a year or two provide against any lack of wood. That is like providing for the farmer's family to live sumptuously on the flesh of the milch cow. [Laughter.] Any farmer can live pretty well for a year if he is content not to live at all the year after. [Laughter and applause] . . .

We are coming to recognize as never before the right of the Nation to guard its own future in the essential matter of natural resources. In the past we have admitted the right of the individual to injure the future of the Republic for his own present profit. In fact there has been a good deal of a demand for unrestricted individualism, for the right of the individual to injure the future of all of us for his own temporary and immediate profit. The time has come for a change. As a people we have the right and the duty, second to none other but the right and duty of obeying the moral law, of requiring and doing justice, to protect ourselves and our children against the wasteful development of our natural resources, whether that waste is caused by the actual destruction of such resources or by making them impossible of development hereafter. . . .

Finally, let us remember that the conservation of our natural resources, though the gravest problem of today, is yet but part of another and greater problem to which this Nation is not yet awake, but to which it will awake in time, and with which it must hereafter grapple if it is to live—the problem of national efficiency, the patriotic duty of insuring the safety and continuance of the Nation. [Applause.] When the People of the United States consciously undertake to raise themselves as citizens, and the Nation and the States in their several spheres, to the highest pitch of excellence in private, State, and national life, and to do this because it is the first of all the duties of true patriotism, then and not till then the future of this Nation, in quality and in time, will be assured. [Great applause]

10

Reclamation Underway
FREDERICK H. NEWELL (1909)

Newell, another protégé of John Wesley Powell (6), did much to transform the reclamation ideal into national policy. In the 1890's, as a member of the United States Geological Survey, he collected the data necessary for the

Frederick H. Newell, "What May Be Accomplished by Reclamation," *Annals of the American Academy of Political and Social Science,* **XXXIII** (1909), 658–663.

beginning of effective dam construction and irrigation. Newell also worked in this decade with Representative (Senator after 1903) Francis G. New- lands of Nevada and with George H. Maxwell of the National Irrigation Association on behalf of federal sponsorship of reclamation. Success came in 1902 when the Reclamation Act created a mechanism for putting the ƿroceeds from the sale of Western lands to use in federal irrigation projects. Newell became the director of the Reclamation Service (the Bu- reau of Reclamation after 1907), organized within the Geological Survey to administer the new program. Within five years he had twenty-five major projects underway, and was rapidly demonstrating the ability of government planners and engineers. But Newell's effort aroused the opposition of Western water users who construed federal involvement as a limitation of their economic opportunity and resented the costs of reclamation. In 1915, he received a curt dismissal from the Bureau of Reclamation, but his vision and enthusiasm helped make the control of water a primary showcase of Progressive conservation.

In the conservation of natural resources reclamation plays a very large part, both directly and indirectly. There is involved in the idea of reclamation not merely the better use of lands otherwise practically valueless, but in connection with this the creation of opportunities for homes; also, but secondary to this, is frequently brought in the storage or disposal of waters in such way as to render possible the use of these waters for power or other industrial purposes, including the manufac- ture of electricity for lighting, heating and transportation.

The word "reclamation" as now commonly employed involves the conception of regulating the water supply for a given area of land, which, under natural conditions, has an excess or deficiency of mois- ture so great that agricultural values are nearly or completely de- stroyed. We speak of reclaiming the swamp or overflowed lands by keeping the waters off them, or of reclaiming arid lands by bringing waters to them at the time and in the quantities best adapted for the development of plants useful to mankind.

The National Government has been and still is an owner of vast areas of reclaimable land. In the early history of the life of the nation, individuals initiated works for draining and reclaiming areas of low- lying but very fertile land. Later, to promote the reclamation of these, Congress passed laws which, in general terms, conveyed to the sep- arate states the title of the swamp and overflowed lands within their borders in order that these lands might be reclaimed by the state through corporate as well as individual activities. The grants were not, however, sufficiently well guarded to secure the desired results, and although practically all of the states eagerly sought and acquired the swamp lands and passed them over to individuals and corporations, very little was ever done to reclaim and utilize these lands. They became objects of speculation, and vast areas still remain in the hands of men who are holding them for rise in prices. . . .

There remains yet to be worked out some feasible scheme by which the vast areas of swamp and overflowed lands whose title is now in private ownership may be reclaimed, subdivided, and put in the hands of men who will cultivate them. The soil of these swamp lands is extremely fertile and with effective systems of drainage the lands are capable not merely of supporting large and prosperous agricultural communities, but will be sources of strength to each commonwealth in which they are situated, instead of being, as now, breeding places of mosquitoes and other pests, centers of disease and a menace to land values in the neighborhood.

It may be possible after diffusing information and stimulating public interest to bring together the diverse interests and ultimately to reclaim the large tracts of the swamp land donated to the states, but this can come about on a broad scale only after careful study of the entire situation and the adoption of far-reaching plans. It is, of course, possible to take up one particular tract and build levees, dikes and drains, but it frequently happens that the plans made for one area are such as seriously to interfere with the development of another or more important piece of land; or the system proposed for several areas may be such as not to provide adequate waterways for tracts higher up, and thus disaster may follow the carrying out of schemes which are not sufficiently broad to take in all the surrounding conditions. Where, on the contrary, plans for reclamation start with a full knowledge of all the conditions as they exist and a comprehension of ideal results to be attained, it should result that with the execution of these plans, great tracts of fertile but water-clogged soil will be made available for agriculture.

The term "reclamation" has of late been popularly used with a somewhat restricted meaning, as applying to the irrigation of arid lands and the bringing on of a needed amount of water at proper seasons. Reclamation in this sense has been undertaken by the National Government under the terms of an act passed June 17, 1902, which creates a special fund in the treasury out of the proceeds of the disposal of public lands. This fund is entirely distinct from the general revenues of the Government, derived by imposts or taxation, and hence it is not subject to many of the constitutional limitations which are imposed upon acts of Congress. The expenditure of the reclamation fund has been placed by Congress in the hands of the Secretary of the Interior for the purpose of making surveys and examinations and later constructing feasible projects for the reclamation by irrigation of arid and semi-arid lands. He is also charged with the duty of maintaining and operating these projects until the charges for water for the major portions of the land have been repaid, when the burden of operation and maintenance passes to the owners of the lands.

The Reclamation Act is very general in character and imposes large discretion upon the secretary. In order to carry it out, he has organized what is known as the Reclamation Service, which is practically a bureau of the Department of the Interior. This service consists of men selected through competitive civil service examinations, based largely on practical experience, and who have made a record for efficiency each in his specialty. This organization has been in existence for a little over six years, and during that time, under the direction of the Secretary of the Interior, has made plans for many important works, and has erected a number of these, the estimated expenditures being in round numbers fifty millions of dollars. Already nearly a million acres have been placed under irrigation, and a third of this has been actually watered. Large dams and other structures for conserving water have been built, so that additional areas can be brought under irrigation by completing other units.

The building of large structures for water conservation and for the reclamation of land is not, however, the ultimate object. These works in themselves are notable, but their importance to the nation comes from the fact that they make possible opportunities for the creation of small farms and building of homes for an independent citizenship. The question of prime interest to the general public is not so much that of how far these works may be extended, but what may be accomplished through them by the reclamation of lands otherwise valueless.

Throughout an extent of land, equalling fully two-fifths of the area of the entire United States, there is not enough rain, at least in the crop season, for the needs of useful plants, and for success in agriculture there must be a constant supply of water, artificially controlled and brought to the fields. Between the two extremes—on the east a humid region with occasional summer droughts, and on the west a truly arid region where all plants need irrigation—lies a broad and somewhat debatable belt of land known as sub-humid or semi-arid region, within which irrigation is valuable, but where the need is not so pressing as to render the practice always successful. In the arid region there is no question as to what may be accomplished by reclamation. The extent of the accomplishments are bounded simply by available water supply, and the acreage which will be reclaimed in the future can be given accurately when facts become available as to the quantity of water which may be stored or pumped to the dry lands.

In the semi-arid region, however, the question is a little more complicated, as the extent to which irrigation may be extended in the future is modified by the possibilities of finding useful drought-resisting plants which can be cultivated on the rich soil where the water supply is now somewhat deficient. Our present knowledge of the water supply available for use in both the arid and semi-arid regions is not sufficient to state accurately the limits which are set by nature to the irrigable areas.

There is more good land in the arid region than there is water for it. If all the run-off waters of this region could be conserved and employed in irrigation, the total reclaimed area might, perhaps, be brought to nearly 60,000,000 acres. This is uncertain, however, as our data on run-off are confined to a portion only of the streams, and are incomplete even for these; furthermore, such an estimate involves assumptions regarding the duty of water that may introduce large errors; that is to say, we do not know in all cases how much land can be irrigated by a given amount of water. It is known, moreover, that large portions of the water of the arid region can not be used in irrigation, as no irrigable land exists upon which it can be brought at feasible cost.

In general it may be stated that the value of irrigated land is increasing while improvements in machinery are tending to decrease costs of construction of reclamation works, so that it is impossible to draw an exact line between the probable and improbable schemes, even if we had full knowledge regarding present costs. This would require elaborate surveys, which have not been made. For these reasons any present estimate of the total irrigable area is necessarily little better than a guess. With present data, the closest statement is probably under 60,000,000 acres . . . .

The subjects of irrigation, forestry, power, domestic water supply, drainage and navigation are all closely interrelated and should be thoroughly studied together, not only in the arid, but in the humid regions. No one of these questions can be properly treated without full regard to all the others. Proper study of these comprehensive subjects should include more extended observations of rainfall and evaporation, especially in high altitudes, and of the annual flow of all streams. Topographic maps should be made showing the areas of drainage basin, the location of reservoir sites, and their relation in altitude and location to irrigable lands and to power and navigation resources. Such maps are the basic information most urgently needed for all land classification, and without them no wise policy can be adopted.

Both state and national laws are incomplete in permitting and encouraging settlement on lands which should be reserved for reservoir sites. Thorough surveys should be made and all feasible reservoir sites, when discovered, should be reserved for development.

The present laws in some states tend to promote irrigation, but in others they do not. The most primitive form of the regulation of water in irrigation is best exemplified by the present laws of the State of California. These declare the principles of priority and beneficial use, and provide that claims to the use of water shall be recorded in the form of a notice of appropriation, and shall be perfected by application to a beneficial use. At the same time they try to recognize as concurrent on the same stream, rights derived by prior appropriation [of water] and rights depending on riparian ownership.* The riparian doctrine of water rights should be definitely and permanently abrogated in all arid regions. . . .

The progress of reclamation in many of the western states will be extremely slow until better laws are passed covering some of the important points above indicated. The uncertainties concerning rights to water are so great that no one would be justified in incurring large expenditures without better safeguards. The conditions are very much as though we had no system for describing or recording land titles, and every man could claim all of the land he desired, leaving it to the courts from time to time to determine how much land was actually used by each man. The litigation which results from this indefinite condition is endless, since it frequently determines only the relative

---

* That is, the rights of a person owning land containing or bordering on a river or lake to its water. Newell is arguing that with respect to water in the arid region, the public interest should take precedence over individual rights. [Ed.]

rights of two men and leaves out of account the rights of third parties or of the public. The confusion which now exists with reference to water titles is indescribable, excepting in those states where a definite system of measuring and recording the amount of water has been adopted.

With larger knowledge of the subject, with better laws, and with skill in handling water, it will be possible to reclaim the vast areas above mentioned, and to make opportunities for at least a million farms and homes, supporting directly five millions of people, and indirectly enabling an equal or greater number of people to be supported through the transportation and manufacturing business which grows up incidental to farming. The yield per acre of the reclaimed land is so great that when completely utilized it is possible that it will support, directly or indirectly, a population averaging very nearly one to the acre. This means communities nearly independent of the effect of fluctuating trade conditions, or of wet or dry weather, and a people more nearly self-supporting than any other similar number in the country. It means a citizenship attached to the soil and with the incentives to the highest patriotism.

11

Ends and Means
GIFFORD PINCHOT (1910, 1947)

When the attitude of Congress and the Taft administration made it apparent that the federal government would not fully accept Progressive conservation, Gifford Pinchot tried to bring public support behind the movement. A clear, compelling statement of purpose and methods was a prerequisite. The way Pinchot attempted to meet such a need is illustrated in the following selections. His utilitarianism as well as his democratic orientation are clearly evident. Yet the grass roots approach proved no more successful in the early twentieth century than had the direct appeal to legislators.

Gifford Pinchot, *The Fight for Conservation* (Garden City, New York, Harcourt, Brace, 1910), 42–50.

Both the National Conservation Congress and the National Conservation Association served chiefly as arenas for conservationists to spar among themselves. Nonetheless, Pinchot made "conservation" a household word, reversed (at least in theory) three centuries of American thinking about the environment, and laid the intellectual foundations for subsequent achievements.

. . . The principles which govern the conservation movement, like all great and effective things, are simple and easily understood. . . .

The first great fact about conservation is that it stands for development. There has been a fundamental misconception that conservation means nothing but the husbanding of resources for future generations. There could be no more serious mistake. Conservation does mean provision for the future, but it means also and first of all the recognition of the right of the present generation to the fullest necessary use of all the resources with which this country is so abundantly blessed. Conservation demands the welfare of this generation first, and afterward the welfare of the generations to follow.

The first principle of conservation is development, the use of the natural resources now existing on this continent for the benefit of the people who live here now. There may be just as much waste in neglecting the development and use of certain natural resources as there is in their destruction. We have a limited supply of coal, and only a limited supply. Whether it is to last for a hundred or a hundred and fifty or a thousand years, the coal is limited in amount, unless through geological changes which we shall not live to see, there will never be any more of it than there is now. But coal is in a sense the vital essence of our civilization. If it can be preserved, if the life of the mines can be extended, if by preventing waste there can be more coal left in this country after we of this generation have made every needed use of this source of power, then we shall have deserved well of our descendants.

Conservation stands emphatically for the development and use of water-power now, without delay. It stands for the immediate construction of navigable waterways under a broad and comprehensive plan as assistants to the railroads. More coal and more iron are required to move a ton of freight by rail than by water, three to one. In every case and in every direction the conservation movement has development for its first principle, and at the very beginning of its work. The development of our natural resources and the fullest use of them for the present generation is the first duty of this generation. . . .

In the second place conservation stands for the prevention of waste. There has come gradually in this country an understanding that waste is not a good thing and that the attack on waste is an industrial necessity. I recall very well indeed how, in the early days of forest fires, they were considered simply and solely as acts of God, against which any opposition was hopeless and any attempt to control them not merely hopeless but childish. It was assumed that they came in the natural order of things, as inevitably as the seasons or the rising and setting of the sun. Today we understand that forest fires are wholly within the control of men. So we are coming in like manner to understand that the prevention of waste in all other directions is a simple matter of good business. The first duty of the human race is to control the earth it lives upon.

We are in a position more and more completely to say how far the waste and destruction of natural resources are to be allowed to go on and where they are to stop. It is curious that the effort to stop waste, like the effort to stop forest fires, has often been considered as a matter controlled wholly by economic law. I think there could be no greater mistake. Forest fires were allowed to burn long after the people had means to stop them. The idea that men were helpless in the face of them held long after the time had passed when the means of control were fully within our reach. It was the old story that "as a man thinketh, so is he"; we came to see that we could stop forest fires, and we found that the means had long been at hand. When at length we came to see that the control of logging in certain directions was profitable, we found it had long been possible. In all these matters of waste of natural resources, the education of the people to understand that they can stop the leakage comes before the actual stopping and after the means of stopping it have long been ready at our hands.

In addition to the principles of development and preservation of our resources there is a third principle. It is this: The natural resources must be developed and preserved for the benefit of the many, and not merely for the profit of a few. We are coming to understand in this country that public action for public benefit has a very much wider field to cover and a much larger part to play than was the case when there were resources enough for every one, and before certain constitutional provisions had given so tremendously strong a position to vested rights and property in general.

. . . [B]y reason of the XIVth amendment to the Constitution, property rights in the United States occupy a stronger position than in any other country in the civilized world. It becomes then a matter of multiplied importance, since property rights once granted are so strongly entrenched, to see that they shall be so granted that the people shall get their fair share of the benefit which comes from the development of the resources which belong to us all. The time to do that is now. By so doing we shall avoid the difficulties and conflicts which will surely arise if we allow vested rights to accrue outside the possibility of governmental and popular control.

The conservation idea covers a wider range than the field of natural resources alone. Conservation means the greatest good to the greatest number for the longest time. One of its great contributions is just this, that it has added to the worn and well-known phrase, "the greatest good to the greatest number," the additional words "for the longest time," thus recognizing that this nation of ours must be made to endure as the best possible home for all its people.

Conservation advocates the use of foresight, prudence, thrift, and intelligence in dealing with public matters, for the same reasons and in the same way that we each use foresight, prudence, thrift, and intelligence in dealing with our own private affairs. It proclaims the right and duty of the people to act for the benefit of the people. Conservation demands the application of common sense to the common problems for the common good.

The principles of conservation thus described—development, preservation, the common good—have a general application which is growing rapidly wider. The development of resources and the prevention of waste and loss, the protection of the public interests, by foresight, prudence, and the ordinary business and home-making virtues, all these apply to other things as well as to the natural resources. There is, in fact, no interest of the people to which the principles of conservation do not apply.

The conservation point of view is valuable in the education of our people as well as in forestry; it applies to the body politic as well as to the earth and its minerals. A municipal franchise is as properly within its sphere as a franchise for water-power. The same point of view governs in both. It applies as much to the subject of good roads as to waterways, and the training of our people in citizenship is as germane to it as the productiveness of the earth. The application of common-sense to any problem for the Nation's good will lead directly to national efficiency wherever applied. In other words, and that is the burden of the message, we are coming to see the logical and inevitable outcome that these principles, which arose in forestry and have their bloom in the conservation of natural resources, will have their fruit in the increase and promotion of national efficiency along other lines of national life.

The outgrowth of conservation, the inevitable result, is national efficiency. In the great commercial struggle between nations which is eventually to determine the welfare of all, national efficiency will be the deciding factor. So from every point of view conservation is a good thing for the American people.

. . . The earth and its resources belong of right to its people.

Without natural resources life itself is impossible. From birth to death, natural resources, transformed for human use, feed, clothe, shelter, and transport us. Upon them we depend for every material necessity, comfort, convenience, and protection in our lives. Without abundant resources prosperity is out of reach.

Therefore the conservation of natural resources is the fundamental material problem. It is the open door to economic and political progress. That was never so true as now.

The first duty of the human race on the material side is to control the use of the earth and all that therein is. Conservation means the wise use of the earth and its resources for the lasting good of men. Conservation is the foresighted utilization, preservation, and/or renewal of forests, waters, lands, and minerals, for the greatest good of the greatest number for the longest time.

Since Conservation has become a household word, it has come to mean many things to many men. To me it means, everywhere and always, that the public good comes first.

To the use of the natural resources, renewable or nonrenewable, each generation has the first right. Nevertheless no generation can be allowed needlessly to damage or reduce the future general wealth and welfare by the way it uses or misuses any natural resource.

Nationally, the outgrowth and result of Conservation is efficiency. In the old world that is passing, in the new world that is coming, national efficiency has been and will be a controlling factor in national safety and welfare.

Internationally, the central purpose of Conservation is permanent

---

peace. No nation, not even the United States, is self-sufficient in all the resources it requires. Throughout human history one of the commonest causes of war has been the demand for land. Land (agricultural land, forest land, coal, iron, oil, uranium, and other mineral-producing land) means natural resources.

Therefore, world-wide practice of Conservation and fair and continued access by all nations to the resources they need are the two indispensable foundations of continuous plenty and of permanent peace.

Conservation is the application of common sense to the common problems for the common good. Since its objective is the ownership, control, development, processing, distribution, and use of the natural resources for the benefit of the people, it is by its very nature the antithesis of monopoly. So long as people are oppressed by the lack of such ownership and control, so long will they continue to be cheated of their right to life, liberty, and the pursuit of happiness, cheated out of their enjoyment of the earth and all that it contains. It is obvious, therefore, that the principles of Conservation must apply to human beings as well as to natural resources.

The Conservation policy then has three great purposes.

First: wisely to use, protect, preserve, and renew the natural resources of the earth.

Second: to control the use of the natural resources and their products in the common interest, and to secure their distribution to the people at fair and reasonable charges for goods and services.

Third: to see to it that the rights of the people to govern themselves shall not be controlled by great monopolies through their power over natural resources.

Two of the principal ways in which lack of Conservation works out in damage to the general welfare are: (A) by destruction of forests, erosion of soils, injury of waterways, and waste of nonrenewable mineral resources. Here is strong reason for Government control. (B) by monopoly of natural and human resources, their products and application, and of the instruments by which these are made available.

Monopoly means power—power not only over the supply of natural resources, but also power to fix prices, and to exact unfair profits which lead to higher living costs for the people. It is the very essence of democracy that the greatest advantage of each of us is best reached through common prosperity of all of us. Monopoly is the denial of that great truth.

Monopoly of resources which prevents, limits, or destroys equality of opportunity is one of the most effective of all ways to control and limit human rights, especially the right of self-government.

Monopoly on the loose is a source of many of the economic, political, and social evils which afflict the sons of men. Its abolition or regulation is an inseparable part of the Conservation policy. . . .

12

The Public Responds to Conservation: Opinion East and West

(1897–1910)

For most Westerners, conservation (they sometimes called it "Pinchotism") was the arbitrary and un-American policy of snobbish Eastern bureaucrats unsympathetic to the needs and desires of the West. Closer to what remained of the frontier, whose myth of inexhaustibility was still alive, Western resource users regarded every reservation or restriction as a "locking up" of raw material and a limitation on individual enterprise. Suspicion exploded into anger in 1897 when President Grover Cleveland, at the suggestion of the Pinchot-dominated National Forestry Commission, created over 21,000,000 acres of new forest reserves. The *first* cartoon, below, appeared in the *Seattle Post-Intelligencer,* March 7, 1897. Cleveland, seated on a horse "blinded" by the Forestry Commission, is using the existence of a single tree to create a reserve and thereby keep Western miners from jobs and profits. Opposition such as this was largely responsible for the passage on June 4 of the Forest Management Act which opened the forest reserves to grazing, mining, commercial lumbering, and hydroelectric development. Federal supervision, however, was retained.

Water was also a sore point in relations between conservationists and many Westerners. By 1910 the federal Bureau of Reclamation had undertaken so many projects as to cause private interests to feel unduly restricted. Calls for automony in resource development, supported by states' rights political theory, were widespread.

The *second* cartoon, which appeared in 1910 in several publications perhaps best summarized Western opinion. Pinchot, with the spats and mustache symbolic of his allegedly aristocratic bearing and background, is using conservation to turn back the progress-minded West.

1. From the *Seattle Post-Intelligencer,* March 7, 1897.

"*And What is to Become of Us?*"

THE WILD AND WOOLLY EAST.

2. From the *Tacoma (Washington) Ledger,* reproduced in the *Literary Digest,* September 17, 1910.

3. J. N. Darling. Reprinted by permission of *The Des Moines Register.*

THE BLAZED TRAIL

4. From the San Francisco Gazz, September 27, 1909.

DISGUISED AS THE FAITHFUL SHEPHERD DOG, A WOLF IS FOUND WITHIN THE CORRAL

5. Louis Wisa, February, 1910. Reprinted by permission of *The Newark News.*

EXPECTING A ROAR FROM THE JUNGLE.

6. From the *Philadelphia Record*, January 10, 1910.

In the East, on the other hand, public opinion generally favored conservation. The *third* cartoon by the well-known Iowa cartoonist (and, under Franklin D. Roosevelt, Director of the Bureau of Biological Survey) Jay N. "Ding" Darling, represents the feeling that conservation as practiced by Theodore Roosevelt was good for the country. It also suggests the vagueness that characterized the public notion of what conservation meant!

The eruption of the controversy between Secretary of the Interior Richard A. Ballinger and Chief Forester Gifford Pinchot in 1909 provided an opening for both critics and supporters of conservation. Although the issue involved personal and political matters quite unrelated to natural resources, many understood it to be the climax of Progressive conservation. The cartoons which follow represent the Ballinger-Pinchot controversy according to the Pinchot sympathizers. In the *fourth* picture Pinchot is guiding President William Howard Taft and the Republican elephant in the direction conservationists hoped they would take: along the Roosevelt trail of resource management. Early in 1909, however, Pinchot realized that without Roosevelt in the White House conservation would not be well treated in Washington, and he began to criticize Ballinger's policies. Pinchot particularly protested the Secretary's alleged cooperation with several large corporations in the acquisition of vast amounts of Alaskan coal lands. The people's rights to the land, Pinchot implied, were being sacrificed to monopolies, and conservation principles utterly disregarded. Moreover, as the *fifth* cartoon suggests, President Taft abrogated his responsibility as custodian of the nation's resources. Only the faithful Pinchot stood between a hypocritical Ballinger and the vulnerable natural wealth of the republic.

In January 1910 Pinchot overtly challenged Ballinger and was immediately dismissed for insubordination by an outraged Taft. It was now impossible to cover the rupture in the Republican party, and the nation, with the symbolic elephant in the *sixth* cartoon, braced itself for the reaction of Roosevelt who was on a safari in Africa. It came, in time, in Roosevelt's decision to run against both Taft and the Democrats, in the Presidential election of 1912. Woodrow Wilson, however, won easily over the divided Republicans, and his initial policy of reducing the federal role to that of a referee among competing private interests proved no more compatible with the conservationists' principles than had Taft's.

Recent scholarship (see the Bibliography, page 228) has revealed that Ballinger was not technically guilty of abusing the power of his office and that Taft had no alternative but to dismiss the unyielding Pinchot. Political realities, rather than conservation policy, determined the outcome of the issue. But in the public mind the Ballinger-Pinchot controversy was either a deserved rebuke of Progressive conservation in the interest of private enterprise, or confirmation that the people must struggle still harder to save the environment from exploitation by big business.

13

Aesthetics and Conservation
ROBERT UNDERWOOD JOHNSON (1910)

Formal, dapper Robert Underwood Johnson represents perfectly the class of genteel Americans for whom conservation meant something quite different than it did for Pinchot and his colleagues. Johnson felt that in their obsession for efficient use of the environment, the national conservation leaders slighted natural beauty. In his opinion conservationists were little better than the exploiters they purported to replace: both gave precedence to the material, as opposed to the spiritual, values of nature. From his editor's desk at Century, Johnson lashed out repeatedly at the preoccupation of his countrymen with the main chance. In 1890 he played a leading role in securing Congressional approval of the act creating Yosemite National Park. Thereafter Johnson championed the National Parks as the embodiment of an enlightened approach to nature. The National Forests, on the other hand, seemed hopelessly utilitarian. Understandably Johnson clashed with Pinchot on this interpretation, a personal break that symbolized the larger schism in American conservation between the developers and the preservationists that persists to this day (see (32) for an example).

Johnson's reference below to the "blot" on the conservation record of the Roosevelt administration and the "scheme for the dismemberment of the Yosemite National Park" concern the 1906 application of San Francisco for the right to construct a dam at the lower end of the Hetch Hetchy Valley, within the park, for the purpose of municipal water supply and hydropower. The resulting controversy is also mentioned in (14) and (18).

Although the declaration of the first White House Conference of Governors included a record of their agreement "that the beauty, healthfulness, and habitability of our country should be preserved and

[Robert Underwood Johnson], "The Neglect of Beauty in the Conservation Movement," *Century,* **LXXIX** (1910), 637–638.

increased," it is much to be regretted that the official leaders of the conservation movement—than which nothing is more important to the country—have never shown a cordial, much less an aggressive, interest in safeguarding our great scenery, or in promoting, in general, this part of their admirable program. When the Appalachian Park reserve was first proposed, a prominent member of Congress embodied his objection to it by saying bluntly, "We are not buying scenery." To meet this criticism, the friends of the bill, instead of boldly insisting upon the value of great scenery, chose to lay stress exclusively upon the material and economic side of the whole movement. The fact is, there is no more popular and effective trumpet-call for the conservation movement than the appeal to the love of beautiful natural scenery. In this matter the idealists are more practical than the materialists, whose mistake is that they never capitalize sentiment. A money valuation of the uses of our great natural scenery, attracting, as it does, a vast number of summer sojourners and the traveling public in general, would make an astonishing showing.

It could easily be proved that the fear of offending the "hard-headed" and "practical" man by such an appeal is without foundation. The first thing that a man does after he obtains a competence is to invest his money in some form of beauty, and it is in the interest of good citizenship that he should have a plot of ground to be proud of. He settles in some town, suburb, or other region mainly because it is beautiful, and he is all the happier if his home can command an attractive natural view. As he grows richer, this desire for beautiful things, and particularly for a beautiful country-place, becomes more dominant, and it is to such a feeling that we owe the development of our sea-coast and hilltops into regions of resort for health and recreation. The American still apostrophizes his country with the lines:

> *I love thy rocks and rills,*
> *Thy woods and templed hills,*

and he is not willing that this sentiment shall be changed to read:

> *I love thy stocks and mills,*
> *Thy goods and crumpled bills.*

It must always be held as a blot upon the lustrous record of the Roosevelt Administration in conservation matters that, in deference to the false sense of what is practical, and, moreover, by a strained construction of law, it gave away a large part of the people's greatest national park for a city's reservoir, confessedly without the slightest inquiry as to the necessity of doing so.* The contention that in fact this necessity does not exist was confirmed when the leader of the scheme acknowledged before the Senate Committee on the Public Lands that San Francisco, without invading the Park, could get an abundant water-supply from a number of other regions by the simple, though sometimes inconvenient, process of paying for it!

The time has come when, if much of what has been gained by the reservation of our great natural monuments is not to be lost, the public must make known its wishes to Congress. The scheme for the dismemberment of the Yosemite National Park, which a year ago was temporarily checked, is to be pushed during the present session. In this contest the recent visit of President Taft to the Yosemite and that of the Secretary of the Interior † to the Hetch-Hetchy will strengthen the defenders of the latter valley, for no one can view the phenomenal beauty of these Sierra gorges without feeling a solemn responsibility for its preservation. Even the San Francisco promoters of the destructive scheme threw up their hands in admiration as they caught sight of the Hetch-Hetchy, and confessed that "something was to be said for the esthetes, after all." And yet they profess to believe that water is "running to waste" if it be simply looked at! And this is said of streams which, after they have been looked at, may be utilized for the irrigation of the great San Joaquin lowlands.

Movements to safeguard Niagara and the Hudson are also impending, and in this connection we respectfully commend to Senators and Representatives, as well as to the members of the New York legislature, these judicious words of Governor [Charles Evans] Hughes, spoken at the dedication of the Palisades Interstate Park:

> *Of what avail would be the material benefits of gainful occupation, what would be the promise of prosperous communities, with wealth of products and freedom of exchange, were it not for the opportunities to cultivate the love of the beautiful? The preservation of the scenery of the Hudson is the highest duty with respect to this river imposed upon those who are the trustees of its manifold benefits. It is fortunate that means have already been taken to protect this escarpment, which is one of its finest features. The two States have joined in measures for this purpose. I hope this is only the beginning*

---

* Actually, the Hetch Hetchy issue was not resolved until 1913: see (18). [Ed.]

† Richard A. Ballinger [Ed.]

of efforts which may jointly be made by these two commonwealths to safeguard the highlands and waters, in which they are both deeply interested. The entire watershed which lies to the north should be conserved, and a policy should be instituted for such joint control as would secure adequate protection.

But it is not merely the colossal beauty of the Sierra, Niagara, and the Hudson that should be preserved and enhanced, but the beauty of city, town, and hamlet. What is needed is the inculcation, by every agency, of *beauty as a principle,* that life may be made happier and more elevating for all the generations who shall follow us, and who will love their country more devotedly the more lovable it is made.

14

A Voice for Wilderness

JOHN MUIR (1901, 1912)

The preservation of wilderness was a favorite cause of "aesthetic" conservationists like Robert Underwood Johnson (13) and John Muir. A Scot by birth, Muir grew up on the central Wisconsin frontier in the 1850's, but unlike most pioneers he formed a love of wilderness that ultimately led him to a lifetime spent close to California's Sierra. By the turn of the century Muir had become the nation's foremost publicizer of the value of wilderness and, as a founder and first president of the Sierra Club (1892), a strong force for its protection. Transcendentalism, gleaned from Ralph Waldo Emerson and Henry David Thoreau (2), shaped his philosophy: undisturbed nature was a "window opening into heaven, a mirror reflecting the Creator." It followed that protecting wilderness was almost an act of worship. In his declining years Muir threw himself into the battle to save Yosemite National Park's wild Hetch Hetchy Valley from alteration by a dam [(13) and (18)]. His failure in this cause was a bitter disappointment, but Muir's efforts did much to call into being a potent national sentiment for preserving wilderness [(23), (32), and (33).]

The tendency nowadays to wander in wildernesses is delightful to see. Thousands of tired, nerve-shaken, over-civilized people are beginning

John Muir, *Our National Parks* (Boston, Houghton, 1901), 1–3.

to find out that going to the mountains is going home; that wildness is a necessity; and that mountain parks and reservations are useful not only as fountains of timber and irrigating rivers, but as fountains of life. Awakening from the stupefying effects of the vice of over-industry and the deadly apathy of luxury, they are trying as best they can to mix and enrich their own little ongoings with those of Nature, and to get rid of rust and disease. Briskly venturing and roaming, some are washing off sins and cobweb cares of the devil's spinning in all-day storms on mountains; sauntering in rosiny pinewoods or in gentian meadows, brushing through chaparral, bending down and parting sweet, flowery sprays; tracing rivers to their sources, getting in touch with the nerves of Mother Earth; jumping from rock to rock, feeling the life of them, learning the songs of them, panting in whole-souled exercise, and rejoicing in deep, long-drawn breaths of pure wildness. This is fine and natural and full of promise. So also is the growing interest in the care and preservation of forests and wild places in general, and in the half wild parks and gardens of towns. Even the scenery habit in its most artificial forms, mixed with spectacles, silliness, and kodaks; its devotees arrayed more gorgeously than scarlet tanagers, frightening the wild game with red umbrellas,—even this is encouraging, and may well be regarded as a hopeful sign of the times.

All the Western mountains are still rich in wildness, and by means of good roads are being brought nearer civilization every year.* To the sane and free it will hardly seem necessary to cross the continent in search of wild beauty, however easy the way, for they find it in abundance wherever they chance to be. Like Thoreau they see forests in orchards and patches of huckleberry brush, and oceans in ponds and drops of dew. Few in these hot, dim, strenuous times are quite sane or free; choked with care like clocks full of dust, laboriously doing so much good and making so much money,—or so little,—they are no longer good for themselves. . . .

---

* At this time (1901) Muir did not foresee the fact that for later preservationists roads and cars would be a major threat. [Ed.]

. . . Hetch Hetchy Valley, far from being a plain, common, rock-bound meadow, as many who have not seen it seem to suppose, is a grand landscape garden, one of Nature's rarest and most precious

---

John Muir, *The Yosemite* (New York, Century, 1912), 255–257, 260–262.

mountain temples. As in Yosemite, the sublime rocks of its walls seem to glow with life, whether leaning back in repose or standing erect in thoughtful attitudes, giving welcome to storms and calms alike, their brows in the sky, their feet set in the groves and gay flowery meadows, while birds, bees, and butterflies help the river and waterfalls to stir all the air into music—things frail and fleeting and types of permanence meeting here and blending, just as they do in Yosemite, to draw her lovers into close and confiding communion with her.

Sad to say, this most precious and sublime feature of the Yosemite National Park, one of the greatest of all our natural resources for the uplifting joy and peace and health of the people, is in danger of being dammed and made into a reservoir to help supply San Francisco with water and light, thus flooding it from wall to wall and burying its gardens and groves one or two hundred feet deep. This grossly destructive commercial scheme has long been planned and urged (though water as pure and abundant can be got from sources outside of the people's park, in a dozen different places), because of the comparative cheapness of the dam and of the territory which it is sought to divert from the great uses to which it was dedicated in the Act of 1890 establishing the Yosemite National Park.

The making of gardens and parks goes on with civilization all over the world, and they increase both in size and number as their value is recognized. Everybody needs beauty as well as bread, places to play in and pray in, where Nature may heal and cheer and give strength to body and soul alike. This natural beauty-hunger is made manifest in the little window-sill gardens of the poor, though perhaps only a geranium slip in a broken cup, as well as in the carefully tended rose and lily gardens of the rich, the thousands of spacious city parks and botanical gardens, and in our magnificent National parks—the Yellowstone, Yosemite, Sequoia, etc.—Nature's sublime wonderlands, the admiration and joy of the world. Nevertheless, like anything else worth while, from the very beginning, however well guarded, they have always been subject to attack by despoiling gain-seekers and mischief-makers of every degree from Satan to Senators, eagerly trying to make everything immediately and selfishly commercial, with schemes disguised in smug-smiling philanthropy, industriously, shampiously crying, "Conservation, conservation, panutilization," that man and beast may be fed and the dear Nation made great. Thus long ago a few enterprising merchants utilized the Jerusalem temple as a place of business instead of a place of prayer, changing money, buying and selling cattle and sheep and doves; and earlier still, the first forest reservation, including only one tree, was likewise despoiled. Ever since the establishment of the Yosemite National Park, strife has been going on around its borders and I suppose this will go on as part of the universal battle between right and wrong, however much its boundaries may be shorn, or its wild beauty destroyed. . . .

That any one would try to destroy [Hetch Hetchy Valley] seems incredible; but sad experience shows that there are people good enough and bad enough for anything. The proponents of the dam scheme bring forward a lot of bad arguments to prove that the only righteous thing to do with the people's parks is to destroy them bit by bit as they are able. Their arguments are curiously like those of the devil, devised for the destruction of the first garden . . . .

These temple destroyers, devotees of ravaging commercialism, seem to have a perfect contempt for Nature, and, instead of lifting their eyes to the God of the mountains, lift them to the Almighty Dollar.

Dam Hetch Hetchy! As well dam for water-tanks the people's cathedrals and churches, for no holier temple has ever been consecrated by the heart of man.

15

The Historical Landscape
THE AMERICAN SCENIC AND HISTORIC PRESERVATION SOCIETY (1914)

One of the factors shaping the environment is the concern, or lack of it, for the past. Possibly because their national history is so short in comparison to Europe's, Americans have been intensely interested in preserving the visible historical record. Preservation of the past began on a major scale in

Nineteenth Annual Report of the American Scenic and Historic Preservation Society, State of New York, Assembly Document 57 (March 24, 1914), 13–16, 18–22.

1858 with the acquisition of George Washington's home at Mount Vernon as a national shrine. The next milestone came in 1895 when Andrew H. Green, president of the Commissioners of the State Reservation at Niagara, formed an organization in New York modeled after Great Britain's National Trust and Monuments Historiques *of France. In 1901 Green's group reconstituted itself as the American Scenic and Historic Preservation Society and began to take an interest in places outside New York. Frequently the antiquarians sided with the wilderness preservationists; indeed the source of support for both crusades was anxiety over the speed with which modern civilization obliterated cherished parts of former environments. The following statement of purpose was most likely the work of George F. Kunz, president of the Society and a New York jeweler.*

. . . [T]he American Scenic and Historic Preservation Society . . . is a national organization of men and women for the protection of natural scenery and the preservation of historic landmarks in the United States. It aims to protect notable features of the landscape in city or country made beautiful by nature or art; to preserve landmarks, objects and other records of the past and present; to erect historical memorials; and generally to promote popular appreciation of the scenic beauties of America and respect for the history of the Nation, its honored names and its physical memorials. . . .

The two fundamental ideas which this Society represents are more closely related than at first appears. Scenery is the work of Nature; history is the work of man. But a moment's reflection will show how intimately one affects the other. Of the three elementary influences which chiefly determine the character of a people, namely, heredity, epoch (the age in which they live) and environment, scenery is an important factor of the latter. The natural surroundings which either by their harshness repress human development and circumscribe the radius of action, or by their opulence tend to promote languor and inactivity, or by their medium between these extremes develop hardihood, activity and progress, present themselves to the mind largely through the sense of sight as scenery. The very sight of the landscape, therefore, affects the character of a people and has its effect upon human history.

Further than this, the great forces of nature, which have lifted the mountain ranges, carved the valleys, set the rivers flowing and the cataracts falling and gathered the waters together in beautiful lakes and expansive seas, have determined the very places where human activity has expressed itself in what we call history. . . .

If space permitted, this theme could be elaborated with a wealth of detail to support the demonstration of the natural connection between the scenic and historic.

The formation of organizations of defenders of natural monuments and human monuments implies that those monuments need protection. And this implication, so far as it relates to human monuments, is sustained by the history of centuries. . . .

The mutilation and disfigurement of notable features of the natural landscape upon a scale calling for restraint may be regarded, perhaps, as a more modern phase of this vandalism. The great advance in the physical sciences generally and in engineering particularly in modern times has led to this commercial assault on nature. In olden times the highways generally followed natural grades and curved around hills and other obstacles. Today, the engineer draws a straight line, and blasts his way along the shortest distance between two points. The highway and the railroad defy Nature and go where they will. The growth of electrical science within twenty-five years has given a new value to waterfalls; and now commercial enterprise seeks to create mill ponds in superb valleys, such as the Hetch-Hetchy in the Yosemite National Park, or to divert the water from its natural course to drive the wheels of industry, as at Niagara Falls. In ancient times the wood-chopper made a prayer of conciliation to the spirit of a tree before he cut it down, so real was his belief that his gods dwelt in the forests. Today the woodsman has no hesitation and in the United States the forests are falling from three to five times as fast as they are growing, not only robbing the landscape of much of its beauty but also vitally affecting the history of the people. As the commerce of ancient Rome has been curtailed by the cutting of forests and the drying up of the affluents of the Tiber, so within the history of living man in the United States, mill streams have disappeared in consequence of the rape of the forests, and our own history is being changed. Sometimes beautiful features of landscape are disfigured by the operation of quarrymen like those which threatened the Palisades of the Hudson before they were rescued by private generosity and public appropriations. When notable features of the scenery are not utilized physically, they are oftentimes disfigured by commercial surroundings or rendered disagreeable by demands for sight-seeing fees, as was the case of Niagara Falls before they were taken under the protection of the State. Again, the shade trees which border our thoroughfares are frequently mutilated by the contractors erecting electric wires, as has been the case notably in Flushing, [Long Island, New York], while glaring billboards and posters, affixed to trees and rocks or erected in conspicuous places, mar some of the finest vistas in city and country.

These operations against historic landmarks and notable landscapes might be permitted to continue unrestrained if they did no harm; but the natural revulsion of intelligent public sentiment against them is a sure indication that they are to be deplored.

. . . No doubt one great reason is the feeling that it is well-nigh criminal to destroy or to undo great works of art and architecture which embody the product of the labor and the genius of so many men of so many ages. It is like nullifying the lives of so many generations of men—like obliterating them from the scroll of time—so far as their productive labors are concerned. It is like setting back the calender of years to the time before those works were made, and creating a condition the same as if the works had never been performed. It is depriving the world of what makes for civilization and of what civilization is entitled to have, namely, the accumulation of the best products of human genius of all preceding generations.

But there is another reason of more universal application than the foregoing. The reason which we have just mentioned is based largely on the consideration that the monuments—architectural or sculptural—are great in themselves; and that they possess intrinsic value, either on account of their magnificence or their artistic refinement. But an historic monument may possess value through an association of ideas irrespective of its intrinsic value, and this is true equally of the palace and the cottage. Indeed, it is frequently truer of the cottage than of the palace. . . . [O]ne may stand before the modest wooden home of a gentleman farmer in Mount Vernon, Va., and feel no stirring of the emotion until he knows that here lived Washington. Then the blood tingles, and the nerves thrill. Then the building loses its insignificance, and the vision of the great patriot, general and statesman transforms it into a shrine of national patriotism. The log cabin in which Lincoln was born in Hodgenville, Ky., and the diminutive cottage of [Edgar Allen] Poe in New York City, lowly in themselves and meaner than any of the more modern habitations in their vicinity, take on, through their associations, a meaning and a value which are inestimable.

And men need these physical objects to stimulate their imaginations and help them fix their thoughts on the ultimate ideas which they represent. The rationale of all elevating symbolism is the rationale of these historic teaching objects, and the humblest of them may be the most inspiring. . . .

When one realizes the influence of tradition, precedent and example upon men's actions,—an influence oftentimes greater than that of written law—it is easy to see a very practical value in the conservation of historic landmarks. But when the advocate of the conservation of *natural scenery* presents himself before a legislative body, especially if he run counter to powerful commerical interests, he is apt to be met with the argument, expressed or implied, that scenic preservation is not a subject of general importance; that it is a matter of aesthetics, and that it is designed to benefit only the refined and highly cultured few. A little reflection, however, cannot fail to show the inadequacy of this view of the subject.

In the first place, the love of natural beauty may be said to be common to both cultured and uncultured people, and with both young people and old people. . . . The conservation of natural scenery . . . is not to be disparaged because it is "aesthetic."

But beautiful scenery has more than an aesthetic value. Science has demonstrated the intimate relation between mental conditions and physical conditions. Our reservations of natural beauty—our great National, State and City parks, where portions of Nature are preserved as they came from the hands of the Creator,—promote the physical welfare of the people. They rest the eye and the mind. In them, the nerves, strained by the tension of life in the crowded city, relax. The lungs inhale air uncontaminated by the germ-laden dust of the pavement. The trees give a grateful shade and the radiation from grass and leaf adds to the coolness of the retreat. If the reservation contains boulders or glaciated rock surfaces as in Central Park, New York City; or a great waterfall like Niagara; . . . or a marvelous canyon like the Grand Canyon, then the mind of the thinking person is set to working and the thoughts are lifted to the contemplation of the wonderful operations of nature. Then the reservations of natural beauty become also open-air universities of the people, teaching them of the working of the great fundamental forces of Nature; and great undenominational cathedrals . . . . Thus these reservations of natural beauty have more than an aesthetic value. Their value is also physical, educational, and, in a broad sense, religious. . . .

16

Conservation as Democracy
J. LEONARD BATES (1957)

In the next selections three historians analyze the Progressive conservation movement. J. Leonard Bates feels that the desire to implement democracy best explains the motives of the conservationists. His people-versus-the-interests interpretation fits neatly into the traditional understanding of Progressivism as a whole. The previous selections from Gifford Pinchot and WJ McGee [(7), (8), and (11)] suggest the type of evidence on which Bates rests his conclusions.

Samuel P. Hays (17), on the other hand, argues that conservation had its origin in a passion for scientific management and efficiency among a relatively small group of planners and technicians. Far from opposing big business, conservation leaders tried to apply its methods to natural resource problems. While Hays' view seems quite different from that of Bates, it must be remembered that Hays has reference to the personal motives of the conservationists while Bates' points might be construed as applying to the public conception of the movement and to the explanations used to secure general support. Undoubtedly both the scientific and the democratic interpretations explain important parts of the motivation of Progressive conservation.

In selection (18) I contend that American attitude toward nature began to change in the late 19th and early 20th centuries. While directed at the rise of the sentiment for preserving wilderness conditions, the essay can be used to understand one reason for the national concern over the exhaustion of natural resources.

Historians of modern reform have given scant attention to a rationale of conservation or to conservation as a democratic movement. In fact the program associated with Theodore Roosevelt and Gifford Pinchot is occasionally disparaged as largely sound and fury. Doubtless the ambiguity and complexity of "conservation" have tended to obscure its democratic implications. Then too, this policy was both a product of

J. Leonard Bates, "Fulfilling American Democracy: The Conservation Movement, 1907–1921," *Mississippi Valley Historical Review*, **XLIV** (1957), 29–31, 38, 42, 47–48, 53–54, 57. Footnotes in the original have been omitted. Reprinted by permission of The Organization of American Historians and the author.

and a stimulant to the larger, so-called Progressive Movement; it shared in certain weaknesses of this epoch of reform and has shared in the criticism. The usual interpretation today is that the Progressive Movement was essentially an uprising of the middle class, protesting against monopoly and boss control of politics, stressing heavily the virtues of competition, freedom, and morality. With respect to conservation this view leads to the criticism that there existed a fundamental inconsistency between the ideas of protecting natural resources and the dominant beliefs in individualism and competition with the resultant low prices, heavy consumption, and waste. . . .

The organized conservationists were concerned more with economic justice and democracy in the handling of resources than with mere prevention of waste. One aspect of the matter was the price and income situation, the actual monetary rewards from the marvelous wealth of this land. Conservationists believed that somehow the common heritage, the socially created resources and institutions, had passed into the hands of vested interests and that the benefits were siphoned into the hands of a few. There were several ways in which this situation might be remedied, as they saw it: first, to hold on to the remaining public lands, at least temporarily, preventing further monopolization; second, to attempt to give the people a fuller share of opportunities and profits; and finally, in that period of low income to keep prices proportionately low. . . .

The conservationists' approach was broad. They believed in government studies and safeguards for the preservation of irreplaceable resources such as petroleum; they recognized and struggled with problems which remain today only partially solved. They understood the need for federal leadership in an organic structure based on the unity of nature itself. . . . They made mistakes, of course. Like most progressives, they concluded easily that the opposition on a particular issue consisted of "robber barons," conspirators, and frauds. . . .

The developing rationale of the conservationists is of the utmost importance in explaining their conduct and influence. By no means were they all alike, but people such as Roosevelt, Pinchot, and La Follette believed that a larger amount of governmental interference and regulation in the public interest was required. They were especially concerned about the remaining public lands, which, according to principles grounded in the Homestead and other acts, belonged to all. Millions of acres had been given away or sold to corporate interests for a trifling price or had been actually stolen. This record of carelessness and exploitation could not be expunged. However, to conserve and use wisely that which remained, to show that civilized man could profit from mistakes of the past, to democratize the handling of a common heritage, would be a genuine consolation. A crisis, they felt, existed. Such an attitude was a compound of idealism, passion, and sober analysis. These men realized that American society in the twentieth century must be increasingly one of cooperative and collective gains.

As progressives they agreed passionately on the need for honesty and a social conscience in the administration of resources. . . . Conservationists were convinced that hostility toward materialism and toward money men and special interests usually was warranted, that history afforded ample justification for suspicion. If nothing else united the conservationists, there was this hatred of the boodler, the rank materialist, the exploiter.

Pinchot and his group therefore believed in using the authority of federal and state government to compel conservation practices ("socialization of management"), even aiming to do this on *private* forest lands. . . .

. . . In [Robert] La Follette's opinion there had been only one great issue in all of history: a struggle "between labor and those who would control, through slavery in one form or another, the laborers." Uppermost in his consideration, therefore, was justice for the exploited. With respect to public resources in general, he argued that there must be a policy of continuing public ownership, of leasing where possible, of price controls, and a degree of government operation depending upon the monopoly situation. Basic raw materials, even though privately owned, must sell at a reasonable price and if they did not he advocated government appropriation. Quite early he had called for leasing rather than selling government properties, and in the conservation fight of the late [Woodrow] Wilson years [1916–1920] he stressed a leasing system for coal and oil and other nonmetalliferous minerals but not without adequate safeguards for democratic development and prevention of waste. He believed, for example, that evidence of collusive bargaining and fixing of prices among the lessees should warrant government cancellation of the lease. . . . The passage of the Water Power Act and the Mineral Leasing Act of 1920 inaugurated a new policy of continuing public ownership and federal trusteeship in which conservation and the national interest seemed to be the winners. . . . Pinchot declared that the major

portion of the Roosevelt program had now been achieved. . . . Undoubtedly [conservationists] had won something of a victory and the
way had been prepared for a larger federal role in the future.
 . . . [T]he conservation policy contained an inner vitality that
could not be obscured or destroyed. Here was an effort to implement
democracy for twentieth-century America, to stop the stealing and
exploitation, to inspire high standards of government, to preserve the
beauty of mountain and stream, to distribute more equitably the
profits of this economy. From McGee, to Pinchot and La Follette, to
George Norris and Harold Ickes, to Wayne Morse and Lister Hill—
there has burned a democratic zeal, a social faith. The faith was
genuine; the propaganda effective. Though a careful evaluation of the
impact upon this country remains to be made, it is difficult to escape
the conclusion that a fighting band of conservationists has made the
United States much richer in material wealth and in the democratic
spirit and faith of its people.

17

Conservation as Efficiency
SAMUEL P. HAYS (1959)

 . . . Conservation neither arose from a broad popular outcry, nor
centered its fire primarily upon the private corporation. . . . In fact,
it becomes clear that one must discard completely the struggle against
corporations as the setting in which to understand conservation history, and permit an entirely new frame of reference to arise from the
evidence itself.

Conservation, above all, was a scientific movement, and its role in
history arises from the implications of science and technology in

Samuel P. Hays, *Conservation and the Gospel of Efficiency: The Progressive
Conservation Movement, 1890–1920* (Cambridge, Mass., Harvard University Press, 1959), 1–4, 265–266. Footnotes in the original have been omitted.
Copyright © 1959 the President and Fellows of Harvard College. Reprinted
by permission of the publishers.

modern society. Conservation leaders sprang from such fields as hydrology, forestry, agrostology, geology, and anthropology. Vigorously active in professional circles in the national capital, these leaders brought the ideals and practices of their crafts into federal resource policy. Loyalty to these professional ideals, not close association with the grass-roots public, set the tone of the Theodore Roosevelt conservation movement. Its essence was rational planning to promote efficient development and use of all natural resources. The idea of efficiency drew these federal scientists from one resource task to another, from specific programs to comprehensive concepts. It molded the policies which they proposed, their administrative techniques, and their relations with Congress and the public. It is from the vantage point of applied science, rather than of democratic protest, that one must understand the historic role of the conservation movement.

The new realms of science and technology, appearing to open up unlimited opportunities for human achievement, filled conservation leaders with intense optimism. They emphasized expansion, not retrenchment; possibilities, not limitations. True, they expressed some fear that diminishing resources would create critical shortages in the future. But they were not Malthusian prophets of despair and gloom. The popular view that in a fit of pessimism they withdrew vast areas of the public lands from present use for future development does not stand examination. In fact, they bitterly opposed those who sought to withdraw resources from commercial development. They displayed that deep sense of hope which pervaded all those at the turn of the century for whom science and technology were revealing visions of an abundant future.

The political implications of conservation . . . grew out of the political implications of applied science rather than from conflict over the distribution of wealth. Who should decide the course of resource development? Who should determine the goals and methods of federal resource programs? The correct answer to these questions lay at the heart of the conservation idea. Since resource matters were basically technical in nature, conservationists argued, technicians, rather than legislators, should deal with them. Foresters should determine the desirable annual timber cut; hydraulic engineers should establish the feasible extent of multiple-purpose river development and the specific location of reservoirs; agronomists should decide which forage areas could remain open for grazing without undue damage to water supplies. Conflicts between competing resource users, especially, should not be dealt with through the normal processes of politics. Pressure group action, logrolling in Congress, or partisan debate could not guarantee rational and scientific decisions. Amid such jockeying for advantage with the resulting compromise, concern for efficiency would disappear. Conservationists envisaged, even though they did not realize their aims, a political system guided by the ideal of efficiency and dominated by the technicians who could best determine how to achieve it.

This phase of conservation requires special examination because of its long neglect by historians. Instead of probing the political implications of the technological spirit, they have repeated the political mythology of the "people versus the interests" as the setting for the struggle over resource policy. This myopia has stemmed in part from the disinterestedness of the historian and the social scientist. Often accepting implicitly the political assumptions of elitism, rarely having an axe of personal interest to grind, and invariably sympathetic with the movement, conservation historians have considered their view to be in the public interest. Yet, analysis from outside such a limited perspective reveals the difficulty of equating the particular views of a few scientific leaders with an objective "public interest." Those views did not receive wide acceptance; they did not arise out of widely held assumptions and values. They came from a limited group of people, with a particular set of goals, who played a special role in society. Their definition of the "public interest" might well, and did, clash with other competing definitions. The historian, therefore, cannot understand conservation leaders simply as defenders of the "people." Instead, he must examine the experiences and goals peculiar to them; he must describe their role within a specific sociological context. . . .

The broader significance of the conservation movement stemmed from the role it played in the transformation of a decentralized, nontechnical, loosely organized society, where waste and inefficiency ran rampant, into a highly organized, technical, and centrally planned and directed social organization which could meet a complex world with efficiency and purpose. This spirit of efficiency appeared in many realms of American life, in the professional engineering societies, among forward-looking industrial management leaders, and in municipal government reform, as well as in the resource management concepts of Theodore Roosevelt. The possibilities of applying scientific and technical principles to resource development fired federal officials with enthusiasm for the future and imbued all in the conservation movement with a kindred spirit. These goals required public management, of the nation's streams because private enterprise could not afford to undertake it, of the Western lands to adjust one resource use to another. They also required new administrative methods, utilizing to the fullest extent the latest scientific knowledge and expert, disinterested personnel. This was the gospel of efficiency—efficiency which could be realized only through planning, foresight, and conscious purpose. The lack of direction in American development appalled Roosevelt and his advisers. They rebelled against a belief in the automatic beneficence of unrestricted economic competition, which, they believed, created only waste, exploitation, and unproductive economic rivalry. To replace competition with economic planning, these new efficiency experts argued, would not only arrest the damage of the past, but could also create new heights of prosperity and material abundance for the future. The conservation movement did not involve a reaction against large-scale corporate business, but, in fact, shared its views in a mutual revulsion against unrestrained competition and undirected economic development. Both groups placed a premium on large-scale capital organization, technology, and industry-wide cooperation and planning to abolish the uncertainties and waste of competitive resource use.

18

Conservation as Anxiety
RODERICK NASH (1966)

On the morning of August 10, 1913, the Boston *Post* headlined its lead story: Naked He Plunges into Maine Woods to Live Alone Two Months. The following article told how six days previously a husky, part-time illustrator in his mid-forties named Joseph Knowles had disrobed in a

Roderick Nash, "The American Cult of the Primitive," *American Quarterly*, **XVIII** (1966), 517–22, 524–25, 534–37. Footnotes in the original have been omitted. Reprinted by permission of the publisher. Copyright, 1966, Trustees of the University of Pennsylvania.

cold drizzle at the edge of a lake in northeastern Maine, smoked a final cigarette, shaken hands around a group of sportsmen and reporters, and trudged off into the wilderness. There was even a photograph of an unclothed Knowles, discreetly shielded by underbrush, waving farewell to civilization. The *Post* explained that Knowles had gone into the woods to be a primitive man for sixty days. He took no equipment of any kind and promised to remain completely isolated, living off the land "as Adam lived."

For the next two months Joe Knowles was the talk of Boston. He provided information about his experiment with periodic dispatches written with charcoal on birchbark. These reports, printed in the *Post*, revealed to an astonished and delighted public that Knowles was succeeding in his planned reversion to the primitive. Using heat from the friction of two sticks, he obtained fire. Clothing came from woven strips of bark. Knowles' first few meals consisted of berries, but he soon varied his diet with trout, partridge and even venison. On August 24 a frontpage banner in the *Post* announced that Knowles had lured a bear into a pit, killed it with a club and fashioned a coat from its skin. By this time newspapers throughout the East and as far away as Kansas City were featuring the story.

When on October 4, 1913 a disheveled but healthy Knowles finally emerged from the Maine woods extolling the values of a primitive way of life, he was swept up in a wave of public enthusiasm. His triumphant return to Boston included stops at Augusta, Lewiston and Portland with speeches before throngs of eight to ten thousand people. The cheers persisted in spite of a fine of $205 which an unyielding Maine Fish and Game Commission imposed on Knowles for killing a bear out of season. But Maine's welcome paled next to Boston's. The city had not had a hero like "the modern primitive man" in a generation. On October 9 a huge crowd jammed North Station to meet Knowles' train and shouted itself hoarse when he appeared. Thousands more lined the streets through which his motorcade passed. Still clad in the bearskin, Knowles went to Boston Common, where an estimated twenty thousand persons waited. His speech was disappointingly brief, but the gathering thrilled at the way he leaped onto the podium with "the quick, graceful movements of a tiger."

In the next few days Knowles even upstaged an exciting World Series. At Harvard physicians reported on the excellence of his physical condition, and there were numerous banquets and interviews, including one with the governor of Massachusetts. Publishers besieged him for the rights to a book version of his experience which, as *Alone in the Wilderness,* sold 300,000 copies, and he toured the vaudeville circuit with top billing. The *Post* published full-page color reproductions of Joe's paintings of wild animals, pointing out that they were suitable for framing and "just the thing to hang in your den." Even when the *Post's* rival newspaper presented substantial evidence that Knowles was a fraud whose wilderness saga had actually occurred in a secret, snug cabin * a vociferous denial arose in reply. Quite a few Americans in 1913 seemed to *want* to believe in the authenticity of the "Nature Man." In fact, the celebration of Joe Knowles was just a single and rather grotesque manifestation of popular interest in the primitive both in man (the savage) and nature (wilderness). Increasingly in evidence after 1890, this enthusiasm attained the dimensions of a national cult in the first years of the present century.

The most significant fact about the Joe Knowles craze was that it occurred at all. One hundred or even fifty years earlier anyone undertaking such an intentional reversion to the primitive would have been thought demented. Apart from a few artists and writers, Americans before Knowles' generation regarded the wild as something alien and hostile. Their energies were largely directed to conquering wilderness and destroying savages in the name of progress, religion and, indeed, survival. The pioneers and their chroniclers frequently employed a military metaphor in discussing the advance of civilization: wild country was an "enemy" which had to be "vanquished" and "subdued" by a "pioneer army." Achievement was defined as winning this battle against the wild. With a ponderous regularity the reminiscences of frontiersmen dwelt on the beneficent effects of the civilizing process. The "unbroken and trackless wilderness" was "reclaimed" by being "transformed into fruitful farms and filled with flourishing cities" which was "always for the better." Others simply said that the wilderness had been made to blossom like a rose. Along with most of his countrymen, the American pioneer looked forward to a future in which Indians had all been made "good" and the wilderness fructified in the manner of a garden.

---

* After his venture in Maine, Knowles tried to repeat his stunt in California and, with a female companion, in New York but without success. Nor did his plan materialize for a wilderness colony where Americans could live close to nature. Ultimately, Knowles retired to an isolated shack on the coast of Washington. He died, Oct. 21, 1942. [Ed.]

During his visit to the United States in 1831 Alexis de Tocqueville observed this aversion to the primitive. The young Frenchman made a special journey to Michigan to satisfy a romantic urge to see wilderness. But when he revealed his desire for a pleasure excursion into the back-country, the frontiersmen thought him mad. It required considerable persuasion on Tocqueville's part to convince them that his interests lay in things other than lumbering or land speculation. He concluded that "living in the wilds, [the pioneer] only prizes the works of man." The settler's eyes were "fixed upon another sight . . . : the . . . march across these wilds, draining swamps, turning the course of rivers, peopling solitudes, and subduing nature." To Tocqueville this was evidence that those farthest removed from the wild valued it the most. He knew his own attraction to wilderness was largely the result of his being a European.

By the late nineteenth century sufficient change had occurred in the conditions of life and thought in the United States to make it possible for increasing numbers of Americans to appreciate Tocqueville's attitude toward the primitive. Civilization had indeed subdued the continent. Labor-saving agricultural machinery and a burgeoning industry coupled with a surge in population turned the American focus from country to city. The census of 1890 gave only statistical confirmation to what most Americans knew first-hand: the frontier was moribund and wilderness no longer dominant. From the perspective of city streets and comfortable homes wildness inspired quite different attitudes than it did when observed from a frontiersman's clearing. No longer did the primeval forest and the Indian have to be battled in hand-to-hand combat. Men might respond to wilderness as vacationers rather than conquerors. Specifically, the solitude and hardship that had intimidated many a pioneer often proved magnetically attractive to his city-dwelling grandchild.

Indicative of the change was the way the new urban environment acquired many of the repugnant connotations of wilderness. By the 1890's cities were frequently regarded with a hostility once reserved for wild forests. In 1898 Robert A. Woods entitled a collection of exposures of Boston's slum conditions *The City Wilderness*. A few years later, Upton Sinclair's *The Jungle* employed a similar metaphor in describing the horrors of Chicago's stockyard. Too much civilization, not too little, seemed at the root of the nation's difficulties. The bugaboos of the time—"Wall Street," "trusts" and "invisible government"—were phenomena of the urban, industrialized East. In regard to primitive man, American opinion was also tending to reverse the flow of two and a half centuries. Increasing numbers joined Helen Hunt Jackson in sympathizing with the Indian and identifying the disease, whiskey and deception of civilization, not his savage state, as the crux of his problem.

Along with the physical change in American life went a closely related intellectual change in temper or mood. The general optimism and hope of the ante-bellum years partially yielded toward the end of the century to more sober assessments, doubts and uncertainties. Many considered the defects of their society evidence that an earlier age's bland confidence in progress was unfounded. Reasons for pessimism appeared on every hand. A flood of immigrants seemed to many to be diluting the American strain and weakening American traditions. Business values and urban living were felt to be undermining character, taste and morality. The vast size and highly organized nature of the economy and government posed obstacles to the effectiveness of the individual. Instead of the millennium, "progress" appeared to have brought confusion, corruption and a debilitating overabundance. The feeling could not be downed that the United States, if not the Western world, had seen its greatest moments and was in an incipient state of decline. There existed, to be sure, a countercurrent in American thought of pride and hope, but the belief persisted that the growth and change of the past century had not been entirely for the better.

As a result of this sense of discontent with civilization, no less uncomfortable because of its vagueness, *fin de siècle* America was ripe for the appeal of the uncivilized on a broad popular basis. The cult had several facets. In the first place there was a growing tendency to associate wilderness with America's frontier and pioneer past that was thought responsible for many desirable national characteristics. Related to this was the appeal of the savage as the embodiment of virility, toughness and a fighting instinct—qualities that defined fitness in Darwinian terms. A third and quite different idea invested wilderness with an aesthetic and ethical value and emphasized the opportunity it afforded for genteel contemplation and worship. Finally, defense of the primitive attracted many Americans as a means of protesting the commercialism and sordidness they observed in their country. . . .

Wilderness preservation was [one] response to the disappearance of the American frontier. The idea of giving large tracts of wild country legal protection had its roots before mid-century, but it was not until 1872 that the first reservation was established. In that year an act of Congress designated three thousand square miles in northwestern Wyoming as Yellowstone National Park. It was the world's first instance of large-scale protection of wilderness in the public interest. But in the 1870's there was no recognition that wilderness had in fact been preserved. Emphasis, rather, was placed on the park's importance in making available Yellowstone's geysers and hot springs as tourist attractions. The original rationale for the second preservation milestone, the establishment of a state forest reservation in New York's Adirondack region in 1885, was similarly unrelated to wilderness. In this case powerful commercial lobbies favored protection because they feared that if the northern forests were cut, water levels in the Erie Canal and Hudson River would fall too low for navigation.

By the 1890's, however, Americans were beginning to attach a new significance to both the Yellowstone and Adirondack reservations. Recognition grew that protecting wilderness had been their most important accomplishment. In 1892 a Congressional defender of the first national park stressed its value as a place where his countrymen could "see primeval nature, simple and pure." Two years later the revisers of New York's Constitution inserted a special provision defining the primary purpose of the Adirondack State Park as protecting a primitive environment. The changed attitude was also apparent in 1890 when the creation of Yosemite National Park was supported with the argument that it would be "a noble mark for the . . . lover of wilderness."

For Theodore Roosevelt the idea of preserving wild country in order to retain a remnant of the frontier was a primary consideration. Immensely influential in such matters, Roosevelt did much to bring wilderness into national prominence. He visited Yellowstone in 1903 and praised it as a region in which "bits of the old wilderness scenery and the old wilderness life are to be kept unspoiled for the benefit of our children's children." According to Roosevelt, modern Americans should covet such reservoirs of wildness because "as our civilization grows older and more complex, we need a greater and not a lesser development of the fundamental frontier virtues." The price, he believed, for forgetting the nation's frontier past would be degeneracy and the loss of messianic idealism. Roosevelt personally led the way in seeking the wild. Fresh out of Harvard, he spent considerable time in the 1880's on a ranch in the Dakota Territories exulting in the pioneer's life. He even had himself photographed posing fiercely in a buckskin hunting suit. A great many Americans must have shared their President's concern about the vanishing wilderness because the preservation movement gained wide support in the second decade of the twentieth century. . . .

For . . . most advocates of wilderness, the controversy over Yosemite National Park's wild and isolated Hetch Hetchy Valley was climactic. The struggle began early in the twentieth century when San Francisco, facing a shortage of fresh water, asked the federal government for permission to dam the Tuolumne River at the end of the high-walled Hetch Hetchy Valley. The Department of the Interior turned to Congress for a decision, and in the ensuing national debate the preservationists saw an opportunity to extend their case from a defense of wilderness to a full-scale critique of their society. Robert Underwood Johnson opened the fusillade when he wrote in *Century* in 1908 that San Francisco's supporters were people who had not advanced beyond the "pseudo-'practical' stage." Their presence, he added, "is one of the retarding influences of American civilization and brings us back to the materialistic declaration that 'Good is only good to eat.' " Later that year at a Congressional hearing on the Hetch Hetchy question, Johnson explained that he was defending wilderness "in the name of all lovers of beauty . . . against the materialistic idea that there must be something wrong about a man who finds one of the highest uses of nature in the fact that it is made to be looked at." Such an argument was intended to embarrass San Francisco's proponents as much as to defend Hetch Hetchy. Paradoxically, according to Johnson, appreciation of the primitive was an indicator of superior cultivation.

Others took up Johnson's theme with even more pointed reference to America's shortcomings. One man, who had camped in Hetch Hetchy, angrily demanded of the House of Representatives' Committee on the Public Lands: "is it never ceasing; is there nothing to be held sacred by this nation; is it to be dollars only; are we to be cramped in soul and mind by the lust after filthy lucre only; shall we be left some of the more glorious places?" Another letter of protest concluded: "may we live down our national reputation for commercialism." At the Senate hearings in 1909 Henry E. Gregory of the American Scenic and Historic Preservation Society appeared in person and spoke of the need to counteract "business and utilitarian motives."

He pointed out that a primitive area like Hetch Hetchy had more than monetary value "as an educator of the people and as a restorer and liberator of the spirit enslaved by Mammon." . . . Because of the more general enthusiasm for the primitive that existed at the time, the preservationists' arguments for Hetch Hetchy found a receptive audience and national concern for the Valley developed at once. After the first set of Congressional hearings, the reservoir bill was killed, according to the House report, by "an exceedingly widespread, earnest, and vigorous protest voiced by scientists, naturalists, mountain climbers, travelers, and others in person, by letters and telegrams, and in newspaper and magazine articles." Resistance gathered momentum in 1913 when another bill granting the Valley to San Francisco was introduced into the Sixty-third Congress. Robert Underwood Johnson and his National Committee for the Preservation of the Yosemite National Park sent protest literature to 1,418 newspapers and published two pamphlets on its own. The public responded, and Hetch Hetchy became a *cause célèbre.* Hundreds of newspapers throughout the country carried editorials on the question, and all but a few West Coast papers took the side of wilderness. Leading magazines, including *Outlook, Nation, Independent* and *Collier's* as well as Johnson's *Century,* published articles protesting the reservoir. A mass meeting on behalf of the Valley took place at the Museum of Natural History in New York City. Meanwhile, mail poured into the offices of Congressmen. Late in November Senator Reed Smoot of Utah estimated he had received five thousand letters opposing the bill while President Woodrow Wilson was besieged with requests that he defend the national park.

In spite of what seemed to be overwhelming national sentiment in favor of keeping Hetch Hetchy wild, the reservoir bill had effective lobbyists in Washington and appeared to have administration backing. After close votes in both houses, Wilson signed it into law December 19, 1913. The only comfort for the preservationists was the thought that on behalf of wilderness "the conscience of the whole country has been aroused from sleep." . . .

Near the close of the Senate debate on Hetch Hetchy, James A. Reed of Missouri arose to confess his incredulity at the entire controversy. How could it be, he wondered, that over such a trivial matter as the future of a piece of wilderness "the Senate goes into profound debate, the country is thrown into a condition of hysteria." Observing that the intensity of resistance to the dam increased with the distance from Yosemite, he remarked that "when we get as far east as New England the opposition has become a frenzy." In Senator Reed's opinion this was clearly "much ado about little." He might have said the same thing about the enthusiastic reception of Joe Knowles, which occurred simultaneously with the climax of the Hetch Hetchy issue. . . . But the point, as Reed himself suggested, was that a great many of his contemporaries *did* regard the primitive as worth getting excited about. The cult, to be sure, was not overwhelming nor was the popularity of primitivism the only manifestation of discontent. In a complex age it was but a single current of thought. Even in the minds of those who championed wilderness, pride in the accomplishments of American civilization and a belief in the virtues of further development of natural resources persisted. Yet by the twentieth century's second decade something of a divide had been passed. Sufficient misgivings about the effects of civilization had arisen to encourage a favorable opinion of the primitive that contrasted sharply with earlier American attitudes.

Part Three

Conservation Between the Wars

Part Three

Conservation Between the Wars

Progressive conservation produced considerably more smoke than fire. There were urgent calls to action, grandiose plans, and elaborate conferences, but relatively little help for the land. Public opinion, however, had been aroused, and after the First World War the American conservation movement resumed. Some of the shrillness disappeared. Conservationists spent more time in action; less in rhetoric and scolding. They talked less about "running out" of resources. The people-versus-the-plutocrats approach gave way to acceptance of the idea that the condition of the environment was a product of American civilization as a whole. Responsibility for land health fell on the entire nation, and it responded with resource programs even more comprehensive than those of the Progressive years.

After conservation 1920 benefited from several new approaches and circumstances. The conservationists' understanding of the interrelation of resource problems was greater than that of the Progressives. The Pinchot school of forest management, for instance, scoffed at the "sentimentalists" who extolled the recreational values of the National Forests. But the next generation of foresters gradually recognized the importance of woodland for both lumber and pleasure, and they adjusted Forest Service policy to accommodate both demands. Indeed in the early 1920's the Forest Service, partially in an effort to prevent the ambitious National Park Service from acquiring some of its land, began to stress recreation as a forest by-product. This unprecedented departure from the utilitarian line even extended to keeping portions of the National Forests undeveloped for their value as wilderness. Similarly, reclamationists started to publicize the boating and fishing potential of reservoirs.

The continued growth of federal power and responsibility, particularly under Franklin D. Roosevelt, had a profound impact on conservation between the wars. State and private efforts were not discouraged, but increasingly Americans recognized that managing the environment was a task requiring a degree of knowledge, power, and money that only the national government could command.

19

The Planned Landscape
BENTON MacKAYE (1928)

Benton MacKaye took a leading role in refining the methods and the goals of American conservation. He was one of the first environmental engineers, a man who sensed that not just natural resources but the whole environment could be planned and managed in society's best interests. MacKaye's reading of Henry David Thoreau (2) and his acquaintance with the ideas of Aldo Leopold (20) and Lewis Mumford, an historian of the city, alerted him to the limitations of urbanization in the United States. His home in Shirley Center, Massachusetts, offered an excellent vantage point from which to observe the spread of megalopolis. In 1921 MacKaye published his first article, "An Appalachian Trail: A Project in Regional Planning" in the Journal of the American Institute of Architects. *He thought of the trail not just as a footpath along the crest of the mountains from Maine to Georgia but as a kind of "indigenous" or natural alternative to the civilized environment. During the 1930's the TVA utilized MacKaye's talents as a regional planner, but he still found time to help found the Wilderness Society (23).*

. . . It takes more than towns and railroads and corn fields to make a nation and a pleasant land to live in. These are enough for the "material fact," but not for the "spiritual form." They are enough for a mechanical state of "civilization," but not for a living "culture." Man needs more than this to cover God's green earth if he would be a *soul*. He needs just one thing further. He needs it in his home and dooryard; he needs it within his community; he needs it throughout his country and his planet. It is the right kind of *environment*.

Environment is to the would-be cultured man what air is to the animal—it is the breath of life. So far as outward matters go, environment is the basic ingredient of living as air is of existence.

Here, then, we have the fields of the old exploration and the new: the outward needs of man engaged merely in a material struggle, and those of cultured man. Pioneer man needs land as the tangible source of bodily existence; he needs the flow of waters to make that source

Benton MacKaye, *The New Exploration: A Philosophy of Regional Planning* (New York, Harcourt, Brace and Co. 1928), 29–30, 45, 50–51, 169–170, 178–181, 226–228. Reprinted by permission of the author.

effective; but above all, he needs air as the constant source and revivifier of his activity. Cultured man needs land and developed natural resources as the tangible source of bodily existence; he needs the flow of commodities to make that source effective; but first of all he needs a harmonious and related environment as the source of his true living.

These three needs of cultured man make three corresponding problems:

(a) The conservation of natural resources.

(b) The control of commodity-flow.

(c) The development of environment.

The visualization of the potential workings of these three processes constitutes the new exploration—and regional planning.

The essentials of the old exploration were *actualities;* the essentials of the new exploration are *potentialities.* The old exploration described *that which is,* while the new exploration projects *that which can be.* The first was based on descriptive science; the second is based on applied science. The one was a recording of actual facts and of nature's laws; the other is a charting of possible facts lying within those laws. . . .

. . . The fundamental problem of regional engineering, comes down to the control and guidance of industrial migration, and control in such wise as to secure the objectives cited regarding resources, commodities, and environment. In this way may a *single engineering* achieve its application, and attain its final goal—"the making of the mold in which future generations shall live."

What approaches offer themselves in the stupendous task of charting the wilderness of civilization and creating the mold for a genuine culture? Well, they are legion, and a few illustrations have been given from present-day engineering practice. But there seem to be two major approaches to the subject. . . .

(1) *The metropolitan world:* a framework of worldwide standardized civilization which forms itself around the traffic stream of modern industry and commerce.

(2) *The indigenous world:* a quiltwork of varied cultures, each with its own environment of racial and regional setting . . . .

. . . On the Times Building [in New York City] (or on its counterpart, the Boston Custom House) we have at our feet the metropolitan world—the "passing streams of traffic" merged in conflux and pouring in from all corners of the land; and we have a glimpse only of the indigenous world—in the distant view of the Hudson Highlands (or of the summit of Mt. Monadnock [New Hampshire]). But when we go and climb this summit, then we have these "worlds" reversed: then we have at our feet the indigenous world; we have the traffic stream not in conflux or midway, but at its two extremes. We have on one hand the field or forest or resource from which the stream arises, and on the other hand we have the home community to which the stream is destined. But we have in this view a *glimpse* only of the metropolitan world—in the distant view of the factory chimney, the screaming locomotive, or the Boston Custom House. . . .

The indigenous world may be said to be *composed* of natural resources, and these may be divided into three great classes:

(1) Material resources (soils, forests, metallic ores).

(2) Energy resources (the mechanical energy resident in falling water, coal seams, and other natural elements).

(3) Psychologic resources (the human psychologic energy, or happiness, resident in a natural setting or environment).

The term "natural resources," as we have used it in previous chapters, has referred to material resources and mechanical energy alone. These resources have been compared with the geographic element of "land": they form the tangible source of man's existence. The psychologic resources (environment) have been compared with the geographic element of "air." Environment, the contours of the landscape, the arrangement of its vegetation, the visible marks of man's efforts in clearings and fences and farms and gardens and cities as well as in wild forests and mountain areas—environment, in one or all of its many forms, is the pervasive source of man's true living. Raw material and mechanical energy relate to the means of life: environment, whether in natural or in humanized forms, relates to the objectives of life. Man (and civilization), considered as a "material fact," is concerned with the means of life: man (and civilization), considered as a "spiritual form," is concerned with the objectives of life, the pursuit of a higher estate in human development. Raw material and mechanical energy form the terrestrial basis of civilization as a material fact, while environment forms the terrestrial basis of civilization as a spiritual form. . . .

. . . Through such developments as the railroad in the [eighteen] sixties, and motor transportation and electric transmission of power, since the nineties, a series of sudden jumps has taken place in this country. The leisurely growth of an American indigenous culture, which promised so much before the Civil War, has been burked, or diverted into purely metropolitan interests and concerns.

This metropolitan invasion is, I believe, in the nature of an interruption, but whether it will amount actually to this or to our permanent undoing depends on what we are going to do about it. The attitude of the regional planner, as conceived in this particular Philosophy of Regional Planning, is to view this phenomenon as an interruption, to cope with it as a distinct intruder, and to proceed with the development of the indigenous America as something belonging to the future as well as to the past. The coming of the metropolitan invasion, overnight as it were, like a flood suddenly set loose from a thousand ruptured reservoirs, may be viewed as the emergent reason, the *occasion* if you please, for the dormant but awakening movement of regional planning and the New Exploration.

The "thousand ruptured reservoirs" refer to the great metropolitan centers (or the thousand and one centers large and small) which are scattered throughout the country. . . .

The flow of metropolitanism we have compared loosely with the flow of waters—but we must now be more precise: we must compare it with the flow of *flood waters*. Metropolitan development is the result of revolution—the industrial revolution. It has come upon us, in its potent form, within a generation. And its potence lies not so much in the particular thing it is as in the *suddenness* of its appearance. This fact is critical: it is critical as to our choice of means for coping with the general problem. One set of means is required for controlling the general normal flow issuing from the upland headwaters; but a different set of means is needed for handling the flow issuing from an upland reservoir which has suddenly broken down. . . .

. . . What manner of embankments (what "dams" and what "levees") can we construct "downstream" to hold our deluge in check? . . .

If left alone, the metropolitan deluge will flow out along the main highways (and the side highways) in the fashion described in the last chapter, distributing the population in a series of continuous strings, which together would make a metropolitan cobweb of the locality. In this way the area with its several villages would become engulfed by the metropolitan flood. What are the barriers and footholds supplied by nature in this locality for narrowing and checking the full workings of this cataclysm? What topographic features are there, and what common public ground, which could be developed as a series of "embankments"?

The outstanding topographic feature consists of the range of hills and mountains encircling the locality, together with the four ridges reaching toward the central city. This could be reserved as a common public ground, serving the double purpose of a public forest and a public playground. It might be called a "wilderness area." It would form a linear area, or belt, around and through the locality, well adapted for camping and primitive travel (by foot or horseback). Overnight, week-end, and vacation trips could be made from the central city and from the adjacent villages by way of a number of varied circuits. This series of open areas and ways would form a distinct realm: it would be a primeval realm (or near-primeval)—the opposite realm from the metropolitan. These open ways (along the crestlines) mark the lines for developing the primeval environment, while the motor ways mark the lines for extending the metropolitan environment. . . .

A system of open ways of this design would form a series of breaks in the metropolitan deluge: it would divide—or tend to divide—the flood waters of metropolitanism into separate "basins" and thereby tend to avert their complete and total confluence. This it would do in two ways—physically and psychologically. . . . [Q]uite as important perhaps as [the] physical control would be the opportunity provided by the open way for carrying out in practical fashion the latent if not evident desire, within a large body of the people, for experiencing the opposite mode of life from that provided for by the channels of metropolitan civilization. The motor way marks a belt of travel devoted to establishing a certain phase of civilization: the open way reveals a belt of travel dedicated to the development of a counter phase of civilization. One opens a channel for the expansion of the "material fact": the other opens a trail for the growth of the "spiritual form." The open way, practically equipped with facilities for camping and for walking or leisurely conveyance, provides definitely for the exercise, and hence for the increased strength, of those cultural powers within human society which would develop the country for the innate ultimate purposes of true *living* and not merely for the routine of mechanical *existence*. In this way we would stimulate within the individual an inner and immediate desire for controlling an over-mechanical civilization—something more potent perhaps than the control alone by outward physical means. . . . . The open way flanking the motor way, even at a remote distance, if equipped for actual use as a zone of primeval sojourn and outdoor living, might form in the public consciousness a forbidding of the metropolitan flood which would be quite as effective as the occasional physical barrier across the flood's path. . . . [H]ere is a means at our disposal—sticking out of the countryside and its topography. It is a means which will prove weak or strong according as you and I—as engineers, as citizens—prove weak or strong. . . .

The forces set loose in the jungle of our present civilization may prove more fierce than any beasts found in the jungle of the continents—far more terrible than any storms encountered within uncharted seas. Here in America . . . we have an area which, potentially, is perhaps the most "volcanic" of any area on earth. It is an area laden with the ingredients of modern industry and civilization: iron, coal, timber, petroleum. It is electric with a high potential—for human happiness or human misery. The coal and iron pockets which lie beneath the surface may be the seeds of freedom or seeds of bitterness; for in them is the latent substance of distant foreign wars as well as deep domestic strife.

These forces are neither "good" nor "bad" but *so.* And they do not stand still, but flow and spread as we have told. Can we control their flow before it controls us? Can we do it *soon enough?* This is a crucial question of our day. What instructions can we issue to our modern-day explorer (whether technician or amateur) to guide him in coping with this modern-day invasion?

The new explorer, of this "volcanic" country of America, must first of all be fit for all-round action: he must combine the engineer, the artist, and the military general. It is not for him to "make the country," but it is for him to know the country and the trenchant flows that are taking place upon it. He must not scheme, he must reveal: he must reveal so well the possibilities of A, B, C, and D that when E happens he can handle it. His job is not to wage war—nor stress an argument: it is to "wage" a determined *visualization.* His attitude in this must be one not of frozen dogma or irritated tension, but of gentle and reposeful power: he must speak softly but carry a big map. He need not be a crank, he may not be a hero, but he must be a scout. . . . And our last instruction to our new explorer and frontiersman is to hold ever in sight his final goal—to reveal within our innate country, despite the fogs and chaos of cacophonous mechanization, *a land in which to live.* . . .

20

An Ethic for Man-land Relations

ALDO LEOPOLD (1949)

Prior to Aldo Leopold, American conservationists had justified their programs in terms of economics or democracy or, less frequently, aesthetics and religion. The emphasis, in each case, was on man's well being. Leopold, however, took as his axiom the right of other forms of life, and ultimately of the environment itself, to a healthy existence. The environment, Leopold pointed out, did not "belong" to man; he shared it with everything alive. And because of his power, man bore the responsibility of maintaining it in the best interests of the life community. Leopold's land ethic had scientific, rather than religious or sentimental roots. He pioneered in the development of an understanding of the complex interrelationships of organisms and the environment known as the science of "ecology." In 1909 Leopold graduated from the Yale Forest School and joined the United States Forest Service. Assigned to the Southwest, he attracted national attention for his efforts on behalf of wildlife management and wilderness preservation. During the 1930's, as a professor at the University of Wisconsin, Leopold formulated the ideas presented here. He lost his life in 1948 while fighting a brush fire along the Wisconsin River, but his collected writings quickly became one of the chief sources of inspiration for the conservation movement. Leopold's ideas on wildlife management form part of selection (22).

When god-like Odysseus returned from the wars in Troy, he hanged all on one rope a dozen slave-girls of his household whom he suspected of misbehavior during his absence.

This hanging involved no question of propriety. The girls were

---

Aldo Leopold, *A Sand County Almanac and Sketches Here and There* (New York, Oxford University Press, 1949), 201–204, 207, 209–210, 223–226. Copyright 1949 by Oxford University Press, Inc. Reprinted by permission.

property. The disposal of property was then, as now, a matter of expediency, not of right and wrong.

Concepts of right and wrong were not lacking from Odysseus' Greece: witness the fidelity of his wife through the long years before at last his black-prowed galleys clove the wine-dark seas for home. The ethical structure of that day covered wives, but had not yet been extended to human chattels. During the three thousand years which have since elapsed, ethical criteria have been extended to many fields of conduct, with corresponding shrinkages in those judged by expediency only. . . .

The first ethics dealt with the relation between individuals. . . . Later accretions dealt with the relation between the individual and society. . . .

There is as yet no ethic dealing with man's relation to land and to the animals and plants which grow upon it. Land, like Odysseus' slave-girls, is still property. The land-relation is still strictly economic, entailing privileges but not obligations.

The extension of ethics to this third element in human environment is, if I read the evidence correctly, an evolutionary possibility and an ecological necessity. It is the third step in a sequence. The first two have already been taken. Individual thinkers since the days of Ezekiel and Isaiah have asserted that the despoliation of land is not only inexpedient but wrong. Society, however, has not yet affirmed their belief. I regard the present conservation movement as the embryo of such an affirmation. . . .

All ethics so far evolved rest upon a single premise: that the individual is a member of a community of interdependent parts. His instincts prompt him to compete for his place in that community, but his ethics prompt him also to co-operate (perhaps in order that there may be a place to compete for).

The land ethic simply enlarges the boundaries of the community to include soils, waters, plants, and animals, or collectively: the land.

This sounds simple: do we not already sing our love for and obligation to the land of the free and the home of the brave? Yes, but just what and whom do we love? Certainly not the soil, which we are sending helter-skelter downriver. Certainly not the waters, which we assume have no function except to turn turbines, float barges, and carry off sewage. Certainly not the plants, of which we exterminate whole communities without batting an eye. Certainly not the animals, of which we have already extirpated many of the largest and most beautiful species. A land ethic of course cannot prevent the alteration, management, and use of these 'resources,' but it does affirm their right to continued existence, and, at least in spots, their continued existence in a natural state.

In short, a land ethic changes the role of *Homo sapiens* from conqueror of the land-community to plain member and citizen of it. It implies respect for his fellow-members, and also respect for the community as such. . . .

Conservation is a state of harmony between men and land. Despite nearly a century of propaganda, conservation still proceeds at a snail's pace; progress still consists largely of letterhead pieties and convention oratory. On the back forty we still slip two steps backward for each forward stride.

The usual answer to this dilemma is 'more conservation education.' No one will debate this, but is it certain that only the *volume* of education needs stepping up? Is something lacking in the *content* as well? . . .

. . . the education actually in progress makes no mention of obligations to land over and above those dictated by self-interest. Land-use ethics are still governed wholly by economic self-interest, just as social ethics were a century ago. . . .

No important change in ethics was ever accomplished without an internal change in our intellectual emphasis, loyalties, affections, and convictions. The proof that conservation has not yet touched these foundations of conduct lies in the fact that philosophy and religion have not yet heard of it. In our attempt to make conservation easy, we have made it trivial. . . .

It is inconceivable to me that an ethical relation to land can exist without love, respect, and admiration for land, and a high regard for its value. By value, I of course mean something far broader than mere economic value; I mean value in the philosophical sense.

Perhaps the most serious obstacle impeding the evolution of a land ethic is the fact that our educational and economic system is headed away from, rather than toward, an intense consciousness of land. Your true modern is separated from the land by many middlemen, and by innumerable physical gadgets. He has no vital relation to it; to him it is the space between cities on which crops grow. Turn him loose for a day on the land, and if the spot does not happen to be a golf links or a 'scenic' area, he is bored stiff. If crops could be raised by hydroponics instead of farming, it would suit him very well. Synthetic substitutes for wood, leather, wool, and other natural land products suit him better than the originals. In short, land is something he has 'outgrown.'

Almost equally serious as an obstacle to a land ethic is the attitude of the farmer for whom the land is still an adversary, or a taskmaster that keeps him in slavery. Theoretically, the mechanization of farming ought to cut the farmer's chains, but whether it really does is debatable.

One of the requisites for an ecological comprehension of land is an understanding of ecology, and this is by no means co-extensive with 'education'; in fact, much higher education seems deliberately to avoid ecological concepts. An understanding of ecology does not necessarily originate in courses bearing ecological labels; it is quite as likely to be labeled geography, botany, agronomy, history, or economics. This is as it should be, but whatever the label, ecological training is scarce. . . .

The 'key-log' which must be moved to release the evolutionary process for an ethic is simply this: quit thinking about decent land-use as solely an economic problem. Examine each question in terms of what is ethically and esthetically right, as well as what is economically expedient. A thing is right when it tends to preserve the integrity, stability, and beauty of the biotic community. It is wrong when it tends otherwise.

It of course goes without saying that economic feasibility limits the tether of what can or cannot be done for land. It always has and it always will. The fallacy the economic determinists have tied around our collective neck, and which we now need to cast off, is the belief that economics determines *all* land-use. This is simply not true. An innumerable host of actions and attitudes, comprising perhaps the bulk of all land relations, is determined by the land-users' tastes and predilections, rather than by his purse. The bulk of all land relations hinges on investments of time, forethought, skill, and faith rather than on investments of cash. . . .

The evolution of a land ethic is an intellectual as well as emotional process. Conservation is paved with good intentions which prove to be futile, or even dangerous, because they are devoid of critical understanding either of the land, or of economic land-use. . . .

The mechanism of operation is the same for any ethic: social approbation for right actions: social disapproval for wrong actions.

By and large, our present problem is one of attitudes and implements. We are remodeling the Alhambra * with a steamshovel, and we are proud of our yardage. We shall hardly relinquish the shovel, which after all has many good points, but we are in need of gentler and more objective criteria for its successful use.

* A royal palace of great beauty in Spain. Leopold is here equating it to the natural world. [Ed.]

21

Soil

HUGH HAMMOND BENNETT (1939)

Soil was the first natural resource in North America to experience the effects of exploitation. Fields "wore out" while still being cleared of trees and stumps. But, with the exception of a few enlightened landowners like Thomas Jefferson, Americans remained unconcerned. Couldn't fresh land be found over the next ridge to the west? Hugh H. Bennett, the father of soil conservation, was one of the first to realize that even if it could it was inviting national disaster to permit the agricultural capacity of the older regions to be destroyed. The son of a North Carolina farmer, Bennett made an early acquaintance with exhausted and eroded land. In 1903 he joined the federal Bureau of Soils and started an investigation of soil conditions in the South. For the next quarter century Bennett crusaded for soil conservation without much success. But in the late 1920's, largely in response to Bennett's incessant urgings, the federal government instituted a program of erosion research. As the Great Depression staggered the country, Bennett continued to press for action and received important assistance from the spectacular dust storms of the early 1930's that darkened skies across half the nation. His efforts were rewarded in 1933 when the Civilian Conservation Corps (24) made erosion control one of its primary tasks. The establishment of the United States Soil Conservation Service in 1935 marked a major victory. With Bennett at its head, the Service quickly launched several hundred demonstration projects and encouraged the states to form soil-conservation districts.

From *Soil Conservation* by Hugh Hammond Bennett. Copyright, 1939, by McGraw-Hill, Inc., New York, pp. v–vii, 1–3, 5–6, 8–9, 11–15. Used by permission of McGraw-Hill Book Company.

In fifteen decades, Americans have transformed a wilderness into a mighty nation. In all the history of the world, no people ever built so fast and yet so well. This will be a land of liberty, they said in the beginning, and as they hacked the forest, drove their ploughshares deep into the earth, and spread their herds across the ranges, they sang of the land of the free that they were making. All that they finally built upon this continent is founded in that faith—that here there would be opportunity and independence and security for any man.

Those things are the power and the hope of this democracy. And they have sprung, very largely, from the goodness of our land, its capacity to produce rewardingly. Yet with astonishing improvidence, Americans have plundered the resource that made it possible to realize their dream.

Moving across this country in the greatest march of occupation ever known, they have exploited and abused this soil. As a result, our vital land supply has been steadily sapped by the heavy drain of soil erosion.

Since the first crude plow uprooted the first square foot of sod, and since man's axe first bit into virgin forest, erosion of the soil has been a problem. It is as old as history. Down through the ages it has influenced the lives of men and the destinies of nations and civilizations. In the United States today, no problem is more urgent.

Millions of acres of our land are ruined, other millions of acres already have been harmed. And not mere soil is going down the slopes, down the rivers, down to the wastes of the oceans. Opportunity, security, the chance for a man to make a living from the land— these are going too. It is to preserve them—to sustain a rewarding rural life as a bulwark of this nation, that we must defend the soil.

This nation is still producing bountiful crops. But many thousands of farmers already feel the pinch of erosion. Tens of thousands of them are finding it increasingly difficult to eke out a living on eroded land almost regardless of agricultural prices.

In other words, even in this young nation, pressure on the land already has become acute in many localities. Many areas have been damaged to such an extent by erosion that not enough productive soil is left for the present population. In Puerto Rico, portions of the Southern Piedmont, and the Rio Grande Valley, for example, erosion already has crowded many people off the land and brought others to the level of precarious subsistence farming. Some of this land can be stabilized, and some severely impoverished areas can be improved, but many land users must seek better soil elsewhere if they are to remain in the business of farming or ranching. Today the nation has an abundance of land, but not enough *good* land. Probably, if there had not been so much good land in the beginning, there would not have developed the early idea that the productive soil of America was limitless and inexhaustible. This erroneous appraisal of the land resource, passed along as a tradition, accounts for much of our costly steep-land tillage, overgrazing, and failure to defend vulnerable soil from the ravage of erosion.

The present plight of the land brings to mind the extremes to which other countries with small areas of arable soil must go in order to make maximum use of every available acre. In southern France, for example, certain poor soils are utilized under a rotation of fish culture with grain production. In Italy, under the program of the *Bonifica Integrale*, many areas of severely gullied steep slopes are being smoothed down with explosives in order to reclaim them for agricultural use. Always, where populations have increased and agricultural lands have been exploited and wasted, people have looked beyond their borders for additional land. This urge has brought about conquests, wars, and migrations to new lands. Permanent agriculture has been achieved in only a few regions, for the most part of relatively small size, throughout the world. Some parts of the world, blessed with gentle rains, favorable soil, moderate slopes, native skills, and inherent love for the soil, have been held securely. Elsewhere . . . people of primitive culture in ancient civilizations, bench-terraced and, in some instances, irrigated steeply sloping land. . . .

A permanent agriculture, then, is possible, even where the land is highly vulnerable to erosion, when people are willing to pay the price of protecting it. Where the price has not been paid, civilizations have disintegrated and disappeared. If necessary for survival, the American people undoubtedly would bench-terrace all their tilled land, as did the Incas, but it would be done at an undreamed of cost. Fortunately, American agriculture is now in a stage where heavy costs may be avoided by consistently working with, rather than against, natural forces, and by provident action based on a thorough diagnosis of the present problems of land use.

All our experience has demonstrated that erosion can be controlled in a practical way. The need is for forthright, determined, nation-wide action. Today's necessity for public action is the outgrowth of yesterday's failure to look more carefully to our land.

Foresight in the last century, during our march of agricultural occupation, would have produced a different result. Today we are simply retracing our steps across this land in a march of agricultural conservation. "Soil Conservation" is primarily concerned with this second march. . . .

The earliest settlers arriving on the North American continent found a land richly endowed by nature and virtually unexploited by man. Except in an inconsequential way, the aborigines had done little to cultivate this land or change its virgin character. Before the gaze of the transplanted Europeans lay a vast wilderness teeming with apparently inexhaustible stores of game, fish, fur, timber, grass, and soil. Across the broad expanses of the country, from semitropical to boreal climates, from humid to arid regions, spread an infinite variety of soil types, topographic and climatic conditions, and vegetative types and patterns. Almost everywhere the fertile land supported some kind of vegetation—trees or grasses, shrubs or chaparral. In all but a few scattered barren areas, dense stands of perennial plants sheltered the ground from the elements and enriched it with their decaying material. Soil nourished vegetation, and vegetation protected soil, in a compact of mutual advantage and growth.

Rains fell on the land, and snows melted with the changing seasons; but water tended to move slowly over the ground surface, checked and kept clear by the tangled canopy of vegetative growth. The deep, humus-charged, granular topsoil, perforated even into the subsoil by decaying plant roots and burrowing earthworms, insects, and animals, soaked up the raindrops, which filtered down to nourish the growth of vegetation or to replenish underground reservoirs and springs. Rivers ran clear, except in flood, when abrasive rushing waters tore soil from the banks, sometimes muddying even the Missouri and the Mississippi. Generally speaking, however, the natural circulation of waters was a uniform and orderly process. Flood heights and silt-laden streams were the spasmodic exceptions in a land of prevailing harmony and balance. Topsoil was removed from the land surface no faster than it was built up from beneath by the slow, complex processes of nature.

Into this virgin land the eager colonists entered with energy and enthusiasm. They began a transformation of the earth's surface that is probably without parallel in the history of the world. The occupation of the continent was accomplished not through steady infiltration of population into undeveloped regions but rather through a remarkably rapid advance over a wide front by farmers, stockmen, prospectors, miners, trappers, loggers, explorers, and adventurers. Along the line of advance, there was little thought of conservation or of depleting resources. With a country of immense potential wealth beckoning for development, it is small wonder that the emphasis lay, unconsciously, on speedy exploitation. . . .

Both the march of land occupation and the ensuing national development were accompanied . . . by a prodigious wastage of the resources with which nature originally stocked the land. The white inhabitants of this country, in their "conquest of the wilderness" and their "subjugation of the West," piled up a record of heedless destruction that nearly staggers the imagination. Slopes once clothed with mighty forests now lie bare and stark. Formerly rich lands are riddled with gullies. Level plains country that once supported lush stands of native "short" grasses is overgrown with weeds or covered with shifting sands left in the wake of dust storms.

What caused this tragic transformation? What happened to the bountiful land that inspired early explorers to enthusiastic comment and rhapsodic description? The answer lies largely in a false philosophy of plenty, a myth of inexhaustibility, which prevailed generally for many years and persists, in some quarters, even at the present time.

Yet in the time of our forefathers this was a normal, perhaps an inevitable, reaction to environmental conditions. Nearly everywhere the early settlers faced rich farm and grazing lands . . . which stretched away as far as the eye could see. There was every reason to conclude that the agricultural domain was limitless and inexhaustible. Free land extended to the far horizons. . . .

. . . [consequently] much of the land was abused, mined, and ravaged. In the turmoil of national growth, abundant resources were reduced to a state of impoverishment or near-extinction. Buffaloes were slaughtered by the thousands, merely for their hides. Trappers took their harvest of pelts without restriction or restraint. Protective forests were cut from sloping hillsides and entire watersheds; immense areas of grassland were broken or bared by the onrushing settlers with their plows and their livestock. Minerals were extracted, and their wealth dissipated in a surge of exploitation.

The story of the passenger pigeon is characteristic. The last of these birds died in a Cincinnati zoo in September, 1914. Ornithologists say that once this species was one of the most abundant game birds ever known in any country. Their flights frequently darkened the skies; the branches of trees are said to have been broken off by the very weight of their numbers settling to roost. Yet within a few generations, the legions of this species have been effaced from the earth. Should man dwell upon this planet for millions of years, he would never behold another passenger pigeon.

In like manner, other valuable resources have been exhausted and continue to be exhausted. What the final result will be in terms of the national economy no one can predict with accuracy. One fact, however, is eminently clear. The potential wealth and living standard of this nation, or of any nation, depend ultimately on its store of natural resources. If, through carelessness and neglect, these resources are wasted beyond a certain point, the whole structure of national achievement must be impaired.

Out of the long list of nature's gifts to man, none is perhaps so utterly essential to human life as soil. And topsoil is the most vital part of soil (made up of topsoil plus the layers beneath). Lying at an average depth of about 7 or 8 inches over the face of the land, this upper layer of the soil is the principal feeding zone of the plants, which provide food for human or livestock consumption, fiber for clothing, and timber for shelter. Soil constitutes the physical basis of our agricultural enterprise; it is a *sine qua non* in the production of practically all food (except fish), of all fiber (without exception), and of all wood (without exception). Under many conditions, however, it is the most unstable of all major natural resources.

Water or wind, in moving across the ground surface, exerts an abrasive force which picks up soil particles and carries them away in suspension. In a natural, undisturbed environment, the dense cover of vegetation retards this surface transposition of soil to a pace so slow, generally, that new soil is formed from the parent materials beneath as rapidly as the finished product (topsoil) is carried away from above. Under such conditions, the removal of topsoil is known as *normal erosion,* sometimes referred to as *geological erosion* or the *geologic norm of erosion.* It is a normal process, proceeding with the tediousness of centuries. It abrades at one place and builds (aggrades) at another. In slowly sculpturing the highlands of the world, it contributes material for the development of alluvial plains, valley fills, and aeolian deposits.

Where the land surface is bared of protective vegetation—as it must be under cultivation—the soil is exposed directly to the abrasive action of the elements. Transposition processes of an extremely rapid order are set in motion. Stripped of the protective cover that normally anchors soil to the landscape, this indispensable material frequently is moved a thousand times faster than under natural conditions. This accelerated phenomenon of soil removal is known as *soil erosion.* Unless steps are taken to check its progress, it becomes the most potent single factor in the deterioration of productive land. . . .

Lack of foresight and restraint, starting in the early Colonial period and continuing through the present day, has created in this country a land problem of tremendous implications. What makes the situation so grave is the irreplaceable nature of soil. Once this valuable asset leaves a field, it is as irretrievably lost as if consumed by fire, as far as that particular field is concerned. It cannot be hauled back economically even though temporarily stranded only a short distance down the slope. A thousand tons would be required to cover one acre to a depth of 7 inches.

Soil is reproduced from its parent material so slowly that we may as well accept as a fact that, once the surface layer is washed off, land so affected is, from the practical standpoint, generally in a condition of permanent impoverishment. As nearly as can be ascertained, it takes nature, under the most favorable conditions, including a good cover of trees, grass, or other protective vegetation, anywhere from 300 to 1,000 years or more to build a single inch of topsoil. When 7 inches of topsoil is allowed to wash away, therefore, at least 2,000 to 7,000 years of nature's work goes to waste. The time involved may be much longer; the building of the second inch may require many more years than the building of the first inch at the surface, and so on downward. Studies of old eroded areas abandoned to trees or other types of vegetation indicate that the building of soil by the natural process generally proceeds from the surface downward. . . .

Available measurements indicate that at least 3,000,000,000 tons of solid material is washed out of the fields and pastures of America every year. It is estimated that about 730,000,000 tons of solid matter is discharged annually into the Gulf of Mexico by the Mississippi River alone. These materials come largely from the farms of the Mississippi Basin; as alluvial deposits, they form land richer than the flood plains of the Nile. But the sediment entering the oceans represents merely a fraction of the soil washed out of fields and pastures. The greater part is piled up or temporarily lodged along lower slopes, often damaging the soil beneath; or it is deposited over rich, alluvial stream bottoms or in channelways, harbors, reservoirs, irrigation ditches, and drainage canals.

Conservative estimates indicate that the annual monetary cost of erosion in the United States amounts to at least $400,000,000 in terms of lost productivity alone. This loss already totals probably not less than $10,000,000,000; and unless erosion is effectively curbed, the probable future costs will be equally gigantic. . . . To this would have to be added huge losses due to (1) clogging of great reservoirs and shoaling of stream channels with the sedimentary products of erosion; (2) the abandonment of irrigated areas dependent on reservoirs; (3) the virtual abandonment of large agricultural sections; (4) the economic devastation of large western areas dependent on grazing; and (5) the disintegration of rural communities and transfer of large farm populations to relief rolls or to new means of livelihood. . . .

In short, little has been left undone to accentuate the gravity of the erosion problem over a large portion of continental United States. The plain truth is that Americans, as a people, have never learned to love the land and to regard it as an enduring resource. They have seen it only as a field for exploitation and a source of immediate financial return. In the days of expanding frontier it was customary, when land was washed, cropped, or grazed to a condition of impoverishment, to pull up stakes and move on to fresher fields and greener pastures. Today such easy migration is no longer possible. The country has expanded to the full limits of its boundaries, and erosion is causing a progressive shrinkage of the tillable area. The early frontier psychology of land treatment must be abandoned once and for all. In its place a new frontier has appeared. A restricted area of land—an indispensable area, subject to still further restriction by the inroads of uncontrolled erosion—has taken the place of a former abundance of land. Now, man must move rapidly over this diminishing area in order to clear away not trees or prairie grasses but old methods of wasteful land use and substitute therefore new methods of conservation that will provide security for the soil and for those living by the soil.

Conservation of the soil, in a national sense, requires the adoption of sound land-use principles and practices by agriculture as a whole. The attainment of this objective involves the widespread use of physical measures of land defense and the adjustment of certain economic and social forces tending to encourage exploitation of the soil. . . .

The responsibility for such a national program falls upon both the nation and the individual. National responsibility involves the protection of society's interest in a natural resource of vital importance to the whole people. Government functions properly in discharging this responsibility. Equally strong, however, is the interest of the individual in the land that he owns. National action may be led and aided by government, but the soil must be conserved ultimately by those who till the land and live by its products. Without a widespread recognition of this latter responsibility, any governmental program of soil conservation must be doomed to eventual futility and failure.

22

Wildlife

WILLIAM T. HORNADAY (1931); ALDO LEOPOLD (1933)

William T. Hornaday, a taxidermist and avid hunter in his youth, matured to become the nation's foremost advocate of absolute protection for wildlife. For Hornaday, limits or seasons restricting hunting were inadequate; all killing of game should stop at once. If not, Hornaday insisted, market hunters and "sportsmen" (he never took the concept seriously) would exterminate the nation's wild animals and birds. Hornaday's evangelical, moralistic approach was a holdover from Progressive conservation. From his headquarters at the New York Zoological Park, he wrote prolifically in support of wildlife conservation and organized several citizens' societies.

By the 1930's, however, a new approach to wildlife conservation had gained many adherents. Aldo Leopold (20) expressed the new philosophy: less panic, more confidence that game could be scientifically managed as a renewable "crop." Hunting could continue under careful regulation and, in fact, would be an important means of eliminating the excess game which the environment could not support. In 1937 the implementation of these ideas was made possible by the revenues provided the states under the

Material from the following work is reprinted with the permission of Charles Scribner's Sons: *Thirty Years War for Wildlife*, pp. 1–2, 11, by William T. Hornaday (copyright 1931 William T. Hornaday; renewal copyright © 1959 Helen Hornaday Fielding).

Pittman-Robertson Act. Three years later the establishment of the United States Fish and Wildlife Service strengthened the federal commitment to game management.

In the United States there are now out hunting, in this very season, 48 *big armies* of men. Their grand total strength is about 7,500,000 well armed, well equipped, and money-supplied killers of "game" and pseudo-game. This means 7,500 *regiments of full strength!* The grand total is composed of 6,493,454 licensed hunters, plus about 1,500,000 unlicensed hunters who legally hunt local game on their own lands without licenses. It far exceeds in number *all of the active standing armies of the world!* How is that for numerical strength and gunpower?

The progressive extinction of all United States game and near-game birds is rapidly proceeding. Ninety per cent of it is due to merciless and determined shooting; and we greatly fear that the leaden-footed Big Stick of the Law will not overtake the 48 huge armies of killers before the game takes its final plunge into oblivion. A deadly contributory trouble is public and private ignorance of the most basic facts of "game management," coupled with many determined and defiant minorities that positively will not voluntarily yield anything more from their present killing privileges as "free hunting" sportsmen, at an average annual fee of a measly $1.50 per head, or about that.

Ever since the coming of man, ignorance and greed have been the world's greatest enemies.

The closed mind is just as deadly as the loaded gun.

The hardened heart is more fatal to game than the automobile.

Even the dullest American shooter should now admit *the fact* that the guns are to blame for about 90 per cent of the scarcity and disappearance of game. And every lawmaker, either federal or state, now should recognize this axiomatic fact, which is no longer open to argument.

Without the fixed law, the regulation, and the Big Stick, no "free" game of any kind, anywhere, can be "saved" from savage slaughter and extinction!

For 200 years the recognition of this fact has been the basis of all successful "game management" in Europe—coupled with iron-hand regulations there of bags and killings. The lack of it has been the curse of the game of North America. All this talk about "enough laws," and "too many laws," is vicious nonsense; and many times it is dishonest!

And yet, even at this late day, with at least 95 per cent of our upland game and marsh and shore birds gone forever, Congress is confronted by strongly organized and vociferous groups of bush-whackers who loudly protest against placing "any more restrictions on sportsmen," and who declaim and print denunciations of any "further curtailment of the privileges" of the killers. I particularly refer to bag limit reductions up to date, and the open-season-reduction campaign now beginning. In another chapter I will set forth some of the achievements of the "conservationists" of the United States who talk and print so much about "saving" game by buying game, "breeding game" on game farms (at $3 per bird!), "drainage," talk about "vermin," and "more perfect law enforcement."

Inasmuch as the now enormous armies of United States game-killers constitute so large a per cent of the causes of the extermination that is savagely pursuing our game and near-game, it is necessary that Congress and the public should be further informed regarding them. It is utterly impossible, however, to fully classify and describe the motley personnel of that mighty host of killers. To hold a mirror up to that vast mass would require an entire volume like this; but we will do our best with the space that we can spare. Our 48 American armies literally stagger the imagination! . . . And "can ye not discern the signs of the times?"

A "game-hog" is a hunter who is ready to kill the last flock or individual of any game-bird species—if he can do it "according to law!" His ambition is to kill "all that the law allows." Now, what percentage of the 7,500,000 game-hunters of the United States belong in that class? It is my estimate that 15 per cent of the *sportsmen* are humane and reasonable conservationists.

Meanwhile, this is the best of all places in which to enter a showing of the armed forces now in the field to hunt down, attack, and kill or wound the remnants of our game birds and mammals, and in places to comb out our last game fishes. The final returns for 1929 are for many states higher than the figures given below for 1928.

In 1927 the increase in hunters was 624,329 and in 1928 it was 711,885.

Can it be possible that any intelligent person really and truly believes that our remnants of killable game can withstand the eager and determined attacks of 6,493,000 "free hunting" hunters on the present basis of destruction? . . .

What does this say for the value of child "education" in bird lore?

As long as game administration consisted merely of limiting the citizen's shooting privileges, there was little room for experimentation. All citizens had to be treated alike. Experiments, if any, had to be made on the state as a whole, or on all portions offering similar conditions. In other words, the technique of restriction was a legal technique which did not admit of experimental procedure. Policies had to be settled in the abstract, and then enacted into law, for better or for worse.

The new idea is different. Its central thesis is not the limitation of rights and privileges, but rather the fostering of effort. The state is just as free to experiment in better cropping methods for game as in better cropping methods for corn or pine trees. In other words the technique of production is a biological or agricultural technique; policies may be settled by concrete trial, and enacted into law, if necessary, *after* it is found whether or not they work.

But the old habit of determining policy in the abstract still persists. It must be broken down.

Our effort to settle biological questions by abstract logic is like that of the doctors who several centuries ago were arguing over the question of whether the blood circulates in the body. They banged the table long and mightily, proving to each other that it must be so, and that it couldn't be so. When they were nearly worn out, one of them had the brilliant idea of trying an experiment to find out whether it were so or not. Thereupon the argument ended, and the doctors had time to tend their patients.

The beginning and the end of this controversy illustrate the two approaches to questions of game policy: (1) the abstract, and (2) the factual or experimental.

Game managers are the doctors of our game supply. The set of ideas which served to string out the remnants of the virgin game supply, and to which many conservationists feel an intense personal loyalty, seems to have reached the limit of its effectiveness. Something new must be done. The different ideas as to what it is are not too numerous to prevent giving all of them a trial. The American Game Policy simply enumerates some of these differences, and urges that they be subjected to the test of experience.

The detail of any policy is an evanescent thing, quickly outdated by events, but the experimental approach to policy questions is a permanent thing, adaptable to new conditions as they arise. Shorn of changeable detail, it might be boiled down to these words:

1) America has the land to raise an abundant game crop, the means to pay for it, and the love of sport to assure that successful production will be rewarded.

2) There are conflicting theories on how to bring the land, the means of payment, and the love of sport into productive relationship with each other. No one can confidently predict which theory is "best." The way to resolve differences is to bring all theories susceptible of local trial to the test of actual experience. The "best" plan is the one most nearly mutually satisfactory to the three parties at interest, namely the landowner, the sportsman, and the general public. No other plan is likely to be actually used.

3) There are some, but not enough, biological facts available on how to make the land produce game. All factions, whatever their other differences, should unite to make available the known facts, to promote research to find the additional facts needed, and to promote training of experts qualified to apply them.

23

Wilderness

ROBERT MARSHALL (1930)

Robert Marshall's personal passion for wild country led him to become one of the greatest recent forces in the movement for preservation of the wilderness. Son of the noted lawyer and philanthropist, Louis Marshall, and

Robert Marshall, "The Problem of the Wilderness," Scientific Monthly, XXX (1930), 142–143, 145–148. Reprinted by permission of Scientific Monthly.

independently wealthy, Robert earned a Ph.D. in plant physiology and worked for the United States Forest Service and the Office of Indian Affairs. In the 1930's he pleaded the case for preservation before develop-, ment-minded New Deal administrators and succeeded in pushing through the Forest Service "U" regulations (September, 1939) which made wilderness recreation the dominant use of fourteen million acres in the western National Forests. In 1935 Marshall carried out the suggestion he makes below and took the lead in organizing and financing the Wilderness Society as a political pressure group. The passage of the Wilderness Act in 1964 (33) was in large part a tribute to the effectiveness of this organization. But Marshall's untimely death in 1939 at the age of thirty-eight (his insistence on continuing strenuous backpacking against medical advice contributed to the fatal heart attack) prevented him from witnessing the culmination of the movement he had done so much to inspire. In this 1930 essay, Marshall attempts to define the values of wilderness for modern civilization.

The Lewis and Clark exploration inaugurated a century of constantly accelerating emigration into the American West such as the world had never known. Throughout this frenzied period the only serious thought ever devoted to the wilderness was how it might be demolished. To the pioneers pushing westward it was an enemy of diabolical cruelty and danger, standing as the great obstacle to industry and development. Since these seemed to constitute the essentials for felicity, the obvious step was to excoriate the devil which interfered. And so the path of empire proceeded to substitute for the undisturbed seclusion of nature the conquering accomplishments of man. Highways wound up valleys which had known only the footsteps of the wild animals; neatly planted gardens and orchards replaced the tangled confusion of the primeval forest; factories belched up great clouds of smoke where for centuries trees had transpired toward the sky, and the ground-cover of fresh sorrel and twinflower was transformed to asphalt spotted with chewing-gum, coal dust and gasoline.

Today there remain less than twenty wilderness areas of a million acres, and annually even these shrunken remnants of an undefiled continent are being despoiled. Aldo Leopold has truly said:

> The day is almost upon us when canoe travel will consist in paddling up the noisy wake of a motor launch and portaging through the back yard of a summer cottage. When that day comes canoe travel will be dead, and dead too will be a part of our Americanism. . . . The day is almost upon us when a pack train must wind its way up a graveled highway and turn out its bell mare in the pasture of a summer hotel. When that day comes the pack train will be dead, the

diamond hitch will be merely a rope and Kit Carson and Jim Bridger will be names in a history lesson. *

Within the next few years the fate of the wilderness must be decided. This is a problem to be settled by deliberate rationality and not by personal prejudice. Fundamentally, the question is one of balancing the total happiness which will be obtainable if the few undesecrated areas are perpetuated against that which will prevail if they are destroyed. For this purpose it will be necessary: first, to consider the extraordinary benefits of the wilderness; second, to enumerate the drawbacks to undeveloped areas; third, to evaluate the relative importance of these conflicting factors, and finally, to formulate a plan of action.

The benefits which accrue from the wilderness may be separated into three broad divisions: the physical, the mental and the esthetic.

Most obvious in the first category is the contribution which the wilderness makes to health. This involves something more than pure air and quiet, which are also attainable in almost any rural situation. But toting a fifty-pound pack over an abominable trail, snowshoeing across a blizzard-swept plateau or scaling some jagged pinnacle which juts far above timber all develop a body distinguished by a soundness, stamina and élan unknown amid normal surroundings.

More than mere heartiness is the character of physical independence which can be nurtured only away from the coddling of civilization. In a true wilderness if a person is not qualified to satisfy all the requirements of existence, then he is bound to perish. As long as we prize individuality and competence it is imperative to provide the opportunity for complete self-sufficiency. This is inconceivable under the effete superstructure of urbanity; it demands the harsh environment of untrammeled expanses.

Closely allied is the longing for physical exploration which bursts through all the chains with which society fetters it. . . . Adventure whether physical or mental, implies breaking into unpenetrated ground, venturing beyond the boundary of normal aptitude, extending oneself to the limit of capacity, courageously facing peril. Life without the chance for such exertions would be for many persons a dreary game, scarcely bearable in its horrible banality. . . .

---

* Leopold's statement appeared in "The Last Stand of the Wilderness," *American Forests and Forest Life*, **XXXI** (1925), 600–604. For Leopold see (20). [Ed.]

One of the greatest advantages of the wilderness is its incentive to independent cogitation. This is partly a reflection of physical stimulation, but more inherently due to the fact that original ideas require an objectivity and perspective seldom possible in the distracting propinquity of one's fellow men. . . .

Another mental value of an opposite sort is concerned not with incitement but with repose. In a civilization which requires most lives to be passed amid inordinate dissonance, pressure and intrusion, the chance of retiring now and then to the quietude and privacy of sylvan haunts becomes for some people a psychic necessity. It is only the possibility of convalescing in the wilderness which saves them from being destroyed by the terrible neural tension of modern existence.

Finally, . . . the wilderness furnishes perhaps the best opportunity for pure esthetic enjoyment. This requires that beauty be observed as a unity and that for the brief duration of any pure esthetic experience the cognition of the observed object must completely fill the spectator's cosmos. There can be no extraneous thoughts—no question about the creator of the phenomenon, its structure, what it resembles or what vanity in the beholder it gratifies. . . . In the wilderness, with its entire freedom from the manifestations of human will, that perfect objectivity which is essential for pure esthetic rapture can probably be achieved more readily than among any other forms of beauty.

But the problem is not all one-sided. Having discussed the tremendous benefits of the wilderness, it is now proper to ponder upon the disadvantages which uninhabited territory entails.

In the first place, there is the immoderate danger that a wilderness without developments for fire protection will sooner or later go up in smoke and down in ashes.

A second drawback is concerned with the direct economic loss. By locking up wilderness areas we as much as remove from the earth all the lumber, minerals, range land, water-power and agricultural possibilities which they contain. In the face of the tremendous demand for these resources it seems unpardonable to many to render nugatory this potential material wealth.

A third difficulty inherent in undeveloped districts is that they automatically preclude the bulk of the population from enjoying them. For it is admitted that at present only a minority of the genus *Homo* cares for wilderness recreation, and only a fraction of this minority possesses the requisite virility for the indulgence of this desire. Far more people can enjoy the woods by automobile. Far more would prefer to spend their vacations in luxurious summer hotels set on well-groomed lawns than in leaky, fly-infested shelters bundled away in the brush. Why then should this majority have to give up its rights? As a result of these last considerations the irreplaceable values of the wilderness are generally ignored, and a fatalistic attitude is adopted in regard to the ultimate disappearance of all unmolested localities. It is my contention that this outlook is entirely unjustified, and that almost all the disadvantages of the wilderness can be minimized by forethought and some compromise.

The problem of protection dictates the elimination of undeveloped areas of great fire hazard. Furthermore, certain infringements on the concept of an unsullied wilderness will be unavoidable in almost all instances. Trails, telephone lines and lookout cabins will have to be constructed, for without such precaution most forests in the west would be gutted. But even with these improvements the basic primitive quality still exists: dependence on personal effort for survival. Economic loss could be greatly reduced by reserving inaccessible and unproductive terrain. Inasmuch as most of the highly valuable lands have already been exploited, it should be easy to confine a great share of the wilderness tracts to those lofty mountain regions where the possibility of material profit is unimportant. . . . The way to meet our commercial demands is not to thwart legitimate divertisement, but to eliminate the unmitigated evils of fire and destructive logging. It is time we appreciated that the real economic problem is to see how little land need be employed for timber production, so that the remainder of the forest may be devoted to those other vital uses incompatible with industrial exploitation.

Even if there should be an underproduction of timber, it is well to recall that it is much cheaper to import lumber for industry than to export people for pastime. The freight rate from Siberia is not nearly as high as the passenger rate to Switzerland. . . .

But the automobilists argue that a wilderness domain precludes the huge majority of recreation-seekers from deriving any amusement whatever from it. This is almost as irrational as contending that because more people enjoy bathing than art exhibits therefore we should change our picture galleries into swimming pools. . . . It is of the utmost importance to concede the right of happiness also to people who find their delight in unaccustomed ways. This prerogative is valid even though its exercise may encroach slightly on the fun of the majority for there is a point where an increase in the joy of the many causes a decrease in the joy of the few out of all proportion to the gain of the former. . . .

These steps of reasoning lead up to the conclusion that the preservation of a few samples of undeveloped territory is one of the most clamant issues before us today. Just a few years more of hesitation and the only trace of that wilderness which has exerted such a fundamental influence in molding American character will lie in the musty pages of pioneer books and the mumbled memories of tottering antiquarians. To avoid this catastrophe demands immediate action. . . .

A thorough study should forthwith be undertaken to determine the probable wilderness needs of the country. Of course, no precise reckoning could be attempted but a radical calculation would be feasible. It ought to be radical for three reasons: because it is easy to convert a natural area to industrial or motor usage, impossible to do the reverse; because the population which covets wilderness recreation is rapidly enlarging and because the higher standard of living which may be anticipated should give millions the economic power to gratify what is today merely a pathetic yearning. Once the estimate is formulated, immediate steps should be taken to establish enough tracts to insure every one who hungers for it a generous opportunity of enjoying wilderness isolation.

To carry out this program it is exigent that all friends of the wilderness ideal should unite. If they do not present the urgency of their view-point the other side will certainly capture popular support. Then it will only be a few years until the last escape from society will be barricaded. If that day arrives there will be countless souls born to live in strangulation, countless human beings who will be crushed under the artificial edifice raised by man. There is just one hope of repulsing the tyrannical ambition of civilization to conquer every niche on the whole earth. That hope is the organization of spirited people who will fight for the freedom of the wilderness.

24

The Civilian Conservation Corps

FRANKLIN D. ROOSEVELT (1933); ROBERT FECHNER (1936)

The Great Depression seemed to awaken Americans to the need for more effort in maintaining the physical basis of prosperity. Not since 1908 had conservation been as important a public issue as it was in the early New Deal. Within two months at the beginning of Franklin D. Roosevelt's first administration in 1933, Congress passed two of the best-known laws in American conservation history, creating the Civilian Conservation Corps and the Tennessee Valley Authority (25). Designed to engage unemployed young men in productive work and to revive local economies, the CCC also reflected national determination to repair some of the damage three centuries of exploitation and neglect had wrought on the American environment. Organized in several thousand "camps," the two million participants in the CCC between 1933 and 1942 engaged in a host of activities on behalf of the land. Moreover, the widespread, nonpartisan sympathy they generated helped create a lasting mood favorable to conservation. In the documents which follow President Roosevelt calls upon Congress to establish the CCC in 1933, and Robert Fechner, CCC director, discusses the accomplishments of his organization after three years.

THE WHITE HOUSE, *March 21, 1933*

To THE CONGRESS: It is essential to our recovery program that measures immediately be enacted aimed at unemployment relief. . . .

. . . I propose to create a civilian conservation corps to be used in simple work, not interfering with normal employment, and confining itself to forestry, the prevention of soil erosion, flood control and similar projects. I call your attention to the fact that this type of work is of definite, practical value, not only through the prevention of great present financial loss, but also as a means of creating future national wealth. This is brought home by the news we are receiving today of vast damage caused by floods on the Ohio and other rivers.

Control and direction of such work can be carried on by existing

Edgar B. Nixon, ed., *Franklin D. Roosevelt and Conservation, 1911–1945* (2 vols. New York, 1957), I, 143–144. Reprinted by permission of National Archives and Records Service, Franklin D. Roosevelt Library.

machinery of the departments of Labor, Agriculture, War and Interior.

I estimate that 250,000 men can be given temporary employment by early summer if you give me authority to proceed within the next two weeks.

I ask no new funds at this time. The use of unobligated funds, now appropriated for public works, will be sufficient for several months.

This enterprise is an established part of our national policy. It will conserve our precious natural resources. It will pay dividends to the present and future generations. It will make improvements in national and state domains which have been largely forgotten in the past few years of industrial development.

More important, however, than the material gains will be the moral and spiritual value of such work. The overwhelming majority of unemployed Americans, who are now walking the streets and receiving private or public relief, would infinitely prefer to work. We can take a vast army of these unemployed out into healthful surroundings. We can eliminate to some extent at least the threat that enforced idleness brings to spiritual and moral stability. It is not a panacea for all the unemployment but it is an essential step in this emergency. I ask its adoption.

WASHINGTON, D.C., *October 24, 1936*

DEAR MR. PRESIDENT: I am sure you will be interested in the results of a recent survey undertaken at my request by the Department of Agriculture and the Department of the Interior to determine the future work opportunities available in our forests, parks, and on other lands for a permanent Civilian Conservation Corps. These departments have reported, following an extensive inquiry covering all sections of the nation, that there is sufficient urgently needed conservation work still to be done to furnish profitable employment for a Civilian Conservation Corps of between 300,000 and 350,000 for many years to come. The departments advised me that notwithstanding the tremendous amount of reforestation, erosion control, and other conservation work accomplished by the CCC during the last three and a half years, much

---

Edgar B. Nixon, ed., *Franklin D. Roosevelt and Conservation, 1911–1945* (2 vols. New York, 1957), I, 591–593. Reprinted by permission of National Archives and Records Service, Franklin D. Roosevelt Library.

work remains to be completed before our forests, parks, agricultural lands, and grazing areas will have been afforded adequate protection and development. The survey indicated that the annual work load ahead for a permanent CCC will increase rather than diminish during the next few years. This will be due largely to the gradual increase in national forest holdings, the acquisition of new forest lands by the states . . . the expansion of state-owned parks, a growing appreciation of the need for erosion control operations on agricultural lands, and an expanded demand for CCC manpower on flood control projects, for wildlife conservation and in the rehabilitation of grazing lands, irrigation systems and drainage projects. Available and planned work for the next several years, as set forth in the survey, may be broadly divided into such classifications as forestry, park development, erosion control, stream, pond and lake improvement, flood control, water conservation, range development, reclamation, wildlife protection, rehabilitation of drainage projects and other types of projects having as their objective the further preservation, improvement and increase in our natural resources.

Our records show that during the last few years the Civilian Conservation Corps has launched the nation on its first broad-gage and effective conservation program. The Civilian Conservation Corps has added enormous tangible values to the country's physical resources through the construction of roads, communication lines and fire detection facilities; through control of insect and disease pests, fire and rodents that injure and destroy natural resources on federal, state and privately owned lands; through the development of new recreational opportunities; through protection of forests, watersheds, agricultural lands and communities against flood and soil erosion; through projects conserving water and improving land drainage; through the protection and increased propagation of game animals and birds; through the planting of nearly one billion trees; through improving range conditions for livestock; through aid to land reclamation projects; through physical improvements to Indian, military and naval reservations; and through many other types of projects of public interest and utility which are noncompetitive with private industry.

The reports from cooperating federal and state agencies indicate that probably the CCC's greatest contribution to conservation has come in the nation-wide defense of our forests and parks from such destructive enemies as forest fires, insects and tree attacking diseases and the protection of agricultural lands from soil wastage due to water and wind erosion. . . .

The past three and one-half years have shown that the continuance of the CCC will be of permanent value to the nation. Public attention has been focused on the need for all types of conservation. The need has long been recognized by conservationists, but now with floods, dust storms and widespread erosion, public insistence on corrective conservation measures is much more widespread. This is particularly true, due to the fact that the effectiveness of corrective measures has been repeatedly demonstrated by CCC accomplishments. A permanent work force, which can carry out the programs of the various agencies interested in the wise use of natural resources, will enable the United States to obtain greater benefits from our heritage of natural resources which has depreciated through carelessness and misuse.

As long as there are young men eager to work, yet idle through no fault of their own, the CCC can continue to be an effective part of our national policy.

I am calling the past record of the CCC, as well as the survey showing future work possibilities for such an organization, to your attention at this time because I desire to express my conviction that steps may well be taken to make the CCC a permanent organization. I, therefore, recommend that this program of conservation work among men and natural resources be adopted as a permanent part of our national governmental activities, the size and extent of the work to be governed by the dual factors of employment conditions among young men and the urgency of the conservation work to be accomplished.

Sincerely yours,

ROBT. FECHNER

25

The Tennessee Valley Authority

DAVID LILIENTHAL (1944)

At Muscle Shoals, Alabama, the Tennessee River used to plunge through a major rapid. During the First World War the government made plans to harness its power. Funds ran out, however, before the work was finished. In 1921 Henry Ford offered to purchase the uncompleted project. Sensing that acquisition by Ford would eliminate the possibility of a multipurpose, public development of the Tennessee watershed, Senator George W. Norris of Nebraska headed the successful fight to block the sale. But Norris could not persuade the Republican administrations of the 1920's to undertake something that seemed socialistic to them. Yet in 1928 the giant Boulder (later Hoover) Dam on the lower Colorado River was authorized and a more favorable political climate was created for federal resource development. On May 18, 1933, President Franklin D. Roosevelt signed Norris' bill establishing the Tennessee Valley Authority, and in the next decade New Deal planners and engineers constructed in the valley the kind of project about which Progressive conservationists had dreamed. The environment of an entire region was reconstructed as a unit in the public interest, and TVA became a byword for regional planning throughout the world.

David Lilienthal was one of the initial directors of TVA. His statements below capture the enthusiasm and confidence that caught up many of those associated with the project. But conservation on this scale involved many difficult problems. The answers Lilienthal gives must not be accepted uncritically. Needing special scrutiny is his contention that federal experts can institute their plans without coercing the people involved.

A new chapter in American public policy was written when Congress in May of 1933 passed the law creating the TVA. For the first time since the trees fell before the settlers' ax, America set out to command nature not by defying her, as in that wasteful past, but by understanding and acting upon her first law—the oneness of men and natural

David E. Lilienthal, *TVA: Democracy on the March* (New York, Harper & Row, 1944), pp. 35–36, 46–51, 117, 120–121, 123–124, 197–198, 200, 217–219, 222, 225. Copyright 1944 by David Lilienthal. Reprinted by permission of Harper & Row, Publishers.

resources, the unity that binds together land, streams, forests, minerals, farming, industry, mankind. . . .

The message of President Roosevelt urging approval of the Norris bill (which became a law with his signature on May 18, 1933) boldly proposed a new and fundamental change in the development of our country's resources. The words of the President's message were not only eloquent; there was in them a creativeness and an insight born of his New York State experience in establishing regional planning as a political reality. That understanding was matured at his Georgia home, in long days of thinking of the problems of the South and its relation to the whole nation.

> *It is clear* [*the message read*] *that the Muscle Shoals development is but a small part of the potential public usefulness of the entire Tennessee River. Such use, if envisioned in its entirety, transcends mere power development: it enters the wide fields of flood control, soil erosion, afforestation, elimination from agricultural use of marginal lands, and distribution and diversification of industry. In short, this power development of war days leads logically to national planning for a complete river watershed involving many states and the future lives and welfare of millions. It touches and gives life to all forms of human concerns.*

The President then suggested

> *legislation to create a Tennessee Valley Authority—a corporation clothed with the power of government but possessed of the flexibility and initiative of a private enterprise. It should be charged with the broadest duty of planning for the proper use, conservation, and development of the natural resources of the Tennessee River drainage basin and its adjoining territory for the general social and economic welfare of the Nation. This authority should also be clothed with the necessary power to carry these plans into effect. Its duty should be the rehabilitation of the Muscle Shoals development and the co-ordination of it with the wider plan.*
>
> *Many hard lessons have taught us the human waste that results from lack of planning. Here and there a few wise cities and counties have looked ahead and planned. But our Nation has "just grown." It is time to extend planning to a wider field, in this instance comprehending in one great project many States directly concerned with the basin of one of our greatest rivers.*

The TVA Act was nothing inadvertent or impromptu. It was rather the deliberate and well-considered creation of a new national policy. For the first time in the history of the nation, the resources of a river were not only to be "envisioned in their entirety"; they were to be developed *in that unity with which nature herself regards her resources*—the waters, the land, and the forests together, a "seamless web" . . . of which one strand cannot be touched without affecting every other strand for good or ill.

Under this new policy, the opportunity of creating wealth for the people from the resources of their valley was to be faced as a single problem. To help integrate the many parts of that problem into a unified whole was to be the responsibility of one agency. The development of the Tennessee Valley's resources was not to be dissected into separate bits that would fit into the jurisdictional pigeon holes into which the instrumentalities of government had by custom become divided. It was not conceded that at the hour of Creation the Lord had divided and classified natural resources to conform to the organization chart of the federal government. The particular and limited concerns of private individuals or agencies in the development of this or that resource were disregarded and rejected in favor of the principle of unity. What God had made one, man was to develop as one.

"Envisioned in its entirety" this river, like every river in the world, had many potential assets. It could yield hydro-electric power for the comfort of the people in their homes, could promote prosperity on their farms and foster the development of industry. But the same river by the very same dams, if they were wisely designed, could be made to provide a channel for navigation. The river could also be made to provide fun for fishermen and fish for food, pleasure from boating and swimming, a water supply for homes and factories. But the river also presented an account of liabilities. It threatened the welfare of the people by its recurrent floods; pollution from industrial wastes and public sewage diminished its value as a source of water supply and for recreation; its current carried to the sea the soil of the hills and fields to be lost there to men forever.

To a single agency, the TVA, the planning for the greatest sum total of these potentialities of the river for good and evil were entrusted. But the river was to be seen as part of the larger pattern of the region, one asset of the many that in nature are interwoven: the land, the minerals, the waters, the forests—and all of these as one—in their relation to the lives of the valley's people. It was the total benefit to all that was to be the common goal and the new agency's responsibility.

That is not the way public resource development had heretofore been undertaken in this country. Congress in creating TVA broke with the past. No single agency had in this way ever been assigned the unitary task of developing a river so as to release the total benefit from its waters for the people. . . . And through the long years there has been a continuing disregard of nature's truth: that in any valley of the world what happens on the *river* is largely determined by what happens on the *land*—by the kind of crops that farmers plant and harvest, by the type of machines they use, by the number of trees they cut down. The full benefits of stream and of soil cannot be realized by the people if the water and the land are not developed in harmony. . . .

The farmers' new pastures and meadows themselves are reservoirs. If the changed farming practices now in use on many tens of thousands of Tennessee Valley farms were applied to all the agricultural area of our watershed (as some day I am confident they will be), the soil might absorb as much as a quarter of the customary 23-inch surface run-off of rain each year.

This is of course nothing new, nothing discovered by the TVA. That a river could offer many benefits and a variety of hazards, that its improvement through engineering structures is inseparable from the development and use of the land of the watershed, has been recognized for many years by scientists and engineers. For over a generation a distinguished line of conservationists had seen this truth and written and spoken of it with great force; not the least among these were President Theodore Roosevelt and Gifford Pinchot. And as a matter of fact almost any farmer, standing in his barn door while he watches a torrential rain beat upon his land and fill his creek, could see that much. The point is that knowledge of this inseparability of land and streams has only once, here on this river, been carried into our national *action*. And though the force of example has compelled the formation of interagency committees in some river basins to carry on conversations about "co-ordination," it is still true that on every other watershed Congress continues to turn our rivers over to engineers of one agency to develop while farm experts of other bureaus or agencies concern themselves with the land. Thus far it is only in the Valley of the Tennessee that Congress has directed that these resources be dealt with as a whole, not separately. . . .

The TVA's collaboration with business and industry is based upon the use of technical skills in the public interest, the skills of public and private experts. . . . One of the tasks of the administrator or executive in public or private affairs who is committed to democratic principles is to devise ways of bringing modern science and technical skills to the hand of the layman. And this it is that TVA's work at the grass roots seeks to bring about. If the technical knowledge can be made to serve the individual in the daily decisions of his life, if it can be made to serve the common purpose of improving opportunity for human beings, that is an achievement of democracy in modern form and application.

This will require some drastic changes in the prevailing relations between experts and the people, both in industry and in government.

First of all, the experts and the people must be brought together. The technicians should live where the people they serve live. There are important exceptions, in highly specialized fields, but they do not affect the principle. An expert ought not to be remote from the problems the people face, and, although physical proximity will not guarantee closeness to the people, it will encourage it, whereas physical remoteness in distance definitely encourages, if it does not actually insure, remoteness in spirit and understanding, particularly in our country of vast area and great diversity in regional customs and natural conditions. . . .

The experts who live with the people's problems are better able to learn of the people's aspirations, what it is that the people want and what they would want if they had available a knowledge of the alternatives from which they could make a choice. The people will not trust the experts and give them their confidence until they are persuaded that technicians in business as well as in government service are not setting up their own standards of what is "good for people." If technicians, by living with people, come to understand what the people want rather than what the experts want, then people will more and more repose confidence in them and their counsel, protect them from partisan and political attacks, and even help them further their specialized professional and scientific interests.

And the physical presence of the expert, the fact that he has elected to live with the people and their problems, to share their physical and social circumstances, will be accepted by laymen as one kind of proof of the sincere devotion of the expert to the improvement of the everyday living of the people, rather than to his own specialized interests and concerns. The technician, whether he be a forester, a social welfare worker, a manager, a financial or farm or mineral expert, has no more excuse to pursue his expertness simply for the pleasure its refinements give him or to increase his own or his profession's repute, than a physician at the bedside or a general in the field would be justified in following a particular course for comparable reasons of a personal or professional character.

Technicians must learn that explaining "why" to the people is generally as important (in the terms in which I am speaking) as "what" is done. To induce the action of laymen, which is the only way resource development is possible, "why" is almost always the key. Experts and managers at central business or government headquarters, isolated and remote, tend to become impatient of making explanations to the people. From impatience it is a short step to a feeling of superiority, and then to irresponsibility or dictation. And irresponsibility or dictation to the people, whether by experts or politicians or business managers or public administrators, is a denial of democracy.

Effective planners must understand and believe in people. The average man is constantly in the mind of the effective planning expert. Planners, whether they are technicians or administrators, must recognize that they are not dealing with philosophical abstractions, or mere statistics or engineering data or legal principles, and that planning is not an end in itself.

In the last analysis, in democratic planning it is human beings we are concerned with. Unless plans show an understanding and recognition of the aspirations of men and women, they will fail. Those who lack human understanding and cannot share the emotions of men can hardly forward the objectives of realistic planning. . . . And it is because of this same conviction that the TVA has never attempted by arbitrary action to "eliminate" or to force reform upon those factors or institutions in the valley's life which are vigorously antagonistic to a plan for unified development. . . .

In the TVA the merging of planning and responsibility for the carrying out of those plans forces our technicians to make them a part of the main stream of living in the region or community; this it is that breathes into plans the breath of life. For in the Tennessee Valley the expert cannot escape from the consequences of his planning, as he can and usually does where it is divorced from execution. This has a profound effect on the experts themselves. Where planning is conceived of in this way, the necessity that experts should be close to the problems with which they are dealing is evident.

In this one of the thousand valleys of the earth the physical setting of men's living has improved. Each day the change becomes more pronounced. The river is productive, the land more secure and fruitful, the forests are returning, factories and workshops and new houses and electric lines have put a different face upon the Tennessee Valley. Is this really genuine improvement? Has it enhanced the quality of human existence? Are men's lives richer, fuller, more "human" as a result of such changes in our physical surroundings? To most people, I am sure, the answer is in the clear affirmative. But, in appraising the meaning of this valley's experience, the doubts on this score can by no means be ignored, nor dealt with out of hand; people not only raise such questions but answer them differently from the way most of us would answer them.

There are those who believe that material progress does not and cannot produce good, and may indeed stand as a barrier to it. To those, and there are many who hold such belief, mechanical progress, technology, the machine, far from improving the lot of men are actually seen as a source of debasement and condemned as "materialism."

The whole theme and thesis of this book challenges these ideas and the philosophy upon which they rest. I do not, of course, believe that when men change their physical environment they are inevitably happier or better. The machine that frees a man's back of drudgery does not thereby make his spirit free. Technology has made us more productive, but it does not necessarily enrich our lives. Engineers can build us great dams, but only great people make a valley great. There is no technology of goodness. Men must make themselves spiritually free.

But because these changes in physical environment in the valley do not in and of themselves make men happier, more generous, kinder, it does not follow that they have no relation to our spiritual life.

We have a choice. There is the important fact. Men are not powerless; they have it in their hands to use the machine to augment the dignity of human existence. True, they may have so long denied themselves the use of that power to decide, which is theirs, may so long have meekly accepted the dictation of bosses of one stripe or another or the ministrations of benevolent nursemaids, that the muscles of democratic choice have atrophied. But that strength is always latent; history has shown how quickly it revives. How we shall *use* physical betterment—that decision is ours to make. We are not carried irresistibly by forces beyond our control, whether they are given some mystic term or described as the "laws of economics." We are not inert objects on a wave of the future. . . .

Whether happiness or unhappiness, freedom or slavery, in short whether good or evil results from an improved environment depends largely upon how the change has been brought about, upon the methods by which the physical results have been reached, and in what spirit and for what purpose the fruits of that change are used. Because a higher standard of living, a greater productiveness and a command over nature are not good in and of themselves does not mean that we cannot make good of them, that they cannot be a source of inner strength.

. . . In this one valley (in some ways the world in microcosm) it has been demonstrated that methods can be developed—methods I have described as grass-roots democracy—which do create an opportunity for greater happiness and deeper experience, for freedom, in the very course of technical progress. Indeed this valley even in the brief span of a decade, supports a conviction that when the use of technology has a moral purpose and when its methods are thoroughly democratic, far from forcing the surrender of individual freedom and the things of the spirit to the machine, the machine can be made to promote those very ends. . . .

We have a long way yet to go in the valley. There are many factories yet to be built, in an area with such great potential wealth and with less than its economic share of the nation's industry and manufacturing. There are many new jobs to be created by the laboratories and businessmen out of the region's dormant resources. There are millions of acres yet to be restored to full productiveness. . . . There are more trees to plant, houses, schools, roads, and hospitals to build. Many new skills have been learned—among farmers, industrial workers in the new factories, the tens of thousands of men and women who have added to their skills in the course of their work for the TVA—but lack of training is still a heavy handicap to be overcome. The task is barely begun—but the Tennessee Valley is certainly on its way.

Democracy is on the march in this valley. Not only because of the physical changes or the figures of increased income and economic activity. My faith in this as a region with a great future is built most of all upon the great capacities and the spirit of the people. . . .

Here in the valley where I have been writing this statement of faith, the people know the job of our time can be done, for they have read the signs and reaped the first token harvest. They know it can be done, not only *for* the people but *by* the people.

26

Conservation Accomplishments, 1921–1933

DONALD C. SWAIN (1963)

For overviews of conservation history in the two decades after the Progressive period, we turn in the next two selections to the accounts of historians Donald C. Swain and Anna Lou Riesch. Clearly, Franklin D. Roosevelt's convictions about the desirability of positive federal action on behalf of the public welfare were more conducive to conservation than the individualistic, free-enterprise philosophies of his three predecessors in the White House. But, as Swain demonstrates, it would be a mistake to discount the 1920's, and especially the Hoover administration, as a time of conservation progress.

The personalities and political philosophies of three Republican Presidents influenced federal resource programs during the 1920's. Executive preference in matters of policy created a milieu of voluntarism, "organized coöperation," and decentralization in which the federal conservation agencies often found it advantageous to soft pedal resource regulation and to emphasize service functions. Warren G. Harding and Calvin Coolidge, while paying scant attention to conservation policy, tended to inhibit positive federal conservation activity. Herbert Hoover, on the other hand, demonstrated throughout the 1920's an active and constructive interest in promoting national conservation programs.

Riding to office on a wave of reaction against wartime restrictions, Harding understood little of the necessity for conserving natural resources. In his view, the conservation issue was unimportant. He stood for rapid resource development within an unfettered private enterprise system. . . . The Teapot Dome scandal,* eventuating from the

Donald C. Swain, *Federal Conservation Policy, 1921–1933*, University of California Publications in History, LXXVI (Berkeley, Calif., 1963), 160–170. Footnotes in the original have been omitted. Reprinted by permission of the University of California Press.

* In 1924 a Congressional investigation revealed that two years previously Secretary of the Interior Albert B. Fall had illegally leased rich oil reserves near Teapot Dome, Wyoming, to private interests in return for financial considerations. [Ed.]

President's own lack of interest in resource administration, is the best example. Without vigorous executive support, the conservation bureaus had to fall back on voluntary programs designed, in general, to appease industrial and commercial interests.

Succeeding to the presidency in 1923, Calvin Coolidge interested himself primarily in trimming the federal budget while largely ignoring natural resources. The era of executive laxity continued. . . . [Coolidge] had almost no aptitude for the subtleties of conservation policy. And his failure to grasp the long-range implications of resource problems might have proved disastrous. It was monumental naïveté, for example, to compare Muscle Shoals * in value to a "first class battleship." With evident pride, he considered himself a "practical" man. But his emphasis on economy in governmental expenditures was impractical in the long run. Among other things it severely hampered the federal conservation program. . . . Although the New Englander promoted coöperative policies in forestry, wildlife, and recreation, his only important influence on conservation came as a result of his insistence on decentralization. He wanted the states to discharge their public functions "so faithfully that instead of an extension on the part of the Federal Government there can be a contraction." When translated into action at the bureau level, this dictum meant less power for the federal conservation agencies, who were expected to stimulate state supervision of resources whenever possible.

Herbert Hoover, in contrast to his immediate predecessors, was a key conservation figure. As Secretary of Commerce, he exerted a large influence in the affairs of both the Harding and Coolidge administrations, demonstrating his personal interest in resource policy-making. From his cabinet office in Washington he crusaded for such conservation causes as the regulation of Alaskan salmon fisheries, the control of water pollution, the establishment of fish nurseries, construction of a St. Lawrence waterway, the improvement of inland navigation, and the authorization of the Boulder Canyon project.† Once in the White House, he concentrated on flood control, waterways development, and oil conservation. That he was a sincere conservationist is beyond question.

The methods by which he chose to implement his conservation ideas remained open to criticism. Believing wholeheartedly that natu-

---

* See the headnote for selection (25). [Ed.]
† Hoover Dam. [Ed.]

ral resources should not be plundered in the name of individualism, he was nevertheless an individualist. How to reconcile his conservation thinking with his individualistic philosophy, therefore, became his personal dilemma. His attempts to solve that dilemma resulted in vigorous programs to reduce waste, to promote coöperation, and to decentralize conservation controls.

Hoover's campaigns against waste and, conversely, for efficiency developed into one of the high lights of the early 1920's. He plugged incessantly for progressive industrial technology and increased scientific research, enlarging the scientific work of the Department of Commerce as a public example. He formed trade associations and arranged voluntary industrial liaisons in which he preached national efficiency at every opportunity. His ideas unquestionably influenced his contemporaries. And the logic of his position led him into conservation. Yet, in regard to the elimination of waste, one may legitimately inquire whether Hoover's primary concern was to conserve natural resources or to stimulate ever greater production. With some inconsistency, both considerations figured prominently in his thinking. Frequently the latter seemed to be the more important.

His quest for efficiency, moreover, led him into the difficult area of governmental reorganization. Attacking the multidepartmental conservation set-up of the federal government, he called for a unification of conservation bureaucracy. He suggested that Congress establish a new organization, grouping resource agencies according to their major purposes. Yet he confined his interest in reorganization almost entirely to administration and methodology. To him, it seemed, conservation results loomed less important than conservation organization. Still, his strong belief in organizational continuity motivated him to appoint the heads of scientific bureaus exclusively from within the bureaus themselves, a policy which had important implications for the federal conservation program.

Hoover championed voluntarism as the method by which the federal government could achieve regulatory results without circumscribing the individual rights. Styling his approach as "Organized Coöperation," he sought to persuade states and individuals to coöperate with the federal government in order to reach certain goals. Even before he became President, his ideas about coöperation permeated the federal establishment. The Forest Service, the Bureau of Fisheries, the Army Engineers, the Biological Survey, the Bureau of Mines, and the Geological Survey all resorted to policies of coöperation during the 'twenties. Later, when Hoover became Chief Executive, he sought assiduously to avoid federal regulation. . . . But on the whole, coöperative tactics failed in the face of strong opposition from resource users. By the time of the New Deal, the policy of coöperation stood generally discredited. Because of his commitment to rugged individualism, Hoover never fully realized the significance to conservation of strong and direct government regulation.

Another characteristic Hoover response during the 1920's was decentralization. Influenced here more than elsewhere by the Republican Party, he consistently advocated states rights and state responsibilities. . . . Hoover's penchant for decentralized organization had a direct effect on his conservation thinking. It caused him to attempt a bold new policy toward the public domain, the range lands of which stood in need of attention.

The arid and semiarid lands of the West, comprising nearly one-third of the total area of the United States, form a valuable natural range for domestic livestock. By the decade of the 'twenties the federal government, true to its easy land policy, had sold the best sections of this vast domain to private individuals and landholding corporations. The government still owned more than 186,000,000 acres of range land, a fact which made it the largest landlord in the West. Despite their lack of title to the land, ranchers and stockmen had become accustomed to free use of these publicly owned areas. Occasionally they claimed exclusive jurisdiction over certain pastures. The trouble was that while supplementary forage on the public domain often became essential to successful grazing operations, the stockmen overused the range. They had little real chance to preserve natural vegetation because the competitive race for free forage forced them to put cattle onto the ranges too early in the spring and encouraged a continual overgrazing. After a time the native grasses tended to disappear, replaced by less desirable varieties or by total barrenness. The Forest Service had brought range lands within the national forests under regulation, but grazers still abused and exploited the unregulated public domain. After conservation organizations made repeated attempts to institute a grazing permit system for the public lands without success, Hoover decided to attack this persistent problem. . . .

As was his custom, he proposed a joint commission to study the problem. The governors agreed to coöperate, and Congress authorized the commission in April, 1930. Chaired by James R. Garfield, Secretary of the Interior under Theodore Roosevelt, and including William B. Greeley, former Forester, the Committee on the Conservation and Administration of the Public Domain commanded respect. Its report of early 1931 reflected Hoover's great influence. It proposed to place the unreserved and unappropriated public domain under responsible administration "for the conservation and beneficial use of its resources." The federal government, it suggested, should maintain jurisdiction over all reclamation projects, national forests, national parks and monuments, wildlife refuges, and any area important to the national defense. The remaining public holdings, valuable primarily as range land, were to be granted to the states. . . . The committee recommended, finally, that the national government pass title to public mineral lands to the states, with the reservation that federal agencies continue to hold the mineral rights. Supported fiercely by the Hoover administration, these proposals nevertheless had no chance of legislative enactment. A sincere attempt to bring effective regulation to the public domain, the plan satisfied too few people.

Conservationists disapproved of Hoover's suggestions for two main reasons. The Roosevelt-Pinchot faction would not sanction the reversal of a principle for which they had fought so hard—federal regulation of the resources of the public domain. Other conservation advocates believed the states incapable of coping with such a large regulatory problem. In the final analysis, the states themselves had little to gain by the committee's proposals. Regulating the public ranges would be a colossal headache, and state governments did not want title to mineral lands so long as the mineral rights resided in the federal government.

In spite of the failure of Hoover's plan for the public domain, his efforts produced a significant negative result. By offering the public lands to the states, and having the states reject the offer, the federal government freed itself to proceed with its own methods of regulation. The states-rights argument, which recurred periodically during grazing and mineral controversies, lost its validity. With the states refusing to act, the federal government had no alternative but to assume responsibility for grazing regulation. The quibbling over methods of range administration had not ended, but the argument over jurisdiction ceased. In 1934 the Taylor Grazing Act—although less than ideal legislation—at last brought conservation regulation to the public ranges of the West.

Hoover's emphasis on decentralization disappointed many conservationists who had hoped for a resurgence of strong and direct federal conservation participation. The old Progressive conservationists, still greatly influenced by Gifford Pinchot, were particularly disenchanted with Hoover.

Instead of being inspired, [Herbert A. Smith wrote] as I had hoped and believed, by a perception of the immense gains to the public welfare that might be realized by applying science, expert knowledge, the engineer's viewpoint, and the principles of business efficiency to the task of making government serve the multitudinous and complex requirements of a highly organized modern world, I believe he [Hoover] draws back in apprehension of what looks to him like an eventual Frankenstein.

During the era of Hoover's national prominence a curious ambivalence characterized his thinking about natural resources. A convert to the conservation philosophy, he was plagued by personal inconsistencies. He announced early in his administration that "conservation of natural resources is a fixed policy of the government," but he refused to pursue certain conservation projects because he objected to their political or economic implications. He became a pioneer advocate of watershed planning, yet he vehemently rejected the idea of comprehensive federal development of Muscle Shoals. He proposed to bring the public domain under regulation, but the method he chose foredoomed his plan to failure. Although he realized fully the imperative of restricting the national production of petroleum, he stubbornly eschewed direct federal intervention. Torn between conservation considerations and strict individualism, he could not bring himself to compromise his individualistic philosophy. He was thus less effective in implementing his conservation plans than he himself had hoped to be. As the first conservationist President since Theodore Roosevelt, Hoover had aroused expectations among conservation partisans. He failed to fulfill their high hopes. His primary contribution, achieved in spite of a severe economic depression, was to rekindle national interest in the orderly development of natural resources. During his administration the era of executive laxity ended. In his hands, the presidency once more became a constructive force in the campaign to conserve public resources. Hoover prepared the way for some of the dramatic conservation successes of Franklin Roosevelt by renewing the image of the President as a conservation leader. . . .

Science had become increasingly important in the federal establishment during the 'twenties. Following the budgetary cut-backs of the post-World War I years, Congress showed a willingness to underwrite federal research programs on a greatly expanded basis. Influenced by the example of private industry, the lawmakers found scientific research increasingly respectable. By the end of Hoover's administration federally supported scientific and technologic research had become more important than ever before. Capitalizing on the generosity of Congress, the conservation bureaus accumulated a large amount of valuable resource data. Soil erosion research progressed so rapidly, for example, that by 1933 Hugh Bennett had the scientific information on which to build his Soil Conservation Service. The Bureau of Fisheries, undertaking a wide range of scientific projects, greatly enlarged its knowledge of the life habits of fishes and made significant advances in the study of fish diseases. The Bureau of Mines perfected important new techniques of mineral extraction and refining, achieving striking technological successes. The Forest Service officially embraced science as the essential preliminary to policy-making. Its nation-wide timber survey, its forest products research, and its studies of forest management improved prospects for increased timber production and decreased timber waste. Even the Army Engineers rose to scientific heights with their excellent investigations of American river basins. By 1933 the federal conservation bureaus had collected the body of data which served as the scientific basis for New Deal resource planning. During the late 1920's government scientists were able to institutionalize a powerful reliance on scientific research. The example of the conservation agencies added impetus to the trend which, in the 1930's, saw research itself win recognition as a national resource. Considerably before the second Roosevelt entered the White House, science and technology had become dominant in resource decisions at the bureau level.

The acceptance of the principle of multiple-purpose resource planning went hand in hand with increased federal reliance on science. The logical use of resource data was developmental planning. As the prestige of research agencies mounted, and as research findings proved more and more valuable in conserving resources, Congress began to lean in the direction of the multiple-purpose approach. In matters of water development, the idea of watershed or river basin planning gained surprisingly wide acceptance. In agriculture, forestry, and soil conservation the concept of planned land utilization became progressively more important. By the time of the New Deal, resource planning had clearly become respectable. Agriculturists had already begun to think in terms of removing farmers from submarginal lands by a "resettlement" process. Congress had already committed itself to the multiple-purpose development of the Muscle Shoals region. Consequently, the Resettlement Administration and the Tennessee Valley Authority followed naturally from pressures which began building before the advent of the New Deal.

The aesthetic conservationists, whom Pinchot had deplored as "nature lovers," gained both strength and prestige during the 1920's. As the National Park Service coalesced and expanded, it furnished the organizational focus for an aesthetic renaissance and for a resurgence of preservationism. Long ignored in national conservation policy, wildlife protection and the preservation of natural beauty became popular causes. Challenging the utilitarians openly and aggressively, aesthetic conservationists forced their powerful opponents to recognize the desirability of protecting certain forms of animal life and to acknowledge the necessity for preserving unique areas of natural beauty. On the rise throughout the decade, "nature lovers" won equality within conservation ranks and received important support at the federal level.

In spite of occasional lapses in federal leadership, the 1920's were productive years in the conservation of natural resources. Stimulated by a heterogeneous group of conservationists, politicians, and resource administrators, the federal government led the way to important conservation achievement. Nation-wide forest fire protection became a reality. Federal soil conservation work began. The Boulder Canyon project, first federally sponsored large-scale multiple-purpose river basin development, won authorization. Giant flood control programs for the Mississippi Valley and other rivers took form. An integrated system of inland waterways intersected the great central section of the United States. The generation of hydroelectric power for the first time received careful consideration in resource planning. A network of migratory bird sanctuaries materialized. The national parks became a great American institution, preserving magnificent natural scenes for the edification of future generations. Left without a dynamic national conservation leader throughout most of the 'twenties, the conservation bureaus carried on unobtrusively and, in general, effectively. They laid foundations for subsequent New Deal conservation achievements. Congress, too, chartered an independent course. Moving largely against the wishes of the Republican chief executives, the federal legislature had by 1933 anticipated the direction of much New Deal conservation policy. Contrary to widely held opinion, the national conservation program did not deteriorate in the 1920's. It expanded and matured.

27

Conservation under Franklin D. Roosevelt

ANNA LOU RIESCH (1952)

The period between the Great Depression of the early 1930's and the World War of the early 1940's is one of great significance in the history of the United States. During these years the economy underwent tremendous changes in the process of recovery from depression and a concurrent and rapid movement toward leadership amongst the nations. On this stage of history Franklin Delano Roosevelt was beyond dispute a central figure. In internal affairs the so-called "New Deal" became associated with his name for it involved changes effected under his Administration. One aspect of this New Deal was a reevaluation and considerable extension of policy directed at the conservation of natural resources. . . .

The principle of conservation was no invention of the Roosevelt Administration. With respect to many resources conservation activities had been introduced by earlier governments both federal and state. Notable examples are the withdrawal of land for National Forests and the National Conservation Conference of Governors called by Theodore Roosevelt. But never before did conservation acquire such a comprehensive character. During the 1930's no resource escaped consideration as a subject for conservation. More significant still is the fact that, although the approach was comprehensive, the record of achievement in the conservation of any single resource surpassed that of any previous administration.

Anna Lou Riesch, "Conservation under Franklin D. Roosevelt" (Unpublished doctoral dissertation, University of Wisconsin, 1952), 340–348. Footnotes in the original have been omitted. Reprinted by permission of the author.

Conservation was taken to be an immediate task by the new Roosevelt Administration of 1933. There was also the important problem of bringing the nation out of depression. The fact that the two problems could be jointly attacked was recognized. This was one of the more important contributions of the Administration. The idea of "pump priming" through government expenditure during depression was itself in its infancy. But in addition political economy owes much to the Roosevelt Administration for the idea that this expenditure could be concentrated on conservation activities, of permanent benefit to the nation with a minimum of interference in the private investment sector of the economy.

Conservation activities, however, were not halted with an improvement in general economic conditions. It was obvious that the Roosevelt Administration had conceived of long-term conservation programs, irrespective of economic conditions, early in its life. This is to say that it believed that the United States had not previously paid sufficient attention to the conservation of natural resources in order to guarantee long-term economic security. This mistake would have to be corrected even if it meant an extended social cost. In seeking support for this belief the Roosevelt Administration was greatly aided by the increasing severity of dust storms, water erosion, floods, and resulting widespread distress. In the years that followed there was to be incorporated within the workings of American democracy what might rightly be termed a permanent conservation policy. This has its basis in the new concepts and procedures whereby effective activities associated with this objective comprised elements of a long-term character.

Important among the new concepts was that of the essential role of the federal government in effective conservation. It came to be recognized that the states as separate entities were no longer capable of coping with the problems alone. They needed financial assistance and leadership from the federal government. In addition it was recognized that many now existing conservation problems and projects transcended state boundaries. In response to these conditions a dynamic federal conservation policy emerged during the 1930's, based on organization, supervision, and financial contribution.

Another important concept was that of coordinated planning. There was the growing appreciation of the fact that the conservation of particular resources could not be set apart from that of other resources. The means available were scarce in relation to the possible conservation projects. There was a question of choosing what resource should receive attention over another, and of determining the scale of conservation activity in respect to a chosen resource. Fortunately it was possible to achieve several purposes at the same time but this was only possible through careful planning. It is here that the Roosevelt Administration made another important contribution. For it was largely responsible for the practical development of the multipurpose approach to resource development and conservation. The idea of the Tennessee Valley Authority involving the planned development of a whole river basin, and the subsequent experience obtained in the practical implementation of this scheme, were critical steps toward the acceptance of multipurpose development as a characteristic feature of the American system.

There is another side to this question of coordination. This involves coordination of the activities of the various governmental agencies concerned with resource work. The conservation activities of the 1930's inevitably resulted in a great expansion of the work of many federal agencies. There did develop a very real danger of an overlapping in the functions of these agencies and even wasteful competition among them. The problem of effective coordination of these agencies, and of these with the various state governments also attained increasing proportion. Although it might well be claimed that much was left to be done in this direction there are notable examples in the record of the Roosevelt Administration of attempts to achieve better coordination between various forms and levels of governmental activity.

Further, governmental action in a democracy has to be coordinated with both the interests and the activities of the citizen. Here the Roosevelt Administration made important contributions. As the recovery program had within it a deep respect for the American tradition of free individual enterprise in economic activities, so in conservation and developmental work there was real appreciation of the tradition of self-determination and respect for the individual. Indeed, in the development of the concept of planning there was involved the idea that this, far from impinging on the freedom of the individual, should provide both greater individual opportunity and greater individual participation in his own improvement. Overall plans were considered essential but not the need to impose schemes against the will of the people. The concept of "grass roots" administration appears throughout the conservation work of the 1930's.

One of the most interesting observations that can be made on the basis of a survey of conservation during the Roosevelt Administration relates to criticisms of this policy. Whether we consider the opinions of the common man, of the press or of opposing political groups the record is one of widespread agreement with Roosevelt's overall policy of conservation. Instances of critical debate revolved around specific proposals rather than general principles. In addition while Roosevelt did not receive a "blank check" for his conservation policy, and at times was disappointed with the extent of appropriations, criticisms of his proposals were more often constructive than destructive. . . .

The question as to whether the conservation policy of the Roosevelt Administration was conducted along sound economic lines, cannot be given a simple answer. There was implied, and generally accepted, the idea that conservation expenditure was warranted even at an immediate economic cost. That is, the profit and loss account of conservation, correctly viewed, should extend beyond the period of this study. The least that can be said is that, so far, history has not offered proof as to a social loss from the conservation policy of the Roosevelt Administration. Rather it would seem that the policy has received social approval. Evidence has been presented to indicate that certain specific measures, such as the Shelter Belt Project and public power development, were closely questioned on economic grounds during the life of the Administration. More generally, however, if questions of social costs and returns are excluded, there remains a creditable record of immediate returns in relation to the costs involved in particular projects.

Finally, the central personality in the record of conservation activity during the 1930's is none other than Franklin Delano Roosevelt. It is true that conditions were ripe for his leadership. It is also true that he had able supporters. Harold Ickes [Secretary of the Interior] in particular, but also Henry Wallace, [Secretary of Agriculture], Senator [George W.] Norris, H. H. Bennett [see (21)] and others, in their own right, made substantial contributions to the developing conservation policy. Further, Roosevelt's task was made easier by a cooperative Congress and the sympathy and support of the scientist, the press, and the average American citizen. However, this does not minimize the importance of Roosevelt as practical conservationist, a man of vision, and a great leader. Examination shows his personal interest in conservation and how he applied this interest to the care of natural resources long before he became President of the United States. In public office as senator, as Assistant Secretary of

Navy, and as governor he was active in promoting conservation. His conservation record as Governor of New York is merely repeated on a larger scale as President of the nation. In New York, he had used conservation as a relief measure, and had urged legislation to protect and fully utilize resources. He had opposed groups bent upon exploitation. During his presidential campaign Roosevelt promised to conserve the country's resources and indicated the procedure he would follow. Promptly after his election, he instigated legislation to that end. Throughout his presidential years he maintained a careful check and an alert supervision. He slighted no phase, no resource, no project, no detail. And while he carried out his determination to develop an all-encompassing conservation policy with diplomatic tact, he did not hesitate to use strong persuasion or pressure to achieve his ends. For he had utmost faith in the objective he sought; an objective that few understood or could express as clearly as himself:

> *We seek to use our natural resources not as a thing apart but as something that is interwoven with industry, labor, finance, taxation, agriculture, homes, recreation, good citizenship. The results of this interweaving will have a greater influence on the future American standard of living than the rest of our economics put together.*

Conservation under Franklin Delano Roosevelt demonstrates the function of mature leadership in a democracy such as the United States, when a multiplicity both of competing interests and of possible techniques requires some courageously far-sighted man, imbued with public spirit, to synthesize and channel the creative forces which must replace those of destruction.

Part Four

Conservation as Quality of the Environment

Part Four

Conservation as Quality of the Environment

Since the Second World War the driving force in the American conservation movement has come increasingly from the quest for *quality* in the environment. At first, to be sure, the familiar theme of providing for man's material needs was much in evidence. Books like Fairfield Osborn's *Our Plundered Planet* (1948), William Vogt's *Road to Survival* (1948), and Osborn's *The Limits of the Earth* (1953) grimly raised the old Malthusian specter of population outreaching the world's productive ability. They contended that birth control, the prevention of needless waste, and the development of new processes of providing food were essential for the survival of the race. From this perspective, conservation was the means of maintaining the physical bases of life. Indeed, this had been the movement's main rationale at the time of its inception.

But the idea of protecting the environment for its *nonmaterial* values also had a long, if usually less potent, history in American thought. And by the 1960's this concept challenged utilitarianism as the central purpose of conservation. Continued improvements in technology, for one thing, eased fears of overpopulation and resource exhaustion. More importantly, many Americans were coming to realize that an environment conducive to survival—even to affluence—was not enough. They demanded that the land had to do more than just keep people alive.

This attitude has made the idea of environmental quality so common in the contemporary discussion of conservation. The concept obviously has a perplexing subjective dimension, but it is generally understood as applying less to particular resources and more to the capacity of the total environment to bring people happiness. Consequently the emphasis of the "new conservation," as President Lyndon B. Johnson labeled it (30), is on such things as beauty and recreational opportunities. The environment is to be groomed for the joy of man.

The new conservation has brought new problems. For one, what economists call benefit–cost analyses are extremely difficult to make in regard to nonmaterial values. The dollar-and-cent worth of a forest, for instance, is relatively easy to calculate compared to its importance as an element in a landscape. Another type of problem results, ironically, from the growing appreciation of nature. Coupled with increasing leisure and mobility, this has created, in Marion Clawson's words, "a crisis in outdoor recreation". It is not that existing parks and recreation areas cannot "hold" all who come, but that after a certain saturation point the degree of the recreational satisfaction decreases. The simple fact of too many people is also responsible for much of the smog, sprawl, blight, and general deterioration of the American environment. Conservationists are recognizing that ultimately they must join hands with those attempting to check the nation's and the world's spiraling population. Malthus may have been right for the wrong reasons.

28

New Directions

JOSEPH L. FISHER (1964)

Resources for the Future, established in 1952 with grants from the Ford Foundation, is dedicated to the advancement of research and education in the development, conservation, and use of natural resources. Through grants to institutions and individuals, as well as by the work of its own staff, RFF has attempted to focus attention on the newest and most challenging problems in conservation. Initially its approach was scientific, economic, and quantitative in the manner of the old Pinchot school, but recently considerations of quality and aesthetics in the environment have received increasing emphasis. In this selection Joseph L. Fisher, president of RFF, uses the occasion of his annual report for 1964 to review his organization's previous accomplishments and anticipate its future work.

. . . [L]ooking ahead to the next five years, what appear to be the major opportunities for Resources for the Future if it is to continue to grow in professional stature and public effectiveness? . . . To what broad problems shall we in Resources for the Future turn our attention in the years ahead? . . .

First let me take a quick look backward to see the road Resources for the Future has traveled thus far. Ten years ago, when our program was getting under way, there was great concern in this country about running out of resources, or at least encountering steeply rising costs for oil, many metals, and lumber and other forest products. The Second World War with its heavy drain on raw materials, the difficulties met in many parts of the world in re-establishing productive economies after the war, the postwar baby boom, the cold war and its requirements for large military programs—all these factors led many observers to the view that even in affluent America the sheer quantity of resource materials would prove to be inadequate to meet needs, let alone expectations. RFF addressed this central issue by preparing a series of studies of the various resources, both on a national and regional scale, in which past trends of demand and supply were

Joseph L. Fisher, "Some New Directions," *Resources for the Future Annual Report* (1964), 1–9. Reprinted by permission of the author.

studied and possibilities for the future were projected. In this way special problems were identified—a prospective shortage of a particular commodity in a particular place or at a particular time, for example—but on the whole we concluded that there would be no shortage in any of the main resource categories. New discoveries, increased yields, development of satisfactory substitutes, more effective conservation, and larger imports could be expected to step into almost any foreseeable breach.

As events have unfolded, the resource outlook for the United States has eased, at least in the time perspective of the next several decades. New discoveries of underground petroleum in various parts of the world, improved prospects for obtaining oil through secondary recovery techniques and from shale and tar sands, the opening of major new iron ore deposits and the upgrading of domestic taconite reserves, improvements in nuclear reactor technology leading to lower costs of nuclear power production, further gains in farm productivity, a much more favorable reappraisal of the nation's forests, and improved prospects for development and management of water supplies have been among the principal features of this change in outlook. Of course the need for vigorous development, wise conservation, and efficient use of natural resources remains, regardless of any shift in the general outlook.

In recent years several other large problems have come more clearly into view—problems no less basic than that of the quantitative adequacy of resources to meet the future demands of the United States which first engaged RFF's attention. One such question arises out of the fact that the broad resource outlook in much of the world, especially in the less developed countries, is far less favorable than it is in the United States. Yet the United States depends on many of these other countries for certain essential raw material imports, as well as for markets and investment outlets. What is the nature of these interdependencies which are so important to all the countries? What international resource policies will nurture fuller development and better relations among the countries? In resources as in other matters the United States is part of a world system; and the livelihood of our citizens is linked with that of people everywhere.

Another problem we are led to is that of declining resource and environmental quality, whether it is water or air pollution, pesticide damage to wildlife or disfigurement of the countryside. Related to this, and to no small extent the cause of it, is the phenomenon of urban and industrial growth which sets a whole series of difficult problems for land use planning, water development, and conservation generally. . . .

During the next few years we plan to give more attention to the resource and economic development problems of the world generally and a few selected countries in particular. Most of our completed studies have been focused primarily on the United States, though it often has been necessary to look abroad at some situations and trends that affect this country directly. Our most comprehensive study to date, *Resources in America's Future*, published in 1963, concluded that, broadly speaking, resources would be adequate to meet the needs of an expanding U.S. population for the next several decades provided scientific and technological progress continued unabated, provided policies were reasonably well chosen and administered, provided adequate programs and investment in resources development and conservation were forthcoming, and provided a reasonably efficient world trading and investing system could be maintained by means of which this country could obtain supplies of certain raw materials from abroad. But in this study, and others that dealt with particular resources, little was said directly or in depth about the resources situation and outlook of other parts of the world. Some two-thirds of the 3.2 billion people in the world at the present time live in economically less developed areas where per capita incomes range from a few hundred dollars a year down to less than fifty dollars. Many of these places are densely populated, and it is obvious that, in the classic Malthusian sense, people press hard on the available natural resources. What about the resources future of India, Pakistan, numerous countries in Africa and the Middle East, and in many parts of Latin America? What policies, developmental investments, training and educational programs, administrative organizations, and international arrangements may be critical in setting these countries on the road to rapid resource development and economic improvement?

Such questions as these will absorb a considerable share of our attention in the period ahead. Important for their own sakes, they also bear significantly and sometimes directly on events and issues in this country. . . .

. . . [Our] reconnaissance survey indicates that in most of the less developed countries during the last ten or fifteen years the level of per capita energy consumption has risen. Coal is fairly widely available over the world, and large reserves await development. Oil has come on rapidly in recent years in the Middle East, in northern South America, and more recently in North Africa and other places. Large hydroelectric potentials await development in Central Africa, the Mekong Basin countries of Southeast Asia, and elsewhere. Nuclear power from fission reactors is crossing the threshold of economic development in this country and is close to the threshold in some of the other economically advanced countries. It may be expected to find application in less developed places once the market justifies installation of large, economical stations or progress is made in developing useable smaller reactors.

Policy problems abound in the international energy field, partly because the sources of supply are not ubiquitous even though fairly widely distributed. For example, Western Europe is becoming increasingly dependent on oil supplies from the Middle East, a politically unstable region. This is of concern because of the obviously close tie between cheap energy and both economic development and national security. Some of these problems are economic; many are political. . . .

The outlook in the less developed countries for food provides less reason for optimism. Here our broad survey is inconclusive; apparently it will be nip and tuck for most of the people of the world whether they will be able to gain significantly in terms of per capita consumption of calories and proteins. The bulk of the population of Asia, Africa, and Latin America is only slightly, if any, better off now than it was twenty-five or thirty years ago. Viewed in world terms, the amount of new land brought into agriculture has been insignificant over the past three decades, while increases in yields have barely managed to keep up with population growth. During the most recent crop year, according to the Food and Agriculture Organization, world production of crops increased less than population. Undoubtedly, the foreign aid in food extended since the war by the United States and other countries has helped, but this can only handle a small part of the problem. Apparently little success has been achieved in the heavily populated and less developed regions of the world in combining more abundant energy supplies, capital equipment, practical technology, and all the rest, with improved farm labor and management so as to enable these countries to achieve any kind of take-off in agriculture. And a take-off in agriculture may prove to be a necessary precondition, or at least accompaniment, of a take-off in industry and the economy generally. . . .

A second line of investigation to which we are drawn concerns the quality of the environment, particularly in the United States. . . . The environment in many places has deteriorated under the pressures of an ever denser population, numerous growing industries, and a set of attitudes carried over from earlier times when good environmental housekeeping may not have been so necessary. Water pollution has become close to pandemic, and air pollution in the urban areas already is a plague. The large increases in agricultural yields over recent decades have resulted in large part from wide-scale application of chemicals to promote growth, kill insects, and eradicate disease. These benefits have been accompanied by costs, one of the heaviest being the loss or threat of loss of animals, birds, and fish. In the long run, the health of people, too, may suffer.

It is important to avoid becoming so alarmed by these matters that capacity for constructive action becomes paralyzed. The need is for objective and careful assessment of the factors and trends, and a patient search for the means of dealing with them. One approach is through systems analysis by means of which the significant factors involved in, say, a problem of water pollution may be considered in an interrelated way and in terms of specified standards of health, economic efficiency, and the like, in a search for the "best" solution to the problem. . . .

Over the coming years we also plan to give some attention to several other kinds of environmental pollution, notably air pollution, pesticides, and the effects of modern civilization on the rural environment. This latter, perhaps the most elusive of them all, recognizes that population growth, large cities, industrial development, increased leisure for outdoor recreation, and the like combine to place new and heavy demands upon the rural and natural landscape in ways hardly dreamed of by our forefathers. Cities thrust out into the countryside frequently in an unplanned manner, with little regard for over-all aesthetic effects. Sheer economic efficiency of metropolitan complexes also leaves something to be desired. The millions of Americans who spend a large portion of their leisure time out-of-doors likewise cause damage to the rural environment, frequently out of ignorance; their search for recreation is slowly eroding away the very values they seek.

Parks are misused and overused, certain fish and wildlife populations are depleted, wilderness is becoming hard to preserve as such, and industries and people alike mess up the landscape. The empty beer can has become almost as much a feature of the rural landscape as the beautiful flower.

The wide variety of threats to the quality of the environment may well embrace the gravest U.S. resources problems of the next generation. The various quantitative resource studies we have made so far indicate that with prudence and foresight there need be no general shortage of resources for the foreseeable future in this country. However, the more we have examined the quantitative outlook the more we have seen that the really difficult resource problems for the future in this country are likely to involve quality. In *Resources in America's Future** we said, "Simply having enough oil, metals, land, and water would not spell a satisfactory life for most people. . . . The relationship of people to resources, which usually has been expressed in terms of quantity, needs to be restated for modern times to emphasize what is happening to the quality of resources."

For these reasons in the years ahead we shall do what we can, within the limitations imposed by our commitments to other important lines of work, to mark out social science approaches to these qualitative problems, to assess the trends and the benefits and costs to society that seem to be involved, and to consider new schemes of management or perhaps even altogether new institutions for dealing more effectively with environmental pollution and disfigurement. . . .

A third problem area which we expect to probe more deeply may be described as urban-resource relations. Already Resources for the Future has undertaken, through its own staff and by means of grants, a number of investigations into those problems of water resources, land use, and outdoor recreation that are urgent today because of the rapid growth of metropolitan population. But so far, we and others with similar interests have only scratched the surface of what is one of the most powerfully moving trends of modern times.

The present outlook for birth and death rates and immigration suggests a population increase in this country from the present figure of 192 million to 245 million in 1980 and to 330 million or more by the year 2000. Virtually the entire increase is expected to be in metropoli-

* [1963]

tan areas. Annually in this country, several hundred thousand acres of farmland are shifting over to urban and suburban uses. That part of the total population classified as rural is static or even declining. The problems of urban living are legion: commuting from home to work, financing local government, maintaining vigorous central cities, providing jobs for more and more young people from rural parts of the country who want to work in cities, maintaining individual and public morality and responsibility in the face of the psychological and cultural shocks imparted by the urban arrangement, and providing both the necessities and the amenities of life for city dwellers in the form of pure water, clean air, and healthful outdoor recreation. These are only some of the problems of growing cities that challenge the imagination of research and the wisdom of decision makers. . . .

We hope to pay special attention to the problems in the suburban and outer fringes of the growing metropolitan areas where shifts in land use are dramatic, conflicts sharp, and monetary stakes high. What are the more sensible patterns for the expansion of cities into the rural countryside? How may the most constructive roles of the land developer, the highway planner, and the local and regional agencies of government be identified? What kinds of guidance of urban growth will be helpful, according to what standards of judgment? What new institutions may be needed if the metropolitan areas of the future are to be more efficient and more pleasant than those we now have? Can the inconsistencies of massive federal aid programs in highways, urban renewal, open space, and welfare be harmonized so that each metropolitan area may become one instead of many—one functioning, liveable, attractive whole instead of a confusion of separate pieces?

In particular, is it possible to identify a few factors a proper understanding and planning of which can guide the development of the whole metropolitan complex? In one speculative paper [we] . . . have suggested that an understanding of the transportation network, the provision of essential utilities, and the arrangement of open space make up the skeleton of metropolitan areas to which all the rest must be related. Underlying any such approach to achieving better urban areas must be the wishes of the inhabitants; consequently it is most important that the people concerned have an adequate knowledge of the trends and possibilities. . . .

These are a few of quite a number of projects in prospect. In pursuing them we look forward to joining forces with individual research scholars and teachers in the universities and elsewhere, many of whom have been concerned with resources for a long time, in our quest for deeper understanding of the part resources play in society. . . . Running through all our activities will be a continued devotion to objective research, to well-chosen educational activities, to understanding those resource problems which must be understood if public and private policies are to be improved. Especially we hope to demonstrate through our program the numerous constructive ways in which research and analysis can put the nation on the road to better conservation, development, and use of natural resources for human welfare. These are our aims for the next five years.

29

Uglification
PETER BLAKE (1964)

With the fervor of the Progressive conservationists, a number of Americans have recently lashed out at the ugliness of modern America. And, as with the Progressives, the targets of their criticism are frequently the rich "interests" whose only objective, allegedly, is the service of their own economic ends. What displeases people like Peter Blake most is the haphazard, unrelated, identity-less "goop" (as an English observer, Ian Nairn, put it in 1962 in The American Landscape) *that results from short-sighted and unresponsible custodianship of the land. Sadly they contrast what is to what might have been, given the potential of the American environment. The most important question conservationists of this persuasion face is how can the material expansion needed to keep pace with population growth be secured without sacrificing the qualities that make existence worthwhile.*

An architect and free lance writer, Blake is foreign born, a circumstance that may partially explain the candor of his attitude. Blake's book,

Peter Blake, *God's Own Junkyard: The Planned Deterioration of the American Landscape* (New York, Holt, Rinehart & Winston, 1964), 7–9, 11, 14, 16–17, 69, 140–142. Copyright © 1964 by Peter Blake. Reprinted by permission of the author and Holt, Rinehart & Winston.

from which the following selection is taken, is largely composed of photographs illustrating the "goulash of environment" (again the phrase is Nairn's) which, he feels, is modern America.

This book is not written in anger. It is written in fury—though not, I trust, in blind fury. It is a deliberate attack upon all those who have already befouled a large portion of this country for private gain, and are engaged in befouling the rest.

Some of these latter-day vandals are well organized and well financed—such as the billboard industry whose profitable creations along our highways have been implicated in a staggering number of automobile accidents . . . . Some of our latter-day vandals are "little people"—tradesmen and shopkeepers trying to make a modest living—people without ties to the landscape or townscape in which they live, people whose eyes have lost the art of seeing. And still others among our latter-day vandals are all the rest of us—all of us who no longer care, or no longer care *enough.*

A very cynical acquaintance of mine said to me recently: "The national purpose of the United States, from the very beginning, has been to let everyone make as much money as he possibly can. If they found oil under St. Patrick's Cathedral, they would put a derrick smack in the center of the nave, and nobody would give the matter a second thought."

This is perhaps a rather naïve book. . . . It is based on the . . . assumption that it is not too late for us to learn to see again, and to learn to care again about the physical aspects of our environment. And it is based, finally, on the assumption that ours could be a reasonably civilized society—if enough of us could be stirred into action.

This is, therefore, a muckraking book, not because muckraking is a particularly enjoyable activity, but because there seems to be so much muck around that needs to be raked so that this country may be made fit again to live in.

❂   ❂   ❂

No people has inherited a more naturally beautiful land than we: within an area representing a mere 6 per cent of the land surface of the globe we can point to mountain ranges as spectacular as those of the Dolomites and to jungles as colorful as those of the Amazon valley; to lake-studded forests as lovely as those of Finland and to rolling hills as gentle as those around Salzburg; to cliffs that rival those of the French Riviera and to sandy beaches that are unexcelled even by the shores of Jutland; in short, to about as varied and thrilling a geography as has ever been presented to man.

The only trouble is that we are about to turn this beautiful inheritance into the biggest slum on the face of the earth. "The mess that is man-made America," as a British magazine has called it, is a disgrace of such vast proportions that only a concerted national effort can now hope to return physical America to the community of civilized nations.

Our towns and cities boast many isolated handsome buildings—but very, very few handsome streets, squares, civic centers, or neighborhoods. . . . Our suburbs are interminable wastelands dotted with millions of monotonous little houses on monotonous little lots and crisscrossed by highways lined with billboards, jazzed-up diners, used-car lots, drive-in movies, beflagged gas stations, and garish motels. Even the relatively unspoiled countryside beyond these suburban fringes has begun to sprout more telephone poles than trees, more trailer camps than national parks. And the shores of oceans, lakes, and rivers are rapidly becoming encrusted with the junkiness of industries that pollute the water on which they depend. . . .

. . . [E]xcept for National and State Parks not much of the natural beauty of this country remains preserved. And unhappily those fine National Forests and State Parks tend to do to the landscape what National and State Museums do to painting and sculpture: that is, embalm it. (They tend to "elevate" us on Sundays and holidays, rather than enrich our lives all year round.) However praiseworthy such conservation efforts may be in helping to protect parts of the American countryside, they do little to protect those areas in which most of us live or spend our free time—the areas nearest to cities and suburbs.

As for the preservation of man-made improvements, this is almost nonexistent: except for a few isolated structures of well-established historic value (or, at any rate, interest), and a few isolated blocks in some of our older cities, none of our impressive architectural heritage is protected. . . . [I]n Buffalo, New York, Frank Lloyd Wright's world-famous Larkin Building, designed in 1904 and honored in every single history book on modern architecture, was sold by the city fathers in 1949 to a wrecking firm for a few thousand dollars; the new owners replaced it with a parking lot.

And so it goes—in St. Louis, San Francisco, Baltimore, Philadelphia, Boston, Pittsburgh—everywhere. When a building—whether handsome or of indifferent quality—has ceased to be a "moneymaker," down it comes to make way for a bowling alley or a supermarket. . . .

Our cities, however, are not alone. When people talk about the flood of ugliness engulfing America, they first think of billboards—and, more specifically, of the billboards that line our highways and dot our landscape.

The problem was stated rather succinctly by Ogden Nash:

> *I think that I shall never see*
> *A billboard lovely as a tree.*
> *Perhaps, unless the billboards fall,*
> *I'll never see a tree at all.*

Mr. Nash may have thought that he was exaggerating just a bit. But the fact of the matter is that in Chicago, for example, the local authorities have recently been busy cutting down the tops of trees that interfere with the view of billboards along one stretch of Lake Shore Drive. . . .

. . . [I]n 1960, a Mr. James M. Crosby, President of something called the "Unexcelled Chemical Corporation," announced that he had acquired the Western hemisphere rights to a Swiss-developed machine named "Skyjector." This little gadget (cost: more than $1.5 million) will project advertising messages on clouds, as well as "such surfaces as skyscrapers, mountainsides, cliffs and dams." The "Skyjector" is mounted on a truck and uses candle power equal to sixty to eighty giant searchlights! (In fact, one bulb in this infernal machine got so hot that it set fire to a stage when the gadget was tried out in a German theater.) There will be no need to drive the "Skyjector" along a highway to achieve the effect of a *moving* advertising sign: the machine can easily project a message on a small slide over a distance of five miles, and it will then appear (on a cloud, the Continental Divide, or the sides of the Grand Canyon, for example) some 25 *million times larger* than the original slide. Presumably the projected image can be shifted around a bit: but even if that problem were to remain unlicked, the illusion of motion could be supplied without trouble, for the "Skyjector" can change slides every five seconds!

Although anti-billboard arguments are, at present, likely to be most effective when advanced on grounds of highway safety, the esthetic argument seems to be gaining adherents. This became evident during the Great Billboard Battle of 1958 . . . which was fought almost exclusively on esthetic grounds.

That battle was a memorable occasion. It was memorable because it represented the first instance in our history that the federal legislature faced up to the problems presented by the systematic "uglification" of the United States by one single-minded private enterprise. It was memorable, too, because after all the rehetoric had died down, the net result of this valiant effort was a feeble compromise. . . .

. . . Unhappily, the evidence before our eyes, every day of the year, in almost every square mile of this country, is proof that the effort, to date, has been almost completely inadequate. There are more billboards—some $1 billion worth—in the United States in 1963 than there were when Senator Ellender feared for America in March, 1958. There are more neon-lit hot dog stands, more garish bowling alleys, more glistening diners, more used car lots, more junk piles. "Yet each man kills the thing he loves," Oscar Wilde once said. Perhaps that is why we are so busy destroying this country. . . .

The next stop on our scenic tour of the United States of America is Suburbia—anywhere! . . .

The massive, monotonous ugliness of most of our Surburbia must be blamed, in part, on those architects and planners who used to advocate a kind of garden-city development in which each family would have its own plot of land and its own house smack in the center of that plot. One of the leading advocates of this ideal was Frank Lloyd Wright, whose "Broadacre City" concept envisaged one-acre plots per family for most Americans. Wright was, of course, greatly influenced by the agrarian traditions of eighteenth- and nineteenth-century America; and while his proposals reflected those traditions and ideals, they hardly faced up to the desperate problems created by recent population growth in this country (an increase of 350 per cent in Wright's lifetime alone) and in the rest of the world.

What happened to *Broadacre City* (with one-family-per-acre), of course, was that it became Suburbia (with about five-families-per-acre). Yet, despite this rather basic change in density, those who proceeded to practice what they thought Wright had preached made no changes in concept; so that Suburbia today is what Wright himself called, in his later years, "a series of anonymous boxes that go into a row on row upon row," and what others have called "the great suburban sprawl."

Suburbia got that way for two simple reasons: first, because the developers who built it are, fundamentally, no different from manufacturers of any other mass-produced product: they standardize the product, package it, arrange for rapid distribution and easy financing, and sell it off the shelf as fast as they can. And, second, because the federal government, through FHA [Federal Housing Administration] and other agencies set up to cope with the serious housing shortages that arose after World War II, has imposed a bureaucratic strait jacket on the design of most new houses, on the placement of these houses on individual lots, on landscaping, on street-planning, and on just about everything else that gives Suburbia its "wasteland" appearance. . . .

There are several ways of looking at our land: there is the choked-up way ("America the Beautiful"); there is the socio-political way ("The land, the earth God gave to man for his home . . . should never be the possession of any man, corporation, (or) society . . . any more than the air or water," as Abraham Lincoln put it); and then there is the point of view . . . that enjoys the sanction of all right-thinking people, of both major political parties, of chambers of commerce and of labor unions: after all, doesn't an owner have the right to do with his land as he pleases (more or less)? If he wants to cut down all the trees, plant billboards and telephone poles, bulldoze the hills into oblivion, turn the place into a village dump, or chop it up into what one California developer calls "ranchettes"—well, isn't that *his* business and isn't this a free country and what right has anyone to try and stop him?

. . . Though we have established the right of individuals to own pieces of land, the implication has always been that this was a trust—not an absolute right. And judging by the manner in which that trust has been abused by many of its present, private owners, a review of this arrangement may be in order. After all, no one has the right to own the American air or the American waters; some have been given permission to *use* these natural resources, and the manner of such uses has been very strictly circumscribed.

The brutal destruction of our landscape is much more than a blow against beauty. Every artist, scientist, and philosopher in the history of mankind has pointed to the laws of nature as his greatest source of inspiration: without the presence of nature, undisturbed, there would have been no Leonardo, no Ruskin, no Nervi, no Frank Lloyd Wright. In destroying our landscape, we are destroying the future of civilization in America. . . .

The trouble is, of course, that there is precious little popular consent or consensus in matters of beauty or in matters of order. Indeed, it can be shown rather convincingly that popular consensus today favors chaos. . . .

Needless to say, it goes against the popular grain to suggest the imposition of limitations on freedom—especially on freedom of taste. . . .

Political and economic freedoms under democracy are (theoretically, at least) absolute—EXCEPT in so far as such freedoms are abused to limit the enjoyment of life, liberty, and the pursuit of happiness by our fellow men. This is obvious, of course: a citizen living in a democracy, under the rule of law, is expected to practice self-restraint in a great many ways. He cannot bump off his personal enemies because that would deprive them of their l., l., and p. of h.; he cannot drive his car through a red light (same reason), cheat his business partners, or, for that matter, build a rock-and-roll emporium next to a church in just about any city in the United States except Houston, Texas. In short, he is free as a lark so long as he does not impair the freedoms of his fellow men.

If and when this citizen in a democracy stops practicing self-restraint, governmental authority rears its ugly head. If and when a large number of citizens stops practicing self-restraint, the federal government may send troops to wherever it is that the citizenry has gone beserk. All of this is tacitly understood, at least in matters of conventional social, political, and economic behavior.

It is not so understood in matters of esthetic behavior. . . .

Where any citizen is permitted a choice between degrading ugliness and beauty, the state has no right to step in and restrain the uglifier. No citizen is *forced* to look at "pop art," or listen to alleged musical compositions consisting of five simultaneously broadcast tape recordings of the mating calls of dromedaries, or watch supposedly prurient movies. He has a choice.

But in America today, no citizen (except for an occasional hermit) has a chance to see anything but hideousness—all around him, day in and day out. We have more art schools than ever before, and more "art appreciation" courses; but how can a child in Gary, Indiana, say, be taught to use his eyes with discrimination, taste, and intelligence? How can he learn without being given a chance to compare? Where can he go even to look at a tree? . . .

Today, whenever architects, artists, writers, and critics gather to deplore, view with alarm, and write manifestos about the planned deterioration of America, there is much talk about hucksters and vulgarians and politicians and special interests. It is pretty good talk, and it is largely true talk—as far as it goes. But it misses one essential point: the point that the "intellectual elite" in America has failed miserably to accept its basic responsibilities, and to set an example for the rest of the country to follow—an example of self-imposed restraint, an example of quality rather than novelty.

It may be possible to create some degree of order in America—and, with it, a *chance* for civilization—by demanding such things as more stringent zoning laws, by taking the profit out of land speculation, by using tax policy to encourage good building and to discourage bad building, by ridding the country of the bureaucrats who have strait-jacketed most government-subsidized architecture, and by getting rid of their moribund agencies.

All this is essential; yet it is no more than preventive medicine. All this will do is *possibly* give us another chance.

But if we intend to do more—to create a great urban civilization in America, for example—then we need something in addition to more stringent laws and more effective controls over bureaucrats. We need creative acts; we need genuine leadership on the part of those capable of creating a new kind of city and a new kind of country. . . .

30

Beautification
LYNDON B. JOHNSON (1965)

On February 8, 1965 President Lyndon B. Johnson sent a special message on natural beauty to the Congress of the United States. A landmark in defining the emphasis of American conservation since World War II, it stimulated action on local, state, and federal levels. The White House

Lyndon B. Johnson, "Natural Beauty—Message from the President of the United States," *Congressional Record*, 89th Cong., 1st Sess., Vol. 111, Pt. 2 (Feb. 8, 1965), 2085–2089.

Conference on Natural Beauty, which Johnson mentions in this message, met on May 24 and 25, 1965. The event resembled Theodore Roosevelt's 1908 conference (9); again the power and prestige of the executive office was used to dramatize the most pressing conservation issue of the time. But aesthetic rather than material concerns received emphasis in the President's "new conservation." Of course Robert Underwood Johnson and John Muir [(13) and (14)] had championed natural beauty a half century earlier, but never before 1965 had it been accorded such enthusiastic official endorsement. The conference chairman Laurance S. Rockefeller, a member of a family whose philanthropy has recently done much to protect and beautify the American landscape, led a panel of experts who reported on subjects ranging from highway billboards and automobile junkyards to the underground installation of utilities. A prominent figure at the conference as well as in the national beautification movement was Mrs. Lyndon B. Johnson.

To the Congress of the United States:

For centuries Americans have drawn strength and inspiration from the beauty of our country. It would be a neglectful generation indeed, indifferent alike to the judgment of history and the command of principle, which failed to preserve and extend such a heritage for its descendants.

Yet the storm of modern change is threatening to blight and diminish in a few decades what has been cherished and protected for generations.

A growing population is swallowing up areas of natural beauty with its demands for living space, and is placing increased demand on our overburdened areas of recreation and pleasure.

The increasing tempo of urbanization and growth is already depriving many Americans of the right to live in decent surroundings. More of our people are crowding into cities and being cut off from nature. Cities themselves reach out into the countryside, destroying streams and trees and meadows as they go. A modern highway may wipe out the equivalent of a 50-acre park with every mile. And people move out from the city to get closer to nature only to find that nature has moved farther from them.

The modern technology, which has added much to our lives can also have a darker side. Its uncontrolled waste products are menacing the world we live in, our enjoyment and our health. The air we breathe, our water, our soil, and wildlife, are being blighted by the poisons and chemicals which are the by-products of technology and industry. The skeletons of discarded cars litter the countryside. The same society which receives the rewards of technology, must, as a cooperating whole, take responsibility for control. To deal with these new problems will require a new conservation. We must not only protect the countryside and save it from destruction, we must restore what has been destroyed and salvage the beauty and charm of our cities. Our conservation must be not just the classic conservation of protection and development, but a creative conservation of restoration and innovation. Its concern is not with nature alone, but with the total relation between man and the world around him. Its object is not just man's welfare but the dignity of man's spirit.

In this conservation the protection and enhancement of man's opportunity to be in contact with beauty must play a major role.

This means that beauty must not be just a holiday treat, but a part of our daily life. It means not just easy physical access, but equal social access for rich and poor, Negro and white, city dweller and farmer.

Beauty is not an easy thing to measure. It does not show up in the gross national product, in a weekly paycheck, or in profit-and-loss statements. But these things are not ends in themselves. They are a road to satisfaction and pleasure and the good life. Beauty makes its own direct contribution to these final ends. Therefore it is one of the most important components of our true national income, not to be left out simply because statisticians cannot calculate its worth.

And some things we do know. Association with beauty can enlarge man's imagination and revive his spirit. Ugliness can demean the people who live among it. What a citizen sees every day is his America. If it is attractive it adds to the quality of his life. If it is ugly it can degrade his existence.

Beauty has other immediate values. It adds to safety whether removing direct dangers to health or making highways less monotonous and dangerous. We also know that those who live in blighted and squalid conditions are more susceptible to anxieties and mental disease.

Ugliness is costly. It can be expensive to clean a soot-smeared building, or to build new areas of recreation when the old landscape could have been preserved far more cheaply.

Certainly no one would hazard a national definition of beauty. But we do know that nature is nearly always beautiful. We do, for the most part, know what is ugly. And we can introduce, into all our planning, our programs, our building, and our growth, a conscious and active concern for the values of beauty. If we do this then we can be successful in preserving a beautiful America.

There is much the Federal Government can do, through a range of specific programs, and as a force for public education. But a beautiful America will require the effort of government at every level, of business, and of private groups. Above all it will require the concern and action of individual citizens, alert to danger, determined to improve the quality of their surroundings, resisting blight, demanding and building beauty for themselves and their children.

I am hopeful that we can summon such a national effort. For we have not chosen to have an ugly America. We have been careless, and often neglectful. But now that the danger is clear and the hour is late this people can place themselves in the path of a tide of blight which is often irreversible and always destructive. . . .

I make the following proposals: . . .

Thomas Jefferson wrote that communities "should be planned with an eye to the effect made upon the human spirit by being continually surrounded with a maximum of beauty."

We have often sadly neglected this advice in the modern American city. Yet this is where most of our people live. It is where the character of our young is formed. It is where American civilization will be increasingly concentrated in years to come.

Such a challenge will not be met with a few more parks or playgrounds. It requires attention to the architecture of building, the structure of our roads, preservation of historical buildings and monuments, careful planning of new suburbs. A concern for the enhancement of beauty must infuse every aspect of the growth and development of metropolitan areas. It must be a principal responsibility of local government, supported by active and concerned citizens. . . .

In almost every part of the country, citizens are rallying to save landmarks of beauty and history. The Government must also do its share to assist these local efforts which have an important national purpose. We will encourage and support the National Trust for Historic Preservation in the United States, chartered by Congress in 1949. I shall propose legislation to authorize supplementary grants to help local authorities acquire, develop, and manage private properties for such purposes.

The Registry of National Historic Landmarks is a fine Federal Program with virtually no Federal cost. I commend its work and the new wave of interest it has evoked in historical preservation.

Our present system of parks, seashores, and recreation areas—

monuments to the dedication and labor of farsighted men—do not meet the needs of a growing population.

The full funding of the land and water conservation fund will be an important step in making this a parks-for-America decade. . . .

More than any country ours is an automobile society. For most Americans the automobile is a principal instrument of transportation, work, daily activity, recreation, and pleasure. By making our roads highways to the enjoyment of nature and beauty we can greatly enrich the life of nearly all our people in city and countryside alike.

Our task is twofold. First, to insure that roads themselves are not destructive of nature and natural beauty. Second, to make our roads ways to recreation and pleasure.

I have asked the Secretary of Commerce to take a series of steps designed to meet this objective. This includes requiring landscaping on all Federal interstate primary and urban highways, encouraging the construction of rest and recreation areas along highways, and the preservation of natural beauty adjacent to highway rights-of-way. . . .

. . . I will recommend legislation to insure effective control of billboards along our highways.

In addition, we need urgently to work toward the elimination or screening of unsightly, beauty-destroying junkyards and auto graveyards along our highways. To this end, I will also recommend necessary legislation to achieve effective control, including Federal assistance in appropriate cases where necessary.

I hope that, at all levels of government, our planners and builders will remember that highway beautification is more than a matter of planting trees or setting aside scenic areas. The roads themselves must reflect, in location and design, increased respect for the natural and social integrity and unity of the landscape and communities through which they pass.

Those who first settled this continent found much to marvel at. Nothing was a greater source of wonder and amazement than the power and majesty of American rivers. They occupy a central place in myth and legend, folklore and literature.

They were our first highways, and some remain among the most important. We have had to control their ravages, harness their power, and use their water to help make whole regions prosper.

Yet even this seemingly indestructible natural resource is in danger.

Through our pollution control programs we can do much to

restore our rivers. We will continue to conserve the water and power for tomorrow's needs with well-planned reservoirs and power dams. But the time has also come to identify and preserve free flowing stretches of our great scenic rivers before growth and development make the beauty of the unspoiled waterway a memory. . . .

The forgotten outdoorsmen of today are those who like to walk, hike, ride horseback, or bicycle. For them we must have trails as well as highways. Nor should motor vehicles be permitted to tyrannize the more leisurely human traffic. . . .

As with so much of our quest for beauty and quality, each community has opportunities for action. We can and should have an abundance of trails for walking, cycling, and horseback riding, in and close to our cities. In the back country we need to copy the great Appalachian Trail in all parts of America, and to make full use of rights-of-way and other public paths.

One aspect of the advance of civilization is the evolution of responsibility for disposal of waste. Over many generations society gradually developed techniques for this purpose. State and local governments, landlords, and private citizens have been held responsible for insuring that sewage and garbage did not menace health or contaminate the environment.

In the last few decades entire new categories of waste have come to plague and menace the American scene. These are the technological wastes—the byproducts of growth, industry, agriculture, and science. We cannot wait for slow evolution over generations to deal with them. . . .

In addition to its health effects, air pollution creates filth and gloom and depreciates property values of entire neighborhoods. The White House itself is being dirtied with soot from polluted air.

Every major river system is now polluted. Waterways that were once sources of pleasure and beauty and recreation are forbidden to human contact and objectionable to sight and smell. Furthermore, this pollution is costly, requiring expensive treatment for drinking water and inhibiting the operation and growth of industry. . . .

In addition to our air and water we must, each and every day, dispose of a half billion pounds of solid waste. These wastes—from discarded cans to discarded automobiles—litter our country, harbor vermin, and menace our health. Inefficient and improper methods of disposal increase pollution of our air and streams.

Almost all these wastes and pollutions are the result of activities

carried on for the benefit of man. A prime national goal must be an environment that is pleasing to the senses and healthy to live in. Our Government is already doing much in this field. We have made significant progress. But more must be done. . . .
I intend to call a White House Conference on Natural Beauty to meet in mid-May of this year. . . .
It is my hope that this Conference will produce new ideas and approaches for enhancing the beauty of America. Its scope will not be restricted to Federal action. It will look for ways to help and encourage State and local governments, institutions and private citizens, in their own efforts. It can serve as a focal point for the large campaign of public education which is needed to alert Americans to the danger to their natural heritage and to the need for action. . . .
In my 33 years of public life I have seen the American system move to conserve the natural and human resources of our land.
TVA transformed an entire region that was "depressed." The rural electrification cooperatives brought electricity to lighten the burdens of rural America. We have seen the forests replanted by the CCC's, and watched Gifford Pinchot's sustained yield concept take hold on forest lands.
It is true that we have often been careless with our natural bounty. At times we have paid a heavy price for this neglect. But once our people were aroused to the danger, we have acted to preserve our resources for the enrichment of our country and the enjoyment of future generations.
The beauty of our land is a natural resource. Its preservation is linked to the inner prosperity of the human spirit.
The tradition of our past is equal to today's threat to that beauty. Our land will be attractive tomorrow only if we organize for action and rebuild and reclaim the beauty we inherited. Our stewardship will be judged by the foresight with which we carry out these programs. We must rescue our cities and countryside from blight with the same purpose and vigor with which, in other areas, we moved to save the forests and the soil.

LYNDON B. JOHNSON.
THE WHITE HOUSE, *February 8, 1965.*

31

Multiple Use
MERRILL K. RIDD (1965)

Although the principle of multiple use has its limitations and ambiguities, it continues to be a popular formula for justifying the allocation of natural resources. The Multiple Use Act of June 12, 1960 gave official sanction to the policy in regard to the National Forests. This stimulated a number of Forest Service land management experts in the United States Forest Service to seek imaginative interpretations of the concept. One of them is offered here by Merrill K. Ridd, a professional geographer in the employ of the Service's Intermountain Forest and Range Experiment Station, Ogden, Utah.

Since the introduction of "conservation" as a resource management slogan, few expressions concerning resources have awakened such interest as "multiple use." And few have raised more questions. Perhaps because of the complexity of multiple use management in action, research has not yet come to grips with some of the vital aspects of the public land manager's problem. . . .

The term "multiple use" may be applied either to areas of land or to particular resources. When applied to land areas, it refers to varied uses; that is, the production and management of various resources or resource combinations on a given land unit . . . . The relation of the several resources in the area to one another may be competitive or complementary.

When applied to individual resources, "multiple use" refers to utilization of a particular resource for various purposes. For example, water may be used for irrigation, municipal and industrial water supply, recreation of various types, and other varied functions. Here again, uses may be competitive or complementary. Timber, in the same sense, may be used for lumber, pulpwood, Christmas trees, or scenery. Forage may be used as feed for cattle or for wildlife, for scenery, watershed stabilization, and so forth. Multiple use land management actually involves both multiple use of individual resources

Merrill K. Ridd, *Area-Oriented Multiple Use Analysis*, U.S. Forest Service Research Paper INT–21 (Ogden, Utah, 1965), 1, 3–6, 9, 14.

and of land areas. Demands on particular resources for specific uses, in turn, place demands on land areas where resources are produced. The object of multiple use management is very simple. It is to manage the resource complex for the most beneficial combination of both present and future uses. The idea of deriving maximum benefit from a given resource base is not new, but it becomes more important as competition increases for limited and interrelated resources. It was not until 1960 that Congress enacted legislation to establish "multiple use" as policy on any of the public lands. For the National Forests, the policy was laid down by Public Law 86-517 of June 12, 1960. The law states in part:

> *The Secretary of Agriculture is authorized and directed to develop and administer the renewable surface resources of the national forests for multiple use and sustained yield of the several products and services obtained therefrom.*

The principle of sustained yield is corollary to multiple use. It is, in fact, implied in the definition of multiple use given in Public Law 88-607 of September 19, 1964, outlining authority for multiple use management of land in the custody of the Bureau of Land Management. This law indicates that:

> *"Multiple use" means the management of the various surface and subsurface resources so that they are utilized in the combination that will best meet the present and future needs of the American people. . . .*

While the doctrine of multiple use is widely accepted, there is still some misunderstanding of how it should be accomplished. The multiple use concept does not demand that every acre in question be utilized for all possible uses and resources simultaneously. Both Acts cited above point out that some land will be used for "less than all of the resources." Designation of a wilderness area, for example, does not necessarily violate the multiple use philosophy. Such use may not provide the greatest dollar return, but when the whole scale of values is considered it is presumed to provide the greatest overall benefit for that particular site. However, highly restrictive use areas will occupy a small percentage of the total acreage of public wildlands. Most of the public land will be utilized, to varying degrees, for a wide array of uses, as dictated by capacity, demand, and prudence.

Multiple use management of the land may be accomplished by any one of the following three options, or by any combination of the three: (1) concurrent and continuous use of the several resources obtainable on a given land unit; (2) alternating or rotational use of the various resources or resource combinations on the unit, so that multiple use is achieved on a time basis; or (3) geographical separation of uses or use combinations so that multiple use is accomplished across a mosaic of units. All of these are legitimate multiple use practices and should be applied in the most suitable combination. . . .

From the public's point of view, regardless of the area in question, multiple use management must become involved in a somewhat broader set of parameters than the private investor is usually concerned with. Whereas the private investor makes decisions based upon the profit motive, a nation interested in preserving benefits for future generations may have to make investments and provide safeguards beyond the dictates of limited business economics. The western range industry illustrates the point. Early stockmen maximized direct, short-run returns, and, as a result, contributed to the eventual deterioration of other resource values as well as to the decline of the range industry itself. Multiple use is the antithesis of this. It provides a plan with vision, a plan that accommodates the full spectrum of today's needs and at the same time provides for tomorrow's requirements, a plan which will keep short-range objectives and short-sighted evaluations from sweeping away opportunities for the future. . . .

The multiple use philosophy is deeply rooted in two axioms. One is that renewable resources belong to all the people (not to selected groups of users) and to all generations. The other is that resources represent capital—just as real as the capital invested in man-made structures. Wise use of this capital generates economic growth and social benefits; unwise use will result at the same time in some drain on the social economy. Consequently, we must be careful to avoid excessive use or mismanagement for current gain, which would lower the productive capacity of the resource base and unduly handicap future generations. . . .

Thus, we must endeavor to provide the combination of products required by the present generation, and at the same time secure production alternatives for the future. The challenge for multiple use research is to help provide not only the data but also the framework on which this type of program must be based.

From a practical standpoint there are two fundamental types of multiple use research: resource-oriented and area-oriented. . . .

The resource-oriented approach seeks to discover interrelations

among the several resources; e.g., how the management of one resource affects production in others or how one use of a particular
resource affects other uses of the same resource. Thus, physical rates of
substitution between resources or resource uses, and even cost and
benefit comparisons of alternative production combinations .may be
taken into account. Resource-oriented studies may deal with a single
resource in alternative uses, with two resources, or with several. They
may range from highly abstract to primarily empirical methods. . . .
The information being developed by resource-oriented studies is
basic to an understanding of resource capacities. Yet from the view-
point of the public land manager something more needs to be
considered — community and regional dynamics. To accomplish
sound management, resources must be related not only to each other
but to settlement patterns, markets, access, and to the changing nature
of these factors. These things are not constants, and cannot be ignored. The public land manager's job is not just to maximize product
output. He must find a balance between resource capacities and
community demands. He needs some guidelines for doing this. Area-
oriented multiple use analysis can provide these guidelines. . . .

The purpose of areal multiple use analysis is to provide an ana-
lytical framework for evaluating the pertinent physical, biological,
economic, and social factors relating to resource development in a
particular place as a basis for making sound land management decisions. . . .

. . . [A]n area is a portion of the landscape where man and his
activities provide a meaningful unit for analysis. The area is outlined
on the basis of land use considerations rather than by political or
ownership lines, except where the latter are fairly well aligned with
patterns of land use.

The area is a sort of functional unit with a high degree of internal
cohesion and interdependence with respect to land use and resource
considerations. Such an area may be regarded as a human ecological
community. Like any biotic community it is at the same time related in
important functions to the outside world. . . .

Benefits may flow from the resources in terms of dollar values or
in some intangible form. To recognize and weigh only dollar values is
quite misleading. Dollar and other values are, in fact, inseparable.
Intangible values contribute to economic growth by stimulating
human energies, which are thus released into the social economy. This
comes in addition to the intrinsic value to the individual involved.

The importance of considering values other than those expressed in dollars is recognized in the two multiple use Acts cited early in this paper. Those documents require that consideration be given to the "relative values of the various resources, and not necessarily the combination of uses that will give the greatest dollar return or the greatest unit output." One of the virtues of the area-oriented approach is that intangibles, despite our inability to measure them adequately, take on a dimension of reality. The mention of intangible value often brings to mind such uses as fishing, hunting, camping, and other outdoor recreation. But some degree of intangible value is associated with all resource activities. For example, cattle raising is commonly considered to have a definable market value. However, a critical audit of the books of many stockmen in the Paunsaugunt Area probably would reveal that in terms of dollars alone these men are fighting a losing battle, partly because of forced livestock reductions resulting from poor range conditions. To most of them, raising cattle is only a secondary source of income. Yet, they justify continuation of their marginal operation on the basis of enjoyment, or of the security of having a few cows on the range. Being a cowboy may not always bring in much money, but it apparently buys a lot of satisfaction. . . .

The aim of areal multiple use analysis as suggested herein is to provide a framework in which available information of importance in the management of a given unit of wildland can be arranged, analyzed, and evaluated for the making of sound decisions. Presently, there is a great deal of useful information which is not easily accessible to the land manager or is not readily applied to his particular area of responsibility. Use of this method should help to close this gap between resource research and problems on the ground. There is a growing need for closer correlation between lands of different ownership and management, in analysis and planning, funding, and action.

Areal analysis is not intended to replace any other form of research, but rather to complement it. Indeed, it relies on other types of multiple use analysis and studies in other fields — physical, biological, economic, and social — for basic data and relationships. However, it is felt there is a need to pull these things together as they apply to particular communities. Only by delineating an area of study can resources be inventoried and analyzed for the purpose of planning and management. Only in an areal context can the dynamic interdependence between the local community and resources and the broader setting be understood. Only in this way can the distribution of values and the reality of intangible values be appreciated. And in an areal context the findings of resource-oriented studies can be made effective. If well chosen and defined, a study area may fairly well represent the conditions of the province and allow the extension of general findings and recommendations across other areas of the same province. In places where use patterns are complex, the opportunity to extend results from one area to another may be more limited.

A study based on [these] considerations should help the public land manager identify his responsibility through broader understanding of the issues involved and how to resolve them.

32

The Echo Park Controversy

JOSEPH C. O'MAHONEY, ULYSSES S. GRANT III,
DAVID BRADLEY (1955)

One of the difficulties with multiple use (31) as a land management principle is that it does not establish a mechanism for deciding between the claims of two incompatible uses of the same area. And when that area is a wild canyon, and the contending interests are wilderness enthusiasts and reclamationists, the conflict can become intense. Both sides believe, with considerable precedent, that they speak for "conservation."

In this situation a political showdown usually replaces rational planning as the means of decision making. A good recent example of such a controversy occurred in the early 1950's over the Dinosaur National Monument, a 200,000 acre reservation on the Green and Yampa Rivers in western Colorado and eastern Utah. The federal Bureau of Reclamation believed a dam at Echo Park, on the Green, was essential to the success of the huge Upper Colorado River Storage Project. Wilderness preservationists were equally determined to keep Dinosaur wild and defend the sanctity of the National Park and Monument system. As the following debate in Collier's *suggests, the controversy reached national proportions.*

"Are You For or Against the Echo Park Dam?" *Collier's*, CXXXV (1955), 78–79, 82.

It was ultimately resolved in 1956 in favor of preservation, thus reversing the Hetch Hetchy verdict [(13), (14), and (18)] and testifying to the growth of both American appreciation of wilderness and the political effectiveness of the wilderness bloc.

At the time these statements were written, Joseph C. O'Mahoney was United States Senator from Wyoming; Ulysses S. Grant III, grandson of the President, a career engineer with the U.S. Army Corps of Engineers (an organization which regarded the Bureau of Reclamation as unwelcome competition in dam-building); and David Bradley, a doctor, writer and wilderness enthusiast living in Hanover, New Hampshire.

Joseph C. O'Mahoney:

Much of Wyoming, my home state, is in an area known as the Upper Colorado River Basin. Important parts of Arizona, Colorado, New Mexico and Utah also are within this area which, in territory, is more extensive than New York, Pennsylvania and New Jersey combined. It is rich in resources. Oil shale is abundant. Sulphur, soda ash, potassium, alumina clays and many nonferrous minerals, including uranium, are found there. Wyoming alone has greater coal deposits than any other state in our Union. Climate is anything you prefer, from the arctic cold of Big Piney in winter to the burning heat of the desert in summer. Scenery is varied and thrilling. But even with these and other great advantages, the population of the basin is only 325,000. Little Rhode Island alone has nearly three times as many people.

The only reason for this sparse population is scarcity of water. That's the one essential resource we do not have in enough quantity. Under such conditions you would think every acre-foot of water would be husbanded with care, but it is not. Water, precious and priceless water, actually is being wasted. It is being allowed to flow on down the Colorado River, over the wonder-working Hoover Dam and finally into the Gulf of California.

Today, after too many years of waiting, Congress has before it again a comprehensive proposal to conserve and use the water of the upper Colorado and its tributaries. Competent engineers and others have evolved what is known as the Upper Colorado River Storage Project. Its nine big dams would be of incalculable benefit to the Upper Basin and, therefore, to the entire United States.

Every member of Congress from the Upper Basin states is in favor of the proposal. But outside the area there is strong opposition, not because of objectives, but because of an incidental and sentimental reason. An essential reservoir in the project requires a dam in Echo

Park, part of Dinosaur National Monument. The dam would be on the Green River, in the northwest corner of Colorado, three miles below the confluence of the Green and the Yampa, two tributaries of the Colorado.

Our opponents, mainly nonresidents of the area, believe—some of them passionately—that this dam would do irreparable damage to the Dinosaur National Monument and to the natural beauty of that wild country. As the name of the monument indicates, dinosaurs once lived and died there millions of years ago; perhaps many of them died in uncontrolled floods such as still wreak havoc as they rush down the mountain canyons when the snows of winter melt.

The bones of these creatures remain, and of course all naturalists are eagerly interested in the site. But these ancient bones would not be disturbed or inundated by the proposed dam and reservoir. In fact, this graveyard of extinct reptiles and the beautiful canyons and mesas of the extended Dinosaur Monument would become easier of access once the necessary road is built to the dam from, I hope, Rock Springs, Wyoming.

The water level in the wild canyon would be raised 520 feet when the reservoir is filled. A crystal-clear lake of 43,400 acres would be created, extending 63 miles up the Green River and 44 miles up the Yampa. It is true that the river beds in the area would be obscured and their dangerous rapids eliminated, but the new crystal-clear reservoir would present to the tourist a calmer beauty of its own. Above the surface of the lake, canyon walls would tower 1,000 feet and more with all the beauty and grandeur now to be found there.

This key Echo Park structure would regulate the flow of these rivers more effectively than any other sites that can be suggested. Six and a half million acre-feet of water would be stored here in high-water season for the year-round benefit of men all the way down the Colorado River Valley, from sources to mouth. One and one-tenth billion kilowatt-hours of electric energy would be generated. Together with others in the project, the reservoir would be not only revenue-producing but self-liquidating over a stretch of 41 years, and at the same time it would create much new wealth in farms, homes and industries.

If you are among those who have opposed the project I ask that you think again about your position. The basic issue here is between the sentimental and aesthetic feelings of some people, mostly outside the area, and the welfare of the several hundred thousand who live there, plus many additional hundreds of thousands who will come if we are allowed to make the most intelligent possible use of our agricultural and mineral resources.

Opponents of the Echo Park reservoir say, in effect, the same results can be achieved by selecting alternate sites in place of some of those now proposed, but their argument is based on theory, not on careful, prolonged and repeated engineering studies. Every one of the proposed variations in the Upper Basin project would reduce the amount of water to be stored, increase the loss by evaporation and decrease the production of electricity. Support for these statements can be found in the official reports of the Department of the Interior, in both Democratic and Republican administrations. . . .

There can be no further important agricultural development in the Upper Basin unless we can have the use of the water that now pours wastefully to the sea. Industrial expansion is stymied. Population is held down. The amount of water will determine our growth and, to get the maximum amount, Echo dam is essential.

Approximately 300,000 acres of never-before-irrigated desert lands is recommended by the Bureau of Reclamation for cultivation after the initial part of the Upper Basin project is completed, and in addition some 470,000 acres of presently inadequately irrigated lands will receive the extra water needed. Also, when all units of the project are completed, nine and four-tenths billion kilowatt-hours of hydro-electric energy will be generated.

What should our goal be—the greatest good of the greatest number, or the sentimental satisfaction of a few? The issue is as plain as that to most of us in the arid-land states. . . .

Ulysses S. Grant III:
There are many ancient treasures in America's national parks, but no scientist would expect to find a Trojan horse in them. Nonetheless there soon may be one. It would be of concrete and steel—a dam which the Bureau of Reclamation proposes to build in the heart of the Dinosaur National Monument. If the American people allow Echo Park dam to be built, it could lead to the destruction of *all* of those stretches of natural beauty set aside for us and our descendants to enjoy as national parks or monuments—just as surely as Troy was destroyed after it allowed another man-made structure within its gates.

No conservationist is against the development of badly needed water resources, and I, for one, am heartily in favor of an over-all plan to harness the waters of the Upper Colorado River Basin. When I observe, however, that the planners of the project can find no site other than one protected under an act of Congress which states that it should be kept "unimpaired for the enjoyment of future generations," I become suspicious.

The inference is plain. Ever since the National Park Service was established by Congress in 1916, there have been repeated attempts to break into the national parks. The same natural features that make them desirable as parks—rushing water, deep canyons, virgin wilderness—only too often also make them favorable locations for dams and commercial exploitation. Up to now when would-be despoilers have made their assaults on the parks, they have been thrown back by an alert and aroused Congress.

This year, however, they may succeed with Trojan-horse tactics. And if they do—watch out. Once the precedent has been set with the Echo Park dam, other already-announced plans may be put into operation. Timbermen are ready to rip into the priceless rain forests of Olympic National Park in northwest Washington State; dam builders have proposed projects that would wash away the foundations of Rainbow Natural Bridge in Utah and drown out much of magnificent Mammoth Cave in Kentucky. Not even Yellowstone in Wyoming, the Grand Canyon in Arizona, or Glacier National Park in Montana would be safe. All already are earmarked as reservoir sites.

Why do I refer to the proposed Echo Park dam as a Trojan horse? For two reasons. First of all, the proponents of the project are trying to infiltrate our national parks in the guise of benefactors. They say that their dam would make remote Dinosaur National Monument more accessible so that additional thousands of Americans could view the beauties of the place. They neglect to mention that when those thousands arrive, they had better come equipped with submarines—the beauties will be under 500 feet of water.

The proponents of the dam insist that the area would be little altered, that much picturesque scenery would remain. Let's look into that claim. The main attractions of the park today are the twin canyons of the Green River and the Yampa River. As in the more famous Grand Canyon, swift-flowing waters have carved ever deeper into the rock beds, leaving beautifully colored sheer rock walls, and among all the scenic canyons in federally protected wilderness areas, these are the only rapids in which people of all ages can ride safely in boats. At the bottom of the gorges are lush meadows for camping areas, turbulent waters and other awesome handiworks of nature— including Steamboat Rock, which looks for all the world like the petrified prow of a Titan's ship.

What would happen if 500 feet of water backed up in the canyons? Their vertical walls average very little above 500 feet, so almost all the scenic attractions in the area would be under water. True, the terrain continues to slope upward and outward from the rims of the vertical cuts, but if the narrow canyons were flooded the rest would become commonplace hills. Buried forever beneath the waves would be the gaily colored walls, the beautiful meadows, the turbulent streams and the Indian hieroglyphs. Steamboat Rock would be just a gaunt little island protruding above the waters.

Proponents of the dam argue that the loss of the canyons would be offset by the creation of a lake on which visitors could sail dinghies to their hearts' content. Moreover, they say, lake recreation is better than river recreation. But the twin canyons provide river recreation which can be found nowhere else in the country, whereas the other dams proposed for the area, along with any of the possible substitutes for Echo Park dam, would create nine or ten similar lakes. And as Bernard De Voto once put it, "Will New Yorkers travel 2,000 miles to sail on a lake? They can do that in Central Park."

It's easy to fool people with idyllic dreams of beautiful reservoir-lakes. Consider California's Hetch Hetchy Dam, which was wrested from Yosemite Park in 1911, before the national parks were protected by law.* Then, too, the cry was the same: "San Francisco will wither without this water. We must have this cheap power. There are no alternatives. The scenery will be enhanced and greater accessibility will result."

The dam builders won out that time. And what happened? One of America's most beautiful glacial canyons was obliterated; its towering granite cliffs and majestic waterfalls vanished. There is nothing there now but an ugly artificial lake; as the water level rises and falls, the banks become covered with slime and debris which smother all grass and trees. There's an excellent paved road from this artificial lake to heavily populated central California, but what good is it? There is no place to camp, and "Keep Out" signs are posted all around the area. The chief irony of all is that cities just across the bay from San

---

* See (13), (14), and (18). The actual date was 1913. [Ed.]

Francisco found abundant, more-easily-obtained water supplies without invading a national park.

From the Bureau of Reclamation's own report, I know there are also alternatives to the Echo Park dam, and the hasty manner in which they have been rejected by the Department of the Interior without adequate investigation leads me to the second of my two reasons for suspecting that the Echo Park dam is a Trojan horse, designed to break into the entire national park system. It's almost as though the proponents don't want to find alternatives.

The bureau's figures and estimates show the possibility of substitute measures that would allow the Upper Colorado Project to be completed without the Echo Park dam and its smaller sister structure, the Split Mountain dam, also in the Dinosaur National Monument. Nearly all the substitutes would cost less, have more water-storage capacity, and produce more electricity. . . .

Some proponents of the Echo Park and Split Mountain dams allege that power could be produced so cheaply there that the profit from its sale would help pay for all the dams in the Upper Colorado River programs. But since this electricity must be sold in the existing market, at six mills a kilowatt-hour, the profit would be only 1/100th of a cent per kilowatt-hour. At that rate, if the estimated cost does not include amortization, it would take more than a thousand years to pay for the Echo Park dam alone, to say nothing of the other eight. If amortization is included, the sale of Echo Park electricity would contribute only about $120,000 a year—a drop in the bucket when you consider that the total cost of the project is anywhere between a billion and a half and five billion dollars. A greater profit could be made by elevating another dam—the Glen Canyon—by some 40 feet.

The second—and main—argument of the dam proponents is that all the alternatives, including mine, would result in excessive evaporation of water. Here, too, they relied on the lack of knowledge of lay people to get their point across, but they have been trapped in their own inaccuracies. At first they announced that, at the alternative sites I had suggested, 350,000 more acre-feet of water would be lost through evaporation than at the Echo Park-Split Mountain sites. When I pointed out the errors in their evaporation estimates, the then under secretary, Ralph Tudor, accepted a revised figure of 100,000 acre-feet, forgetting that the greater storage capacity would more than make up the loss. . . .

Actually, such evaporation computations are at best only approximate estimates, and the Bureau of Reclamation figures were based on inadequate observations. The evaporation argument has indeed evaporated.

Why, then, do the dam proponents use such erroneous or incomplete data in their attempt to destroy this unique federally protected recreation area? They have fought with such bitterness and tenacity that one may suspect something more than river control is involved. In fact, the Upper Colorado River Project, with noncontroversial dams much closer to the central Utah district which most desperately needs the water, might have been started four years ago but for this obstinate insistence on the Echo Park-Split Mountain dams.

It leads one to ask why the errors, why the specious arguments, why such a reluctance to make a more thorough study of the matter so that we do not have to invade the national parks? The Dinosaur National Monument contains natural, geological, archaeological and recreational features that are unique and irreplaceable. These are treasures which our generation holds in trust for posterity. There is a moral obligation upon us to preserve them undamaged for our grandchildren and our great-grandchildren.

A precedent is a precedent, no matter what people say, and that's why we conservationists are resisting so fervently the admission of the Trojan horse into the Dinosaur National Monument, and so into the national park system.

David Bradley:

I made my first trip into a national park—my father back-packing me into Yosemite in a knapsack—at the age of a year and a half. Since then, I have visited most of our scenic parks and monuments with my family—just as my father did, and his father, who was one of the first explorers of the Sierra Nevada.

Two summers ago my family was among the hundreds of people who took the river trip down through the canyons of Dinosaur National Monument. In all, 14 of us—my four brothers and I, our wives and children, and our seventy-six-year-old father—traveled down the Yampa and Green Rivers in pontoon rafts and small folding kayaks.

For six days the rivers did all the work. We ran many rapids and, unexpectedly, found no great danger. The West is blessed with much magnificent scenery, but none is more remarkable than the canyons of Dinosaur.

The Yampa River at first was silent, beautiful, intimate, as it flowed through its deep sandstone convolutions. It led us down from open parks to overhanging cliffs, from ice-cream domes and sunburned terraces to the arched and polished contours of the canyons. There were beaches of brilliant sand where we stopped to swim. There were shady recesses where we drifted and ate lunch. There were bank beaver, Canada geese, deer and the prints of big cats whose presence was felt but never seen.

There were riffles and minor rapids too—Teepee and Big Joe—leading on to bigger water mills. In the rough sections, the rocks came by like swimming hippos.

On the fourth day the Yampa carried us to its junction with the larger Green River in the famous Echo Park, two miles upstream from the proposed dam. In the center towered Steamboat Rock, rising sheer from its sea of river sand. On three sides, beyond the green meadows and box-elder groves, climbed the white walls of the park, layer upon layer.

It was one of those perfect sanctuaries which inspire awe from the moment one enters, a temple which has been in building for a hundred times the life of man on earth. Buttressed by the arched mountains, tiled by the wide green grass, illuminated by the stained-glass windows of the sunset, Echo Park commands silence. As with all temples, its value is not in the sounds one may startle from its ledges, but rather in the echoes which it may awaken within oneself.

There were two more days on the pell-mell Green River, and more canyons, more rapids, but we will always remember best the ageless silence of Echo Park. It was this memory that impelled my nine-year-old daughter Kim, the youngest member of our expedition, to take up her pen and laboriously write:

> *Dear President Eisenhower:*
> *Please don't build a dam in Dinosaur Park. It is beautiful and exciting and fun riding on rubber rafts on the huge waves.*
> *I went there once and want to go again. If you had been down it, you would not build a dam.*
> *Sincerely, Kim Bradley*

In her simple way Kim had touched the truth which so far has preserved this and all our other national parks.

33

The Meaning of Wilderness in American Civilization

WALLACE STEGNER (1960)

Victory in the Echo Park controversy (32) and the growing emphasis on quality of the environment gave wilderness preservation unaccustomed influence in American conservation. On September 3, 1964, after eight years of hearings and revisions, the bill establishing the National Wilderness Preservation System became law. While failing to satisfy preservationists' demands completely, the act made most disturbances of wilderness conditions on selected federal lands illegal. Ultimately the Wilderness System could contain approximately fifty-million acres, chiefly in the National Forests and National Parks.

While the wilderness bill was under Congressional consideration, Wallace Stegner, novelist, university professor, and the biographer of John Wesley Powell (6), tried to articulate the meaning of wild country in modern American life. His statement appeared initially, and in a condensed form, in the report of the Wildland Research Center to the Outdoor Recreation Resources Review Commission, a body created by Congress in 1958 to determine the recreational needs of Americans in the years 1976 and 2000. Secretary of the Interior Stewart L. Udall read the version below at the Sierra Club's Seventh Biennial Wilderness Conference.

I should like to urge some arguments for wilderness preservation that involve recreation, as it is ordinarily conceived, hardly at all. Hunting, fishing, hiking, mountain-climbing, camping, photography, and the enjoyment of natural scenery will all, surely, figure in your report. So will the wilderness as a genetic reserve, a scientific yardstick by which we may measure the world in its natural balance against the world in its man-made imbalance. What I want to speak for is not so much the wilderness uses, valuable as those are, but the wilderness *idea*, which is a resource in itself. Being an intangible and spiritual resource, it will seem mystical to the practical-minded—but then anything that cannot be moved by a bulldozer is likely to seem mystical to them.

Wallace Stegner, "The Wilderness Idea" in *Wilderness: America's Living Heritage*, ed. David Brower (San Francisco, Sierra Club, 1961), 97–102. Reprinted by permission of the publisher.

I want to speak for the wilderness idea as something that has helped form our character and that has certainly shaped our history as a people. It has no more to do with recreation than churches have to do with recreation, or than the strenuousness and optimism and expansiveness of what historians call the "American Dream" have to do with recreation. Nevertheless, since it is only in this recreation survey that the values of wilderness are being compiled, I hope you will permit me to insert this idea between the leaves, as it were, of the recreation report.

Something will have gone out of us as a people if we ever let the remaining wilderness be destroyed; if we permit the last virgin forests to be turned into comic books and plastic cigarette cases; if we drive the few remaining members of the wild species into zoos or to extinction; if we pollute the last clear air and dirty the last clean streams and push our paved roads through the last of the silence, so that never again will Americans be free in their own country from the noise, the exhausts, the stinks of human and automotive waste. And so that never again can we have the chance to see ourselves single, separate, vertical and individual in the world, part of the environment of trees and rocks and soil, brother to the other animals, part of the natural world and competent to belong in it. Without any remaining wilderness we are committed wholly, without chance for even momentary reflection and rest, to a headlong drive into our technological termite-life, the Brave New World of a completely man-controlled environment. We need wilderness preserved—as much of it as is still left, and as many kinds—because it was the challenge against which our character as a people was formed. The reminder and the reassurance that it is still there is good for our spiritual health even if we never once in ten years set foot in it. It is good for us when we are young, because of the incomparable sanity it can bring briefly, as vacation and rest, into our insane lives. It is important to us when we are old simply because it is there—important, that is, simply as idea.

We are a wild species, as Darwin pointed out. Nobody ever tamed or domesticated or scientifically bred us. But for at least three millennia we have been engaged in a cumulative and ambitious race to modify and gain control of our environment, and in the process we have come close to domesticating ourselves. Not many people are likely, any more, to look upon what we call "progress" as an unmixed blessing. Just as surely as it has brought us increased comfort and more material goods, it has brought us spiritual losses, and it threatens now to become the Frankenstein that will destroy us. One means of sanity is to retain a hold on the natural world, to remain, insofar as we can, good animals. Americans still have that chance, more than many peoples; for while we were demonstrating ourselves the most efficient and ruthless environment-busters in history, and slashing and burning and cutting our way through a wilderness continent, the wilderness was working on us. It remains in us as surely as Indian names remain on the land. If the abstract dream of human liberty and human dignity became, in America, something more than an abstract dream, mark it down at least partially to the fact that we were in subtle ways subdued by what we conquered.

The Connecticut Yankee, sending likely candidates from King Arthur's unjust kingdom to his Man Factory for rehabilitation, was overoptimistic, as he later admitted. These things cannot be forced, they have to grow. To make such a man, such a democrat, such a believer in human individual dignity, as Mark Twain himself, the frontier was necessary, Hannibal and the Mississippi and Virginia City, and reaching out from those the wilderness: the wilderness as opportunity and as idea, the thing that has helped to make an American different from and, until we forget it in the roar of our industrial cities, more fortunate than other men. For an American, insofar as he is new and different at all, is a civilized man who has renewed himself in the wild. The American experience has been the confrontation of old peoples and cultures by a world as new as if it had just arisen from the sea. That gave us our hope and our excitement, and the hope and excitement can be passed on to newer Americans; Americans who never saw any phase of the frontier. But only so long as we keep the remainder of our wild as a reserve and a promise—a sort of wilderness bank.

As a novelist, I may perhaps be forgiven for taking literature as a reflection, indirect but profoundly true, of our national consciousness. And our literature, as perhaps you are aware, is sick, embittered, losing its mind, losing its faith. Our novelists are the declared enemies of their society. There has hardly been a serious or important novel in this century that did not repudiate in part or in whole American technological culture for its commercialism, its vulgarity, and the way in which it has dirtied a clean continent and a clean dream. I do not expect that the preservation of our remaining wilderness is going to cure this condition. But the mere example that we can as a nation apply some other criteria than commercial and exploitative considerations would be heartening to many Americans, novelists or otherwise. We need to demonstrate our acceptance of the natural world, including ourselves; we need the spiritual refreshment that being natural can produce. And one of the best places for us to get that is in the wilderness where the fun houses, the bulldozers, and the pavements of our civilization are shut out.

Sherwood Anderson, in a letter to Waldo Frank in the 1920s, said it better than I can. 'Is it not likely that when the country was new and men were often alone in the fields and the forest they got a sense of bigness outside themselves that has now in some way been lost? . . . Mystery whispered in the grass, played in the branches of trees overhead, was caught up and blown across the American line in clouds of dust at evening on the prairies . . . I am old enough to remember tales that strengthen my belief in a deep semi-religious influence that was formerly at work among our people. The flavor of it hangs over the best work of Mark Twain . . . I can remember old fellows in my home town speaking feelingly of an evening spent on the big empty plains. It had taken the shrillness out of them. They had learned the trick of quiet . . .'

We could learn it too, even yet; even our children and grandchildren could learn it. But only if we save, for just such absolutely nonrecreational, impractical, and mystical uses as this, all the wild that still remains to us.

It seems to me significant that the distinct downturn in our literature from hope to bitterness took place almost at the precise time when the frontier officially came to an end, in 1890, and when the American way of life had begun to turn strongly urban and industrial. The more urban it has become, and the more frantic with technological change, the sicker and more embittered our literature, and I believe our people, have become. For myself, I grew up on the empty plains of Saskatchewan and Montana and in the mountains of Utah, and I put a very high valuation on what those places gave me. And if I had not been able periodically to renew myself in the mountains and deserts of Western America I would be very nearly bughouse. Even when I can't get to the back country, the thought of the colored deserts of southern Utah, or the reassurance that there are still stretches of prairie where the world can be instantaneously perceived as disk and bowl, and where the little but intensely important human being is exposed to the five directions and the thirty-six winds, is a positive consolation. The idea alone can sustain me. But as the wilderness areas are progressively exploited or 'improved,' as the jeeps and bulldozers of uranium prospectors scar up the deserts and the roads are cut into the alpine timberlands, and as the remnants of the unspoiled and natural world are progressively eroded, every such loss is a little death in me. In us. Nevertheless I am not moved by the argument that those wilderness areas which have already been exposed to grazing or mining are already deflowered, and so might as well be 'harvested.' For mining I cannot say much good except that its operations are generally short-lived. The extractable wealth is taken and the shafts, the tailings, and the ruins left, and in a dry country such as the American West the wounds men make in the earth do not quickly heal. Still, they are only wounds; they aren't absolutely mortal. Better a wounded wilderness than none at all. And as for grazing, if it is strictly controlled so that it does not destroy the ground cover, damage the ecology, or compete with the wildlife it is in itself nothing that need conflict with the wilderness feeling or the validity of the wilderness experience. I have known enough range cattle to recognize them as wild animals; and the people who herd them have, in the wilderness context, the dignity of rareness; they belong on the frontier, moreover, and have a look of rightness. The invasion they make on the virgin country is a sort of invasion that is as old as Neanderthal man, and they can, in moderation, even emphasize a man's feeling of belonging to the natural world. Under surveillance, they can belong; under control, they need not deface or mar. I do not believe that in wilderness areas where grazing has never been permitted, it should be permitted; but I do not believe either that an otherwise untouched wilderness should be eliminated from the preservation plan because of limited existing uses such as grazing which are in consonance with the frontier condition and image. . . .

So are great reaches of our western deserts, scarred somewhat by prospectors but otherwise open, beautiful, waiting, close to whatever God you want to see in them. Just as a sample, let me suggest the Robbers' Roost country in Wayne County, Utah, near the Capitol Reef National Monument. In that desert climate the dozer and jeep tracks will not soon melt back into the earth, but the country has a way of making the scars insignificant. It is a lovely and terrible wilderness, such a wilderness as Christ and the prophets went out into; harshly and beautifully colored, broken and worn until its bones are exposed, its great sky without a smudge or taint from Technocracy, and in hidden corners and pockets under its cliffs the sudden poetry of springs. Save a piece of country like that intact, and it does not matter in the slightest that only a few people every year will go into it. That is precisely its value. Roads would be a desecration, crowds would ruin it. But those who haven't the strength or youth to go into it and live with it can still drive up onto the shoulder of the Aquarius Plateau and simply sit and look. They can look two hundred miles, clear into Colorado; and looking down over the cliffs and canyons of the San Rafael Swell and the Robbers' Roost they can also look as deeply into themselves as anywhere I know. And if they can't even get to the places on the Aquarius where the present roads will carry them, they can simply contemplate the *idea,* take pleasure in the fact that such a timeless and uncontrolled part of earth is still there.

These are some of the things wilderness can do for us. That is the reason we need to put into effect, for its preservation, some other principle than the principles of exploitation or usefulness or even recreation. We simply need that wild country available to us, even if we never do more than drive to its edge and look in. For it can be a means of reassuring ourselves of our sanity as creatures, a part of the geography of hope.

34

Pesticides

RACHAEL CARSON (1962)

In 1960 a distinguished naturalist and best-selling nature writer, Rachael Carson, published a series of articles in The New Yorker *which generated widespread discussion. The series concerned the effects of chemical insecticides on the balance of nature. Miss Carson was less concerned about the "ethics" of pesticides, as Aldo Leopold (20) might have been, and more about the possible consequences for man's health of unenlightened use of his ability to kill lower forms of life. Keyed to react strongly to Miss*

Carson's message by the radioactive "fall-out" scare that occurred simultaneously, many Americans were horrified at her revelations. But some scientists and, of course, the chemical companies that manufactured pesticides dismissed her fears as unfounded.

The history of life on earth has been a history of interaction between living things and their surroundings. To a large extent, the physical form and the habits of the earth's vegetation and its animal life have been molded by the environment. Considering the whole span of earthly time, the opposite effect, in which life actually modifies its surroundings, has been relatively slight. Only within the moment of time represented by the present century has one species— man—acquired significant power to alter the nature of his world.

During the past quarter century this power has not only increased to one of disturbing magnitude but it has changed in character. The most alarming of all man's assaults upon the environment is the contamination of air, earth, rivers, and sea with dangerous and even lethal materials. This pollution is for the most part irrecoverable; the chain of evil it initiates not only in the world that must support life but in living tissues is for the most part irreversible. In this now universal contamination of the environment, chemicals are the sinister and little-recognized partners of radiation in changing the very nature of the world—the very nature of its life. Strontium 90, released through nuclear explosions into the air, comes to earth in rain or drifts down as fallout, lodges in soil, enters into the grass or corn or wheat grown there, and in time takes up its abode in the bones of a human being, there to remain until his death. Similarly, chemicals sprayed on croplands or forests or gardens lie long in soil, entering into living organisms, passing from one to another in a chain of poisoning and death. Or they pass mysteriously by underground streams until they emerge and, through the alchemy of air and sunlight, combine into new forms that kill vegetation, sicken cattle, and work unknown harm on those who drink from once pure wells. As Albert Schweitzer has said, "Man can hardly even recognize the devils of his own creation."

It took hundreds of millions of years to produce the life that now inhabits the earth—eons of time in which that developing and evolving and diversifying life reached a state of adjustment and balance with its surroundings. The environment, rigorously shaping and directing the life it supported, contained elements that were hostile as well as supporting. Certain rocks gave out dangerous radiation; even within the light of the sun, from which all life draws its energy, there were short-wave radiations with power to injure. Given time—time not in years but in millennia—life adjusts, and a balance has been reached. For time is the essential ingredient; but in the modern world there is no time.

The rapidity of change and the speed with which new situations are created follow the impetuous and heedless pace of man rather than the deliberate pace of nature. Radiation is no longer merely the background radiation of rocks, the bombardment of cosmic rays, the ultraviolet of the sun that have existed before there was any life on earth; radiation is now the unnatural creation of man's tampering with the atom. The chemicals to which life is asked to make its adjustment are no longer merely the calcium and silica and copper and all the rest of the minerals washed out of the rocks and carried in rivers to the sea; they are the synthetic creations of man's inventive mind, brewed in his laboratories, and having no counterparts in nature.

To adjust to these chemicals would require time on the scale that is nature's; it would require not merely the years of a man's life but the life of generations. And even this, were it by some miracle possible, would be futile, for the new chemicals come from our laboratories in an endless stream; almost five hundred annually find their way into actual use in the United States alone. The figure is staggering and its implications are not easily grasped—500 new chemicals to which the bodies of men and animals are required somehow to adapt each year, chemicals totally outside the limits of biologic experience.

Among them are many that are used in man's war against nature. Since the mid-1940's over 200 basic chemicals have been created for use in killing insects, weeds, rodents, and other organisms described in the modern vernacular as "pests"; and they are sold under several thousand different brand names.

These sprays, dusts, and aerosols are now applied almost universally to farms, gardens, forests, and homes—nonselective chemicals that have the power to kill every insect, the "good" and the "bad," to still the song of birds and the leaping of fish in the streams, to coat the leaves with a deadly film, and to linger on in soil—all this though the intended target may be only a few weeds or insects. Can anyone believe it is possible to lay down such a barrage of poisons on the surface of the earth without making it unfit for all life? They should not be called "insecticides," but "biocides."

The whole process of spraying seems caught up in an endless spiral. Since DDT was released for civilian use, a process of escalation has been going on in which ever more toxic materials must be found. This has happened because insects, in a triumphant vindication of Darwin's principle of the survival of the fittest, have evolved super races immune to the particular insecticide used, hence a deadlier one has always to be developed—and then a deadlier one than that. It has happened also because, for reasons to be described later, destructive insects often undergo a "flareback," or resurgence, after spraying, in numbers greater than before. Thus the chemical war is never won, and all life is caught in its violent crossfire.

Along with the possibility of the extinction of mankind by nuclear war, the central problem of our age has therefore become the contamination of man's total environment with such substances of incredible potential for harm—substances that accumulate in the tissues of plants and animals and even penetrate the germ cells to shatter or alter the very material of heredity upon which the shape of the future depends.

Some would-be architects of our future look toward a time when it will be possible to alter the human germ plasm by design. But we may easily be doing so now by inadvertence, for many chemicals, like radiation, bring about gene mutations. It is ironic to think that man might determine his own future by something so seemingly trivial as the choice of an insect spray.

All this has been risked—for what? Future historians may well be amazed by our distorted sense of proportion. How could intelligent beings seek to control a few unwanted species by a method that contaminated the entire environment and brought the threat of disease and death even to their own kind? Yet this is precisely what we have done. . . .

It is not my contention that chemical insecticides must never be used. I do contend that we have put poisonous and biologically potent chemicals indiscriminately into the hands of persons largely or wholly ignorant of their potentials for harm. We have subjected enormous numbers of people to contact with these poisons, without their consent and often without their knowledge. If the Bill of Rights contains no guarantee that a citizen shall be secure against lethal poisons distributed either by private individuals or by public officials, it is surely only because our forefathers, despite their considerable wisdom and foresight, could conceive of no such problem.

I contend, furthermore, that we have allowed these chemicals to be used with little or no advance investigation of their effect on soil, water, wildlife, and man himself. Future generations are unlikely to condone our lack of prudent concern for the integrity of the natural world that supports all life. There is still very limited awareness of the nature of the threat. This is an era of specialists, each of whom sees his own problem and is unaware of or intolerant of the larger frame into which it fits. It is also an era dominated by industry, in which the right to make a dollar at whatever cost is seldom challenged. When the public protests, confronted with some obvious evidence of damaging results of pesticide applications, it is fed little tranquilizing pills of half truth. We urgently need an end to these false assurances, to the sugar coating of unpalatable facts. It is the public that is being asked to assume the risks that the insect controllers calculate. The public must decide whether it wishes to continue on the present road, and it can do so only when in full possession of the facts. . . .

35

Pollution
Herblock (*1967*);
PRESIDENT'S SCIENCE ADVISORY COMMITTEE (1965)

The pesticide menace that Rachael Carson described (34) *was only a portion of the problem that Americans of the 1960's referred to as "pollution." Its scope was suggested by the Herblock cartoon, below, which appeared in April, 1967, in many newspapers. The total environment appears cluttered with civilization's wastes. Billboards and automobile junkyards dominate the landscape. The oil slicks in the water reminded viewers of the devastation caused by the wrecking of the American oil freighter Torrey Canyon off the British coast the previous March. The dark, polluted air, or "smog," in the cartoon had recently made headlines, especially as it enveloped large metropolitan areas such as Los Angeles and New York City. Herblock's title "On the Beach" was the same as that of a popular 1957 novel by Nevil Shute which depicted the human race on the verge of extinction as the result of a nuclear world war.*

Indicative of the degree of national concern over pollution was the appointment of an Environmental Pollution Panel by the President's Science

On The Beach

Copyright 1967 Herblock in *The Washington Post,* from *The Herblock Gallery* (Simon & Schuster, 1968).

Advisory Committee. In 1965 the Panel made its report, significantly entitled Restoring the Quality of Our Environment.

The production of pollutants and an increasing need for pollution management are an inevitable concomitant of a technological society with a high standard of living. Pollution problems will increase in importance as our technology and standard of living continue to grow.

Our ancestors settled in a fair and unspoiled land, easily capable of absorbing the wastes of its animal and human populations. Nourished by the resources of this continent, the human inhabitants have multiplied greatly and have grouped themselves to form gigantic urban concentrations, in and around which are vast and productive industrial and agricultural establishments, disposed with little regard for state or municipal boundaries.

Huge quantities of diverse and novel materials are dispersed, from city and farm alike, into our air, into our waters and onto our lands. These pollutants are either unwanted by-products of our activities or spent substances which have served intended purposes. By remaining in the environment they impair our economy and the quality of our life. They can be carried long distances by air or water or on articles of commerce, threatening the health, longevity, livelihood, recreation, cleanliness and happiness of citizens who have no direct stake in their production, but cannot escape their influence.

Pollutants have altered on a global scale the carbon dioxide content of the air and the lead concentrations in ocean waters and human populations. Pollutants have reduced the productivity of some of our finest agricultural soils, and have impaired the quality and the safety of crops raised on others. Pollutants have produced massive mortalities of fishes in rivers, lakes and estuaries and have damaged or destroyed commercial shellfish and shrimp fisheries. Pollutants have reduced valuable populations of pollinating and predatory insects, and have appeared in alarming amounts in migratory birds. Pollutants threaten the estuarine breeding grounds of valuable ocean fish; even Antarctic penguins and Arctic snowy owls carry pesticides in their bodies.

The land, water, air and living things of the United States are a heritage of the whole nation. They need to be protected for the benefit

Environmental Pollution Panel, President's Science Advisory Committee, *Restoring the Quality of Our Environment* (Washington, D.C., Government Printing Office, 1965), 1–2, 5–7, 10–15.

of all Americans, both now and in the future. The continued strength and welfare of our nation depend on the quantity and quality of our resources and on the quality of the environment in which our people live.

The pervasive nature of pollution, its disregard of political boundaries including state lines, the national character of the technical, economic and political problems involved, and the recognized Federal responsibilities for administering vast public lands which can be changed by pollution, for carrying out large enterprises which can produce pollutants, for preserving and improving the nation's natural resources, all make it mandatory that the Federal Government assume leadership and exert its influence in pollution abatement on a national scale. . . .

Man is but one species living in a world with numerous others; he depends on many of these others not only for his comfort and enjoyment but for his life. Plants provide the principal mechanism whereby energy from the sun can serve the earth's inhabitants. In doing so, they maintain the oxygen content of the air and furnish the basic habitat and food of animals and men. Microorganisms—bacteria, algae, fungi, and protozoa—perform a myriad of essential functions including the purification of air, soil, and water, and the recycling of nutrients. Animals serve man as great converters, changing plant-stored energy into forms of food he prefers and supplying him with a wide variety of materials: leather and furs, oils and pharmaceuticals, ivory and pearls, bristles and wool. Many insects are beneficial, some as pollinators; others as predators on harmful forms; some as makers of silk and honey.

As contributors to happiness and the quality of life, plants and animals provide opportunities for enjoyment of natural beauty, for hunting, fishing, gardening, scientific study, entertainment, and the satisfaction of our human curiosity.

In the control of pollution, plants, animals and microorganisms are directly useful in two ways: First, living things, especially microorganisms, have a capacity for absorption and decomposition of pollutants, with resulting purification of air, water and soil. Second, many species of organisms, each with its own particular range of sensitivity to each pollutant, stand as ready-made systems for environmental bioassay and monitoring, and for warnings of danger to man and his environment.

Because living things are interdependent and interacting, they form a complex, dynamic system. Tampering with this system may be desirable and necessary, as in agriculture, which involves artificial manipulation of the balances of nature on a huge scale. But such tampering often produces unexpected results, or side effects, and these are sometimes very damaging. Many of the effects of pollution fall into this category.

In small amounts, pollution can produce effects so subtle as to escape notice. Small changes in the reproductive rates of birds or fish, for example, can result from pesticide pollution at low levels, yet be very difficult to detect in nature. At high levels, damaging effects of pollution become clearly evident, as when fish are killed in large numbers or bees disappear from a locality.

Pollution affects living things in many different ways: In high concentrations, the sulfur dioxide in stack fumes kills trees and crop plants. The mixture of pollutants in urban smog damages spinach, tobacco, and other valuable plants. Domestic sewage and animal wastes can act as fertilizers, stimulating the growth of algae, but creating unfavorable conditions for game fish. Heating of rivers and lakes by return of waters used to cool industrial processes or power plants can favor some living forms and devastate others. Soils and waters can be polluted by radioactive materials derived from weapons testing, from industrial release, or from naturally contaminated fertilizers or spring waters. Once in soils or water, the radioactivity may then become concentrated in organisms. Sediments released into streams or lakes can reduce the supply of light for plants, and smother fish eggs and other useful forms.

The effects of pollution on livestock and crop plants often show up clearly because farmers quickly notice any impairment of health or yield. Effects on wild forms are much less likely to be detected and are harder to measure. Disappearance or catastrophic diminution of a wild population often occurs before the effects of a pollutant are recognized.

The effects of pollutants on living things are usually complicated and seldom well understood. Organisms are subjected to many different pollutants at the same time, pollutants that may enhance one another, partially compensate for one another, or act side by side.

Because different species react differently, and because the living world is so thoroughly interdependent, pollution produces profound indirect effects. A pesticide directed at a certain insect pest may, as a side effect, destroy a population of beneficial predator insects, so that a population of aphids that the predators had kept small suddenly multiplies and becomes highly destructive. A pollutant may fertilize a lake, creating vigorous algal growth near the surface, which shuts off the supply of sunlight from deeper-growing plants. The latter then consume the oxygen dissolved in the water, so that microscopic animals perish, and fish, depending on them for food and on dissolved oxygen for respiration, either starve or suffocate.

Pollutants tend to reduce the numbers of species, and to make the relationships of those that remain less stable. Large bodies of water, such as Lake Erie, may be depleted of many useful living forms. Pollution typically reduces the variety and abundance of wildlife serving our recreation and enjoyment.

From the economic point of view, pollution may produce serious adverse effects on living things used by man. Useful crops have been damaged by air and soil pollution, valuable commercial fisheries have been destroyed or diminished, as in the Great Lakes, Raritan Bay, and Long Island Sound, and wild populations of game fish and game birds valued for human recreation have been reduced. In a few instances, milk from herds of cattle fed on polluted forage has been so contaminated as to be unmarketable. . . .

Deliberate disposal of wastes is a more or less systematized activity. Most such wastes are not toxic, though some may carry disease. But odors, excess fertility of waters, and offenses against natural beauty are widespread. . . .

A frequently quoted estimate for the annual output of urban solid wastes, containing such things as paper, grass and brush cuttings, garbage, ashes, metal, and glass, is 1600 pounds per capita. Currently, this means 125 million tons each year, whose collection and disposal costs about 2.5 billion dollars a year. . . .

The combustion of coal, oil, and gas in our homes, vehicles, and factories results in the discharge into the air of sulfur dioxide, carbon dioxide, carbon monoxide, oxides of nitrogen, and partially burned hydrocarbons. Some of these gases, together with gasoline and natural gas vapors, undergo chemical change in air and in sunlight, and become the noxious constituents of smog; others, like carbon dioxide, are accumulating in such large quantities that they may eventually produce marked climatic change. Large amounts of lead are dispersed into the atmosphere from motor vehicle exhausts. Indeed, the pollution from internal combustion engines is so serious, and is growing so fast, that an alternative nonpolluting means of powering automobiles, buses and trucks is likely to become a national necessity. . . .

Pollution touches us all. We are at the same time pollutors and sufferers from pollution. Today, we are certain that pollution adversely affects the quality of our lives. In the future, it may affect their duration.

Present levels of pollution of air, water, soils and living organisms are for the most part below the levels that have been demonstrated to cause disease or death in people. At the same time we recognize a number of episodes where air pollution has caused deaths, where disease has been spread by water, where accidental poisonings have occurred from pesticides. The documented cases of pollution-caused injuries to plants, fish, birds and mammals are extensive and the economic loss from these injuries has been considerable. Some waters no longer support any useful fish or invertebrates. Some areas have been rendered unsuitable for useful plants. Many natural waters throughout the country are becoming continually less beautiful and less usable. Air in some of our cities is unpleasant to breathe and obscures our surroundings; our buildings are dirtied and sometimes rapidly weathered. Pollution has denied to some of our farmers the most desirable uses of parts of their lands. Prudence and self interest dictate that we exert ourselves not only to prevent further buildup of pollutants but to reduce present burdens of pollution in our air, our waters, and our land.

Arrangements to deal with pollution have grown on a piecemeal basis, with organizations, programs and legislation created when problems became evident or critical. With this background it is not surprising that current organization is a hodge-podge, with responsibilities widely separated among government agencies, and some unassigned. Some pollutants are dealt with on the basis of the environmental medium in which they occur, for example, pollutants in air and water; others are dealt with on the basis of the kinds of effect they have, for example toxic materials in food; some are dealt with on the basis of their sources, for example artificially radioactive materials.

With some pollutants there is no Federal authority to act until a problem exists. Such is the case with water pollution and air pollution. With some pollutants there is no Federal authority to act at all, as is the case with pesticide residues on tobacco. With some pollution problems existing Federal authorities constrain the type of action that can be taken, as with water pollution problems that can be approached by the Corps of Engineers only through providing excess water storage for low-flow augmentation (usually a costly and inefficient process). With some pollutants such as radionuclides, extreme caution is exercised to assure that unwanted effects in the environment will be prevented; with other materials, such as pesticides, consideration of side effects has been scant in the past.

The situation at the Federal level is more or less duplicated in the states and other jurisdictions.

Careful attention to organization of pollution-related activities in the Federal Government, to the relation of Federal activities and organizations to other political jurisdictions, and to the relations among agencies below the Federal level will be necessary to enable us to cope with pollution in the future.

There are many areas in which ignorance constrains our ability to deal effectively with pollution problems. Examples lie in the deficiencies of our knowledge of the behavior of important carriers of pollution, such as atmospheric gases, surface and ground waters, oceanic currents, and soil particles. Basic research on these topics is necessary in order to clarify our understanding of the movement of pollutants. Some pollutants are carried extensively in living things, moving from one plant or animal to another as food, moving from place to place with the plant or animal. Such movements of pollutants in and through living organisms are important, for example, when we consider means of protecting wildlife, fisheries, and shellfish from pollution. Basic ecological research is necessary if we are to cope effectively with these serious problems.

We now know that the full effects of environmental changes produced by pollution cannot be foreseen before judgments must be made. The responsible judgment, therefore, must be the conservative one. Trends and indications, as soundly based as possible, must provide the guidelines; demonstration of disaster is not required. Abnormal changes in animal populations, however small, at whatever stage in the life history of the individual, or in whatever niche of the species complex, must be considered warnings of potential hazard.

Many kinds of pollution problems could be prevented by the exercise of ecological foresight. Given a reasonable knowledge of persistence, biological effect and expected initial distribution and amount, at least part of the impact on living things can be predicted. In the future, such advance evaluations will be essential.

Disposal of wastes is a requisite for domestic life, for agriculture, and for industry. Traditionally waste disposal was accomplished in the cheapest possible way, usually by dumping in the nearest stream. This tradition is no longer acceptable—we believe industrial and agricultural waste disposal must now be accomplished in such a way that pollution is avoided, and that the higher costs of such disposal should be borne by industry and agriculture, and considered as a part of the cost of operation. The pressure to pollute in the past has been an economic one; the pressure to abate must in the future also be economic.

Much can be done by enforcement of today's regulatory laws, and by modifying the administrative policy under which Federal assistance is provided. For example, pollution from farm animal wastes could be alleviated by vigorous enforcement without technological advances. The same is true of particulate materials in air and sewage effluents in water.

As a basis for pollution abatement, we need to establish environmental quality standards. Such standards imply that the community is willing to bear certain costs or to enforce these costs on others in order to maintain its surroundings at a given level of quality and utility. For each pollutant the elements that must be taken into account are: its effects; technological capabilities for its control; the costs of control; and the desired uses of the resources that pollutants may affect.

These complex problems cannot be handled without a sufficient number of trained technicians, engineers, economists, administrators and scientists, and without the requisite scientific, technical and economic knowledge. The manpower and knowledge now at hand are insufficient for the complete task, though much can be accomplished with present resources. Our government has a clear responsibility to insure that persons of ability and imagination are attracted into this broad field and trained in its intricacies, and that scientists and engineers are enabled to produce the knowledge and technology that will give the people of our country a clean, healthy, and happy environment.

36

Prospects for the Land

STEWART L. UDALL (1963)

*In this concluding selection Stewart L. Udall reflects on American conserva-
tion's history and anticipates its future. Born in Arizona and a Representative of that state in Congress in the 1950's, Udall became President John F.
Kennedy's Secretary of the Interior in 1961 and remained in office under
Lyndon B. Johnson. Thus far his term has been marked by an unprecedented degree of concern for the quality of the environment. Udall believes that a society cannot regard itself a success if, in spite of its material
abundance, it permits the land it occupies to become blighted and uninspiring. And he feels much of his own country is uncomfortably close to this
situation. The best corrective, Udall believes, is the development of a sense
of ethical responsibility for the land, and, in a portion of his book not quoted
here, he singles out Aldo Leopold (20), as the prophet of this attitude.
With Leopold's philosophy as his ideal, and the record of conservation
achievement in the past century as an indication of progress toward it,
Udall, like most of his countrymen, manages to retain a guarded optimism
for the American environment despite the presence of staggering problems.*

If the forester and reclamation engineer symbolized the conservation
effort during Theodore Roosevelt's time, and the TVA [Tennessee
Valley Authority, see (25)] planner and the CCC [Civilian Conservation Corps, see (24)] tree planter typified the land·program of the
New Deal, the swift ascendancy of technology has made the scientist
the surest conservation symbol of the 60's. His instruments are the
atom-smasher, the computer, and the rocket—tools that have opened
the door to an ultimate storehouse of energy and may yet reveal the
secrets of the stars.

TR partially stopped the waste of resources, and his pilot conservation programs were a solid success. A generation later, Franklin D.
Roosevelt's new agencies set out to rebuild the land, and the dams and
development projects he instituted became the keystone of the conser-

Stewart L. Udall, *The Quiet Crisis* (New York, Holt, Rinehart & Winston,
1963), 173–191. Copyright © 1963 by Stewart Udall. Reprinted by permission of Holt, Rinehart & Winston.

vation effort. However, when the cadence of history accelerated with the onset of World War II, resource problems were either downgraded or transformed. FDR marshaled a maximum science-industry effort to produce the goods and weapons needed to win a global war. The supreme conservation achievement of this century, the fashioning of an almost self-renewing source of energy by the atomic scientists, was a direct result of the war effort. The first dramatic testing of an atomic pile at Chicago, in 1942, introduced the new role of scientists as the midwives of conservation. A hundred years of resource history were telescoped. The atomic physicists who uncovered the edge of an infinite dynamo brought fire, like the gods of Greek mythology, from seemingly inert elements, and allayed our fears of fuel shortage once and for all.

The surge of science was a boon to many areas of resource conservation. During the war years and those that followed, the alchemies of research brought new metals such as beryllium, germanium, columbium, molybdenum, and titanium into use, created synthetics and substitute products, and increased the usefulness of many raw materials. Investments in basic research in agriculture paid off with discoveries that gave wider insights into agronomy, while plant genetics and plant pathology yielded new strains, which, with new fertilizers and pesticides, made the granaries of American farmers overflow and gave us an opportunity to share our surplus and our science with other nations. Similarly, research in animal husbandry increased our ability to raise livestock, and science encouraged the owners of public and private forest lands to apply the tree-farming techniques fostered by the successors of Gifford Pinchot [(7), (11)].

These triumphs of technology have, in the 1960's, lent a note of optimism to the reports of most resource experts. Today, we are told, technology carries in its hands the keys to a kingdom of abundance, and sound solutions to many conservation problems rest largely on adequate research and efficient management. At last, long-range resource planning is becoming an indispensable aide to science in assuring an abundance of resources for human use.

Ironically, however, these very successes of science have presented a new set of problems that constitute the quiet crisis of conservation in this decade. It began with the inrush to the cities at the outset of World War II, and intensified with each new advance of technology. Our accomplishments in minerals and energy, in electronics and aircraft, in autos and agriculture have lifted us to new heights of affluence, but in the process we have lost ground in the attempt to provide a habitat that will, each day, renew the meaning of the human enterprise. A lopsided performance has allowed us to exercise dominion over the atom and to invade outer space, but we have sadly neglected the inner space that is our home. We can produce a wide range of goods and machines, but our manipulations have multiplied waste products that befoul the land, and have introduced frightening new forms of erosion that diminish the quality of indispensable resources and even imperil human health. The hazards appear on every hand; many new machines and processes corrupt the very air and water; in what Rachel Carson [(34).] has called "an age of poisons," an indiscriminate use of pesticides threatens both man and wildlife; and the omnipresent symbol of the age, the auto, in satisfying our incessant demand for greater mobility, has added to the congestion and unpleasantness of both cities and countrysides.

The conservation effort was confused and side tracked by the cataclysmic events that began in 1939. In the two decades that followed, public men were so preoccupied by the urgent issues of the hot and cold wars that none tried, as Pinchot and the two Roosevelts had done, to expand the conservation concept and apply it to the new world of natural resources and the new problems of land stewardship.

As a result of this failure to keep the conservation idea abreast of the times, such successful conservers as the scientific industrialists and scientific farmers seldom consider themselves conservationists at all, while many modern disciples of [Henry David] Thoreau [(2)] and [John] Muir [(14)] have narrowed their concern to park, forest, wildlife, or wilderness problems.

With the passing of each year neglect has piled new problems on the nation's doorstep. Some brilliant successes—in electronics, atom physics, aerodynamics, and chemistry, for example—encouraged a false sense of well-being, for our massive ability to overpower the natural world has also multiplied immeasurably our capacity to diminish the quality of the total environment. Our water husbandry methods have typified these failures. At the same time that our requirements for fresh water were doubling, our national sloth more than doubled our water pollution. We now are faced with the need to build 10,000 treatment plants and to spend $6,000,000,000 to conserve water supplies.

Much of our river development proceeded on an uncoordinated basis (although regional planning, which Major Powell [(6)] would have applauded, had an inning when the Upper Colorado River Storage Project was passed in 1956). The incursions of industry, agriculture, and urbanization into the marshlands were reducing waterfowl populations. Acreage in new parklands created by federal and state governments was too sparse to be significant: in 1940, 130,000,000 Americans had a spacious National Park system of 22,000,000 acres; twenty years later, a population which had grown to a more mobile 183,000,000 inherited an overcrowded system that had been enlarged by only a few acres. Of 21,000 miles of ocean shore line in the contiguous 48 states, only 7 per cent was cent was reserved for public recreation.

In addition, the most eroded lands in the United States—the overused grasslands of the Western public domain—were not restored to full fertility despite the new American awareness of the importance of soil conservation. Asphalt inroads of city subdividers in search of quick profits were so ill-conceived that stream valleys and open space were obliterated.

In the postwar period, unfortunately, most Americans took their out-of-doors for granted. It was a fact that pressures were growing each year to despoil our few remaining wilderness areas; Americans who were accustomed to outdoor recreation as a way of life—with access to public areas for hunting, fishing, hiking, and swimming— found overcrowding increasing each year. Most state and city governments faced so many growth problems that they had little time for foresight in planning their over-all environment. It was a sad fact, also, that the men, women, and children of America the Beautiful became the litter champions of the world. Each year about 5,000,000 battered autos are added to our junk yards. Aided by industries that produce an incredible array of boxes, bottles, cans, gadgets, gewgaws, and a thousand varieties of paper products, our landscape litter has reached such proportions that in another generation a trash pile or piece of junk will be within a stone's throw of any person standing anywhere on the American land mass. Our irreverent attitudes toward the land and our contempt for the Indians' stewardship concepts are nowhere more clearly revealed than in our penchant to pollute and litter and contaminate and blight once-attractive landscapes.

The promised land of thousands of new products, machines, and services has misled us—and the conservation movement, which should have become an intricate and interlocking effort on a hundred fronts, was itself disorganized and outdated.

Simultaneously, the steep upsurge of population and the pell-mell rush to enlarge our cities changed our people-to-people ratio and our attitudes toward the land with it. Indifference to the land was also accelerated by new seductions of spectatorship, the requirements of industrial growth, and air-conditioned advantages that made glassed-in living so appealing. The predictable result was that sedentary, city-bound citizens were encouraged to acquiesce in the diminution of the spaciousness and freshness and green splendor of the American earth.

Intoxicated with the power to manipulate nature, some misguided men have produced a rationale to replace the Myth of Superabundance. It might be called the Myth of Scientific Supremacy, for it rests on the rationalization that the scientists can fix everything tomorrow.

The modern land raiders, like the public-land raiders of another era, are ready to justify short-term gains by seeking to minimize the long-term losses. "Present the repair bill to the next generation" has always been their unspoken slogan.

As George Perkins Marsh [(3)] pointed out a century ago, greed and shortsightedness are conservation's mortal enemies. In the years ahead, the front line of conservation will extend from minerals to mallards, from salmon to soils, from wilderness to water, but most of our major problems will not be resolved unless the resource interrelationships are evaluated with an eye on long-term gains and long-term values.

Large-scale conservation work can no longer be accomplished by the flourish of a president's pen or through funds appropriated to fight a business depression. If we are to preserve both the beauty and the bounty of the American earth, it will take thoughtful planning and a day-in and day-out effort by business, by government, and by the voluntary organizations.

If the area of individual involvement is enlarged, if enough modern Muirs step forward to fight for "legislative interference" to save land and check its despoilment, the conservation movement can become a sustained, systematic effort both to produce and to preserve.

Full-fledged collaboration of science and industry and government, quickened by the spur of business competition, will enable us to write bright new chapters in the conservation of some resources. The continuing revolution in research should give us the means to harness the tides of Passamaquoddy, interconnect the electric-power systems of whole regions, economically extract fresh water from the seas, turn vast oil shale beds into oil, and, by discovering the innermost secrets of fission and fusion, allow us to "breed" energy from rocks.

Government leadership and government investment, however, must continue to play the larger role in traditional conservation work. In a matter of decades many regions will confront an insistent water crisis. Water conservation must always be primarily a public endeavor. It is already plain that regional planning, basin-wide water regimens, transmountain diversions of water from areas of surplus to more arid watersheds, sustained yield management of underground aquifers, and the development of techniques for pollution control and the re-use and recycling of water will be needed to save the day for water-short areas of the United States. To achieve this we must begin now to train a fully adequate corps of hydroscientists and to develop an awareness of the vital elements of a water-conservation program.

In addition, the forested land of our country must be managed more intensively to achieve much higher wood yields, and public forest lands must have much wider use if we are to provide adequate outdoor opportunities for our citizens. Likewise, our efforts to save soil, to control stream pollution, and to repair the land damage of the past must be enlarged and intensified.

The quiet conservation crisis is the end product of many forces. Its threat is all the more serious because most harm involves subtle erosion and contamination, and because motives of commercial profit do not enlist public support. Quick action can be expected only when threats to the public health or public convenience are imminent. The larger task will not be undertaken unless a quickening conscience brings us to act now to protect the land for future generations.

President Kennedy's preservation-of-environment program is a response to the quiet crisis, and it points the way toward the main arenas of conservation action in the years ahead. It concerns wilderness and wildlife and parklands and the whole spectrum of outdoor resources. The American out-of-doors was studied with thoroughness and vision from 1959 to 1962 by the Outdoor Recreation Resources Review Commission. Its report is a landmark analysis of our past failures and present opportunities in the use and protection of our environment.

As inheritors of a spacious, virgin continent we have had strong roots in the soil and a tradition that should give us special understanding of the mystique of people and land. It is our relationship with the

American earth that is being altered by the quiet crisis, our birthright of fresh landscapes and far horizons. Unless we are to betray our heritage consciously, we must make an all-out effort now to acquire the public lands which present and future generations need. Only prompt action will save prime park, forest, and shore line and other recreation lands before they are pre-empted for other uses or priced beyond the public purse.

The Land and Water Conservation Fund proposed by President Kennedy * may mark a turning point in conservation history. If the states are to provide leadership before it is too late, if the few remaining spacious seashores are to be preserved for all of the people, if wildlife values are to be permanently protected and our National Park, Forest, and Wildlife Refuge systems are to be rounded out by the addition of the remaining suitable lands, the task must begin immediately and be completed within the next three decades.

The status we give our wilderness and near-wilderness areas will also measure the degree of our reverence for the land. American pioneering in establishing National Parks and in promoting the wilderness concept is already being emulated in many parts of the world today. Many nations no longer have the option of preserving part of their land in its pristine condition. We must take ours up before it is too late. A wilderness system [see (33)] will offer man what many consider the supreme human experience. It will also provide watershed protection, a near-perfect wildlife habitat, and an unmatched science laboratory where we can measure the world in its natural balance against the world in its man-made imbalance. . . .

In Alaska we have a magnificent opportunity to show more respect for wilderness and wildlife values than did our forebears. The wonders of the wilderness still abound there; if we spoil them, we cannot excuse their defilement with pleas of ignorance.

We have an opportunity, too, to take a leaf from FDR's book and establish a permanent Conservation Corps to rehabilitate and renew our public lands. Generations to follow will judge us by our success in preserving in their natural state certain rivers having superior outdoor recreation values. The Allagash of Maine, the Suwannee of Georgia and Florida, the Rogue of Oregon, the Salmon of Idaho, the Buffalo of Arkansas, and the Ozark Mountain rivers in the State of Missouri are

---

* Passed in 1964, this measure is designed to raise revenue for the acquisition of parkland and open space for recreation. [Ed.]

some of the waterways that should be kept as clean, wild rivers—a part of a rich outdoor heritage. We must act to provide a habitat in which the fish and wildlife sharing our planet may thrive. Our environment-preservation work will lack balance unless our highway building includes a national system of scenic roads.

The quiet crisis demands a rethinking of land attitudes, deeper involvement by leaders of business and government, and methods of making conservation decisions which put a premium on foresight. With the acumen of our scientists we can achieve optimum development of resources that will let us pluck the fruits of science without harming the tree of life. Once we decide that our surroundings need not always be subordinated to payrolls and profits based on short-term considerations, there is hope that we can both reap the bounty of the land and preserve an inspiriting environment.

The Muirs and Olmsteds [(4)] and Pinchots of the decades ahead will surely fail unless both our business and public budgets embrace conservation values. Enlightened leaders of the business community are already pointing the way: such companies as Lever Brothers, Johnson's Wax, and the Connecticut General Life Insurance Company have demonstrated that a beautifully designed building is the most attractive form of advertising. Conservation will make headway when it is patently good business for companies to invest in programs of education and practices of production which emphasize both conservation and industrial efficiency. Conservation statesmen must prove that profits and the conservation cause are compatible if we are to succeed in making an attractive and orderly environment part of our national purpose. At present, many of our policies actively conspire against conservation, and the conservation-minded businessman too often finds himself at an intolerable competitive disadvantage if he implements his convictions.

The proper control of waste products or polluting materials, or the reclamation of strip-mine areas, cost money. For any one state or any one region to allow its enterprisers an economic advantage by permitting damage illegal elsewhere is a repetition of the nineteenth-century story of the forest raiders and hydraulic miners. Our air and water resources are essential to life. Water and the air masses are in constant motion, and it will take uniform laws, national in scope, to put competing industries on an equal footing. Where our laws make land reclamation and pollution abatement a normal part of the cost of doing business, enlightened businessmen are already working with the conservation cause. Once intolerable competitive advantages are eliminated, researchers will quickly devise machines and gadgets to minimize the damage. But environment restoration and preservation can succeed only if we pay as we go.

We have reached the point in our history where it is absolutely essential that all resources, and all alternative plans for their use and development, be evaluated comprehensively by those who make the over-all decisions. As our land base shrinks, it is inevitable that incompatible plans involving factories, mines, fish, dams, parks, highways, and wildlife, and other uses and values will increasingly collide. Those who decide must consider immediate needs, compute the values of competing proposals, and keep distance in their eyes as well. For example, technical innovations which will have a widespread effect on other resources and on living values shared by all must be assessed in advance. Chemical contamination, the disposal of radioactive wastes, and sonic boom are examples of present or coming problems which will require the careful measurement of social costs against social benefits.

Our mastery over our environment is now so great that the conservation of a region, a metropolitan area, or a valley is more important, in most cases, than the conservation of any single resource. Complex decisions will require sophisticated judgments that weigh all elements and explore all possible alternatives. Slum valleys and regional slums will be the result, unless we put our resources to their highest and best use.

As the area of conflict and overlap increases we must constantly improve our decision-making techniques. Nor must' we be afraid to decide the toughest of issues: practices that defer necessary decisions can also be a threat to the national welfare.

Geography has always been a global science and conservation must now become a truly global concept if the optimum use of resources is to be achieved. Nature's rules still obtain, and all parts of the natural world, from minerals and marine life to the gulf streams of the ocean and jet streams of the upper atmosphere, obey a single set of laws. It is the seven seas themselves, the one remaining largely unspoiled, untapped resource, which now represent the largest remaining frontier of conservation on this earth.

The atmosphere and the oceans are the two resources that are owned by all of the people of the world. Yet, save for a few farsighted treaties, we have no plan of management for these common resources, and oceanographers are still at the outer edge of the secrets of the sea. The ocean domain includes the submerged 71 per cent of the earth's surface, and in its depths are an immense reserve of mineral and marine resources for the future: for example, once the enormous schools of "trash" fish are converted into edible food or fish flour, the protein diet deficiency afflicting two-thirds of the people of the world can be partially alleviated.

Inadequate research into marine resources and the absence of international planning have meant that some resources are overexploited while others remain underdeveloped. With the exception of a few notable agreements the law of hunt-and-kill is still the code of the sea. Only timely international conservation agreements will avert the spectacle of a resource raid to dwarf those of the past on the fur seal and the sea otter. The oceans can be the most fruitful field for international co-operation in conservation, if the nations will turn in time to the principles of sustained-yield management.

The one factor certain to complicate all of our conservation problems is the ineluctable pressure of expanding population. Our resource planners operate in a bureaucratic trance, assuming that the population of the United States will inevitably double by the year 2000. An all-too-common corollary assumption is that life in general—and the good, the true, and the beautiful in particular—will somehow be enhanced at the same time. We have growth room in this country, but the time has come for thoughtful men and women to ask some basic questions about our land-people equation. Our whole history demonstrates that his physical environment has an enormous influence upon man. Are not such inquiries as these, then, pertinent to the future course of human enterprise: What is the ideal "ecology of man," the ideal relationship of the human population to environment? Is man subject to the laws of nature, which hold that every species in any environment has an optimum population? How much living space do human beings need in order to function with maximum efficiency and to enjoy maximum happiness?

It is obvious that the best qualities in man must atrophy in a standing-room-only environment. Therefore, if the fulfillment of the individual is our ultimate goal, we must soon determine the proper man-land ratio for our continent.

Our future will be linked increasingly with the success of other peoples in dealing with their resources. The American economy already consumes over 30 per cent of the world's raw material production, and resource interdependence among nations increases each year. The Peace Corps program and the second phase of our foreign aid effort largely involve the export of conservation know-how. That foreign students already outnumber Americans in the mining courses offered by our graduate schools serves to measure the extent of our educational contributions. We are generous enough and practical enough to share our resource insights with the farmer in Pakistan, the Peruvian fisherman, and the game warden of east Africa. In return, we ought to accept gladly the land lessons they can teach us. The region of the river valley is now the proper setting for resource planning, but technology will soon make international conservation planning a necessity. The treaty that made the Antarctic a scientific preserve, and the world-wide co-operation evinced by the International Geophysical Year, are signposts of hope for the future.

In the years ahead, nations can either compete ruthlessly for resources, in a context of scarcity, or co-operate, respect the laws of nature, and share its abundance. Resource interdependence and the common management of those resources owned in common will enlarge the area of unified action and do much to encourage world order. The growth of a world-wide conservation movement might be a gyroscopic force in the world politics. The most influential countries of the future surely will be those that bring desalted water to arid lands and use their scientific discoveries to advance the welfare of all mankind.

Internationally, we need new forms of co-operation in order to realize the full potential of all natural resources. Domestically, we must have a ground swell of concern over the quiet crisis, which could culminate in a third wave of the conservation movement. . . .

❊ ❊ ❊

Beyond all plans and programs, true conservation is ultimately something of the mind—an ideal of men who cherish their past and believe in their future. Our civilization will be measured by its fidelity to this ideal as surely as by its art and poetry and system of justice. In our perpetual search for abundance, beauty, and order we manifest both our love for the land and our sense of responsibility toward future generations.

Most Americans find it difficult to conceive a land ethic for tomorrow. The pastoral American of a century ago, whose conservation insights were undeveloped, has been succeeded by the asphalt

American of the 1960's, who is shortsighted in other ways. Our sense of stewardship is uncertain partly because too many of us lack roots in the soil and the respect for resources that goes with such roots. Too many of us have mistaken material ease and comfort for the good life. Our growing dependence on machines has tended to mechanize our response to the world around us and has blunted our appreciation of the higher values.

There are many uprooting forces at work in our society. We are now a nomadic people, and our new-found mobility has deprived us of a sense of belonging to a particular place. Millions of Americans have no tie to the "natural habitat" that is their home. Yet the understanding of the grandeur and simplicity of the good earth is the umbilical cord that should never be cut. If the slow swing of the seasons has lost its magic for some of us, we are all diminished. If others have lost the path to the wellsprings of self-renewal, we are all the losers.

Modern life is confused by the growing imbalance between the works of man and the works of nature. Yesterday a neighbor was someone who lived next door; today technology has obliterated old boundaries and our lives overlap and impinge in myriad ways. Thousands of men who affect the way we live will always remain strangers. An aircraft overhead or an act of air or water pollution miles away, can impair an environment that thousands must share. If we are to formulate an appropriate land conscience, we must redefine the meaning of "neighbor" and find new bonds of loyalty to the land.

One of the paradoxes of American society is that while our economic standard of living has become the envy of the world, our environmental standard has steadily declined. We are better housed, better nourished, and better entertained, but we are not better prepared to inherit the earth or to carry on the pursuit of happiness.

A century ago we were a land-conscious, outdoor people: the American face was weather-beaten, our skills were muscular, and each family drew sustenance directly from the land. Now marvelous machines make our lives easier, but we are falling prey to the weaknesses of an indoor nation and the flabbiness of a sedentary society.

A land ethic for tomorrow should be as honest as Thoreau's *Walden,* and as comprehensive as the sensitive science of ecology. It should stress the oneness of our resources and the live-and-help-live logic of the great chain of life. If, in our haste to "progress," the economics of ecology are disregarded by citizens and policy makers alike, the result will be an ugly America. We cannot afford an America where expedience tramples upon esthetics and development decisions are made with an eye only on the present.

Henry Thoreau would scoff at the notion that the Gross National Product should be the chief index to the state of the nation, or that automobile sales or figures on consumer consumption reveal anything significant about the authentic art of living. He would surely assert that a clean landscape is as important as a freeway, he would deplore every planless conquest of the countryside, and he would remind his countrymen that a glimpse of grouse can be more inspiring than a Hollywood spectacular or color television. To those who complain of the complexity of modern life, he might reply, "If you want inner peace find it in solitude, not speed, and if you would find yourself, look to the land from which you came and to which you go."

We can have abundance and an unspoiled environment if we are willing to pay the price. We must develop a land conscience that will inspire those daily acts of stewardship which will make America a more pleasant and more productive land. If enough people care enough about their continent to join in the fight for a balanced conservation program, this generation can proudly put its signature on the land. But this signature will not be meaningful unless we develop a land ethic. Only an ever-widening concept and higher ideal of conservation will enlist our finest impulses and move us to make the earth a better home both for ourselves and for those as yet unborn.

Part Five

The Gospel of Ecology

Part Five

The Gospel of Ecology

By the early 1970s hardly anyone in the United States was unaware of conservation even if they called it by a different name. "Environment" was in vogue. "Ecology" also became a household word, although those capable of defining it correctly were in a decided minority. The words took their places in the American reverential vocabulary alongside "home" and "mother" and "church"; for some persons they were synonymous. Riding the crest of a wave of public interest and support, the conservation-turned-environment movement attained an unprecedented political and cultural power. During the years 1969 and 1970, which marked the zenith of environmental concern, it was a rare issue of a magazine or newspaper that did not feature some aspect of man's relationship to the earth. Santa Barbara, California captured headlines early in 1969 with an offshore oil well blowout and subsequent oil spill whose impact was as much symbolic as physical. In July Neil Armstrong walked on the moon, dramatizing as an important by-product a new perspective of the earth as fragile, finite, and beautiful beyond man's landbound imagination.

Emphasizing the priorities of the time, President Richard M. Nixon's first official act of the 1970s was the signing into law of the National Environmental Policy Act. It established a Council on Environmental Quality in the Executive Office of the President, required "environmental impact statements" for all federal expenditures, and officially recognized, in the words of the act, the necessity of achieving "harmony between man and his environment." Despite precedents for such ideals in the work of George Perkins Marsh (3) and Aldo Leopold (20), NEPA was epoch-making in terms of official recognition of ecological realities. The camp-meeting atmosphere associated with the first Earth Day, 22 April 1970, revealed a similar recognition at a broad public level. Supporting it was a mounting tendency, particularly evident in younger persons, to question traditional American ideals, like unlimited growth and unnecessary affluence, which did not take ecologi-

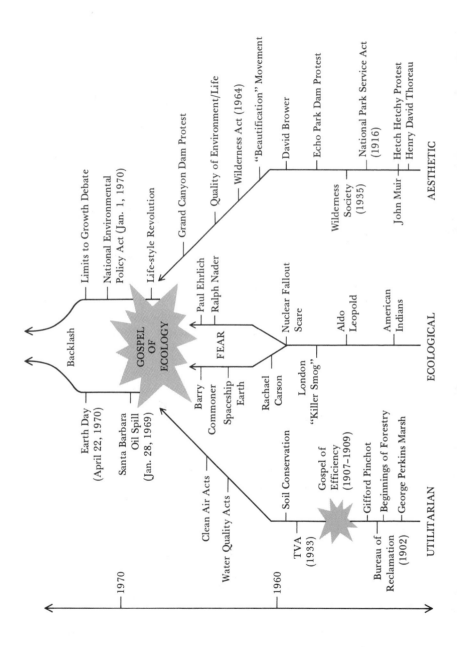

cal imperatives into account. In this respect the so-called "counterculture" of the late 1960s and the recent environment movement were clearly supportive.

The explosion of American concern for conservation was rooted in shifting attitudes and values and, in view of its intensity and evangelical character, might be termed a *gospel of ecology*. It can best be explained as a convergence, around ecological concepts, of the major rationales already existing for conservation. Visually, what took place can be depicted in the diagram on page 226.

The lower levels of the diagram separate and highlight the three major rationales for conservation that have been advanced in the United States. Their coming together in the 1960s was the result of a catalytic agent: fear. But it was not the old fear of running out of useful resources which had impelled the utilitarians and produced its own minor explosion of public concern in 1907–1909. Nor was it the fear of making the world ugly and uninspiring, which figured as the mainstay of aesthetic conservation. The fear implicit in the ecological rationale stems from the recognition of threats to the health of the entire ecosytem. Of course there is concern about man's future but as part of a broader concern for the well-being of the whole. Man recedes to a position of mere membership in the life community, and *its* welfare, not exclusively man's, becomes the new criterion for judging man-land relationships. This is still an expression of anthropocentrism, but the new self-interest is qualitatively different since it demands the subordination of the old self-interest to ecological imperatives. The ecological perspective helped man discover the irony of selfishness.

The gospel of ecology itself can be seen as an intellectual collision between scientific and what might be called *theological* ecology. The logic of the scientist was fused to the intuition of the poet; Western analysis to Eastern mysticism. The result was a holistic sense of oneness, of community, that could stand the test of both fact and feeling. The combination was powerful enough to impel many Americans to find in ecology the essence of a world view tantamount to a religion.

Inevitably the intensity of environmental concern characteristic of the late 1960s and early 1970s cooled. The constriction of the broad arrow emerging in the diagram from the top of the gospel-of-ecology explosion represents this recession, which in some quarters approached a backlash. But the legacy is certainly a conservation/environment movement both broader and deeper than ever before.

37

Restructuring American Thinking for Harmony with the Environment
GARY SNYDER (1969)

A poet and early member of what came in the late 1960s to be called the "counterculture," Gary Snyder's experience has included logging, university study of anthropology, bohemianism in San Francisco, and an extended visit to Japan where he steeped himself in non-Western ways of thinking about the natural world. Four Changes, written in the summer of 1969 during the zenith of the gospel of ecology, brings together in succinct form many of the ideals of the environmental movement. Acceptance of Snyder's principles leads away from many traditional American values and objectives. His thoughts constitute a manifesto for the new lifestyle that is widely thought to be a prerequisite for any meaningful, long-term reform in man-land relations in the United States. Snyder himself currently shares a quasi hunting-gathering existence with a group of friends in a wilderness setting. In the tradition of American messianism, he sees his role as providing an example for others to follow. Document 46, later in the text, expresses the philosophy and method of this lifestyle revolution.

I. POPULATION

The Condition

Position: Man is but a part of the fabric of life—dependent on the whole fabric for his very existence. As the most highly developed tool-using animal, he must recognize that the unknown evolutionary destinies of other life forms are to be respected, and act as gentle steward of the earth's community of being.

Situation: There are now too many human beings, and the problem is growing rapidly worse. It is potentially disastrous not only for the human race but for most other life forms.

Goal: The goal would be half of the present world population, or less.

Gary Snyder, *Turtle Island* (New York: New Directions, 1974), 91–102. Reprinted by permission.

Action

Social/political: First, a massive effort to convince the governments and leaders of the world that the problem is severe. And that all talk about raising food-production—well intentioned as it is—simply puts off the only real solution: reduce population. Demand immediate participation by all countries in programs to legalize abortion, encourage vasectomy and sterilization (provided by free clinics)—free insertion of intra-uterine loops—try to correct traditional cultural attitudes that tend to force women into child-bearing—remove income tax deductions for more than two children above a specified income level, and scale it so that lower income families are forced to be careful too—or pay families to limit their number. Take a vigorous stand against the policy of the right wing in the Catholic hierarchy and any other institutions that exercise an irresponsible social force in regard to this question; oppose and correct simple-minded boosterism that equates population growth with continuing prosperity. Work ceaselessly to have all political questions be seen in the light of this prime problem.

[The governments are the wrong agents to address. Their most likely use of a problem, or crisis, is to seize it as another excuse for extending their own powers. Abortion should be legal and voluntary, but questions about vasectomy side-effects still come up. Great care should be taken that no one is ever tricked or forced into sterilization. The whole population issue is fraught with contradictions: but the fact stands that by standards of planetary biological welfare there are already too many human beings. The long-range answer is steady low birth rate. Area by area of the globe, the criteria of "optimum population" should be based on the sense of total ecological health for the region, including flourishing wildlife populations.]

The community: Explore other social structures and marriage forms, such as group marriage and polyandrous marriage, which provide family life but many less children. Share the pleasures of raising children widely, so that all need not directly reproduce to enter into this basic human experience. We must hope that no woman would give birth to more than one [two?] child, during this period of crisis. Adopt children. Let reverence for life and reverence for the feminine mean also a reverence for other species, and future human lives, most of which are threatened.

Our own heads: "I am a child of all life, and all living beings are my brothers and sisters, my children and grandchildren. And there is a child within me waiting to be brought to birth, the baby of a new and wiser self." Love, Love-making, a man and woman together, seen as the vehicle of mutual realization, where the creation of new selves and a new world of being is as important as reproducing our kind.

II. POPULATION

The Condition

Position: Pollution is of two types. One sort results from an excess of some fairly ordinary substance—smoke, or solid waste—which cannot be absorbed or transmitted rapidly enough to offset its introduction into the environment, thus causing changes the great cycle is not prepared for. (All organisms have wastes and by-products, and these are indeed part of the total biosphere: energy is passed along the line and refracted in various ways, "the rainbow body." This is cycling, not pollution.) The other sort is powerful modern chemicals and poisons, products of recent technology, which the biosphere is totally unprepared for. Such is DDT and similar chlorinated hydrocarbons—nuclear testing fall-out and nuclear waste—poison gas, germ and virus storage and leakage by the military; and chemicals which are put into food, whose long-range effects on human beings have not been properly tested.

Situation: The human race in the last century has allowed its production and scattering of wastes, by-products, and various chemicals to become excessive. Pollution is directly harming life on the planet: which is to say, ruining the environment for humanity itself. We are fouling our air and water, and living in noise and filth that no "animal" would tolerate, while advertising and politicians try and tell us we've never had it so good. The dependence of the modern governments on this kind of untruth leads to shameful mind-pollution: mass media and much school education.

Goal: Clean air, clean clear-running rivers, the presence of Pelican and Osprey and Gray Whale in our lives; salmon and trout in our streams; unmuddied language and good dreams.

Action

Social/political: Effective international legislation banning DDT and other poisons—with no fooling around. The collusion of certain scientists with the pesticide industry and agri-business in trying to block this legislation must be brought out in the open. Strong penalties for water and air pollution by industries—"Pollution is somebody's profit." Phase out the internal combustion engine and fossil fuel use in general —more research into non-polluting energy sources; solar energy; the tides. No more kidding the public about nuclear waste disposal: it's impossible to do it safely, and nuclear-generated electricity cannot be seriously planned for as it stands now. [Energy: we know a lot more about this problem now. Non-polluting energy resources such as solar or tides, would be clearly inadequate to supply the power needs of the world techno-industrial cancer. Five hundred years of strip-mining is not acceptable. To go into the liquid metal fast breeder reactor on the gamble that we'll come out with the fusion process perfected is not acceptable. Research should continue on nuclear power, but divorced from any crash-program mentality. This means, conserve energy. "Do more with less." "Convert Waste into Treasure."] Stop all germ and chemical warfare research and experimentation; work toward a hopefully safe disposal of the present staggering and stupid stockpiles of H-bombs, cobalt gunk, germ and poison tanks and cans. Laws and sanctions against wasteful use of paper etc. which adds to the solid wastes of cities—develop methods of recycling solid urban wastes. Recycling should be the basic principle behind all waste-disposal thinking. Thus, all bottles should be reusable; old cans should make more cans; old newspapers back into newsprint again. Stronger controls and research on chemicals in foods. A shift toward a more varied and sensitive type of agriculture (more small-scale and subsistence farming) would eliminate much of the call for blanket use of pesticides.

The community: DDT and such: don't use them. Air pollution: use less cars. Cars pollute the air, and one or two people riding lonely in a huge car is an insult to intelligence and the Earth. Share rides, legalize hitch-hiking, and build hitch-hiker waiting stations along the highways. Also—a step toward the new world—walk more; look for the best routes through beautiful countryside for long-distance walking trips: San Francisco to Los Angeles down the Coast Range, for example. Learn how to use your own manure as fertilizer if you're in the country—as the Far East has done for centuries. There's a way, and it's safe. Solid waste: boycott bulky wasteful Sunday papers which use up trees. It's all just advertising anyway, which is artificially inducing more energy consumption. Refuse paper bags at the store. Organize Park and Street clean-up festivals. Don't work in any way for or with an industry which pollutes, and don't be drafted into the military. Don't waste.

(A monk and an old master were once walking in the mountains. They noticed a little hut upstream. The monk said, "A wise hermit must live there"—the master said, "That's no wise hermit, you see that lettuce leaf floating down the stream, he's a Waster." Just then an old man came running down the hill with his beard flying and caught the floating lettuce leaf.) Carry your own jug to the winery and have it filled from the barrel.

Our own heads: Part of the trouble with talking about something like DDT is that the use of it is not just a practical devise, it's almost an establishment religion. There is something in Western culture that wants to totally wipe out creepy-crawlies, and feels repugnance for toadstools and snakes. This is fear of one's own deepest natural inner-self wilderness areas, and the answer is, relax. Relax around bugs, snakes, and your own hairy dreams. Again, we all should share our crops with a certain percentage of buglife as "paying our dues." Thoreau says: "How then can the harvest fail? Shall I not rejoice also at the abundance of the weeds whose seeds are the granary of the birds? It matters little comparatively whether the fields fill the farmer's barns. The true husbandman will cease from anxiety, as the squirrels manifest no concern whether the woods will bear chestnuts this year or not, and finish his labor with every day, relinquish all claim to the produce of his fields, and sacrificing in his mind not only his first but his last fruits also." In the realm of thought, inner experience, consciousness, as in the outward realm of interconnection, there is a difference between balanced cycle, and the excess which cannot be handled. When the balance is right, the mind recycles from highest illuminations to the muddy blinding anger or grabbiness which sometimes seizes us all; the alchemical "transmutation."

III. CONSUMPTION

The Condition

Position: Everything that lives eats food, and is food in turn. This complicated animal, man, rests on a vast and delicate pyramid of energy-transformations. To grossly use more than you need, to destroy, is biologically unsound. Much of the production and consumption of modern societies is not necessary or conducive to spiritual and cultural growth, let alone survival; and is behind much greed and envy, age-old causes of social and international discord.

Situation: Man's careless use of "resources" and his total dependence on certain substances such as fossil fuels (which are being exhausted, slowly but certainly) are having harmful effects on all the other members of the life-network. The complexity of modern technology renders whole populations vulnerable to the deadly consequences of the loss of any one key resource. Instead of independence we have overdependence on life-giving substances such as water, which we squander. Many species of animals and birds have become extinct in the service of fashion fads—or fertilizer—or industrial oil—the soil is being used up; in fact mankind has become a locustlike blight on the planet that will leave a bare cupboard for its own children—all the while in a kind of Addict's Dream of affluence, comfort, eternal progress—using the great achievements of science to produce software and swill.

Goal: Balance, harmony, humility, growth which is a mutual growth with Redwood and Quail; to be a good member of the great community of living creatures. True affluence is not needing anything.

Action

Social/political: It must be demonstrated ceaselessly that a continually "growing economy" is no longer healthy, but a Cancer. And that the criminal waste which is allowed in the name of competition—especially that ultimate in wasteful needless competition, hot wars and cold wars with "Communism" (or "Capitalism")—must be halted totally with ferocious energy and decision. Economics must be seen as a small subbranch of Ecology, and production/distribution/consumption handled by companies or unions or co-operatives, with the same elegance and spareness one sees in nature. Soil banks; open spaces; [logging to be truly based on sustained yield; the U.S. Forest Service is—sadly—now the lackey of business.] Protection for all scarce predators and varmints: "Support your right to arm bears." Damn the International Whaling Commission which is selling out the last of our precious, wise whales; absolutely no further development of roads and concessions in National Parks and Wilderness Areas; build auto campgrounds in the least desirable areas. Consumer boycotts in response to dishonest and unnecessary products. Radical Co-ops. Politically, blast both "Communist" and "Capitalist" myths of progress, and all crude notions of conquering or controlling nature.

The community: Sharing and creating. The inherent aptness of communal life—where large tools are owned jointly and used efficiently.

The power of renunciation: If enough Americans refused to buy a new car for one given year, it would permanently alter the American economy. Recycling clothes and equipment. Support handicrafts, gardening, home skills, mid-wifery, herbs—all the things that can make us independent, beautiful and whole. Learn to break the habit of unnecessary possessions—a monkey on everybody's back—but avoid a self-abnegating anti-joyous self-righteousness. Simplicity is light, carefree, neat and loving—not a self-punishing ascetic trip. (The great Chinese poet Tu Fu said, "The ideas of a poet should be noble and simple.") Don't shoot a deer if you don't know how to use all the meat and preserve that which you can't eat, to tan the hide and use the leather—to use it all, with gratitude, right down to the sinew and hooves. Simplicity and mindfulness in diet is a starting point for many people.

Our own heads: It is hard to even begin to gauge how much a complication of possessions, the notions of "my and mine," stand between us and a true, clear, liberated way of seeing the world. To live lightly on the earth, to be aware and alive, to be free of egotism, to be in contact with plants and animals, starts with simple concrete acts. The inner principle is the insight that we are interdependent energy-fields of great potential wisdom and compassion—expressed in each person as a superb mind, a handsome and complex body, and the almost magical capacity of language. To these potentials and capacities, "owning things" can add nothing of authenticity. "Clad in the sky, with the earth for a pillow."

IV. TRANSFORMATION

The Condition

Position: Everyone is the result of four forces: the conditions of this known-universe (matter/energy forms and ceaseless change); the biology of his species; his individual genetic heritage and the culture he's born into. Within this web of forces there are certain spaces and loops which allow to some persons the experience of inner freedom and illumination. The gradual exploration of some of these spaces is "evolution" and, for human cultures, what "history" could increasingly be. We have it within our deepest powers not only to change our "selves" but to change our culture. If man is to remain on earth he must transform the five-millenia-long urbanizing civilization tradition into a new ecologically-sensitive harmony-oriented wild-minded scientific-spiritual culture. "Wildness is the state of complete awareness. That's why we need it."

Situation: Civilization, which has made us so successful a species, has overshot itself and now threatens us with its inertia. There also is some evidence that civilized life isn't good for the human gene pool. To achieve the Changes we must change the very foundations of our society and our minds.

Goal: Nothing short of total transformation will do much good. What we envision is a planet on which the human population lives harmoniously and dynamically by employing various sophisticated and unobtrusive technologies in a world environment which is "left natural." Specific points in this vision:

—A healthy and spare population of all races, much less in number than today.

—Cultural and individual pluralism, unified by a type of world tribal council. Division by natural and cultural boundaries rather than arbitrary political boundaries.

—A technology of communication, education, and quiet transportation, land-use being sensitive to the properties of each region. Allowing, thus, the Bison to return to much of the high plains. Careful but intensive agriculture in the great alluvial valleys; deserts left wild for those who would live there by skill. Computer technicians who run the plant part of the year and walk along with the Elk in their migrations during the rest.

—A basic cultural outlook and social organization that inhibits power and property-seeking while encouraging exploration and challenge in things like music, meditation, mathematics, mountaineering, magic, and all other ways of authentic being-in-the-world. Women totally free and equal. A new kind of family—responsible, but more festive and relaxed—is implicit.

Action

Social/political: It seems evident that there are throughout the world certain social and religious forces which have worked through history toward an ecologically and culturally enlightened state of affairs. Let these be encouraged: Gnostics, hip Marxists, Teilhard de Chardin Catholics, Druids, Taoists, Biologists, Witches, Yogins, Bhikkus, Quakers, Sufis, Tibetans, Zens, Shamans, Bushmen, American Indians, Polynesians, Anarchists, Alchemists . . . the list is long. Primitive cultures, communal and ashram movements, co-operative ventures. Since it doesn't seem practical or even desirable to think that direct bloody force will achieve much, it would be best to consider this a continuing "revolution of consciousness" which will be won not by guns but by seizing the key images, myths, archetypes, eschatologies, and ecstasies so that life won't seem worth living unless one's on the transforming energy's side. We must take over "science and technology" and release its real possibilities and powers in the service of this planet—which, after all produced us and it.

[More concretely: no transformation without our feet on the ground. Stewardship means, for most of us, find your place on the planet, dig in, and take responsibility from there—the tiresome but tangible work of school boards, county supervisors, local foresters—local politics. Even while holding in mind the largest scale of potential change. Get a sense of workable territory, learn about it, and start acting point by point. On all levels from national to local the need to move toward steady state economy—equilibrium, dynamic balance, inner-growth stressed—must be taught. Maturity/diversity/climax/creativity.]

The community: New schools, new classes, walking in the woods and cleaning up the streets. Find psychological techniques for creating an awareness of "self" which includes the social and natural environment. "Consideration of what specific language forms—symbolic systems— and social institutions constitute obstacles to ecological awareness." Without falling into a facile interpretation of McLuhan, we can hope to use the media. Let no one be ignorant of the facts of biology and related disciplines; bring up our children as part of the wildlife. Some communities can establish themselves in backwater rural areas and flourish—others maintain themselves in urban centers, and the two types work together—a two-way flow of experience, people, money and home-grown vegetables. Ultimately cities may exist only as joyous tribal gatherings and fairs, to dissolve after a few weeks. Investigating new life-styles is our work, as is the exploration of Ways to explore our inner realms—with the known dangers of crashing that go with such. Master the archaic and the primitive as models of basic nature-related cultures—as well as the most imaginative extensions of science—and build a community where these two vectors cross.

Our own heads: Is where it starts. Knowing that we are the first human beings in history to have so much of man's culture and previous ex- perience available to our study, and being free enough of the weight of traditional cultures to seek out a larger identity; the first members of a civilized society since the Neolithic to wish to look clearly into the eyes of the wild and see our self-hood, our family, there. We have these advantages to set off the obvious disadvantages of being as screwed up as we are—which gives us a fair chance to penetrate some of the riddles of ourselves and the universe, and to go beyond the idea of "man's survival" or "survival of the biosphere" and to draw our strength from the realization that at the heart of things is some kind of serene and ecstatic process which is beyond qualities and beyond birth-and-death. "No need to survive!" "In the fires that destroy the universe at the end of the kalpa, what survives?"—"The iron tree blooms in the void!"

Knowing that nothing need be done, is where we begin to move from.

38

The Broader Context of the Environmental Movement
BARRY COMMONER (1970)

The gospel of ecology was part of a broader and deeper unrest in American society. The values and attitudes that lay behind environmental problems also produced social discontent and international disorder. The gospel, in fact, must be seen as drawing part of its force from a more general cultural questioning. In the following selection Barry Commoner, the biologist whose allegation that Lake Erie had "died" from pollution caused a minor sensation in 1968, draws the connections between the environmental movement and other troubling issues of the 1960s such as war, racial equality, and poverty. Behind these comments is a recurrent theme in Commoner's writing, particularly in his book The Closing Circle *(1971), concerning the need to weigh the liabilities of scientific and technological progress against their advantages.*

Barry Commoner, "Beyond the Teach-In," *Saturday Review* LIII (1970), 50–52, 62–64. Reprinted by permission.

The sudden public concern with the environment has taken many people by surprise. After all, garbage, foul air, putrid water, and mindless noise are nothing new; the sights, smells, and sounds of pollution have become an accustomed burden of life. To be sure, the mess has worsened and spread in the last decade, but not at a rate to match the dramatic, nearly universal reaction to it that has hit the country in the past year.

Although the growing demand for action against environmental pollution is very clear, it is not so clear how the movement came about and where it is going. This is a particularly crucial time to find out. For the environmental teach-ins that are being planned on thousands of campuses this month are both the chief evidence of the origins of the movement and the main force that will determine its future.

Several environmental teach-ins have already taken place, the largest of them being that of March 11–14 at the University of Michigan, where the roster of speakers and participants was dramatic evidence that the environmental movement has become a meeting place for major and divergent elements of American society.

The kick-off rally for the teach-in, attended by 15,000 enthusiastic students, was addressed by Michigan's Governor Milliken, and a number of other municipal, state, and federal officials were present— testimony to the importance government figures attach to voter interest in the environment.

Among the teach-in speakers were a variety of scientists with a professional interest in the environment: biologists, ecologists, engineers, sociologists, urban analysts, and public health experts. This reflects one of the earliest origins of the environmental movement—the work of those of us in the scientific community who, some years ago, began to detect in our own studies evidence that pollution is not only a nuisance but a threat to the health, even the survival, of mankind.

The well-known performers Arthur Godfrey and Eddie Albert— both ardent conservationists and anti-pollutionists—were teach-in participants, lending the prestige of the world of entertainment. Ralph Nader, another teach-in participant, spoke for the consumer and dealt with the failure of our technological society to meet the real needs of those who live in it.

Industry was represented by officers of the Detroit Edison Company, Ford Motor Company, Dow Chemical Company, and others—all industries that bear a large responsibility for serious pollution problems. The interest of these companies in public concern with the environment has become a matter of direct corporate necessity.

Labor was represented by Walter Reuther, whose union—the United Automobile Workers—opposed the construction about five years ago of Detroit Edison's Fermi reactor, located about five miles outside Detroit. Through an educational program, the UAW has developed a broad interest in environmental quality, and that consideration is now included among UAW contract demands.

That the president of the Dow Chemical Company was invited to speak at Michigan reveals another important element in the environmental movement. Dow has been, of course, a prime target of the antiwar movement; its campus recruiting program has triggered many demonstrations by student activists, who cite the hold of the military-industrial complex on U.S. policy as a reason why our social system must be radically changed. And the activists had *their* representatives on the roster of teach-in speakers—one being Murray Bookchin, an environmental analyst who takes a socio-revolutionary approach to this and other social ills. Finally, the speech that closed the teach-in was given by Richard Hatcher, mayor of Gary, Indiana, a city that suffers the specially intense environmental problems of a largely black population.

The Michigan teach-in epitomized the remarkable convergence around the environmental issue of a number of earlier, separate concerns: conservation, scientists' responsibility for the social consequences of science and technology, the consumer movement, the young generation's feeling for a more humane life-style, the businessman's worries over the impact of all of these on industrial profits, the problem of the ghetto and urban decay, the antiwar movement, and student activism against the nation's social and economic system. Somehow, the issue of environmental quality touches all these separate facets of the crisis of American society.

I can report from my own experience that there is a close link between the problem of war and the problem of the environment. My concern with the environment does not stem from my professional training: I was trained as a cellular biologist, not as an ecologist. But I also learned that science is part of society and that every scientist owes it to himself, and to the society that supports him, to be concerned with the impact of science on social problems. And it was the problem of war that first introduced me to the environmental crisis. In the 1950s, when nuclear tests first showered the world with fallout, and the Atomic Energy Commission showered the nation with assurances that radiation was "harmless," I studied, along with many other scientists, the path that fallout takes in the environment from the bomb to man. And I was shocked to learn that nuclear radiation is never harmless, to the ecosystem or to man. That is when I began to appreciate the importance of the environment to man. It was the AEC that turned me into an ecologist.

There are specific links between the environmental crisis, the evils of war in general, and the war in Vietnam in particular. One link can be seen in the economics of war and of pollution. That our industrial system is heavily sustained by the military diversion of human and natural resources from human needs has been demonstrated cogently by numerous observers; the military-industrial complex was not a myth to President Eisenhower, nor is it to the stockholders in major American industries. What is less known, but can be equally well documented, is that the profitability of most American industry and agriculture has been related significantly to their avoidance of a large cost of doing business—environmental deterioration. For example, the power industry, a major cause of urban air pollution, sells electricity to its consumers for a certain amount of money, but those same consumers pay an added cost for the environmental consequences of the power they buy—in laundry bills caused by soot, and in doctor bills (and some reduction in their life expectancy) caused by sulfur dioxide and organic air pollutants from power plants. The dollar value alone of these "social costs" of air pollution that we now know of—and many remain unknown—adds about 25 per cent to the city dweller's electric bill.

Some economists assert that the economic system could readily adjust itself to this situation by undertaking the cost of preventing pollution and adding that cost to the real price of its products. Such a readjustment would affect the cost to the consumer, not only of power but of all manufactured goods (nearly every factory pollutes the air and water), of transportation (cars, trucks, and airplanes are major polluters of air), and of food (U.S. agriculture, through its use of intensive fertilization and feedlots for fattening cattle to high-priced grades, bears a major responsibility for water pollution; organic wastes from U.S. feedlots exceed those produced by the total U.S. urban population). It may be that the economic system *can* get along without the crutch provided by the diversion of environmental costs to the people, and that it *can* get along without the crutch of military production. But thus far it hasn't, and one can at least suspect that in both cases the crutch has become a support essential to the system's stability.

Another close link between the problems of war and the environment is that both represent the inability of our technology to foresee its own inherently fatal environmental flaws. Like detergents—which, much to their developers' surprise, failed to be accommodated by natural water systems and bloomed into unsightly mounds of foam on our rivers—or the unanticipated ecological backlash of DDT, the nation's war program can be viewed as a vast technological blunder. When, in the 1950s, the Pentagon and its scientific advisers decided to hang the nation's defense on nuclear weapons, they did not know what the scientific community has since told them: It will not work; no nation can survive a nuclear war. Remember that in 1956 Eisenhower campaigned for continued nuclear tests in part because "by the most sober and responsible scientific judgment they do not imperil the health of man." Eight years later, Johnson praised the nuclear test ban treaty, because it "halted the steady, menacing increase of radioactive fallout." The Pentagon also told scientists that it would not use herbicides in Vietnam if it believed that these agents would have "long-term ecological effects" on that tortured land. Now we know from scientific evidence that mangrove areas of Vietnam will not recover from herbicide attacks for at least twenty years. Indeed, because of herbicide attacks not only on forest areas but on food crops, together with the massive assaults by more conventional weapons, the war in Vietnam represents, in my opinion, the first ecological warfare conducted by the United States since the attacks on American Indians. The technological failure of biological warfare as a suitable means of defense (for there is no way to test artificial infectious agents, much less use them, without incurring serious risks to ourselves) was recently acknowledged when the government ordered the abandonment of its entire biological warfare program.

If there is little reason to regard the environmental movement as a diversion from the antiwar movement, its relation to the racial issue is less clear. Some approaches to the environmental problem seem to run counter to the interests of the blacks. This was dramatized recently at San Jose State College, where, as a symbol of environmental rebellion, a student program was climaxed by the burial of a brand new car. The event was picketed by black students who believed the $2,500 paid for the car could have been better spent in the ghetto.

The San Jose burial reflects a personalized attack on the environmental crisis, an approach that is now fairly common among some student groups. They reason that pollution in the United States is caused by the excessive consumption of goods and resources, a favorite statistic being that the U.S. contains about 6 per cent of the world's population but consumes half of the planet's total goods and resources. Since the wastes generated by this intense consumption pollute our environment, the eco-activist is advised to "consume less." In the absence of the added statistic that in the United States the per capita consumption by blacks is much lower than that of whites, such observations are not likely to arouse the enthusiasm of blacks.

Disaffiliation of blacks from the environmental movement would be particularly unfortunate, because in many ways blacks are the special victims of pollution and have much to teach whites about survival. A white suburbanite can escape from the city's dirt, smog, carbon monoxide, lead, and noise when he goes home; the ghetto dweller not only works in a polluted environment, he lives in it. And in the ghetto he confronts added environmental problems: rats and other vermin and the danger of his children's suffering lead poisoning when they eat bits of ancient, peeling paint. To middle-class Americans, survival is not a familiar issue. They have not yet learned how to face such a soul-shaking threat, as demonstrated by the continued failure to appreciate that the existence of ready-armed nuclear weapons may bring doomsday as close as tomorrow. For blacks, the issue of survival is 200 years old. If they have not yet mastered it, they at least have had a good deal of experience that may be enormously valuable to a society that now, as a whole, must face the threat of extinction. Blacks need the environmental movement, and the movement needs the blacks.

Confusion between certain aspects of the environmental movement and other social issues is also generated by the view that the former is closely connected to the population crisis. In one sense, this belief is valid, for clearly the world population cannot continue to grow at its present rapid rate (largely in underdeveloped countries) without eventually outrunning the capacity of the planetary ecosystem to produce sufficient food to sustain it. But some environmentalists hold that in an advanced country like the United States "the pollution problem is a consequence of population." This view leads to the idea that the environmental crisis in the U.S., which clearly calls for drastic action, can be solved only if we take strong action to stop the growth of the U.S. population.

A good deal of the confusion surrounding priorities can be cleared up by some facts. Nearly all of the stresses that have caused the environmental breakdown here—smog, detergents, insecticides, heavy use of fertilizers, radiation—began about 20 to 25 years ago. That period saw a sharp rise in the *per capita* production of pollutants. For example, between 1946 and 1966 total utilization of fertilizer increased about 700 per cent, electric power nearly 400 per cent, and pesticides more than 500 per cent. In that period the U.S. population increased by only 43 per cent. This means that the major factor responsible for increasing pollution in the U.S. since 1946 is not the increased number of people, but the intensified effects of ecologically faulty technology on the environment.

So the environmental movement—and the teach-ins that signal its emergence as a major political force—has become a meeting place for the major issues that trouble American society. This is its strength, and this is the importance of its future course.

Demands for *action* dominate the environmental movement, and wide-ranging programs of action are being organized. Some are direct, personal efforts to clear up the environment, such as community-wide campaigns to remove the junk from a stream bed. Some are politically oriented demonstrations, such as the delivery of a mass of beer cans to the lawn of a can manufacturer's home. Petition campaigns directed at remedial legislation abound, and legislators have been busy trying to reflect in law the new desire of their constituents for a clean environment. There are strong indications that on most campuses the current teach-ins will lead to environmental action's becoming a major, continuing feature of campus life.

Of course, there are those who regard the environmental movement as only the latest in a series of ephemeral fads for political action, doomed like its predecessors—civil rights, the antiwar movement, and student power—to rise to an enthusiastic peak and fade away before the hard, intransigent realities of political life. I disagree.

That danger does exist, for there are no easy solutions to the *fundamental* problems of the environmental crisis. Some of the superficial symptoms can be attacked directly: Creeks can be cleared of junk and beer cans can be collected. But no band of activists can return a river to an unpolluted state when the polluting agent is fertilizer draining from the surrounding farmland. And if farmers were abruptly required to halt their intensive use of fertilizer, often crucial to the solvency of their operation, they would simply go out of business.

Once we look beyond its immediate accessible symptoms, the environmental crisis confronts us with very hard, inescapable choices. If we really want to cure the evil of water pollution, we will have to make drastic revisions in present waste-treatment methods, for these overfertilize the algae in the water, which soon die, reimposing on rivers and lakes the very burden of organic waste that the treatment was supposed to remove. The natural ecological system that can accommodate organic waste is not in the water, but in the soil, and no lasting solution to the deterioration of both surface waters and the soil can be achieved until organic waste is returned to the soil. For the same reason no scheme of handling garbage that fails to meet this fundamental requirement of nature can, in the long run, succeed. And since these and similar violations of the demands of the ecosystem have become embedded in our ways of productivity, any effort to change them will encounter the massive economic, social, and political forces that sustain that system. Our major technologies—power production, transport, the metal and chemical industries, and agriculture—are a threat to the ecosystems that support them and to our very lives. Because we reckon the value of a technology by the value of its marketable products, we have neglected their cost to society—which is, potentially, extinction.

President Nixon has spoken of the need for "the total mobilization of the nation's resources" in order to pay our "debt to nature." But the resources needed to roll back pollution remain immobilized by the cost of the Vietnam war and the huge military budget, by the talent- and money-gulping space program, by the disastrous cuts in the federal budget for research support, by the reduction in funds for the cities and for education. The environmental crisis, together with all of the other evils that blight the nation—racial inequality, hunger, poverty, and war—cries out for a profound revision of our national priorities. No national problem can be solved until that is accomplished.

Confronted by the depth of this multiple crisis, it is easy to respond with a spate of studies, reports, and projections for future action. But, however essential they may be, more than plans are needed. For the grinding oppression of environmental deterioration— the blighted streets and uncollected garbage, the rats and the cock- roaches, the decaying beaches and foul rivers, the choking, polluted air—degrades the hope of our citizens for the future and their will to secure it. To unwind this spiral of despair, we must take immediate steps against the symptoms as well as the fundamental disorder. Community efforts to clean up rivers and beaches, to build parks, to insist on enforcement of anti-pollution ordinances and to improve them can give tangible meaning to the spirit of environmental revival.

All of our problems seem to have a common root. Something is wrong with the way this nation uses its human and natural resources. And I believe that it is always healthy to reexamine, to test, the basic mechanism we have created to run our affairs. Those who are 'already convinced that our social system is in need of radical revision will welcome this opportunity to discuss the prospect. Those who are convinced that the system is fundamentally sound and can be adjusted to the new stresses should welcome this opportunity to demonstrate their conviction. Here, then, is good reason to bring the social revolutionary and the industrialist onto the same platform. Both need to face the same question: How should our society be organized to resolve the crisis of survival?

It is fitting that these issues are being called to our attention by the nation's youth—in the teach-ins and in the student movement that will surely follow them. For young people, our future generations, are the real victims of the impending environmental catastrophe. They are the first generation in human history to carry strontium 90 in their bones and DDT in their fat; their bodies will record, in time, the effects on human health of the new environmental insults. It is they who face the frightful task of seeking humane knowledge in a world that has, with cunning perversity, transformed the power knowledge generates into an instrument of catastrophe. And during the coming months, I think, our young people will demonstrate that they are, in fact, equal to this task, as their environmental teach-ins and ecological actions begin to mobilize the knowledge of our schools and universities and the civic zeal of our communities for a real attack on the environmental predicament.

We have long known that ours is a technological society, a society in which the knowledge generated by science is a chief source of wealth and power But what the environmental crisis tells us is that the future of our society now depends on new, profoundly fundamental judgments of how this knowledge, and the power that it endows, is to be used. If power is to be derived from the will of the people, as it should be in our democracy, then the people need to have the new knowledge—about strontium 90, DDT, herbicides, smog, and all the other elements of the environmental crisis—that must be the source of the grave new judgments and sweeping programs this nation must undertake. Here, then, is an urgent task that must follow the teach-ins. Let us take our knowledge about the environmental plight to the people; let us help them learn what they need to know to decide the future course of our society.

The obligation that our technological society forces upon all of us is to discover how humanity can survive the new power engendered by science. Every major advance in man's technological competence has enforced new obligations on human society. The present age is no exception to this rule of history. We already know the enormous benefits technology can bestow, and we have begun to perceive its frightful threats.

The environmental peril now upon us is a grim challenge. It also represents a great opportunity. From it we may yet learn that the proper use of science is not to conquer nature but to live in it. We may yet learn that to save ourselves we must save the world, which is our habitat. We may yet discover how to devote the wisdom of science and the power of technology to the welfare and survival of man.

39

Environmental Priorities for the 1970s
RICHARD M. NIXON AND
THE COUNCIL ON ENVIRONMENTAL QUALITY (1970)

The Council on Environmental Quality was among the most important institutional consequences of the gospel of ecology. Established in the Executive Office of the President by the National Environmental Policy Act (January 1, 1970), the three-person council and modest supporting staff had an impossible task. The act required them to report immediately on the condition of the American environment and the effects upon it of federal, state,

Council on Environmental Quality, *Environmental Quality: The First Annual Report of the Council on Environmental Quality* (Washington, D.C., 1970), v–vii, xi–xv, 5–18.

local, corporate, and individual actions. Undaunted, the council produced by August of its first year a book-length overview of environmental issues facing the nation. Although unauthored, it is safe to say that the opening chapter, reproduced here, was a joint effort of the council members, Russell E. Train, Robert Cahn, and Gordon J. MacDonald. These same men and their staff probably had a hand in drafting the message President Richard M. Nixon delivered to Congress on the occasion of transmitting the council's report in August 1970. President Nixon's message opened the report and appears first below. Selections from the Council's introduction follow. Together the documents provide a comprehensive overview of the national assessment of man-environment relations as the 1970s began.

This first report to the Congress on the state of the Nation's environment is an historic milestone. It represents the first time in the history of nations that a people has paused, consciously and systematically, to take comprehensive stock of the quality of its surroundings.

It comes not a moment too soon. The recent upsurge of public concern over environmental questions reflects a belated recognition that man has been too cavalier in his relations with nature. Unless we arrest the depredations that have been inflicted so carelessly on our natural systems—which exist in an intricate set of balances—we face the prospect of ecological disaster.

The hopeful side is that such a prospect *can* be avoided. Although recognition of the danger has come late, it has come forcefully. There still are large gaps in our environmental knowledge, but a great deal of what needs to be done can be identified. Much of this has already been begun, and much more can be started quickly if we act now.

The accompanying report by the Council on Environmental Quality seeks to describe the conditions of our environment, and to identify major trends, problems, actions under way and opportunities for the future. This first report by the Council is necessarily incomplete in some respects, especially in the identification of trends. The National Environmental Policy Act, which created the Council, became law only at the beginning of this year. Existing systems for measuring and monitoring environmental conditions and trends, and for developing indicators of environmental quality, are still inadequate. There also is a great deal yet to be learned about the significance of these facts for the human condition.

However, the report will, I think, be of great value to the Congress (and also to the Executive Branch) by assembling in one comprehensive document a wealth of facts, analyses and recommendations concerning a wide range of our most pressing environmental challenges. It should also serve a major educational purpose, by clarifying for a broad public what those challenges are and where the principal dangers and opportunities lie.

Substantively as well as historically, this first report is an important document. No one can read it and remain complacent about the environmental threats we confront, or about the need both to do more and to learn more about those threats.

"Environment" is not an abstract concern, or simply a matter of esthetics, or of personal taste—although it can and should involve these as well. Man is shaped to a great extent by his surroundings. Our physical nature, our mental health, our culture and institutions, our opportunities for challenge and fulfillment, our very survival— all of these are directly related to and affected by the environment in which we live. They depend upon the continued healthy functioning of the natural systems of the Earth.

Environmental deterioration is not a new phenomenon. But both the rate of deterioration and its critical impact have risen sharply in the years since the Second World War. Rapid population increases here and abroad, urbanization, the technology explosion and the patterns of economic growth have all contributed to our environmental crisis. While growth has brought extraordinary benefits, it has not been accompanied by sufficiently foresighted efforts to guide its development.

At the same time, in many localities determined action has brought positive improvements in the quality of air or water—demonstrating that, if we have the will and make the effort, we can meet environmental goals. We also have made important beginnings in developing the institutions and processes upon which any fundamental, long-range environmental improvement must be based.

The basic causes of our environmental troubles are complex and deeply imbedded. They include: our past tendency to emphasize quantitative growth at the expense of qualitative growth; the failure of our economy to provide full accounting for the social costs of environmental pollution; the failure to take environmental factors into account as a normal and necessary part of our planning and decision-making; the inadequacy of our institutions for dealing with problems that cut across traditional political boundaries; our dependence on conveniences, without regard for their impact on the environment; and more fundamentally, our failure to perceive the environment as a totality and to understand and to recognize the fundamental interdependence of all its parts, including man himself.

It should be obvious that we cannot correct such deep-rooted causes overnight. Nor can we simply legislate them away. We need new knowledge, new perceptions, new attitudes—and these must extend to all levels of government and throughout the private sector as well: to industry; to the professions; to each individual citizen in his job and in his home. We must seek nothing less than a basic reform in the way our society looks at problems and makes decisions.

Our educational system has a key role to play in bringing about this reform. We must train professional environmental managers to deal with pollution, land planning, and all the other technical requirements of a high quality environment. It is also vital that our entire society develop a new understanding and a new awareness of man's relation to his environment—what might be called "environmental literacy." This will require the development and teaching of environmental concepts at every point in the educational process.

While education may provide ultimate answers to long-range environmental problems, however, we cannot afford to defer reforms which are needed now. We have already begun to provide the institutional framework for effective environmental improvement. . . .

Lately, our attention as a people has repeatedly and insistently been seized by urgent concerns and immediate crises: by the sudden blanketing of cities or even whole regions with dense clouds of smog, for example, or the discovery of mercury pollution in rivers. But as we take the longer view, we find another challenge looming large: the mounting pressures of population. Both the size and the distribution of our population have critical relevance to the quality of our environment and thus to the quality of our lives.

Population growth poses an urgent problem of global dimensions. If the United States is to have an effective voice in world population policies, it must demonstrate willingness to face its own population problems at home.

The particular impact of any given level of population growth depends in large measure on patterns of land use. Three quarters of our people now live in urban areas, and if present trends continue most of them in the future will live in a few mammoth urban concentrations. These concentrations put enormous pressure on transportation, sanitation and other public services. They sometimes create demands that exceed the resource capacity of the region, as in the case of water supply. They can aggravate pollution, overcrowd recreation facilities, limit open space, and make the restorative world of nature ever more remote from everyday life. Yet we would be blind not to recognize that for the most part the movement of people to the cities has been the result neither of perversity nor of happenstance, but rather of natural human aspirations for the better jobs, schools, medical services, cultural opportunities and excitement that have traditionally been associated with urban life.

If the aspirations which have drawn Americans to the city in the first instance and subsequently from the city core to the suburbs are often proving illusory, the solution does not lie in seeking escape from urban life. Our challenge is to find ways to promote the amenities of life in the midst of urban development: in short, to make urban life fulfilling rather than frustrating. Along with the essentials of jobs and housing, we must also provide open spaces and outdoor recreation opportunities, maintain acceptable levels of air and water quality, reduce noise and litter, and develop cityscapes that delight the eye and uplift the spirit.

By the same token, it is essential that we also make rural life itself more attractive, thus encouraging orderly growth in rural areas. The creation of greater economic, social, cultural, and recreational opportunities in rural parts of the country will lead to the strengthening of small cities and towns, contributing to the establishment of new growth centers in the nation's heartland region.

Throughout the nation there is a critical need for more effective land use planning, and for better controls over use of the land and the living systems that depend on it. Throughout our history, our greatest resource has been our land—forests and plains, mountains and marshlands, rivers and lakes. Our land has sustained us. It has given us a love of freedom, a sense of security, and courage to test the unknown.

We have treated our land as if it were a limitless resource. Traditionally, Americans have felt that what they do with their own land is their own business. This attitude has been a natural outgrowth of the pioneer spirit. Today, we are coming to realize that our land is finite, while our population is growing. The uses to which our generation puts the land can either expand or severely limit the choices our children will have. The time has come when we must accept the idea that none of us has a right to abuse the land, and that on the contrary society as a whole has a legitimate interest in proper land use. There is a national interest in effective land use planning all across the nation.

I believe that the problems of urbanization which I have described, of resource management, and of land and water use generally can only be met by comprehensive approaches which take into account the widest range of social, economic, and ecological concerns. I believe we must work toward development of a National Land Use Policy to be carried out by an effective partnership of Federal, State and local governments together, and, where appropriate, with new regional institutional arrangements.

The prospect of increasing population density adds urgency to the need for greater emphasis on recycling of "waste" products. More people means greater consumption—and thus more rapid depletion— of scarce natural resources; greater consumption means more "waste" to dispose of—whether in the form of solid waste, or of the pollutants that foul our air and water.

Yet much of this is unnecessary. Essentially, waste is a human invention: Natural systems are generally "closed" systems. Energy is transformed into vegetation, vegetation into animal life, and the latter returns to the air and soil to be recycled once again. Man, on the other hand, has developed "open" systems—ending all too often in an open sewer or an open dump.

We can no longer afford the indiscriminate waste of our natural resources; neither should we accept as inevitable the mounting costs of waste removal. We must move increasingly toward closed systems that recycle what now are considered wastes back into useful and productive purposes. This poses a major challenge—and a major opportunity—for private industry. The Council on Environmental Quality is working to foster development of such systems. Establishment of the proposed Environmental Protection Agency would greatly increase our ability to address this need systematically and creatively.

As our government has moved ahead to improve our environmental management, it has been greatly heartening to me to see the extent and effectiveness of citizen concern and activity, and especially the commitment of young people to the task. The job of building a better environment is not one for government alone. It must engage the enthusiasm and commitment of our entire society. Citizen organizations have been in the forefront of action to support strengthened environmental programs. The Citizens Advisory Committee on Environmental Quality, under the chairmanship of Laurance S. Rockefeller, has provided an important link between the Federal Government's effort and this broad-ranging citizen activity.

Similarly, the active participation of the business community is essential. The government's regulation and enforcement activities will continue to be strengthened. Performance standards must be upgraded as rapidly as feasible. But regulation cannot do the whole job. Forward-looking initiatives by business itself are also vital—in research, in the development of new products and processes, in continuing and increased investment in pollution abatement equipment.

On the international front, the level of environmental concern and action has been rapidly rising. Many of our most pressing environmental problems know no political boundaries. Environmental monitoring and pollution of the seas are examples of major needs that require international cooperation, and that also provide an opportunity for the world's nations to work together for their common benefit.

In dealing with the environment we must learn not how to master nature but how to master ourselves, our institutions, and our technology. We must achieve a new awareness of our dependence on our surroundings and on the natural systems which support all life, but awareness must be coupled with a full realization of our enormous capability to alter these surroundings. Nowhere is this capability greater than in the United States, and this country must lead the way in showing that our human and technological resources can be devoted to a better life and an improved environment for ourselves and our inheritors on this planet.

Our environmental problems are very serious, indeed urgent, but they do not justify either panic or hysteria. The problems are highly complex, and their resolution will require rational, systematic approaches, hard work and patience. There must be a *national* commitment and a *rational* commitment.

The accompanying report by the Council describes the principal problems we face now and can expect to face in the future, and it provides us with perceptive guidelines for meeting them. These deserve the most careful consideration. They point the directions in which we must move as rapidly as circumstances permit.

The newly aroused concern with our natural environment embraces old and young alike, in all walks of life. For the young, it has a special urgency. They know that it involves not only our own lives now but the future of mankind. For their parents, it has a special poignancy—because ours is the first generation to feel the pangs of concern for the environmental legacy we leave to our children.

At the heart of this concern for the environment lies our concern for the human condition: for the welfare of man himself, now and in the future. As we look ahead to the end of this new decade of heightened environmental awareness, therefore, we should set ourselves a higher goal than merely remedying the damage wrought in decades past. We should strive for an environment that not only sustains life but enriches life, harmonizing the works of man and nature for the greater good of all.

Historians may one day call 1970 the year of the environment. They may not be able to say that 1970 actually marked a significant change for the better in the quality of life; in the polluting and the fouling of the land, the water, and the air; or in health, working conditions, and recreational opportunity. Indeed, they are almost certain to see evidence of worsening environmental conditions in many parts of the country.

Yet 1970 marks the beginning of a new emphasis on the environment—a turning point, a year when the quality of life has become more than a phrase; environment and pollution have become everyday words; and ecology has become almost a religion to some of the young. Environmental problems, standing for many years on the threshold of national prominence, are now at the center of nationwide concern. Action to improve the environment has been launched by government at all levels. And private groups, industry, and individuals have joined the attack.

No one can say for sure just how or why the environment burst into national prominence in 1970. Certainly national concern had been mounting for a long time, and the tempo has increased greatly in the last decade.

Early environmentalists—Henry David Thoreau, George Perkins Marsh, John Muir, Gifford Pinchot, Theodore Roosevelt, Aldo Leopold—and a legion of dedicated citizens contributed to the rise in awareness. In its early days, the conservation movement aimed primarily at stemming the exploitation of natural resources and preserving wildlife and important natural areas. By the 1950's, Federal air and water pollution laws had been enacted, and the pace of environmental legislation quickened dramatically in the decade of the 1960's. Now the conservation movement has broadened to embrace concern for the totality of man's environment, focusing on pollution, population, ecology, and the urban environment.

The public has begun to realize the interrelationship of all living things—including man—with the environment. The Santa Barbara oil spill in early 1969 showed an entire nation how one accident could temporarily blight a large area. Since then, each environmental issue— the jetport project near Everglades National Park, the proposed pipeline across the Alaskan wilderness, the worsening blight of Lake Erie, the polluted beaches off New York and other cities, smog in mile-high Denver, lead in gasoline, phosphates in detergents, and DDT—flashed the sign to Americans that the problems are everywhere and affect everyone. Millions of citizens have come to realize that the interdependent web of life—man, animals, plants, earth, air, water, and sunlight—touches everyone.

A deteriorating environment has awakened a lively curiosity in Americans about exactly what is meant by an ecosystem, a biome, or the biosphere. Citizens who are now aware of environmental problems want to know the full extent of the environmental crisis and the nature of the factors that have contributed to it. They are anxious to learn what can be done to correct the mistakes that have led to the current condition of the environment. This report attempts to answer some of these questions.

Ecology is the science of the intricate web of relationships between living organisms and their living and nonliving surroundings. These interdependent living and nonliving parts make up *ecosystems*. Forests, lakes, and estuaries are examples. Larger ecosystems or combinations of ecosystems, which occur in similar climates and share a similar character and arrangement of vegetation, are *biomes*. The Arctic tundra, prairie grasslands, and the desert are examples. The earth, its surrounding envelope of life-giving water and air, and all its living things comprise the *biosphere*. Finally, man's total *environmental system* includes not only the biosphere but also his interactions with his natural and manmade surroundings.

Changes in ecosystems occur continuously. Myriad interactions take place at every moment of the day as plants and animals respond to variations in their surroundings and to each other. Evolution has produced for each species, including man, a genetic composition that limits how far that species can go in adjusting to sudden changes in its surroundings. But within these limits the several thousand species in an ecosystem, or for that matter, the millions in the biosphere, continuously adjust to outside stimuli. Since interactions are so numerous, they form long chains of reactions. Thus small changes in one part of an ecosystem are likely to be felt and compensated for eventually throughout the system.

Dramatic examples of change can be seen where man has altered the course of nature. It is vividly evident in his well-intentioned but poorly thought out tampering with river and lake ecosystems. The Aswan Dam was primarily built to generate electric power. It produced power, but it also reduced the fish population in the Mediterranean, increased the numbers of disease-bearing aquatic snails, and markedly lowered the fertility of the Nile Valley.

In the United States, the St. Lawrence Seaway has contributed significantly to the economic growth of the Great Lakes region. Yet it has done so at a high and largely unforeseen cost to the environment. The completion of the Welland Canal let the predatory sea lamprey into the Great Lakes. Trout, which had been the backbone of the lakes' fishing industry, suffered greatly from the lamprey invasion. By the mid-1950's the trout and some other large, commercial predatory fish were nearly extinct. And with their near extinction, smaller fish, especially the alewife, normally kept under control by these predators, proliferated. The aggressive alewife dominated the food supply and greatly reduced the numbers of small remaining native fish, such as the lake herring. The alewife became so numerous, in fact, that on occasion great numbers died and the dead fish along the shore caused a major public nuisance.

Man attempted to restore the ecological balance by instituting sea lamprey control in the 1950's and 1960's and by stocking the lakes with coho salmon beginning in 1965—to replace the lost native predatory fish. Feeding on the abundant alewife, the salmon multiplied rapidly and by 1969 had become important both as a commercial and sport resource. Some of the salmon, however, were contaminated by excessive concentrations of DDT and were taken off the commercial market.

The lesson is not that such activities as the St. Lawrence Seaway must be halted, but that the consequences of construction must be carefully studied in advance of construction. Planners and managers must begin to appreciate the enormous interrelated complexity of environmental systems, weigh the tradeoffs of potential environmental harm against the benefits of construction, look at alternatives, and incorporate environmental safeguards into the basic design of new developments.

The stability of a particular ecosystem depends on its diversity.

The more interdependencies in an ecosystem, the greater the chances that it will be able to compensate for changes imposed upon it. A complex tropical forest with a rich mosaic of interdependencies possesses much more stability than the limited plant and animal life found on the Arctic tundra, where instability triggers frequent, violent fluctuations in some animal populations, such as lemmings and foxes. The least stable systems are the single crops—called monocultures—created by man. A cornfield or lawn has little natural stability. If they are not constantly and carefully cultivated, they will not remain cornfields or lawns but will soon be overgrown with a wide variety of hardier plants constituting a more stable ecosystem.

The chemical elements that make up living systems also depend on complex, diverse sources to prevent cyclic shortages or oversupply. The oxygen cycle, which is crucial to survival, depends upon a vast variety of green plants, notably plankton in the ocean. Similar diversity is essential for the continued functioning of the cycle by which atmospheric nitrogen is made available to allow life to exist. This cycle depends on a wide variety of organisms, including soil bacteria and fungi, which are often destroyed by persistent pesticides in the soil.

Although pollution may be the most prominent and immediately pressing environmental concern, it is only one facet of the many-sided environmental problem. It is a highly visible, sometimes dangerous sign of environmental deterioration. Pollution occurs when materials accumulate where they are not wanted. Overburdened natural processes cannot quickly adjust to the heavy load of materials which man, or sometimes nature, adds to them. Pollution threatens natural systems, human health, and esthetic sensibilities; it often represents valuable resources out of place. DDT, for instance, is a valuable weapon in combating malaria. But DDT, when out of place—for example in lakes and streams—concentrates in fish, other wildlife, and the smaller living things on which they depend.

Historically, man has assumed that the land, water, and air around him would absorb his waste products. The ocean, the atmosphere, and even the earth were viewed as receptacles of infinite capacity. It is clear now that man may be exceeding nature's capacity to assimilate his wastes.

Most pollutants eventually decompose and diffuse throughout the environment. When organic substances are discarded, they are attacked by bacteria and decompose through oxidation. They simply rot. However, some synthetic products of our advanced technology resist natural decomposition. Plastics, some cans and bottles, and various persistent pesticides fall into this category. Many of these materials are toxic, posing a serious health danger. . . .

Radioactive fallout from the air also concentrates through food chains. Arctic lichens do not take in food through their roots but instead absorb mineral nutrition from dust in the air. Radioactive fallout tends therefore to collect in the lichens and is further concentrated by grazing caribou, which eat huge quantities of lichen. Caribou meat is a major part of the Eskimo's diet. Although reconcentration of radioactive fallout at low levels has not been proved damaging to health, the effects of long-term, low-level exposure to radioactive pollutants are still not well known.

Water pollution is a problem throughout the country, but is most acute in densely settled or industrial sections. Organic wastes from municipalities and industries enter rivers, where they are attacked and broken down by organisms in the water. But in the process, oxygen in the river is used up. Nutrients from cities, industries, and farms nourish algae, which also use up oxygen when they die and decompose. And when oxygen is taken from the water, the river "dies." The oxygen is gone, the game fish disappear, plant growth rots, and the stench of decay reaches for miles.

Air pollution is now a problem in all parts of the United States and in all industrialized nations. It has been well known for some time to Los Angeles residents and visitors who have long felt the effect of highly visible and irritating smog from automobile exhaust. Now Los Angeles's local problem is becoming a regional problem, because noxious air pollution generated in the Los Angeles Basin has spread beyond the metropolitan area. This same problem, which seemed unique to Los Angeles in the 1950's is today common to major cities in the United States and abroad. Smog is but one of the many types of air pollution that plague the United States, especially its cities.

Urban land misuse is one of today's most severe environmental problems. The character of our urban areas changes rapidly. Old buildings and neighborhoods are razed and replaced by structures designed with little or no eye for their fitness to the community's needs. A jumble of suburban developments sprawls over the landscape. Furthermore, lives and property are endangered when real estate developments are built on flood plains or carved out along unstable slopes.

Unlimited access to wilderness areas may transform such areas into simply another extension of our urban, industrialized civilization.

The unending summer flow of automobiles into Yosemite National Park has changed one of nature's great wilderness areas into a crowded gathering place of lessened value to its visitors. The worldwide boom in tourism, teamed with rapid and cheap transportation, threatens the very values upon which tourist attraction is based.

The proposed jetport west of Miami and north of the Everglades National Park raised a dramatic land use problem. The jetport, together with associated transportation corridors, imperiled a unique ecological preserve. Planners for the jetport had considered density of population, regional transportation needs, and a host of other related variables. But they gave slight consideration to the wildlife and recreational resources of the Everglades. The jetport could have spawned a booming residential, commercial, and industrial complex which would have diminished water quality and without question drastically altered the natural water cycle of Southern Florida. This in turn would have endangered all aquatic species and wildlife within the park and beyond.

Natural resource depletion is a particular environmental concern to a highly technological society which depends upon resources for energy, building materials, and recreation. And the methods of exploiting resources often create problems that are greater than the value of the resources themselves.

A classic case was the Federal Government's decision to permit oil drilling in California's Santa Barbara Channel. There, primary value was placed on development of the oil resources. The commercial, recreational, esthetic, and ecological values, which also are important to the residents of Santa Barbara and to the Nation, were largely ignored. The President recently proposed to the Congress that the Federal Government cancel the 20 Federal leases seaward from the State sanctuary extending 16 miles along the Santa Barbara Channel. This is where the blowout erupted in January 1969, spreading a coat of oil across hundreds of square miles including the sanctuary. This action illustrates a commitment to use offshore lands in a balanced and responsible way.

Environmental problems seldom stem from simple causes. Rather they usually rise out of the interplay of many contributing circumstances.

Many individuals cite selfish profit seekers for environmental degradation, rather than laying much of the blame—where it belongs—to misplaced incentives in the economic system. Progress in environmental problems is impossible without a clearer understanding of how the economic system works in the environment and what alternatives are available to take away the many roadblocks to environmental quality.

Our price system fails to take into account the environmental damage that the polluter inflicts on others. Economists call these damages—which are very real—"external social costs." They reflect the ability of one entity, e.g., a company, to use water or air as a free resource for waste disposal, while others pay the cost in contaminated air or water. If there were a way to make the price structure shoulder these external costs—taxing the firm for the amount of discharge, for instance—then the price for the goods and services produced would reflect these costs. Failing this, goods whose production spawns pollution are greatly underpriced because the purchaser does not pay for pollution abatement that would prevent environmental damage. Not only does this failure encourage pollution but it warps the price structure. A price structure that took environmental degradation into account would cause a shift in prices, hence a shift in consumer preferences and, to some extent, would discourage buying pollution-producing products.

Another type of misplaced incentive lies imbedded in the tax structure. The property tax, for example, encourages architectural design that leans more to rapid amortization than to quality. It may also encourage poor land use because of the need for communities to favor industrial development and discourage property uses, such as high-density housing, which cost more in public services than they produce in property taxes. Other taxes encourage land speculation and the leap-frog development that has become the trademark of the urban-rural fringe.

Americans have placed a high priority on convenience and consumer goods. In recent times they have learned to value the convenience and comfort of modern housing, transportation, communication, and recreation above clean earth, sky, and water. A majority, like a prodigal son, have been willing to consume vast amounts of resources and energy, failing to understand how their way of life may choke off open space, forests, clean air, and clear water. It is only recently that the public has become conscious of some of the conflicts between convenience and a deteriorating environment.

In the early days of westward expansion, a period in which many national values were shaped, choices did not seem necessary. The forests, minerals, rivers, lakes, fish, and wildlife of the continent seemed inexhaustible. Today choices based on values must be made at every turn. Values can be gauged to some degree by the costs that the Nation is collectively willing to incur to protect them. Some of the costs of environmental improvements can be paid with local, State, and Federal tax money. But paying taxes and falling back on government programs is not enough. People may ultimately have to forgo some conveniences and pay higher prices for some goods and services.

Americans are just beginning to measure the magnitude of the impact of population and its distribution on their environment. The concept that population pressures are a threat to the Nation's well-being and to its environment is difficult to grasp in a country which, during its formative decades, had an ever receding western frontier. That frontier ended at the Pacific many years ago. And it is at the western end of the frontier that some of the most serious problems of population growth emerge most clearly.

California continues to lure large numbers of Americans from all over the country, in large part because of its climate and its beauty. But as the people come, the pressures of population mount. Smog, sprawl, erosion, loss of beaches, the scarring of beautiful areas, and the congestion of endless miles of freeways have caused thoughtful Californians to consider stemming the continued uncontrolled development of their State. When the Governor's Conference on California's Changing Environment met last fall, it agreed that there was now a need "to deemphasize growth as a social goal and, rather, to encourage development within an ideal and quality environment."

The magnitude of the press of population, although significant, must be put in perspective. This is a vast country, and its potential for assimilating population is impressive, although there is disagreement over what level of population would be optimum. Some authorities believe that the optimum level has already been passed, others that it has not yet been reached. More troublesome, population control strikes at deeply held religious values and at the preference of some Americans for large families.

Population density outside metropolitan areas is not high. There is a desire—indeed an almost inevitable compulsion—to concentrate population in urban areas—primarily in the coastal and Great Lakes regions. If the trend continues, 70 to 80 percent of all Americans will be concentrated in five large urban complexes by the year 2000. The pressures that cause environmental problems that the Nation now confronts—water and air pollution and inefficient land use—will only increase.

Population growth threatens the Nation's store of natural resources. Currently the United States, with about 6 percent of the world's population, uses more than 40 percent of the world's scarce or nonreplaceable resources and a like ratio of its energy output. Assuming a fixed or nearly fixed resource base, continued population growth embodies profound implications for the United States and for the world.

The major environmental problems of today began with the Industrial Revolution. Belching smoke from factory stacks and the dumping of raw industrial wastes into rivers became the readily identified, but generally ignored hallmarks of "progress" and production. They are no longer ignored, but the extraordinary growth of the American economy continues to outpace the efforts to deal with its unwanted by-products.

The growth of the economy has been marked not just by greater production but also by an accelerating pace of technological innovation. This innovation, although it has provided new solutions to environmental problems, has also created a vast range of new problems. New chemicals, new uses for metals, new means of transportation, novel consumer goods, new medical techniques, and new industrial processes all represent potential hazards to man and his surroundings. The pace of technological innovation has exceeded our scientific and regulatory ability to control its injurious side effects. The environmental problems of the future will increasingly spring from the wonders of 20th-century technology. In the future, technology assessment must be used to understand the direct and secondary impacts of technological innovation.

The extraordinary, growing mobility of the American people constitutes another profound threat to the environment—in at least three major ways. The physical movement of people crowds in on metropolitan centers and into recreation areas, parks, and wild areas. Mobility permits people to live long distances from their places of employment, stimulating ever greater urban and suburban sprawl. The machines of this mobility—particularly automobiles and aircraft—themselves generate noise, air pollution, highways, and airports—all in their way affecting the environment.

The automobile freed Americans from the central city and launched the flight to the suburbs. As a consequence, thousands of acres of undeveloped land fall prey each year to the bulldozer. More single-family, detached homes shoulder out the open spaces. Many of these developments are drab in design and wasteful of land. They denude the metropolitan area of trees and thus affect climate; they cause erosion, muddy rivers, and increase the cost of public services. Most government agencies charged with solving environmental problems were not originally designed to deal with the severe tasks they now face. And their focus is often too narrow to cope with the broad environmental problems that cut across many jurisdictions. Agencies dealing with water pollution, for example, typically do not have jurisdiction over the geographic problem area—the watersheds. Control is split instead among sewerage districts, municipalities, and a multitude of other local institutions. To attack water pollution effectively may require establishing new river basin authorities or statewide basin agencies with the power to construct, operate, and assess for treatment facilities.

Public decisions, like private decisions, suffer from the inadequate balancing of short-run economic choices against long-term environmental protection. There is a nearly irresistible pressure on local governments to develop land in order to increase jobs and extend the tax base—even if the land is valuable open space or an irreplaceable marsh. The problem is amplified by the proliferation of agencies, all competing narrowly, without consideration of broader and often common goals. The development that generates economic benefits in a town upstream may create pollution and loss of recreation in a town downstream.

Sometimes people persist in actions which cause environmental damage because they do not know that they are causing it. Construction of dams, extensive paving of land surfaces, and filling of estuaries for industrial development have in many cases been carried out with incomplete or wrong information about the extent of the impact on the environment. Furthermore, change in the environment has often been slow and exceedingly difficult to detect, even though piecemeal changes may eventually cause irreversible harm. Widespread use of certain types of pesticides, mercury pollution, and the use of dangerous substances such as asbestos occurred without advance recognition of their potential for harm.

The impact of environmental deterioration on health is subtle, often becoming apparent only after the lapse of many years. The speed of change in a rapidly altering technological society and the complex causes of many environmental health problems produce major uncertainty about what environmental changes do to human well-being.

Nevertheless, it is clear that today's environment has a large and adverse impact on the physical and emotional health of an increasing number of Americans.

Air pollution has been studied closely over the past 10 years, and its tie to emphysema and chronic bronchitis is becoming more evident. These two diseases are major causes of chronic disability, lost workdays, and mortality in industrial nations. Estimates of deaths attributable to bronchitis and emphysema are beset with doubts about cause; nevertheless, physicians have traced 18,000 more deaths in the United States to these two causes in 1966 than 10 years earlier—an increase of two and one-half times. The increase of sulfur oxides, photochemical oxidants, and carbon monoxide in the air is related to hospital admission rates and length of stay for respiratory and circulatory cases.

Whether the accumulation of radioactive fallout in body tissues will eventually produce casualties cannot be predicted now, but close surveillance is needed. Nor has a direct correlation between factors in the urban environment and major malignancies of the digestive, respiratory, and urinary tracts been established. But the frequency of these diseases is much higher in cities than in nonurban environments.

The impact of the destruction of the environment on man's perceptions and aspirations cannot be measured. Yet today citizens are seeking better environments, not only to escape pollution and deterioration but to find their place in the larger community of life. It is clear that few prefer crowding, noise, fumes, and foul water to esthetically pleasing surroundings. Objections today to offensive sights, odors, and sounds are more widespread than ever. And these mounting objections are an important indicator of what Americans are unwilling to let happen to the world about them.

The economic costs of pollution are massive—billions of dollars annually. Paint deteriorates faster, cleaning bills are higher, and air filtering systems become necessary. Direct costs to city dwellers can be measured in additional household maintenance, cleaning, and medical bills. Air pollution causes the housewife to do her laundry more often. The farmer's crop yield is reduced or destroyed. Water pollution prevents swimming, boating. fishing, and other recreational and commercial activities highly valued in today's world.

Vast natural systems may be severely damaged by the improvident intervention of man. The great Dust Bowl of the 1930's was born in the overuse of land resources. Many estuarine areas have been altered and their ecology permanently changed. On a global scale, air pollution could trigger large-scale climatic changes. Man may also be changing the forces in the atmosphere through deforestation, urban construction, and the spilling of oil on ocean waters.

In the short run, much can be done to reverse the deadly downward spiral in environmental quality. Citizens, industries, and all levels of government have already begun to act in ways which will improve environmental quality. The President's February 10 Message on the Environment spelled out some specific steps which can be taken now.

It is clear, however, that long-range environmental improvement must take into account the complex interactions of environmental processes. In the future, the effects of man's actions on complete ecosystems must be considered if environmental problems are to be solved.

Efforts to solve the problems in the past have merely tried—not very successfully—to hold the line against pollution and exploitation. Each environmental problem was treated in an ad hoc fashion, while the strong, lasting interactions between various parts of the problem were neglected. Even today most environmental problems are dealt with temporarily, incompletely, and often only after they have become critical.

The isolated response is symptomatic of the environmental crisis. Americans in the past have not adequately used existing institutions to organize knowledge about the environment and to translate it into policy and action. The environment cuts across established institutions and disciplines. Men are beginning to recognize this and to contemplate new institutions. And that is a hopeful sign.

40

Loving Wilderness to Death
THE CONSERVATION FOUNDATION (1972)

In 1972 the United States celebrated the hundredth anniversary of the world's first national park: Yellowstone. Part of the commemoration of this American contribution to world civilization involved a look into the future. What would, and more importantly, what should national parks be like in

The Conservation Foundation, *National Parks for the Future: An appraisal of the National Parks as they begin their second century in a changing America* (Washington, D.C., 1972), 31–39. Reprinted by permission.

2072? To shed light on the question, the National Park Service commissioned The Conservation Foundation to prepare an analysis of park policy and submit recommendations for changes. The Foundation, in turn, invited individuals representative of both the scholarly community and the general public to draft text for the centennial report. One of the issues that arose repeatedly in the ensuing discussions was the possibility of destroying the parks by too much recreational use; of loving them to death. The irony of the situation was inescapable: for most of the first century of the parks' existence, their supporters believed that preservation depended on getting Americans to appreciate parks. Now the success of this endeavor constitutes the gravest challenge to the maintenance of park quality. The section of the centennial report that follows analyzes this problem and suggests solutions. But Department of the Interior officials, preferring a parks-are-for-people approach, criticized the report as exclusive and elitist.

A group of explorers a century ago, sitting around their campfire at Madison Junction in northwestern Wyoming, could hardly have foreseen the vigor of the idea that sprang from their conversation about the Yellowstone country. They could not have anticipated that their idea would flower into a new dimension of the American dream and would capture the imagination of men around the world.

The national park concept, conceived at Madison Junction and given birth by the President of the United States 100 years ago, has been nurtured in the very essence of the democratic principle. This concept, first enunciated for Yellowstone, says that some areas of remarkable value are too special, too precious ever to be reduced to private ownership and exploitation, but that those areas should instead be retained for the enjoyment and inspiration of all the people.

Yet, over the decades, the concept has come under assault at Yellowstone and elsewhere because of the democratic principle—if the asset is publicly owned, it should be accessible and useable by all the people. Certainly, those who first held the Yellowstone Park vision could not have anticipated the practical difficulties of park use a hundred years later—difficulties brought on by an exploding population, new forms of transportation, and new wealth and leisure made available through the hard labor of a people dedicated to conquering and subverting the wilderness.

With the end of World War II, a booming economy, greater mobility, and longer vacations combined to power a move to the outdoors such as America had never experienced before. Restraints heretofore imposed by geography, time, distance and cost were, for the most part, swept aside and with them the original simple principle from which the national park ideal was born. The national park visit became a casual thing—of little more significance to many than a visit to any other place that provides a scenic backdrop for everyone's outdoor thing. Appreciated? Of course, in some way—one of a dozen vacation stops, one more decal on the window, one more place for later comparison as to efficiency of trailer hook-up, quality of cafeteria, variety of souvenirs and congestion of highway and campground. The national park was fast becoming a playground, a bland experience little different from what the visitor can and does find at a thousand other areas.

The visitor has almost lost something else of enormous importance, a crucial ingredient of the democratic ideal—the opportunity for choice. He is in danger of losing the opportunity to choose the remarkable experience which the national parks were established to save for him, because it is in danger of disappearing.

But the opportunity has not been wholly lost. There remains a spark of the original concept. More and more people are leaving the gadgetry and comforts of technology behind and striking out for the wilderness to find solitude and adventure with what they can carry on their backs. There in the backcountry of our natural area parks the wilderness persists, little changed in a century. There man can find and be a partner once again in the elementary processes of an undisturbed ecosystem and recapture the awe, the spiritual exaltation, the acute awareness of the very roots of life from which he sprang. The basic choice remains with us—whether we circle back to the original concept, or permit further spin-off into stultifying mediocrity. The choice is ours, whether the parks shall remain the "crown jewels" of our outdoor heritage to be cherished, protected, preserved and worthy of our rigorous self-imposed restraints, or permitted to degenerate into the commonplace.

It is a difficult choice, but it must be made. And nobody else can make it. The choice is ours alone.

PRESERVATION OF VALUES

The Act of 1872 creating Yellowstone National Park coupled two purposes: preservation of the remarkable environment and use of the area preserved as a pleasuring ground. The National Park Service Act of 1916 also stressed both preservation and value of the parks as a source of pleasure for the people. Over the years, the National Park Service has developed a variety of interpretations of those purposes, including the belief that they are in conflict, even incompatible. That is partially the result of the enormous recent popularity of the parks. Changes in transportation and in patterns of wealth and leisure as well as in popular attitudes toward nature contributed to the outdoor recreation explosion. Congress could not have anticipated those changes, and attendant pressures on the parks, when it passed the organic laws of 1872 and 1916. Consequently, the seeds of a dilemma between recreation and preservation appear in the legislation. We believe the dilemma is more apparent than real, and can be resolved, if the meaning of Congress in the organic acts is understood to be preservation for the enjoyment of the people in the natural values being preserved.

The early parks, in other words, were established for the purpose of protecting and displaying certain special environments. Visitors expected to take their pleasure from experiencing those environments. It follows that the parks can only be enjoyed fully if they are preserved unimpaired. In the national parks, there is no dichotomy between preservation and pleasuring. Consequently, the preservation function, not the recreation function, should be the central focus of the National Park Service in the next hundred years.

We therefore recommend:

Recreation in and enjoyment of the national parks must be in the terms of their preservation function.

Recognizing the rarity of wilderness in the United States in 1972 compared to 1872, preservation of what remains should be given the top priority in all policy decisions affecting national parks.

Criteria other than the number of visitors should be used as measurements of park performance and as yardsticks for allocating appropriations; for example, the quality of the visitors' experience and success in preserving integrity of ecosystems.

Although the first national parks were great wilderness areas, in recent years the jurisdiction of the National Park Service has expanded to include several other kinds of units, such as recreation areas. This expansion is welcome, but only if distinctions between the varieties of units is kept in mind by both management and the public. One way to approach the problem is to consider the varieties of value inherent in the natural world. We might detail the values, with a simple illustrative analogy, as follows:

Material use—A tree can provide lumber.

Beauty—A tree can be scenic and decorative.

Spiritual-symbolic—A tree can be worshipped, and it can be understood as a symbol of an idea or concept. This category of use does not necessarily involve the physical presence of man.

Recreation—A tree can be climbed.

Knowledge—A tree can be studied as a biological organism with a role in the ecosystem, or an historical object, for instance, a landmark tree on a trail.

The National Park Service has jurisdiction over environment that contains these five values. The overriding problem in today's National Park System is the delineation and, in cases of conflict, separation of those values. To that end, we recommend yet another categorization of areas under National Park Service administration. The objective of the restructuring is to establish clearly in the public mind the dominant purpose and appropriate uses of the various units in the National Park System. That is related to the need of protecting the dominant values of each unit. Our schema follows:

National Wilderness Parks. This category embraces the larger "national parks" and most parts of many "national monuments," as well as appropriate portions of some other kinds of units. A National Wilderness Park has as its dominant purpose the preservation of an intact ecosystem. People visiting this kind of park expect to derive their enjoyment from the wilderness being preserved. That expectation resolves any ambiguity in the 1872 and 1916 organic legislation with respect to park preservation and the pleasure of the people. It follows that visitors to the National Wilderness Parks must be prepared to accept a wilderness life-style if they intend to stay in the park more than a single day. Those desiring more civilized accommodations, particularly hotels and motels and their own mobile homes, have to accept the necessity of leaving the park at the end of the day to find such accommodations outside its boundaries. However, given the general excellence of major park roads and the speed of modern motorized transportation, this requirement does not exclude anyone from, say, a view of Old Faithful. Stated another way, this is a recommendation that the National Park Service get out of the hotel and motel business. Instead, it should be left to private enterprise—the accommodations industry surely flourish immediately outside the parks if its in-park competition ceases. As a corollary, the National Wilderness Parks should specialize in camping.

National Recreation Areas.   Included here would be the present National Recreation Areas plus some National Seashores (although some, like Cape Hatteras, should surely be placed in the first category, above, with its present intrusions eliminated) and the National Riverways and Parkways. As opposed to the National Wilderness Parks, such areas would stress high density recreation rather than nature preservation. Motorized transportation, including off-road vehicles such as powerboats and dune buggies, might be permitted under appropriate regulations. Many more of these areas need to be established, especially near urban areas. Their presence as an alternative recreational opportunity would reduce visitor pressure on the National Wilderness Parks.

National Landmarks.   This category would include natural, historic, and environmental education landmarks as currently conceived by the National Park Service. Management in certain cases might be intensive and highly specialized. A National Landmark might occasionally exist as an "island" within a larger National Wilderness Park. The quarry in Dinosaur National Monument or the archaeological ruins in Bandalier National Monument come to mind in this respect.

In sum, we recommend that the management of the various parklands conform to their dominant values.

CARRYING CAPACITY

The simplest meaning of this concept is the ability of something to absorb outside influence and still retain its essence. When carrying capacity is exceeded, that essense is lost. The problem is already crucial in many national parks.

Carrying capacity may be understood to have three parts:

Physical Carrying Capacity.   This relates to the effect of visitation on the nonliving aspects of the habitat. The ability of a particular terrain to resist trail erosion is one factor. So is its ability to "absorb" trails, roads, and other man-made objects. Conversely, when man-made features dominate the scene, the physical carrying capacity is exceeded and, in the case of park, the preservation function aborted. Space also determines carrying capacity, notably in the case of a national landmark where the visitor objective is limited. Only a few visitors can stand in a ruin at a time.

Ecological Carrying Capacity. This concerns the effect of visitors on park ecosystems. When the natural plant and animal features are substantially altered, ecological carrying capacity is exceeded and the preservation function aborted. More particularly, when the presence of visitors causes a particular bird or animal to vacate its normal habitat or behave abnormally (grizzlies come to mind), ecological carrying capacity has been exceeded. The "fishing-out" of a lake or stream is another illustration, as is the effect on flora of pasturing a horse on a mountain meadow. The ability to dispose of visitor wastes without damage to park ecosystems may prove to be the ultimate measure of ecological carrying capacity.

Psychological Carrying Capacity. The most subtle and difficult, but in many ways the most important, component of carrying capacity concerns the effect of other visitors on the mind of the individual visitor. The assumption is that a certain atmosphere or setting is necessary in order that certain attributes of an environment be perceived and enjoyed. Levels of tolerance for other people vary, of course. At one extreme is the person for whom the sight (and even the knowledge) of one other camper or camping party in the vicinity detracts from the quality of the experience. At the other extreme are those whose chief delight in a park experience comes from association with fellow visitors. For them an empty campground would not only be a disappointment but a positively frightening prospect.

Although more concrete data are badly needed, most visitors seem able to accept the presence of others up to a point (the psychological carrying capacity for them).

Campground capacities already in effect at many parks reflect cognizance of the physical and psychological carrying capacity. Similarly, the closure of nesting areas to visitor use (the eagle nests along the Snake River in Grand Teton, for example) is a recognition of ecological carrying capacity. The routine of trails around fragile high Sierra meadows is an instance of physical carrying capacity. More restrictions of those types, based on careful environmental inventories of the parks, are recommended.

The concept of psychological carrying capacity becomes crucial in regard to the preservation of wilderness. It is now indisputable that wilderness can be loved to death. Its worst enemies are its friends. Wilderness by definition is a region where man's presence is minimized. When securing a campsite becomes a matter of competition between several parties, the perception of wilderness vanishes. That points up the need for user quotes based on the physical, ecological, and especially, on the social. At first glance such restrictions seem abhorrent, totally out of keeping with the freedom wild country should entail. But on second thought, we accept quota-type restrictions on almost every form of recreational activity. We buy tickets for the theater, and when the performance is sold out we wait for the next one or even for the next season. We don't insist on the right to sit on each other's laps. Similarly in regard to tennis, if the courts are occupied we wait our turn. Even in the case of public courts, which we support as taxpayers, we wait. We understand that if sixteen people crowd the court the result is not tennis. So we make reservations, we wait, perhaps we don't even get to play that day. We may be displeased, but we accept it because we respect the integrity of the game.

Wilderness is also a "game" that can't be played at any one time at any specific place by more than a few people. Respect for the quality of a wilderness experience demands that we accept more regulated use and quotas. The time is not far distant when the "right" to enter wild country may be distributed much like tickets to a concert or permits to hunt big game. There will be inconveniences and some people will inevitably be disappointed, but, like the tennis analogy, acceptance will result from an understanding and appreciation of the meaning of wilderness.

We therefore recommend that:

High priority should be given to research directed at finding the physical, ecological and psychological carrying capacity of every unit under the jurisdiction of the National Park Service.

This information should be the basis for the establishment and enforcement of user quotas to prevent visitation from exceeding the carrying capacity of the environment.

In setting quotas and accepting reservations, the National Park Service must realize that certain segments of American society are likely to be discriminated against. Special measures must be taken to insure this does not occur.

Recognizing that preservation has top priority, the National Park Service should not encourage visitation in excess of carrying capacity.

The National Park Service should explore means of visitor management consistent with carrying capacity standards, such as the use of earphone touring, binocular and telescope stations, alternate-day visiting, and dispersal of visitors into alternate areas.

The National Park Service should educate citizens and visitors on the meaning of and need for the carrying capacity and quota concepts to gain a broader basis of public support in its preservation function.

Because noise is destructive of solitude, the National Park Service should seek to have overflights by aircraft regulated, and explore other means to minimize noise intrusions on the ground, such as playing radios, which reduces psychological carrying capacity.

VISITOR MANAGEMENT

The adoption of a National Wilderness Park concept would challenge the National Park Service with questions of visitor management. As hotel-type accommodations are phased out of all National Park Service units, camping would obviously have to be provided for to a far greater extent than now exists. The National Park Service should adopt a policy of phasing out car camping as an activity incompatible with park purposes even before the more general exclusion of private autos. Two kinds of camping situations seem appropiate.

Shortwalk Camping. The concept here is to get visitors out of the sight, sound, and smell of mechanized civilization by camping a short distance (generally no more than one-half mile) from a road access. The possibilities are exciting. Consider the way dead-end spur roads and feeder trails could disperse visitors along the rim of a canyon, or along a river, or through a valley. In each case the road would be kept away from the prime camping areas. Wood and water might constitute problems in some locales, but dry camping (carrying water from the road access) and provision of wood by the National Park Service are possible solutions. The concept of "fallow campgrounds," periodically rested from use, might also be fruitfully employed to sustain the quality of shortwalk camping. A spur road could simply be closed to camping for a season or more so that the land and vegetation could recover. Mass-transit access is a desirable alternative to cars for the shortwalk camper.

Backcountry Camping and the Exploration Station. Like the weather, everyone complains about the concentration of visitors in small portions of the parks, but few steps have been taken to do something about this situation. As an aid in assisting backcountry campers, we recommend the establishment of Exploration Stations in the National Wilderness Parks. Located in park visitor centers, the Exploration Station would be prepared to rent or sell complete backpacking (or canoe camping) equipment, including maps, dehydrated foods, even hiking boots. The Exploration Station would include staff who could instruct visitors in the use of equipment, plan trip itineraries, and dispense a substantial dose of land ethic that would help insure safe and responsible backcountry use. That last task might be facilitated by a tape-slide presentation aimed at environmental education and wilderness courtesy.

The Exploration Station might best be compared to the familiar ski school where a complete novice can secure all the equipment and instruction he needs to enjoy skiing. Another analogy is the canoe country outfitters of the Boundary Waters Canoe Area in northern Minnesota. One of those establishments boasts that you can enter the store stark naked and within two hours be paddling away from the landing fully equipped for a two-week trip.

For a backcountry trip, guides would not be required; the idea is to prepare visitors to discover wilderness by themselves. However, if a guide is desired, one would be available. This is really only an extension of the current park "interpretation" program, particularly aspects such as Yosemite's cross-country skiing and rock climbing schools. Even more to the point is the wilderness tent camp program along Yosemite's High Sierra Loop Trail which is filled to capacity every season. Former Secretary of the Interior Walter J. Hickel's directive of June 18, 1969, to the Director of the National Park Service singled out this undertaking as a model for visitor management. However, the presence of those permanent tent camps must be recognized as a prior nonconforming use of wilderness and should be replaced by backpacked tents. In some places, secluded Adirondack-type shelters might be appropriate, those at Isle Royale National Park, for example.

The Exploration Station would be an aid in defining the purpose of the National Wilderness Parks in the public mind. Their existence would underscore the idea that the enjoyment of this kind of park consists of visiting wilderness on its own terms and not on those of civilization. When Secretary of the Interior Rogers C. B. Morton directed the National Park Service on June 17, 1971, to "seek a new perspective of just how camping fits into our mission of protecting park resources for future generations, while providing today's and tomorrow's visitors with a quality experience," we believe he had in mind the kind of imaginative visitor assistance that Exploration Stations represent. There can be no more appropriate application of the National Wilderness Park concept than helping visitors enjoy wilderness camping. But here, as elsewhere in this report, it is intended that the concept of carrying capacity must be strictly observed. Exploration Stations should not be located where their presence is likely to stimulate visitor use beyond the carrying capacity—particularly the psychological carrying capacity—of any part of a park.

Transportation is another key aspect of visitor management.

In the National Wilderness Parks, as opposed to the National Recreation Areas, backcountry motor travel should be categorically prohibited. That problem has crept up on the National Park Service before full awareness of its consequences existed. Rafts using outboard motors now regularly run the Colorado River in the heart of the backcountry of Grand Canyon National Park. Powerboating is the dominant form of off-road travel in Everglades National Park. Snowmobiles are permitted in Yellowstone and elsewhere. The age of individual minihelicopters, which could place a visitor anywhere in a park within minutes, is almost here. Cars are no longer the only threat to wilderness values.

The converse of prohibiting motorized vehicles is that unmechanized off-road travel should be encouraged and actively facilitated by the National Wilderness Parks to an extent consistent with the concept of carrying capacity. The Exploration Stations can obviously play a role here and so can the expansion of such current rental programs as rentals of bicycles and cross-country skis in Yosemite. Canoes and horses in selected places might also figure in this program. The objective would be to make it easy for the visitor to exchange his car for alternate, unmechanized means of transportation, which do not dilute the pleasure of discovering it yourself, the essence of a wilderness experience.

Under the category of visitor management, particularly with reference to the National Wilderness Parks, we recommend:

The National Wilderness Parks should categorically exclude backcountry motorized transportation.

In keeping with the directives of Congress and Secretaries of the Interior, the Service should proceed rapidly in its wilderness classification program with emphasis on maximum preservation and protection of wilderness values inside the parks and with full public participation at all stages, not just when the master plan is presented for final approval.

The concept of a ⅛ mile "buffer" zone around wilderness should be rejected in favor of a boundary that begins at the edge of civilization (at roads, etc.).

In keeping with the determination to maximize the amount of wilderness in the National Wilderness Parks, the "enclave" concept, which excludes "islands" in wilderness for more intensive development, should be abandoned. If overuse becomes a problem, quotas rather than enclaves should be turned to as solutions. Those who enter wilderness must be prepared to do so on the terms of wilderness.

Shortwalk camping opportunities should be expanded in all categories of parks.

The National Park Service should give the Exploration Station concept a trial in several National Wilderness Parks.

41

The Force of Public Awareness
RALPH NADER (1970)

In 1965, lawyer Ralph Nader began his crusade against the human and environmental irresponsibility of big business with the publication of Unsafe At Any Speed. *The book's attack on General Motors was first ignored, then featured in congressional hearings, and later made the subject of litigation which Nader won. But more importantly for his cause, he won the interest and admiration of millions of Americans who saw in him a countervailing force to profits at any price. By the end of the 1960s Nader had gathered around him a group of young, tough-minded researchers and lawyers dubbed "Nader's Raiders." Some of their exposures did not concern environmental problems, but many did. In recent years Nader has turned the spotlight of his criticism on pesticides, air pollution, and water pollution. His principal tactic in every instance is to alert and arouse the citizenry who, through*

Ralph Nader, "The Profits in Pollution," *The Progressive* XXXIV (1970), 19–22. Reprinted by permission from *The Progressive*, 408 West Gorham Street, Madison, Wisconsin 53703. Copyright © 1970, The Progressive, Inc.

pressure on their government, can force reforms on even the most powerful organizations. Few would question that in the arena of public opinion there has not been a more effective performer for conservation than Ralph Nader since the Progressive heyday of Gifford Pinchot (7,9,11).

The modern corporation's structure, impact, and public accountability are the central issues in any program designed to curb or forestall the contamination of air, water, and soil by industrial activity. While there are other sources of pollution, such as municipalities dumping untreated or inadequately treated sewage, industrial processes and products are the chief contributors to the long-term destruction of natural resources that each year increases the risks to human health and safety.

Moreover, through active corporate citizenship, industry could soon overcome many of the obstacles in the way of curbing noncorporate pollution. The mighty automobile industry, centered around and in Detroit, never thought it part of its role to press the city of Detroit to construct a modern sewage treatment plant. The automobile moguls, whose products, according to Department of Health, Education and Welfare data, account for fifty-five to sixty per cent of the nation's air pollution, remained silent as the city's obsolete and inadequate sewage facilities dumped the wastes of millions into the Detroit River. Obviously, local boosterism does not include such elementary acts of corporate citizenship.

The toilet training of industry to keep it from further rupturing the ecosystem requires an overhaul of the internal and external levers which control corporations. There are eight areas in which policies must be changed to create the pressures needed to make corporate entities and the people who run them cease their destruction of the environment:

One—The conventional way of giving the public a share in private decisions that involve health and safety hazards is to establish mandatory standards through a public agency. But pollution control standards set by governmental agencies can fall far short of their purported objectives unless they are adequately drafted, kept up to date, vigorously enforced, and supported by sanctions when violated. Behind the adoption of such standards, there is a long administrative process, tied to a political infrastructure. The scientific-engineering-legal community has a key independent role to play in this vital and complex administrative-political process. Almost invariably, however, its talents have been retained on behalf of those to be regulated. Whether in Washington or in state capitals around the country, the experts demonstrate greater loyalty to their employers than to their professional commitments in the public interest.

This has been the regular practice of specialists testifying in behalf of coal and uranium mining companies on the latters' environmental contamination in Appalachia and the Rocky Mountain regions. Perhaps the most egregious example of willing corporate servility was a paper entitled "We've Done the Job—What's Next?" delivered by Charles M. Heinen, Chrysler's vehicle emissions specialist, at a meeting of the Society of Automotive Engineers last spring.

Heinen, whose paper bordered on technical pornography, said the auto industry had solved the vehicle pollution problem with an eighty per cent reduction of hydrocarbons and a seventy per cent reduction of carbon monoxide between the 1960 and 1970 model years. He avoided mentioning at least four other vehicle pollutants—nitrogen oxides, lead, asbestos, and rubber tire pollutants. He also failed to point out that the emissions control performance of new cars degrades after a few thousand miles, and that even when new they do not perform under traffic conditions as they do when finely tuned at a company test facility. The overall aggregate pollution from ever greater numbers of vehicles in more congested traffic patterns also escaped Heinen's company-indentured perceptions.

Two—Sanctions against polluters are feeble and out of date, and, in any case, are rarely invoked. For example, the Federal air quality act has no criminal penalties no matter how willful and enduring the violations. In New Jersey, New York, and Illinois, a seventy-one year old Federal anti-water pollution law was violated with total impunity by industry until the Justice Department moved against a few of the violators in recent months. Other violators in other states are yet to be subjected to the law's enforcement. To be effective, sanctions should come in various forms, such as non-reimbursable fines, suspensions, dechartering of corporations, required disclosure of violations in company promotional materials, and more severe criminal penalties. Sanctions, consequently, should be tailored to the seriousness and duration of the violation.

It is expressive of the anemic and nondeterrent quality of existing sanctions that offshore oil leaks contaminating beaches for months, as in Santa Barbara, brought no penalty to any official of any offending company. The major controversy in Santa Barbara was whether the company—Union Oil—or the Government or the residents would bear the costs of cleaning up the mess. And even if the company bore the costs initially, the tax laws would permit a considerable shifting of this cost onto the general taxpayer.

Three—The existing requirements for disclosure of the extent of corporate pollution are weak and flagrantly flouted. The Federal Water Pollution Control Administration (FWPCA) has been blocked since 1963 by industrial polluters (working with the Federal Bureau of the Budget) from obtaining information from these companies concerning the extent and location of discharges of pollutants into the nation's waterways. For three years, the National Industrial Waste Inventory has been held up by the Budget Bureau and its industry "advisers," who have a decisive policy role. Led by the steel, paper, and petroleum industries, corporate polluters have prevented the FWPCA from collecting specific information on what each company is putting into the water. Such information is of crucial importance to the effective administration of the water pollution law and the allocation of legal responsibility for violations.

Counties in California have been concealing from their citizens the identity of polluters and the amounts of pollution, using such weak, incredible arguments to support their cover-up as the companies' fear of revealing "trade secrets." California state agencies have refused to disclose pesticide application data to representatives of orchard workers being gradually poisoned by the chemicals. Once again the trade secret rationale was employed.

The real reason for secrecy is that disclosure of such information would raise public questions about why government agencies have not been doing their jobs—and would facilitate legal action by injured persons against the polluters. What must be made clear to both corporate and public officials is that no one has the right to a trade secret in lethality.

Massive and meticulous "fish bowl" disclosure requirements are imperative if citizens are to be alerted, at the earliest possible moment, to the flow of silent violence assaulting their health and safety, and that of unborn generations as well. This disclosure pattern, once established, must not lapse into a conspiracy between private and public officials, a conspiracy of silence against citizens and the public interest. A good place to start with such company-by-company disclosure is in the corporation's annual report, which now reveals only financial profits or losses; it should also reveal the social costs of pollution by composition and tonnage.

Four—Corporate investment in research and development of pollution controls is no longer a luxury to be left to the decision or initiative of a few company officers. Rather, such research and development must be required by law to include reinvestment of profits, the amount depending on the volume of pollution inflicted on the public. For example, in 1969 General Motors grossed $24 billion, yet last year spent less than $15 million on vehicle and plant pollution research and development, although its products and plants contribute some thirty-five per cent of the nation's air pollution by tonnage. A formula proportional to the size of a company and its pollution could be devised as law, with required periodic reporting of the progress of the company's research and its uses. A parallel governmental research and development program aimed at developing pollution-free product prototypes suitable for mass production, and a Federal procurement policy favoring the purchase of less-polluting products, are essential external impacts.

Five—Attention must be paid to the internal climate for free expression and due process within the corporate structure. Again and again, the internal discipline of the corporate autocracy represses the civic and professional spirit of employees who have every right to speak out or blow the whistle on their company after they have tried in vain, working from the inside, to bring about changes that will end pollution practices. Professional employes—scientists, engineers, physicians— have fewer due process safeguards than the blue collar workers in the same company protected by their union contract.

When Edward Gregory, a Fisher Body plant inspector for General Motors in St. Louis, publicly spoke out in 1966 on inadequate welding that exposed Chevrolet passengers to exhaust leakage, the company ignored him for a few years, but eventually recalled more than two million cars for correction. GM knew better than to fire Gregory, a member of the United Auto Workers.

In contrast, scientists and engineers employed by corporations privately tell me of their reluctance to speak out—within their companies or outside them—about hazardous products. This explains why the technical elites are rarely in the vanguard of public concern over corporate contamination. Demotion, ostracism, dismissal are some of the corporate sanctions against which there is little or no recourse by the professional employe. A new corporate constitutionalism is needed, guaranteeing employes' due process rights against arbitrary reprisals, but its precise forms require the collection of data and extensive study. Here is a major challenge to which college faculty and students can respond on the campus and in field work.

Six—The corporate shareholder can act, as he rarely does, as a prod and lever for jolting corporate leaders out of their lethargy. The law and the lawyers have rigged the legal system to muffle the voice of shareholders, particularly those concerned with the broader social costs of corporate enterprise. However, for socially conscious and determined stockholders there are many functions that can be performed to help protect the public (including themselves) from industrial pollution.

Shareholders must learn to take full advantage of such corporate practices as cumulative voting, which permits the "single-shot" casting of all of a shareholder's ballots for one member of the board of directors. Delegations of stockholders can give visibility to the issues by lobbying against their company's ill-advised policies in many forums apart from the annual meeting—legislative hearings, agency proceedings, town meetings, and the news media, for example. These delegations will be in a position to expose company officers to public judgment, something from which executives now seem so insulated in their daily corporate activities.

Seven—Natural, though perhaps unexercised, countervailing forces in the private sector can be highly influential incentives for change. For example, the United Auto Workers have announced that pollution will be an issue in the collective bargaining process with automobile company management this year; the union hopes to secure for workers the right not to work in polluting activities, or in a polluted environment. Insurance companies could become advocates for loss prevention in the environmental field when confronted with policyholder, shareholder, and citizen demonstrative action. Through their political influence, their rating function in evaluating risks and setting premium charges, and their research and development capability, insurance companies could exert a key countervailing stress on polluters. Whether they do or not will first depend on citizen groups to whip them into action.

Eight—Environmental lawsuits, long blocked by a conservative judiciary and an inflexible judicial system, now seem to be coming into their own—a classic example of how heightened public expectations, demands, and the availability of facts shape broader applications of ancient legal principles. Environmental pollution is environmental violence—to human beings and to property. The common law has long recognized such violence against the person as actionable or enjoinable. What has been lacking is sufficient evidence of harm and avoidability to persuade judges that such hitherto invisible long-range harm outweighed the economic benefits of the particular plant activity in the community.

It now appears that such lawsuits will gain greater acceptance, especially as more evidence and more willing lawyers combine to breathe contemporary reality into long-standing legal principles. An amendment to the U.S. Constitution providing citizens with basic rights to a clean environment has been proposed; similar amendments to state constitutions are being offered. Such generic provisions can only further the judicial acceptance of environmental lawsuits. Imaginative and bold legal advocacy is needed here. The *forced consumption* of industrial pollutants by 200 million Americans must lead to a recognition of legal rights in environmental control such as that which developed with civil rights for racial minorities over the last two decades.

Three additional points deserve the attention of concerned citizens:

First, a major corporate strategy in combating anti-pollution measures is to engage workers on the company side by leading them to believe that such measures would threaten their livelihood. This kind of industrial extortion in a community—especially a company town—has worked before and will again unless citizens anticipate and confront it squarely.

Second, both industry spokesmen and their governmental allies (such as the President's Science Adviser, Lee DuBridge) insist that consumers will have to pay the price of pollution control. While this point of view may be an unintended manifestation of the economy's administered price structure, it cannot go unchallenged. Pollution control must not become another lever to lift up excess profits and fuel the fires of inflation. The costs of pollution control technology should come from corporate profits which have been enhanced by the use of the public's environment as industry's private sewer. The sooner industry realizes that it must bear the costs of cleanups, the more likely it will be to employ the quickest and most efficient techniques.

Finally, those who believe deeply in a humane ecology must act in accordance with their beliefs. They must so order their consumption and disposal habits that they can, in good conscience, preach what they actually practice. In brief, they must exercise a personal discipline as they advocate the discipline of governments and corporations.

The battle of the environmentalists is to preserve the physiological integrity of people by preserving the natural integrity of land, air, and water. The planet earth is a seamless structure with a thin slice of sustaining air, water, and soil that supports almost four billion people. This thin slice belongs to all of us, and we use it and hold it in trust for future earthlings. Here we must take our stand.

42

Technology Assessment: The Case of the SST
JAMES RAMSEY (1971); ROBERT HOTZ (1971)

By narrow margins in March 1971 Congress refused to approve further supersonic transit (SST) development funding, thus reversing its decade-long, three-quarter-billion-dollar support for the revolutionary airplane. The defeated "airplane of the future" was to have flown at 1800 mph, or nearly three times the speed of sound, instead of the mere 500–600 mph jets presently achieve. During the early 1960s few questioned the SST's impact on the environment since Americans had long carried on a love affair with machines and technology. But hard questions were raised as the decade closed —about cost, sonic booms, possible adverse modifications of the earth's atmosphere, and even the need for flying so fast. Eventually these considera-

James Ramsey, "The SST Fight in Perspective," *Sierra Club Bulletin* LVI (1971), inside cover. Reprinted by permission.

tions caused the project to be dropped. The defeat held heavy symbolic meaning for both sides. Supporters of the SST tended to view it as evidence of eccentric, antitechnological bias. Environmentalists, on the other hand, saw it as a major and long overdue step in a national reassessment of technology and priorities. The short statements below summarize these two positions and allude to the meaning of the defeat for America's future.

Now that the celebrations of victory and the lamentations of defeat have subsided in the wake of the Super Sonic Transport battle, it is appropriate to examine the significance of its outcome. First, its defeat in both the House and Senate (by narrow margins, it should be noted) was not as much a national statement of ecological concern as many environmentalists would like to believe; nor was it a blind, emotional, anti-science reaction as some SST proponents claim. The SST was grounded by a number of complex circumstances, the paramount one being a change in congressional priorities between 1970 and 1971. Representative Art Link (D-ND) was no doubt echoing in a general way the feelings of many others who voted against the SST when he told *The New Republic* that he wasn't opposed to the SST, *per se*, but that he couldn't explain a pro-SST vote back home when the new Railpax system was cutting out passenger service to many small communities in his district because of lack of funds, the Farmers Home Administration was cutting back on loans, education funds were in short supply, and medical research was being short-changed.

There were other non-environmental reasons for the defeat of the SST. Ironically, a critical one may have been the boomerang effect of the massive campaign waged for the SST by the Nixon Administration, the aerospace industry and the unions. Prior to the House and Senate votes, James Reston described how the Administration was "paying little attention to the evidence of the economists and scientists who oppose the project, but is using every argument, no matter how feeble or false, to overwhelm rather than to persuade the opposition." Congress, as it turned out, was not overwhelmed.

None of the foregoing is to deny the environmental movement its proper credit for a sustained and courageous effort in combatting the SST. Although the majority of anti-SST votes in Congress may not have been "ecology" votes, it is a matter of historical fact that without the environmental movement the SST could not have been stopped.

The question raised here is not who should get credit for stopping the SST, but has it in fact, been stopped? If it was denied funds based primarily on economic priorities, then in a year or two, or three, when priorities will have changed, what is to stop it from rising up phoenix-like to confront environmentalists again? (Immediately after the Senate vote plans to issue public stock to finance SST development were reported in many of the nation's newspapers.)

It may be that the SST vote represents the first hesitant step by the most technologically advanced nation on earth to seriously question the environmental impact of unbridled technology. Should this be true, then the SST, or rather its continued absence, will truly be a cause for national pride. If, on the other hand, SST proponents are simply waiting in the wings for an upturn in the economy, environmentalists had better concentrate now on both state and federal legislation to prohibit SST overflights and landings. In the end this may be the only way to kill the beast.

The rejection of further funding for development of two supersonic transport prototypes by Congress this month marks a fundamental watershed in government policy that portends a national skid into the hopeless poverty of a technological Appalachia. For more than a half century, it has been U.S. government policy to fund research and development for advancing aerospace technology. Now, by a relatively slim margin in both House and Senate, the Congress has abandoned that policy and the very substantial benefits that accrued from it.

Many legislators who voted against further SST funding would deny this is what they had in mind, citing continued federal funding of military aeronautical research. But it is a sad fact that there are no military aircraft now under development that even approach the advanced state of the art embodied in the Boeing 2707 supersonic transport. So the technological spearhead will be blunted, and the commercial aircraft market of the future will be passed into other hands.

This initial victory of the sociologists over technology is only the beginning of this great battle over the future course of this nation. Sen. Henry Jackson (D.-Wash.) warned that a defeat for continued SST research would presage an attack on every other major technological program this nation attempts. Already there are signs that the victorious sociologists are girding for a similar assault on the space shuttle, the B-1 supersonic bomber and the entire advanced technology base that supports this nation.

Robert Hotz, "Toward a Technological Appalachia," *Aviation Week and Space Technology* XCIV (1971), p. 9. Reprinted by permission.

The forces that killed the SST development program are out to stamp out technology. Listen to Sen. Charles Percy (R.-Ill.) when he rants on the Senate floor that 40,000 unemployed aerospace engineers and scientists should be converted to fill a shortage of 50,000 doctors: "If we continue in our universities to turn out physicists and chemists that we do not need . . . something is wrong with our society." When challenged by Sen. Gordon Allott (R.-Colo.) as to how aeronautical engineers could be converted to doctors, the senator from Illinois mouthed some vague persiflage about a study being made by the University of Chicago.

We noted that Sen. Percy did not repeat his ridiculous statement made in the previous Senate SST debate equating a vote for the program with endorsing the spread of skin cancer. As Sen. Percy abandoned this untenable position, many of his colleagues embraced it, citing an avowed believer in flying saucers who also happens to own a Ph.D. as their principal authority. We suggest that unemployed aerospace engineers write personally to Sen. Percy to solicit his aid in finding jobs for them in the medical profession.

There were some curious developments in the Senate vote. Sen. Stuart Symington (D.-Mo.) reversed an earlier vote and supported the SST funding. Sen. Clinton Anderson (D.-N.M.), a steady SST supporter, voted against it in justifiable pique over the Nixon Administration's evisceration of the Nerva nuclear-powered space stage. Sen. Hubert Humphrey (D.-Minn.), who once presided over the National Aeronautics and Space Council and loved to bask in the limelight at Apollo dinners, voted against technology and labor in a decision we predict will haunt him in the pursuit of his rekindled political ambitions. Freshman Sen. John Tunney (D.-Calif.) said that California aerospace workers who thought cancellation of the SST would create more unemployment in California were being misled. We urge all those Californians who lose their jobs on the SST subcontracting programs to write Sen. Tunney directly and express their opinions on his perspicacity.

Aerospace is by far the largest employer in the state of Connecticut. Both its senators, Abraham Ribicoff and Freshman Lowell Weicker, voted against the SST.

In contrast to the earlier Senate SST debate last November, the ecological issue was soft-pedaled, and the main thrust of the opposition was concentrated on economics. None of those arguing the economic case against the SST agreed on any single aspect of their case.

Nor could they define the economy involved in washing a $1-billion investment down the drain without any tangible achievement and forfeiting all future benefits from the program including sales royalty payments that would return about 4% on the government's original investment. The kind of economics espoused by the opponents of the SST extrapolated to the rest of the national scene will lead this nation to bankruptcy and, in the words of Sen. Warren Magnuson (D.-Wash.), to a "technological Appalachia that will create a third-rate nation."

The aerospace industry made some semblance of a political fight, but it was another sad case of "too little, too late." The fate of the SST should serve notice, if any is needed, that the aerospace industry can no longer survive with its political naivete and aloofness from the fray.

The supersonic transport program is not completely dead. Various groups are working to put together new patterns to try to continue prototype development, but a major obstacle is the defeatist attitude of Boeing. The Boeing mandarins in their walled city of Seattle have apparently learned little from their shattering experience of the past year.

It is a sad day when a deliberate national decision is made to abandon a major frontier of technological advance. But it will be even sadder when the victors in this significant debate gird for their next assault on the space shuttle program.

43

To Grow or Not to Grow

GARRETT HARDIN (1972); R. STEPHEN BERRY (1972)

Growth has been as American as apple pie. For a nation that expanded for three centuries, "growth" was so inextricably involved with "progress" as to be almost synonymous. It was a tenet of the national faith that went unquestioned. But the finitude of the earth, noted by Fairfield Osborn and

Garrett Hardin, "We Live on a Spaceship," *Bulletin of the Atomic Scientists* XXIII (1972), 23–25. Reprinted by permission of the *Bulletin of the Atomic Scientists*. Copyright © 1972 by the Educational Foundation for Nuclear Science.

others in the 1950s (see p. 155), inevitably caught up with and destroyed the illusion of endless expansion. Clearly the advent of the space age, with its dramatic photographs and television images of a tiny earth, hastened the new awareness. So did computer-assisted projections of growth trends. The most widely discussed of these, sponsored by the Club of Rome, bore the title The Limits to Growth *(1972). The book was not only a commentary; for many it became an historical fact with an influence on thought and feeling that added new dimensions to its scholarly format and tone. Among the many discussions of* The Limits to Growth *were the two reviews below. Garrett Hardin, a professor of human ecology at the University of California, Santa Barbara, has long been in the forefront of iconoclasts with regard to man-environment relations. The second reviewer, R. Stephen Berry, is a professor of chemistry at the University of Chicago and a member of the editorial board of the* Bulletin of the Atomic Scientists.

The first problem of human ecology is to determine the facts: how do population, technology and environment interact? And how can we move toward the best possible arrangement of things? This is a fiendishly difficult intellectual problem.

The second problem of human ecology is no less difficult: as we reach each partial answer, how do we get the general body politic to accept the truth? In the twentieth century, Julian Huxley, Aldous Huxley, Karl Sax, William Vogt, Robert C. Cook and the Paddock brothers have each, in their time, publicized shocking and irrefutable facts. Each has had his moment of glory, and then his contribution has been drowned in the unending torrent of printed words as mankind has continued in its thoughtless way to make a shambles of the world. Paul Ehrlich is the latest to make a splash; but already his message is being suppressed. To date, all population prophets have been Cassandras: the price for their vision of the truth has been public disbelief in what they say.

Now come some more candidates for the Cassandra corps: a research group at MIT headed by Jay Forrester. By computer simulation they have produced a large number of plausible "scenarios" of the future course of population, prosperity and pollution. Their conclusions were described first in mimeographed inhouse documents, then in rather weighty books put out by an obscure publisher, and in hearings before Congressional committees. With the publication of "The Limits to Growth," their findings reach a much larger audience. A financially well-endowed group called the Club of Rome has sponsored this work and bought 10,000 copies for distribution to influential business leaders, statesmen and journal editors. The book is receiving wide notice and thoughtful discussion. Perhaps this time the message will be remembered. Perhaps this time Cassandra will be believed. Let us hope so.

The message can be summarized in five words (though the authors never explicitly say as much): We live on a spaceship. All the rest is an extended gloss on this simple text. The method of elaboration is well-chosen for our day: computer read-outs. The pronouncements of computers are the magic of our time: it is well to use them. The authors are not deceived; as they state repeatedly, none of the computer outputs is a prediction. Each merely shows the interaction of the important variables on each other during the next few seconds of historic time, i.e., for roughly the next 200 years. Many different assemblages of arbitrary rate-constants are worked out, all yielding qualitatively the same picture: "The basic mode of the world system is exponential growth of population and capital, followed by collapse." The conclusion proves to be astonishingly insensitive to variation in the parameters. Collapse follows even with the most optimistic assumptions, e.g., an infinite supply of energy.

We should not be surprised at this conclusion (and we do not really need a computer to reach it). The same thing was said by Sir Geoffrey Vickers in a BBC broadcast that was published in "The Listener" for October 28, 1965. The title of this article on population could not have been more graphic: "The End of Free Fall." To anyone who has taken Physics 1A the imagery is frightening.

Picture a man who has jumped off a very high building. His falling corresponds to the growth of population, and of the gross national product. It is not in the least painful; on the contrary, the feeling is one of excitement and exhilaration. But if he is one of those oddballs who insist on looking ahead, he sees the ground approaching and realizes he really ought to do something about decelerating his rate of descent.

He could reach out and grab a cornice of the building and stop his fall. What would you think if he reacted to this suggestion in the following way? "No, I won't do it, because if I do my legs will slam against the building and that will hurt." So he continues to fall and to accelerate; consequently, by the time he's fallen another story his speed is even greater, and the pain of stopping would be still worse. This mode of thought is a trap which insures that the end, when it comes, will be devastating.

Is this a far-fetched analogy? I think not. The demographer Ansley

J. Coale, belaboring the Zero Population Growth people, has pointed out that achieving ZPG instantly would produce, within a few years, an age-distribution like that of St. Petersburg, Florida. One can grant Coale's point that the thought of living in such a gerontocracy is frightening. But does that mean that we should reconcile ourselves to descending a few more stories in a state of free fall? And then more? The demographer never spells out this implication of his position; he contents himself with pointing out that stopping will be painful. Indeed it will. But not stopping will be worse.

The biological situation is, if anything, more dangerous than the physical one because of time-lags built into the system. Each child that is born threatens the world with a further increase in population about 16 years later when it becomes sexually mature. DDT (with some other pollutants) percolates its way through the ecosystem slowly and may produce the maximum kill of peregrine falcons (and perhaps harm man as well) a decade after the pollutant has been outlawed (if it ever is). Radioactive garbage may overwhelm mankind generations after it is produced as a result of "accidents." (Definition: "An accident is a low-frequency event that is certain to happen sooner or later, but I don't want to think about it.") It is not easy to feed such considerations into the computer, but it is clear that the results of doing so would be even more frightening than those graphed by Meadows, et al.

Considerations like these throw new light on the meaning of "conservatism." Usually we think of conservative action as one of no interference with current practices. Change is regarded as nonconservative action, and the old-fashioned conservative advises us to take no such positive action until we have made exhaustive studies of the phenomena involved. But when human survival is at stake, is clinging to the status quo conservative? As the theologian Harvey Cox has said: "Not to decide is to decide." To continue on our present course, while we gather more facts about DDT, atmospheric carbon dioxide, the permeability of rock salt to radioactive atoms, etc., is neither conservative nor wise. We don't have to know exactly how far away the ground is, or exactly what the value of g is, to know that we had better put brakes on our free fall. Waiting for the report of another committee is not the most conservative course to follow.

Some of the poorly educated commentators who man the mikes of TV stations and peck at the typewriters of the popular press have defended inaction in the usual way. Malthus has been buried again. (This is the 174th year in which that redoubtable economist has been interred. We may take it as certain that anyone who has to be buried 174 times cannot be wholly dead.) It is futile to cross swords with the ignorant; but better informed critics who assume that true conservatism is the defense of the status quo deserve a reply. I will deal with two such critics at some length because the way in which they badger the authors of this book throws light on the mechanisms whereby dangerous inaction is defended.

In the Washington Post for March 2, 1972, Allen Kneese and Ronald Ridker of Resources for the Future did their best to see to it that no one should take Meadows, et al., seriously (or become too concerned about the future). Early on, they used the time-honored reviewers' ploy of undermining confidence by pointing out errors which in fact are not crucial to the development of the argument. In the third paragraph, Kneese and Ridker say that the MIT group is mistaken in thinking that any species of whales have been hunted to extinction. This is a quibble; several species have been brought so near to extinction that they are now not worth hunting—but the animals are still killed when found. (Playing the reviewers' game, let me point out that Kneese and Ridker, in paragraph four, identify 1826 as the year of publication of Malthus' "Essay on Population." They are wrong by 28 years. So what?)

More important are the rhetorical arts the reviewers use to insure that their audience remains immobile in the face of approaching catastrophe. Consider this passage: "New discoveries and technological improvements over the past 100 years fully kept up with the demand. In other words, the effectively useful resource base has been expanding exponentially too. Although it cannot be expected to do so indefinitely, it does seem reasonable that a model explicitly based on past tendencies would incorporate this."

The "although" denigrates to second-class status the admission that follows. The essential truth becomes a truth "in passing." To appreciate the effect of this rhetorical ploy, let's return to our man in free fall. He has just passed the 30th story, counting from the top downward. We ask him how he views his prospects. Calmly he replies: "Well, the wind is rushing past me, but I've learned how to adjust to it without discomfort. Although I can't expect to do so indefinitely, still any theory about free fall must be explicitly based on this past tendency to adjust."

In a court of law, such a statement might be defended. But how long can we safely be advised by men who use an "although" clause in this way?

Further on, the reviewers point out that the authors did not—

which Meadows, et al., admit—program their computer for the "social-adaptation, learning, and institution-building process," and go on to say that "One can't help but believe that this failure accounts for the fact that almost all of the scenarios considered result in collapse. This is not to assert that collapse is unlikely. . . ."

Again, we are confronted with the rhetoric of the belittling "although." And again the reviewers are on safe ground, legally speaking. At Judgment Day, if it turns out that the MIT crowd has been right, and the RFF crowd wrong, Kneese and Ridker will still get off the hook—if the Lord is a lawyer. They've hedged their bets astutely. But is such cleverness part of the great tradition of science?

There also is a paradoxical aspect to this second criticism coming from RFF. By implying that an unspecified "social-adaptation, learning, and institution-building process" will appear on the scene as a deus ex machina to save mankind, the writers in fact encourage inaction of all sorts. Their verbal tranquilizer inhibits the active search for such processes (which presumably will appear spontaneously). In contrast, the targets of their criticism, by restricting themselves to a frightening description of what will happen in the absence of such processes, actually stimulate research in social engineering.

It's curious that spokesmen for an organization named "Resources for the Future" should, in fact, throw so many roadblocks in the way of planning for the future. They sometimes seem to act as if they had a vested interest in nonaction. If they were part of the R&D arm of a great industrial concern this would be understandable, but they are not. One would hope that the millions of dollars they receive from the Ford Foundation would give them the feeling of intellectual independence that is needed to prepare for the future in the face of monumental opposition by a multitude of vested interests, both public and private. Yet I am afraid that this admirably endowed organization deserves the name I have heard the geologist Preston Cloud bestow on it—Resources for the Near Future. The label may be a bit unkind because occasionally RFNF does look beyond the near future. Not, however, in the present instance, in which Kneese and Ridker seem more interested in "putting down" their rivals in futurology at another institution than in preparing the public for change. The point of view of their criticism is a narrowly near one. Unconsciously, the critics admit as much in their closing paragraph:

Our assessment? An interesting framework upon which to hang some types of resources and environmental research? We think so. A help-

*ful near-term tool for strengthening and deepening our understand-
ing of man's predicament and what to do about it? We think not.*

It is doubtful if much needed light will be thrown on man's predicament by minds in which the adjective "near term" reverberates so
strongly. In contrast, the authors of "The Limits to Growth" march to a
different drummer. Wisely so, I think.

It is remarkable what a clamor has been raised by "The Limits to
Growth." Somehow the sonority of the name of the sponsor, The Club
of Rome, and the status of its members in the business world seem to
give an authority to this work that other dire and oracular statements
have failed to capture. The thesis of the work is simple: it starts with
the assumption that population, resource use and pollution are rising
exponentially, that these factors are linked in a way that can be represented by a set of differential equations, and that these equations, with
present rates and levels (or 1900 levels) as initial conditions, can be
solved to make projections of the reasonable possibilities for the next
century or so. Moreover the model has been run with a number of the
rates and constraints adjusted to various values that presumably cor-
respond to modes of behavior different from our present one, to see
what range of outcomes one might expect.

The model itself is unfortunately not described in sufficient detail
in the book to allow one to evaluate what the authors have actually
done. However they do say that it is similar to the models used by Jay
Forrester in "Urban Dynamics" (MIT Press, 1969) and "World Dynamics" (Wright-Allen Press, 1971), so that familiarity with Forrester's
work at least gives one some sense of how the "Limits" model was constructed. On this basis, we can go ahead to look critically at just what
"Limits to Growth" says.

First, let us examine the question of the input data, and of the assumption that the current rates of growth are exponential. This is one
ground on which the work has been criticized; some demographers,
for example, insist that population has not grown exponentially, except

---

R. Stephen Berry, "Reflections on 'The Limits to Growth'," *Bulletin of the
Atomic Scientists* XXIII (1972), 25–27. Reprinted by permission of the
Bulletin of the Atomic Scientists. Copyright © 1972 by the Educational
Foundation for Nuclear Science.

perhaps during the past century or century and a half. Is this criticism really cogent? I think it is probably not; population and resource use now are rising at increasing rates, even though not everywhere, and not without fluctuations. On a time scale of about 40 years, there is probably no simple function better than an exponential to fit the data of the recent past. Representing the data by a simple mathematical function is a straightforward way to determine the apparent rate co-efficients and to make projections for behavior of the system over some future time interval. The extent of the interval of validity of the extrapolation is one of the sensitive quantities we must examine. However one cannot fault the authors for their approximating the data the way they do as a way to infer near-term consequences.

The model itself and its use, as a device to test various effective rates and policies, is interesting but, as the authors are aware, it is only a model. It is terribly important to be aware of the subtle ways in which such models can induce a feeling of their reality. A particularly vivid example arose in connection with Forrester's urban model. Leo Kadanoff (American Scientist, 60 (1972), 74–79) compared the inferences regarding the impact of slum clearance and job training on the underemployed and labor force populations. Kadanoff carried out two calculations; the first was essentially a replication of Forrester's own model calculations, with the same conclusions. The second was a variation in which Forrester's single open city system was replaced with a collection of interacting cities, each open but with the entire set forming a closed system. The calculation was particularly striking because the two models give, in essence, diametrically opposite conclusions.

The authors of "Limits to Growth" have varied a number of rate coefficients and initial quantities to try to probe the sensitivity of both the society and the model to such variations. I fear that the experience of Kadanoff's analysis indicates that the probing has not gone as far as it should. The change of a rate coefficient may change the behavior of a system of coupled rate equations, but unless one is very near a critical region, trajectories are often very insensitive to such changes. On the other hand, changes in boundary conditions or of the form of dependence of one variable on another can have drastic effects.

Computer Experiment

It is a pity that neither Forrester nor the four authors of "Limits to Growth" have written out their model as concise sets of coupled equations. I personally find it very hard to relate a model expressed in its entirety only as a computer code to the sorts of models whose behavior has been studied in more than an experimental fashion. And I do think we can charge "The Limits to Growth" with being a set of computer experiments, in contrast to being an analysis of the behavior of the model. By contrast to the method of computer experiment, one might expect world modelers to adopt the methods of Prigogine, Nicolis and their coworkers, of Cowan, Winfree, Goodwin, Kerner and many others; methods exemplified in simplest form by the analyses of the predator-prey model of Volterra and Lotka. It is surprising, for example, that the "Limits" model seems to have no room for limit cycles, which Poincare pointed out are characteristic of nonlinear, nonconservative systems of which the Earth is clearly an example. One would suspect that many realistic trajectories of our society would in fact lead to true or quasi-oscillatory behavior (as in limit cycles), and that not all trajectories would display monotonic approach toward an asymptote or a single rise and sharp fall, as do the trajectories shown in "Limits to Growth." One would expect to see world models showing quasiperiodic motion around one point and, then, with a change of parameter, to shift suddenly to an alternative cycle around an altogether different point.

The basic difference between the most vehement advocates of "Limits to Growth" and its most violent critics lies in an implicit difference in the beliefs of these two groups about the nature of the trajectories. The advocates believe that the exponential model (as I shall call the model used by the authors of "Limits") is valid up to and beyond the point at which the curves turn over and plummet downward. The critics believe that the exponential model is inaccurate, at least by the time at which the maxima are predicted; they believe, usually implicitly and diffusely, that some less cataclysmic behavior, perhaps oscillatory, is far more likely.

The Same Answers

It is clearly true that the exponential model is a valid representation for projecting into next week or next month. This is true because essentially all reasonable methods of extrapolation give the same answers for sufficiently short intervals of extrapolation. It is also clearly true that if one assumes an incorrect form for the dependence of one variable on others, then an extrapolation will go awry if it is pushed far enough. When should one look for symptoms to decide whether a relation and an extrapolation are valid? Clearly, the most sensitive time is one at which the initial mode of dependence undergoes a drastic change; in other words, if the exponential model is correct, and if we do not change the system in a basic way (by changing our values, for example), then we will learn of its validity most clearly precisely because we shall experience a cataclysmic turnover of the sort indicated by the "Limits" model. If, on the other hand, the model is inadequate, we can expect to experience some leveling or downward trend before we reach a critical maximum predicted by the "Limits" model. For it is hard to refute the assertion that if we were to follow the exponential model until we reached a point very near a critical maximum, then we should almost assuredly follow it closely for at least a short while— even over the precipice—because the behavior of the system is very insensitive to the model over short ranges.

Should we expect the exponential behavior to be valid up to the point of the critical maxima and beyond? Hardly. Surely when a system with as much feedbacks as our society approaches a singular point on its trajectory, one should expect to see a change in the essential relationships, at least on the farther side of the singularity, and presumably a bit before. Perhaps this very debate is itself part of an adaptation and change of relationships symptomatic of the society veering away from "exponential behavior." Rational inquiry and response is, after all, one of our favorite feedback mechanisms. We cannot really expect the simple relationships of the model that apply for short extrapolations to be valid into the range in which the model itself predicts behavior violently different from that on which the model is based. If we had a sound external basis for believing in the validity of the model under a variety of conditions, then we could consider trusting it through a region of drastic change; without this external validation, I fear we have no reason to accept or reject the model in regions where things are different from the way they are now. In plain words, the model may give us danger signals; but, in its present form, it should not be used in a positive way to select policies.

This prompts me to take the empirical and historically-inclined social scientists to task. It is striking and very disappointing that models are not more frequently tested against historical data. I have in mind, in particular, Forrester's urban model, for which a rather good test can be made, I suspect, from historical data alone. So far as I am aware, this model is still essentially untested against real data.

If we cannot trust the exponential model in the regions that lead to its major implications, are we to chuck out the model and the method and sit back, waiting for the inevitable comfortable down-trend? The very phraseology suggests my answer; certainly, we must pay attention to the cataclysmic predictions of the "Limits" model. The patient should be put under observation because of possible illness, and we should be exploring the contingencies with vigor; but it is hardly appropriate to put the poor creature into intensive care when the diagnosis is prone to serious mistakes and the side effects of intensive treatment can be so debilitating.

A Warning

It would be a grievous but real possibility to let ourselves be carried along up a rising exponential or unstable trajectory until the only path back involved a cataclysmic change in our life style. The role of "The Limits to Growth" should not be, and need not be, to show us that we are on such a trajectory, but only to warn us that we may be. As I have often argued myself, we should be watching carefully, avoiding the obviously foolhardy courses and preparing for contingencies. We should be moving as fast as we can away from the obviously untenable dichotomy between the conditions of developed and underdeveloped nations, we should be reducing population growth at a rapid but not catastrophic rate, we should be learning how to make increasingly effective use of resources, both recoverable and nonrecoverable, and we should be building a sinking fund of knowledge of how to cope with these problems in increasingly severe ways, if and when the symptoms don't respond to our gentler treatments.

Let me close with the warning that a fast response can itself be a destabilizing factor. Trying to adjust society to a stable trajectory in a time interval faster than the society can respond will surely have the effect that a sudden impulse has in almost any complex system: the system responds with a series of sharp oscillations. Sometimes these oscillations are damped and the system recovers. Sometimes the oscillations increase in amplitude until the system breaks. We must understand not only the way the system works and identify its weaknesses; we must carefully find out how it responds to therapy, lest we kill the patient with overzealous care.

44

The Santa Barbara Oil Spill
RODERICK NASH (1970); ROSS MACDONALD (1972)

A year after the oil spill that blackened their channel, the citizens of Santa Barbara, California arranged an anniversary celebration to assess the significance of the event. On January 28, 1970, Roderick Nash read the following before national television from a meeting room overlooking the scene of the event that helped shock the nation into an awareness of environmental problems. "The Santa Barbara Declaration of Environmental Rights" owes much to both Thomas Jefferson's and Aldo Leopold's (20) ideas. Amounting to a declaration of interdependence, it represents a summation of environmental problems and solutions as many perceived them at the start of the 1970s.

Further assessment of the significance of the Santa Barbara oil spill came in 1972 with the publication of Robert Easton's Black Tide. *The book was introduced by Ross Macdonald, the mystery writer and an environmentally concerned Santa Barbaran. His interpretation helps explain how a relatively minor event came to symbolize serious problems and to elicit deep-rooted anxieties among thoughtful Americans.*

THE SANTA BARBARA DECLARATION OF ENVIRONMENTAL RIGHTS

ALL MEN have the right to an environment capable of sustaining life and promoting happiness. If the accumulated actions of the past become destructive of this right, men now living have the further right to repudiate the past for the benefit of the future. And it is manifest that centuries of careless neglect of the environment have brought mankind to a final crossroads. The quality of our lives is eroded and our very existence threatened by our abuse of the natural world.

"The Santa Barbara Declaration of Environmental Rights" was published by the January 28 Committee on January 28, 1970. It had previously been read into the *Congressional Record,* CXVI, no. 2, on January 20, 1970, by Senator John V. Tunney with several minor changes.

MOVED by an environmental disaster in the Santa Barbara Channel to think and act in national and world terms, we submit these charges:

We have littered the land with refuse.

We have encroached upon our heritage of open space and wild-land.

We have stripped the forests and the grasses and reduced the soil to fruitless dust.

We have contaminated the air we breathe for life.

We have befouled the lakes and rivers and oceans along with their shorelines.

We have released deadly poisons into earth, air, and water, imperiling all life.

We have exterminated entire species of birds and animals and brought others close to annihilation.

We are overpopulating the earth.

We have made much of the physical world ugly and loud, depriving man of the beauty and quiet that feeds his spirit.

RECOGNIZING that the ultimate remedy for these fundamental problems is found in man's mind, not his machines, we call on societies and their governments to recognize and implement the following principles:

We need an ecological consciousness that recognizes man as member, not master, of the community of living things sharing his environment.

We must extend ethics beyond social relations to govern man's contact with all life forms and with the environment itself.

We need a renewed idea of community which will shape urban environments that serve the full range of human needs.

We must find the courage to take upon ourselves as individuals responsibility for the welfare of the whole environment, treating our own back yards as if they were the world and the world as if it were our back yard.

We must develop the vision to see that in regard to the natural world private and corporate ownership should be so limited as to preserve the interest of society and the integrity of the environment.

We need greater awareness of our enormous powers, the fragility of the earth, and the consequent responsibility of men and governments for its preservation.

We must redefine "progress" toward an emphasis on long-term quality rather than immediate quantity.

WE, THEREFORE, resolve to act. We propose a revolution in conduct toward an environment which is rising in revolt against us. Granted that ideas and institutions long established are not easily changed; yet today is the first day of the rest of our life on this planet. We will begin anew.

This is the first full account of an ecological crime—a crime without criminals but with many victims—and a community's response to it. The eruption of the oil well on Union Platform A off Santa Barbara on January 28, 1969, has had profound effects, and could be described as the blowout heard around the world.

The blowout shook the industry and the federal bureaucracy, whose rules and safeguards had failed to prevent it, and is gradually forcing the reform of those rules and safeguards. It triggered a social movement and helped to create a new politics, the politics of ecology, which is likely to exert a decisive influence on future elections and on our lives. It brought to a head our moral and economic doubts about the American uses of energy and raised the question of whether we really have to go on polluting the sea and land and air in order to support our freeway philosophy of one man, one car.

The book begins with basic physical events: the rupture of the well under the sea floor, its running wild for ten days, and the attempts of industry and government to get it stopped. Perhaps the central figure of the early chapters is a young Coast Guard officer, Lieutenant George H. Brown, III, who found himself to be the responsible authority at the scene of the spill, and the human fulcrum of almost incredible weights and pressures. Gradually, the threatened Santa Barbara

Ross Macdonald, "Introduction" in Robert Easton, *Black Tide: The Santa Barbara Oil Spill and Its Consequences* (New York, 1972), ix–xvi. Copyright © 1972 by Ross Macdonald. Used with permission of Delacorte Press.

community becomes the main protagonist, and its life intensifies like that of a city under siege. The drama mounts and expands onto the national stage. There are congressional investigations and debates, and repercussions in senatorial and presidential politics. The book as a whole asks whether and how the American people can control what government and industry, oil and accident, may do to them, and suggests some intelligent answers to these questions.

It was no accident that Robert Easton wrote this book. He is a third-generation Californian and a grandson of Warren Olney, one of the founders of the Sierra Club. His father was a nature-loving cattle rancher, and conservation was a second religion in his household. Bob was raised near Santa Barbara in Santa Maria, which already in the early years of the century had been the scene of a major oil strike, and a major spill.

When I first met Bob in the years just after the war, he was a young ex-infantry officer with a successful first novel and a mass of serious journalism already behind him. The war novel he was writing at night was related to his personal experiences—so closely related, indeed, that he found it difficult to finish: too many men of his company had died. The daytime work with which he supported his wife and family had been chosen as if in unconscious preparation for the present book. He was employed as a foreman by the Richfield Oil Company, helping to build an artificial island on the Rincon, some twenty miles east of Santa Barbara, from which underwater oil wells could be drilled.

The oil operations on the Rincon were not pretty, in spite of the palm trees that were brought in to decorate the artificial island. Still, few Santa Barbarans realized that such operations might some day constitute a threat to the city itself. There had been an oil strike just east of Santa Barbara some fifty years before, and the Summerland shore was still a wasteland being cleaned up at state expense. But such enormities seemed a thing of the past.

In those early postwar years, Santa Barbara was a quiet seaport facing south across white public beaches to blue waters reflecting a clear sky. A boat trip to the Channel Islands was like a voyage to Eden. The channel was alive with fish and dolphins, sea lions, whales in season, birds on the water and in the air. There was so little traffic in town that traffic lights were unnecessary and I could ride my bicycle down the main street with my black dog Skipper carelessly trailing me. There was a sense of freedom and ease in the untainted atmosphere. The city had so many trees and gardens that it seemed to be interfused with live green nature.

Santa Barbara's tradition of living at respectful ease with nature went back a long way. For a thousand years before the white man came, the Indians had built their villages on the coastal slope. They lived on acorns and fish, and decorated their ceremonial caves with some of the finest primitive art in the world. The Santa Barbara pueblo was founded by the Spanish in 1782, the year after Los Angeles. A gradual immigration from the east changed the graceful Spanish character of the city without destroying it, and strengthened it with rigor and independence of thought.

Santa Barbara became a center of West Coast civilization, a place that leading American writers knew and referred to in their books. Naturalists, impressed by the equable climate, transplanted flowers and trees from other continents. Santa Barbara's Museum of Natural History was founded by William L. Dawson. whose *Birds of California* is still the classic on that subject. The Museum, the Botanic Garden, and the nearby branch of the University of California have made the city a center for the study of natural history, and attracted nature-loving residents from all over the country and the world. The local branch of the Audubon Society, in this city of 70,000, has over 750 members.

The Audubon emblem, the common egret, is a reminder that the national society was founded to save that bird from extinction. Similarly, the Santa Barbara Audubon Society has a special interest in preserving the California condor. It is not too much to say that in Southern California that great threatened bird is a symbol of survival, and of warning. The condor is our canary in the mine—the mine slowly filling with pollutants which is a possible image of our world—and if the condor survives, perhaps we may too.

This was one of the central ideas of the book about the condor which Bob Easton wrote with Dick Smith in the mid-1960s. This slim book marked a milestone in Bob's life, pointing toward his future as a historian of Santa Barbara's ecological disaster, and grounded in his personal and family past. When Bob was a small boy, his father had taken him into the wilderness near his ranch and shown him condors. In the 1930s, the elder Easton led a successful national campaign to set up the Sisquoc Condor Sanctuary in that wilderness. But in the 1960s, the condor was still in trouble, having declined to a population of forty or so. Now it was Bob who took the lead in trying to save it.

The issue was not only the survival of the condor, but the preservation of the wilderness over which the condor flew. Both were threatened by Forest Service plans to build a paved road along the Sierra Madre Ridge, which marks the northern rim of the Sisquoc wilderness and is itself part of the condor flyway. Bob fought mightily for the endangered wilderness and its birds.

During this time I came to know Bob Easton well and saw him grow into first a community and ultimately a national leader. Our little "wilderness campaign" group was largely made up of leaders: Fred Eissler of the Sierra Club, Dick Smith of the *Santa Barbara News-Press*, Jim Mills, now president of the Santa Barbara Audubon Society, and our gray eminence Ian McMillan of Shandon, perhaps California's most effective conservationist. Over a period of several years we met irregularly. The Sierra Madre Ridge road was put to sleep, only to be replaced by a larger but related issue.

This was the establishment of the San Rafael Wilderness Area, the first under the Wilderness Act of 1964. In its final dimensions, on which our group insisted and held firm, this national wilderness covers some 140,000 acres in the Santa Barbara back country. After many months of educational and political activity, Fred Eissler and Bob went to Washington to see the expanded wilderness bill through Congress. They came back proud, feeling that Santa Barbara had established itself as a center of conservation in the west. This wilderness campaign helped to determine the strategy and tactics of the massive and continuing campaign against oil in our channel.

Santa Barbara had had to fight continually to preserve both her amenities and her reputation as a conservation center. Like most other Southern California cities, it had more than doubled in size since the war. It was faced with serious traffic problems and accompanying air and noise pollution. The overhead freeway proposed by the State Highway Division threatened to broadcast this pollution further, and to cut the downtown business section in two. Visible decay in the central part of the city called for rehabilitation and restoration.

The city resisted many threats. The wild growth that overran San Jose and other cities in this period was checked in Santa Barbara by the city's refusal to accept any but smokeless industry. The overhead freeway has been stalled for years, and plans for it are being gradually and reluctantly altered by the Highway Division. An enlightened citizen force led by Miss Pearl Chase prevented the building of high-rise apartments in the city, and had held back a later plan which would lead to suburban sprawl.

It was an ecologically aware citizen force that held the city together during the oil crisis. Though the city is quite conservative politically, and backed Nixon and Reagan in recent elections, it is far from devoid of intellectual activism. This activism can be reminiscent of a New England town meeting, where citizens are a functioning and vocal part of government. The civic life of Santa Barbara has been punctuated, loudly, by such meetings.

The oil crisis crept up on us in near silence. Concentrating on protecting the city and the surrounding lands, we didn't fully realize that the sea could be in danger. In my early years in Santa Barbara, I had made the narrator of a novel say: "I turned on my back and floated, looking up at the sky, nothing around me but cool clear Pacific, nothing in my eyes but long blue space. It was as close as I ever got to cleanliness and freedom, as far as I ever got from all the people. They had jerrybuilt the beaches from San Diego to the Golden Gate, bulldozed super-highways through the mountains, cut down a thousand years of redwood growth, and built an urban wilderness in the desert. They couldn't touch the ocean. They poured their sewage into it, but it couldn't be tainted."

My narrator and I were wrong. A series of oil drilling platforms had been erected in the state tidelands southeast of Santa Barbara. Now there was pressure for further platforms in the deeper and more treacherous federal waters outside the three-mile limit. The pressure was intensified by the federal government's need for money to finance the war in Indochina, and local government was unable to withstand it. A number of citizens, including Fred Eissler and Bob Easton, tried to open public discussion on the matter, but the decision had already been made in Washington, based on Interior Department findings which were rather loosely related to local reality. Without a public hearing, or any serious examination of the dangers of deep-water drilling in the earthquake-prone channel, oil rights in large sections of the channel were auctioned off to the oil companies. After the damage was done, we learned why there had been no public hearings: a permanent official in the Interior Department had vetoed it on the grounds that it might "stir up the natives."

At this time, Bob was employed as a senior writer in the U.S. Naval Laboratory at Port Hueneme. By a neat twist of fate, he was putting together a massive anonymous tome on underwater construction which gave him further preparation for writing the present book. At the same time, he was researching and writing a biography of Max

Brand, his father-in-law and literary mentor. His working life was relieved by long walks in the wilderness he had helped to preserve. When he had a moral or intellectual or political problem—and more and more the conservation problems of the community tended to migrate to him—he would carry it into the back country for a day or two and come out with a solution or at least a fresh approach.

The walks Bob took with me and my dog Brandy were shorter. During those walks, we talked about the things that men in their fifties are ordinarily concerned with—our past lives, children and grandchildren, our work, and how to preserve the country we were walking through.

The great oil spill that began on January 28, 1969, failed to interrupt our walks, but it displaced other topics of conversation. I remember a day, about two weeks after the eruption, when we stopped on Mountain Drive and looked out over the contaminated sea. The flowing oil had been partly choked off, but it was still leaking up through the ruptured sea floor. Thousands of diving birds had died, and the quality of human life in the area was being threatened. The beaches were black for forty miles along the coast, and reblackened every day as the tides came in. The odor of crude oil reached us like the whiff of a decaying future.

It seemed to us that if the spill was to have a meaning, that meaning would have to be created by the men on the scene. Somehow the black disaster of Santa Barbara must be converted into a turning point in our history, a signpost marking the end of such ruinous environmental carelessness. This view was presented in an article for the *New York Times Magazine* which Bob Easton and I collaborated on. Then I turned back to my fiction. Bob went on by himself to traverse a wilderness of fact and write this book about the blow to Santa Barbara's life and her historic response—the book his entire life had prepared him to write.

Like those ancient Greek historians who fought in the wars they later chronicled, the author is a witness as well as a recorder. He shared with the other residents of Santa Barbara, and shares with the reader, the sickening uncertainties of the early days of the spill, when it appeared that this beautiful city would be degraded into an industrial slum. He shared the months of conflict and doubt, as it became clear that the lessons of the spill were being lost on the federal government and its favored industry, and that the sellout of the Santa Barbara Channel would be allowed to proceed. He shared, and contributed to, the realization that our fate was in our own hands, that only the people on the spot could hope to counter and change a self-destructive national policy. He describes from firsthand knowledge the organization and use of citizen movements like GOO (Get Oil Out!) without whose advice and dissent both big government and big industry seem to be one-eyed giants. He is one of the citizen-litigants who are still seeking in the federal courts a full disclosure from the government of the uncertain physical situation in the channel.

Yet the reader will be pleasantly surprised to find that this book is in no sense a work of special pleading. It was written after laborious and detailed research by a trained historian who does not let his personal views distort the record. The scientific evidence was derived from and checked by competent biologists and ecologists, and other experts. The clear and detailed explanation of how the spill came to occur and how it was eventually checked is based on all available reports, including those of the U.S. Geological Survey, and on the testimony of eyewitnesses and participants. Weeks and months of interviewing underlie the day-to-day account. For example, before writing the story of Lieutenant Brown's activities, the author spent some days talking to the young Coast Guard lieutenant and recording everything he said.

Since then, Lieutenant Brown has been detached from his Santa Barbara command and has begun work, under Coast Guard auspices, toward an advanced degree in the ecological field. The people of Santa Barbara had hoped that a similarly enlightened response to the city's near tragedy would be made by other agencies of the federal government. But the Department of the Interior, staffed by many of the same permanent officials whose recommendations and decisions precipitated the disaster, is persisting in its determination to convert the Santa Barbara Channel into an oil field.

The issue, as it appears to local residents, is whether their environment can be bought and sold over their objections, or whether there is an inalienable right to the use and enjoyment of air and water. It is a test case, between a pervasive new form of tyranny and an ancient freedom, which will help to determine the future conditions of life throughout the United States.

45

The International Dimension
THE UNITED NATIONS CONFERENCE ON THE HUMAN ENVIRONMENT (1972); EARTHCARE (1975)

As early as 1908 Gifford Pinchot (9) entertained hopes that the conservation movement could transcend national boundaries. Advancing knowledge in the field of systems ecology has made such transcendence imperative if conservation is to succeed at all. Space exploration provided dramatic evidence of the unity of the environment. Everything was connected; there were no environmental islands.

Using as a theme "Only One Earth," the United Nations Conference on the Human Environment, held in Stockholm June 5–16, 1972, marked the movement of environmental concern into the world arena. One hundred and fourteen delegations, including a large and enthusiastic one from the United States, participated. Given the divergent social and economic viewpoints of the conferees, tension was inevitable. Most conflict centered on the issue of growth and development, pitting the "haves" (who could afford conservation) and the "have-nots" (for whom it was an obstacle to short-term material progress). Still the conference managed to draft a Declaration and produce a set of Principles. Both appear below as does an abridged version of the conference-closing remarks of Canadian Maurice Strong who chaired the proceedings and, later, assumed direction of the United Nations Environment Programme. UNEP, as it came to be called, was based, significantly, in a developing nation: Kenya.

On World Environment Day, 5 June 1975, the organizers of the EARTHCARE Conference pursued the objectives of Stockholm by circulating the second document below. Sharper and less anthropocentric than the Stockholm statement, EARTHCARE's petition will, after worldwide signature, be submitted to the Secretary-General of the United Nations.

"Declaration on the Human Environment" and "A Strong Reason for Hope," *Not Man Apart* II (1972), 1, 3. "Declaration of Principles" from a leaflet distributed by the United Nations Environment Programme, Nairobi, © 1973.

DECLARATION ON THE HUMAN ENVIRONMENT

1. *Man is both creature and moulder of his environment* which gives him physical sustenance and affords him the opportunity for intellectual, moral, social and spiritual growth. In the long and tortuous evolution of the human race on this planet a stage has been reached when through the rapid acceleration of science and technology, man has acquired the power to transform his environment in countless ways and on an unprecedented scale. Both aspects of man's environment, the natural and the man-made, are essential to his well-being and to the enjoyment of basic human rights—even the right of life itself.

2. *The protection and improvement of the human environment is a major issue which affects the well-being of peoples and economic development* throughout the world; it is the urgent desire of the peoples of the whole world and the duty of all governments.

3. *Man has constantly to sum up experience and go on discovering, inventing, creating and advancing.* In our time man's capability to transform his surroundings, if used wisely, can bring to all peoples the benefits of development and the opportunity to enhance the quality of life. Wrongly or heedlessly applied, the same power can do incalculable harm to human beings and the human environment. We see around us growing evidence of man-made harm in many regions of the earth: dangerous levels of pollution in water, air, earth and living beings; major and undesirable disturbances to the ecological balance of the biosphere; destruction and depletion of irreplaceable resources; and gross deficiencies harmful to the physical, mental and social health of man, in the man-made environment; particularly in the living and working environment.

4. *In the developing countries most of the environmental problems are caused by under-development.* Millions continue to live far below the minimum levels required for a decent human existence, deprived of adequate food and clothing, shelter and education, health and sanitation. Therefore the developing countries must direct their efforts to development, bearing in mind their priorities and the need to safeguard and improve the environment. For the same purpose, the industrialized countries should make efforts to reduce the gap between themselves and the developing countries. In the industrialized countries, environmental problems are related to industrialization and technological development.

5. *The natural growth of population continuously presents prob-*

lems on the preservation of the environment, but with the adoption of appropriate policies and measures these problems can be solved. Of all things in the world people are the most precious. It is the people that propel social progress, create social wealth, develop science and technology and through their hard work, continuously transform the human environment. Along with social progress and the advance of production, science and technology, the capability of man to improve the environment increases with each passing day.

6. *A point has been reached in history when we must shape our actions throughout the world with a more prudent care for their environmental consequences.* Through ignorance or indifference we can do massive and irreversible harm to the earthly environment on which our life and well-being depend. Conversely, through fuller knowledge and wiser action, we can achieve for ourselves and our posterity a better life in an environment more in keeping with human needs and hopes. There are broad vista for the enhancement of environmental quality and the creation of a good life. What is needed is an enthusiastic but calm state of mind and intense but orderly work. For the purpose of attaining freedom in the world of nature, man must use knowledge to build in collaboration with nature a better environment. To defend and improve the human environment for present and future generations has become an imperative goal for mankind—a goal to be pursued together with, and in harmony with, the established and fundamental goals of peace and of world-wide economic and social development.

7. *To achieve this environmental goal will demand the acceptance of responsibility by citizens and communities and by enterprises and institutions at every level,* all sharing equitably in common efforts. Individuals in all walks of life as well as organizations in many fields, by their values and the sum of their actions, will shape the world environment of the future. Local and national governments will bear the greatest burden for large-scale environmental policy and action within their jurisdictions. International co-operation is also needed in order to raise resources to support the developing countries in carrying out their responsibilities in this field. A growing class of environmental problems, because they are regional or global in extent or because they affect the common international realm, will require extensive co-operation among nations and action by international organizations in the common interest. The Conference calls upon the Governments and peoples to exert common efforts for the preservation and improvement of the

human environment, for the benefit of all the people and for their posterity.

DECLARATION OF PRINCIPLES

Principle 1.   Man has the fundamental right to freedom, equality and adequate conditions of life, in an environment of a quality that permits a life of dignity and well-being, and he bears a solemn responsibility to protect and improve the environment for present and future generations. In this respect, policies promoting or perpetuating apartheid, racial segregation, discrimination, colonial and other forms of oppression and foreign domination stand condemned and must be eliminated.

Principle 2.   The natural resources of the earth including the air, water, land, flora and fauna and especially representative samples of natural ecosystems must be safeguarded for the benefit of present and future generations through careful planning of management, as appropriate.

Principle 3.   The capacity of the earth to produce vital renewable resources must be maintained and, wherever practicable, restored or improved.

Principle 4.   Man has a special responsibility to safeguard and wisely manage the heritage of wildlife and its habitat which are now gravely imperiled by a combination of adverse factors. Nature conservation including wildlife must therefore receive importance in planning for economic development.

Principle 5.   The non-renewable resources of the earth must be employed in such a way as to guard against the danger of their future exhaustion and to ensure that benefits from such employment are shared by all mankind.

Principle 6.   The discharge of toxic substances or of other substances and the release of heat, in such quantities or concentrations as to exceed the capacity of the environment to render them harmless, must be halted in order to ensure that serious or irreversible damage is not inflicted upon ecosystems. The just struggle of the peoples of all countries against pollution should be supported.

Principle 7.   States shall take all possible steps to prevent pollution of the seas by substances that are liable to create hazards to human health, to harm living resources and marine life, to damage amenities, or to interfere with other legitimate uses of the sea.

Principle 8. Economic and social development is essential for ensuring a favourable living and working environment for man and for creating conditions on earth that are necessary for the improvement of the quality of life.

Principle 9. Environmental deficiencies generated by the conditions of underdevelopment and natural disasters pose grave problems and can best be remedied by accelerated development through the transfer of substantial quantities of financial and technological assistance as a supplement to the domestic effort of the developing countries and such timely assistance as may be required.

Principle 10. For the developing countries, stability of prices and adequate earnings for primary commodities and raw material are essential to environmental management since economic factors as well as ecological process must be taken into account.

Principle 11. The environmental policies of all States should enhance and not adversely affect the present or future development potential of developing countries, nor should they hamper the attainment of better living conditions for all, and appropriate steps should be taken by States and international organizations with a view to reaching agreement on meeting the possible national and international economic consequences resulting from the application of environmental measures.

Principle 12. Resources should be made available to preserve and improve the environment, taking into account the circumstances and particular requirements of developing countries and any costs which may emanate from their incorporating environmental safeguards into their development planning and the need for making available to them, upon their request, additional international technical and financial assistance for this purpose.

Principle 13. In order to achieve a more rational management of resources and thus to improve the environment, States should adopt an integrated and co-ordinated approach to their development planning so as to ensure that development is compatible with the need to protect and improve the human environment for the benefit of their population.

Principle 14. Rational planning constitutes an essential tool for reconciling any conflict between the needs of development and the need to protect and improve the environment.

Principle 15. Planning must be applied to human settlements and urbanization with a view to avoiding adverse effects on the environment and obtaining maximum social, economic and environmental benefits for all. In this respect projects which are designed for colonialist and racist domination must be abandoned.

Principle 16. Demographic policies, which are without prejudice to basic human rights and which are deemed appropriate by Governments concerned, should be applied in those regions where the rate of population growth or excessive population concentrations are likely to have adverse effects on the environment or development, or where low population density may prevent improvement of the human environment and impede development.

Principle 17. Appropriate national institutions must be entrusted with the task of planning, managing or controlling the environmental resources of States with the view to enhancing environmental quality.

Principle 18. Science and technology, as part of their contribution to economic and social development, must be applied to the identification, avoidance and control of environmental risks and the solution of environmental problems and for the common good of mankind.

Principle 19. Education in environmental matters, for the younger generation as well as adults, giving due consideration to the underprivileged, is essential in order to broaden the basis for an enlightened opinion and responsible conduct by individuals, enterprises and communities in protecting and improving the environment in its full human dimension. It is also essential that mass media of communications avoid contributing to the deterioration of the environment, but, on the contrary, disseminate information of an educational nature, on the need to protect and improve the environment in order to enable man to develop in every respect.

Principle 20. Scientific research and development in the context of environmental problems, both national and multinational, must be promoted in all countries, especially the developing countries. In this connexion, the free flow of up-to-date scientific information and transfer of experience must be supported and assisted, to facilitate the solution of environmental problems, environmental technologies should be made available to developing countries on terms which would encourage their wide dissemination without constituting an economic burden on the developing countries.

Principle 21. States have, in accordance with the Charter of the United Nations and the principles of international law, the sovereign right to exploit their own resources pursuant to their own environmental policies, and the responsibility to ensure that activities within their jurisdiction or control do not cause damage to the environment of other States or of areas beyond the limits of national jurisdiction.

Principle 22. States shall co-operate to develop further the international law regarding liability and compensation for the victims of pollution and other environmental damage caused by activities within the jurisdiction or control of such states to areas beyond their jurisdiction.

Principle 23. Without prejudice to such criteria as may be agreed upon by the international community, or to standards which will have to be determined nationally, it will be essential in all cases to consider the systems of values prevailing in each country, and the extent of the applicability of standards which are valid for the most advanced countries but which may be inappropriate and of unwarranted social cost for the developing countries.

Principle 24. International matters concerning the protection and improvement of the environment should be handled in a co-operative spirit by all countries, big or small, on an equal footing. Co-operation through multilateral or bilateral arrangements or other appropriate means is essential to effectively control, prevent, reduce and eliminate adverse environmental effects resulting from activities conducted in all spheres, in such a way that due account is taken of the sovereignty and interests of all States.

Principle 25. States shall ensure that international organizations play a co-ordinated, efficient and dynamic role for the protection and improvement of the environment.

Principle 26. Man and his environment must be spared the effects of nuclear weapons and all other means of mass destruction. States must strive to reach prompt agreement, in the relevant international organs, on the elimination and complete destruction of such weapons.

A STRONG REASON FOR HOPE

Secretary-General Maurice Strong

When this Conference convened two weeks ago, the tasks before it seemed almost impossible of achievement. But it has faced up to the challenge—much of it controversial, all of it difficult, none of it with precedent for guidance—with a determination to find solutions. . . .

We have taken the first steps on a new journey of hope for the future of mankind. But the journey before us is long and difficult, and we have barely begun it. What is most important of all, however, is that we leave Stockholm with a program of action to cope with the critical relationships between the natural and the man-made systems of Planet Earth. . . .

Non-governmental organizations in particular have stimulated a two-way exchange of ideas and information that have made major contributions to the success of our deliberations. I now look forward to their initiatives and co-operation in the future environmental work of the UN. . . .

I believe we must leave here with an awakened sense of this new dynamic breaching the barriers between those who make the official decisions and those who are affected by such decisions. If we do that, it may well have a more far-reaching impact on the affairs of Planet Earth than any of the more technical decisions we have reached. . . . This Conference has emphasized both in word and in deed that deep and pervasive changes are needed in the way man looks at his world, at the role of man within nature, and at his relations with other men. It has asserted its conviction that man cannot manage his relations with nature unless he learns to manage better the relations between man and man—that if he is to preserve Planet Earth for future generations, he must also make it a better home for present generations. . . .

This Conference has done more than recognize the urgent need for a change in man's priorities. It has achieved a heartening consensus to the effect that no fundamental conflict exists between the goal of environmental quality on the one hand and economic and social progress on the other.

So there is reason for hope in the work it has done—in the programs it has adopted—in the awareness it has expressed of our global unity—in the affirmation that the problems of the human environment can only be resolved if we place man at the center of our concerns—and in the convictions that we must liberate ourselves from the outdated and outworn habits of the past. . . .

RIGHTS TO EARTHCARE: A PETITION

Three years ago, acting upon the recommendations of the United Nations Stockholm Conference on the Human Environment the General Assembly declared that safeguarding the environment is a prerequisite to "the enjoyment of basic human rights—even the right to life itself." Each Government is responsible for securing such rights.

For the first time in Earth's history, our species has the capacity to violate the environment on a scale that endangers the existence of all species. The heedless exploitation of nature and the careless use of resources already threaten our inheritors with a world physically and spiritually impoverished. We must act now to renounce such a perilous course and to conduct our affairs in harmony with nature.

We have little time to reshape our global community. The next thirty years will produce a doubling of world population and an even greater explosion of expectations. We shall not cope with the consequent stresses on social organization without first reordering our values in recognition that human life is a part of nature. Our decisions must be grounded in ecological principles.

The biosphere comprises myriad interrelations between plants and animals, land, air and water. We can modify some ecosystems, even enhance them, but we may not abuse them. Given our elementary knowledge, we cannot press the limits and capacities of natural systems without incurring the gravest danger. We are not immune to the hazard of ecological breakdown resulting from irreparable acts.

Regardless of our political, economic or social organization, the lessons of natural science must guide all human affairs. Despoliation of natural environments denies science keys to better understanding and enriching all life. Without environmental protection, short-term economic gain impairs economic stability in the longer span of time. No

---

"Rights to EARTHCARE: A Petition," Released by the Sierra Club and the Audubon Society at the United Nations, New York City, 5 June 1975.

new development should proceed until its environmental impact has been appraised. The drive to exploit, regardless of consequences, must yield to rational use of natural resources. Human needs must be met, excessive demands rejected.

The nations gathered at the 1972 Stockholm Conference on the Human Environment proclaimed that protection of the human environment is the "duty of all Governments." They also agreed that their responsibility to secure natural systems from disruption is a necessary condition to achieving fundamental human rights. Too seldom have these commitments been honored.

Daily, Governments violate our human rights by ignoring the intimacy between the natural and human environments. Such behavior threatens the security of nations, individually and collectively.

After the Stockholm Conference we hoped that Governments would move quickly to avert harm to Nature and adopt a policy of Earthcare which creates the conditions for assuring human rights. Too little has been done.

Members of the United Nations have welcomed petitions seeking assurance of fundamental rights. We add our own, as basic as any received before. Our right to receive protection of our common global environment must be honored.

46

Experiments in Returning to Nature
ED KISSAM (1972)

In 1971 Charles Reich wrote a book about changing American attitude and behavior in the direction of peace, freedom, and harmony. Its title, The Greening of America, *is significant in its suggestion that the remedial process involved nature and naturalness. Expression of the same point of view can be found in the diverse attempts of younger Americans of the late 1960s and early 1970s to go back to the land. Some of the energy for this trend came from countercultural phenomena (from "beatniks" to "hippies") which shared*

Ed Kissam, "Nomads," *Clear Creek* XV (1972), 29–33.

a disgust with established American ends and means. Rejecting civilization meant turning back toward nature. It also meant simplicity and self-suffi-ciency. The commune, or the nomadic existence described in the following selection, was appealing from this perspective. Involved too was the recovery of nonrational modes of relating to the natural world. Some of them amounted to pantheistic religions, and most entailed revolutionary attitudes toward animals, Indians, and the earth itself. Permeating most of the ide-ology of contemporary back-to-nature experiments are the principles of ecology—particularly cooperation, community, and a holistic point of view. The frequently cryptic nature of the following essay can be seen as an expression of the rejection of orthodox ways of thought and communication.

It begins this way: Turtle brought earth up from the bottom of the sea. Just enough. Just barely enough, like a sheet of thin ice, to move across, to move on. . .

How to move on Turtle Island? Charles Olson says:

he who walks with his house on
his head is heaven he
who walks with his house
on his head is heaven he who walks
with his house on his head

We do not ask for reasons to move. The motion is its own reward—take only what you need, move on, fast, light, as on snowshoes: dress as the animal you hunt, in him. This here is Turtle Island, this here continent, earth . . .

Slowly, in America, some of us are learning how little we need and how much is given, not always freely but often for free. We are learn-ing to search out the truths contained in the nomadic life. That lazy wildness of slow Arab coffee, the frizzy-haired freak lying with thumb in air by freeway, the all-night jam sessions of the BaMbuti pygmies, these possibilities which infuriate our industrious neighbors serve to give us ease in the wilderness. Yes, we will yet be nomads.

For the nomad is a lazy man. But tough, precise. He says to the treadmill, "Slow down and get there, somewhere." We are cultivating our "laziness." We learn from the gypsies that when the environment is entirely human rather than natural, you domesticate the *human* animals who surround you. Fortune-telling, horse-trading and intermittent rip-off. Protection in an aura of darkness and magic which terrifies day-light farmers into submission.

All of them, the Saharan nomad, the Eskimo, the gypsy, each knows exactly where he is: the Arab, by the texture of the sand, the signature of the horizon; the gypsy by the subtle gestural clues of face or body on the transparent peasant. For the Australian, the map is given by an encyclopedic tradition of places visited in dreamtime, a spring for each ancestor: the landscape is built into the texture of all talk, the net of memory. The caribou bone breaks open in fire giving the Eskimo an image, a map of the path the caribou will follow in their migration; or the feel of the air tells where the seal will be.

It is a precarious existence, this nomadic life. But there are meaner threats hidden in the bowels of skyscrapers, in the dead air that curls around a television antenna. Nomads are in constant danger of starvation or overexposure to the elements; yet these dangers are perhaps less menacing because anywhere is home, and all places, equally well known, are potential sources of equilibrium. Tundra, ocean, desert, and grassland are all open. Moving over them, there are few boundaries, only gradations of detail. For the nomad, the range is communal, shared among everyone; networks of expanded kinship encompass the wanderers to make them always near a known place. As a mark of this, powerful traditions of hospitality emerge. Even a stranger is welcome to food, shelter, and, in some instances, sex. When men share the belief that one wants only what he needs, there is little fear in giving freely.

We are learning, in our own time, the timeless lessons.

When a Lapp comes into a room with a ceiling he understands next to nothing, as the wind cannot blow into his nostrils. He cannot think when there are walls and a roof about his head. Nor is it good for him to be in thick forest when there is warmth in the air; but when a Lapp is in the high mountains then he has quite a clear brain and if there were a meeting-place up there on some mountain or another then a Lapp could possibly explain his own case quite well.

—Johan Turi

There is an insidious bias in our values which is evident even when we try to free ourselves from our own culture. To a century of Victorians who despised their own textile factories, the ziggurats and pyramids of Mesopotamia and Egypt were wondrous, foreign though they were. But this liberalism guaranteed scorn for those whose attention was concentrated on light design, textures, geometric art—until recently, the Bushmen were barely human since size (Big!) was not of value to them. Australian aborigines, who have a similarly austere culture, were thought "primitive" because the profusion and intricacy of that culture had, as its only artifacts, the trained memories of dreamers and storytellers.

This "Victorian" preference for the megalith to the micro-lith, the empire to tripe, the lushness of alluvial valley cultivation with irrigation to opportune gatherers, the epic to the epigram, leads to a dead-end question taking the form—"Where did we go wrong?" (As though one could tidy up those few sloppy mistakes.) And the answer, just as absurd, is nowhere, really, but in this titanic business of accumulation. Where nomads left stones to the spirits of trees a cairn grew, and a holy hut and then what is it, the Dome of the Rock, and Jerusalem, a modern city. No nomad did more than leave rocks or later, perhaps, undertake a pilgrimage, a cosmic dance to the Qabah. The nomad seems most perceptive when it comes to limitations. He is fortunately a robber, not a conquerer or a builder.

However, the nomad is not anti-technological. Most nomadic cultures separated from their agricultural, sedentary brothers not in Paleolithic times, but rather at a level of Neolithic sophistication. The dog, the camel, the horse are all the results of carefully selective breeding as much as are the corn and wheat of Jarmo and Tenochtitlan, those Gotham Cities of antiquity. The Eskimo's dog and sled, the Bedouin's camel, the Mongol's horse, are elegant, efficient animals, greatly beloved by the humans with whom they lived. The personal care devoted to each makes it obvious that they would never be "mass-produced."

Those animals which were herded—sheep, goats, reindeer and cattle, were owned not by the individual, but by the community. Without the temptation of unlimited personal profit and the tiresome commitment of raising feed, it seems that no major accumulation could take place.

The concept of ownership is, of course, the central contrast between nomads and squatting businessmen. The difference between a community in ecological balance and our leviathan ecological "sinks" is easily erased by a slight shift in values. The Navaho discovery of a market for sheep, coupled with white encouragement of the status value of riches, led to serious overgrazing throughout much of Navaho land. Presumably, the introduction of a market economy to the Plains in which a "product" (buffalo skins) was defined, the political imposition of "reservation" life and consequent value on pumps, roofing, and cast iron stoves, forced the Plains Indians to join their conquerors, the railroad men, in finishing off the buffalo in 20 years.

No community is self-denying, nor need be, if the delicate "ecological" checks and balances within the society which maintain an ecological equilibrium with nature are not disturbed. And who could possibly disturb them? What outside force? Only one, by definition colonial, colonial because its own ecological imbalance required take-over of not only other areas of the earth, but even the hearts and minds of other human beings who are the "prime materials" of commerce.

In the comfort of our urban environment where our energy is im-ported from "marginal" areas such as the Hopi Black Mesa desert or Eskimo North Shore tundra, we wonder, some of the worst of us do, how any community could really want to live in a marginal environ-ment. And that makes nomadic peoples the most wondrous. The Eski-mos and Lapps living entirely north of the Arctic Circle; the Arabs of the Sahara and the desert east of the Levant and Al-JHijaz; the Aus-tralians of Arnhem Land; the Pygmies of sunless rain forest. But then it becomes obvious that our own urban environments with population densities up to three million per square mile, as compared to .2 per square mile for typical nomadic range, are as "marginal" psychologi-cally, biologically, and economically, as any place on earth. Are they lonely, are they poor? Well, try hitting New York City and providing yourself with friends, lovers, family, food, and shelter, plus something you might happen to enjoy doing. Pity the poor subway-token collector.

Slowly, here in America, some of us are learning how little we need and how much is given, not always freely but often for free. And where. Recently a nomad friend, Tim, took me on a two-minute detour off 101 in an old car which he had salvaged from the Arizona desert. Where we went was one Safeway garbage bin. Which gave us: 3 lbs figs, 20 lbs carrots, 12 eggplants, 2 ripe tomatoes, 10 lbs squash, 3 lbs potatoes, 5 lbs limes, 2 cauliflower, 5 pears, parsley, and ½ gal. eggnog with which Tim lounged down in the bottom of the bin to finish off. A Chicano nomad who wandered up was "given" all he could carry and kindly recommended to us a Purity. Twenty miles up the road I gave away most of the carrots, eggplants, and pears and ended up with a gift chicken. Recycled food.

In addition to everyday food-scrounging, Tim has five caches of found objects scattered over 150 miles, from Half Moon Bay up the coast to Geyserville, which are given away when someone mentions they could use them. There is also a larger map of piles of firewood, car parts, abandoned cabins, baby toys, blackberry patches, abandoned or-chards, all of eventual interest, remembered with total precision.

Similarly, the Hog Farm, that legendary bus tribe, thrived on good memories, charm, tricks, and exchange of shaman kindnesses for what-ever else was needed.

The ecological pressure in America is perhaps less physical, though that's obviously intolerable, than psychic. So the "road," the open, that magic itinerary, litany of place names which mean, really, the spaces in-between, is irresistible. Hitchhiking. You do get your kicks on Route 66. No nameless hitchhiker is "alienated" from any other nameless human being who is there synchronistically to provide the information, the human shape of the country, the new visions, to take "home," to take in. Moving on is finding out. We are all technicians of the sacred if humans, brothers and sisters of the communal house, if the earth house itself is—sacred.

Lying back in the flatbed truck about eight humans flashing on Truckee on past Reno on each other. Winnemucca, night (summer), billowing nylon of sleeping bag 75 mph. Salt Lake up changing gears, eventually Denver, shivering but joyful, all honor to Jack Kerouac.* This trip goes on: she arrives at the wedding 2000 miles away in Newark; he heads south to Albuquerque: she forgets her boyfriend in jail by Kansas City; he comes back from a particular field of dope in South Dakota, a branching tree of incantations.

My incantation for last week was: "Big Sur," a "place-name" (which you will discover is not a place, despite the map) which was unknown to me at the time I dreamed it. It became a camping site under cypress trees at the mouth of the river, one of many, right under a *No Trespassing* sign, hearthstones left by previous inhabitants, then the herons, gulls, and ducks, snow down to the head of the canyon, long night wine talk and ocean. Prospect of abalones, which turned out to be safely under a high tide, became vision-knowledge of a particular tilted strata cupping translucent boulders licked shiny by waves, as the river carried sandbar into the ocean after light night rain.

Our American nomadism of hitchhiking is random. For that reason it leads to a peculiar knowledge of land, specific but undirected. Such knowledge is not luxury: the knowledge of the traditional nomad is not really more pragmatic. In neither case does a man demand immediate returns in the profane realm. That is more a corporate concept of profit. Sacred knowledge eventually comes to be of practical use. Neither mind is linear. The nomad's tough precision is a field, a context, where the isolating question, "what is happening here?", need not be phrased. You all know where to go, what to see, whom to meet,

---

* Kerouac, author of *On the Road* (1957), was a leading early spokesman of countercultural values and lifestyles.

what to get. The discipline is mental: the style may be austere, or lavish as with the bus people: embroidered Arab tent of textures or Eskimo igloo whose marvels are all geometrical as it is an improvised geodesic net. "Lazy" and full of care as Smohalla declaring: "My young men will never work."

This here is Turtle Island. This here continent, earth.

47

The Trans-Alaska Pipeline
(1971–1973)

The cartoons below represent a variety of proenvironment views on one of the most controversial environment planning decisions of the early 1970s. In February 1968, exploratory drilling rigs on the Alaskan North Slope, near Prudhoe Bay, struck one of the largest concentrations of oil ever located by the United States. The leases awarded September 10, 1969, brought over $900 million into the federal treasury. The oil industry wanted to begin development at once, but a problem remained: how to get the oil from the North Slope to the refineries in southern Alaska or in the lower 48 states. An 800-mile pipeline to the ice-free seaport of Valdez, Alaska, was one answer, but the prospect of building a developed corridor featuring hot oil through some of the wildest and most fragile country in the United States horrified environmentalists. After 1970, the discussions focused on the newly required environmental impact statement that the Trans-Alaska Pipeline System had to provide. Hasty initial drafts of the statement did not satisfy reviewing agencies or the courts. At length, two developments opened the way for the construction of the pipeline. One was the modification of the plans by the pipeline companies to include environmental safeguards. The other was the advent of the so-called "energy crisis" in the winter of 1973–74, which underscored the need for a domestic oil supply. On November 16, 1973, an act of Congress authorized pipeline construction. The disappointment in some quarters was lessened by the knowledge that the opposition had succeeded in making an industry known for its economic focus admit ecological considerations into its thinking and planning. In this sense, the environmental impact statement requirement of the National Environmental Policy Act served its purpose.

*"... And For The Main Course We Have
Alaskan King Pipeline, Fresh Atlantic and
Pacific Leases ..."*

Tom Engelhardt in *St. Louis Post Dispatch*. Reprinted
by permission.

"Admit it, Muntley, . . . you're a conservationist!"

"Fine, Cousin—And How Are Things With You?"

Copyright 1972 by Herblock in *The Washington Post.*

Moment of Truth

Frank Williams in *Detroit Free Press*. Reprinted with permission.

Bill Sanders in the *Milwaukee Journal*. Reprinted with permission.

48

Mineral King and the Rights of Rocks
WILLIAM O. DOUGLAS (1972)

In 1965 the United States Forest Service, as part of its multiple-use management program (see Document 31), offered the Mineral King Valley of Sequoia National Forest in California's Sierra to prospective developers of ski resorts. Walt Disney Enterprises' bid for a $35 million complex was eventually accepted, but the Sierra Club, concerned with destruction of the aesthetics and ecology of the fragile valley, contested the decision. The battle for Mineral King began. The weapons were years of tedious and costly court proceedings. Many of them centered on the question of legal "standing." Disney and the Forest Service, arguing that the Sierra Club had no property in the area, challenged its right to be a participant in the proceedings. When the case reached the Supreme Court in 1972, Justice William O. Douglas, long a defender of wilderness, argued that the land itself had rights (compare Document 20). The Sierra Club, Douglas said, should have standing in court as the legal spokesman for the rights of the environment. Exciting as the Douglas doctrine was for proponents of environmental ethics, in the end the opponents of Disney's plans for Mineral King won by a war of attrition. The complex legal actions sapped the developer's patience and drained its treasury. In the fall of 1973 Disney announced it was withdrawing its proposal, and would look elsewhere for a winter resort locale.

The critical question of "standing" would be simplified and also put neatly in focus if we fashioned a federal rule that allowed environmental issues to be litigated before federal agencies or federal courts in the name of the inanimate object about to be despoiled, defaced, or invaded by roads and bulldozers and where injury is the subject of public outrage. Contemporary public concern for protecting nature's ecological equilibrium should lead to the conferral of standing upon environmental objects to sue for their own preservation.

Inanimate objects are sometimes parties in litigation. A ship has a

Supreme Court of the United States, *Sierra Club* v. *Morton*, 70–34, April 19, 1972.

legal personality, a fiction found useful for maritime purposes. The corporation sole—a creature of ecclesiastical law—is an acceptable adversary and large fortunes ride on its cases. The ordinary corporation is a "person" for purposes of the adjudicatory processes, whether it represents proprietary, spiritual, aesthetic, or charitable causes.

So it should be as respects valleys, alpine meadows, rivers, lakes, estuaries, beaches, ridges, groves of trees, swampland, or even air that feels the destructive pressures of modern technology and modern life. The river, for example, is the living symbol of all the life it sustains or nourishes—fish, aquatic insects, water ouzels, otter, fisher, deer, elk, bear, and all other animals, including man, who are dependent on it or who enjoy it for its sight, its sound, or its life. The river as plaintiff speaks for the ecological unit of life that is part of it. Those people who have a meaningful relation to that body of water—whether it be a fisherman, a canoeist, a zoologist, or a logger—must be able to speak for the values which the river represents and which are threatened with destruction.

I do not know Mineral King. I have never seen it nor travelled it, though I have seen articles describing its proposed "development". . . . The Sierra Club in its complaint alleges that "One of the principal purposes of the Sierra Club is to protect and conserve the national resources of the Sierra Nevada Mountains." The District Court held that this uncontested allegation made the Sierra Club "sufficiently aggrieved" to have "standing" to sue on behalf of Mineral King.

Mineral King is doubtless like other wonders of the Sierra Nevada such as Tuolumne Meadows and the John Muir Trail. Those who hike it, fish it, hunt it, camp in it, or frequent it, or visit it merely to sit in solitude and wonderment are legitimate spokesmen for it, whether they may be a few or many. Those who have that intimate relation with the inanimate object to be injured, polluted, or otherwise despoiled are its legitimate spokesmen. . . .

The voice of the inanimate object, therefore, should not be stilled. That does not mean that the judiciary takes over the managerial functions from the federal agency. It merely means that before these priceless bits of Americana (such as a valley, an alpine meadow, a river, or a lake) are forever lost or are so transformed as to be reduced to the eventual rubble of our urban environment, the voice of the existing beneficiaries of these environmental wonders should be heard.

Perhaps they will not win. Perhaps the bulldozers of "progress" will plow under all the aesthetic wonders of this beautiful land. That is not the present question. The sole question is, who has standing to be heard?

Those who hike the Appalachian Trail into Sunfish Pond, New Jersey, and camp or sleep there, or run the Allagash in Maine, or climb the Guadalupes in West Texas, or who canoe and portage the Quetico Superior in Minnesota, certainly should have standing to defend those natural wonders before courts or agencies, though they live 3,000 miles away. Those who merely are caught up in environmental news or propaganda and flock to defend these waters or areas may be treated differently. That is why these environmental issues should be tendered by the inanimate object itself. Then there will be assurances that all of the forms of life which it represents will stand before the court—the pileated woodpecker as well as the coyote and bear, the lemmings as well as the trout in the streams. Those inarticulate members of the ecological group cannot speak. But those people who have so frequented the place as to know its values and wonders will be able to speak for the entire ecological community.

Ecology reflects the land ethic; and Aldo Leopold wrote in *A Sand County Almanac* (1949), "The land ethic simply enlarges the boundaries of the community to include soils, waters, plants, and animals, or collectively, the land."

That, as I see it, is the issue of "standing" in the present case and controversy.

49

Friendship with the Earth
DAVID BROWER (1973)

With his appointment as executive director of the Sierra Club in 1952, David Brower assumed the role of one of the nation's leading witnesses to the gospel of ecology. During the next seventeen years the club's membership grew from 7,000 to 77,000. Brower's first major involvement in environ-

New York Times, 16 April 1967.

mental politics came during the Echo Park Controversy (32). He followed that victory with an abortive attempt to prevent a dam in Glen Canyon of the Colorado River. This experience sharpened Brower's recognition of the need to create an intense and politically directed concern in the American people for cherishing and protecting the earth's wild places. One consequence was the publication in 1962 by the Sierra Club of In Wildness *is the Preservation of the World. The book was an exhibit-quality combination of the photographs of Eliot Porter and the words, including the title, of Henry David Thoreau (2). Similar publications followed as Brower spared no effort or expense in his crusade to preserve wilderness and enhance environmental quality everywhere. A test of his determination came in the mid-1960s in the form of federal Bureau of Reclamation proposals to dam the Colorado River in the Grand Canyon. Brower went all out in opposition, placing full-page advertisements such as the one below in nationally prominent newspapers. The Grand Canyon was not dammed, but in 1969 Brower was ousted from his position in the Sierra Club by a segment of the board of directors that feared he had pushed too far, too fast, and too irresponsibly. Others, to be sure, felt he had not gone far enough, and these persons formed the organizing nucleus of Brower's new organization, Friends of the Earth. In the interview following the advertisement below, Brower expresses himself on a variety of environmental issues of the past, present, and the future.*

SHOULD WE ALSO FLOOD THE SISTINE CHAPEL SO TOURISTS CAN GET NEARER THE CEILING?

Earth began four billion years ago and Man two million. The Age of Technology, on the other hand, is hardly a hundred years old. . . .

It seems to us hasty, therefore, during this blip of time, for Man to think of directing his fascinating new tools toward altering irrevocably the forces which made him. Nonetheless, in these few brief years among four billion, wilderness has all but disappeared. And now these:

1) There are proposals before Congress to "improve" Grand Canyon. Two dams would back up artificial lakes into 148 miles of canyon gorge. This would benefit tourists in power boats, it is argued, who would enjoy viewing the canyon wall more closely. See headline. Submerged underneath the tourists would be part of the most revealing single page of earth's history. The lakes would be as deep as 600 feet, deeper for example than all but a handful of New York buildings are high, but in a century, silting would have replaced the water with that much mud, wall to wall.

There is no part of the wild Colorado River, the Grand Canyon's sculptor, that would not be maimed.

Tourist recreation, as a reason for the dams, is in fact an after-thought. The Bureau of Reclamation, which has backed them, has called the dams "cash registers." It expects the dams would make money by sale of commercial power.

They will not provide anyone with water.

2) In Northern California, four lumber companies have nearly com-pleted logging the private virgin redwood forests, an operation which to give you an idea of its size, has taken fifty years.

Where nature's tallest living things have stood silently since the age of the dinosaurs, much further cutting could make creation of a redwood national park absurd.

The companies have said tourists want only enough roadside trees for the snapping of photos. They offered to spare trees for this purpose, and not much more. The result would remind you of the places on your face you missed while you were shaving.

3) And up the Hudson, there are plans for a power complex—a plant, transmission lines, and a reservoir near and on Storm King Mountain—effectively destroying one of the last wild and high and beautiful spots near New York City.

4) A proposal to flood a region in Alaska as large as Lake Erie would eliminate at once the breeding grounds of more wildlife than con-servationists have preserved in history.

5) In San Francisco, real estate interests have for years been filling a bay that made the city famous, putting tract houses over the fill; and now there's a new idea—still more fill, enough for an air cargo terminal as big as Manhattan.

There exists today a mentality which can conceive such destruc-tion, giving commerce as ample reason. For 74 years, the Sierra Club has opposed that mentality. But now, when even Grand Canyon is en-dangered, we are at a critical moment in time.

This generation will decide if something untrammelled and free remains, as testimony we had love for those who follow.

We have been taking ads, therefore, asking people to write their Congressmen and Senators; Secretary of the Interior Stewart Udall; The President; and to send us funds to continue the battle. Thousands have written, but meanwhile, Grand Canyon legislation still stands a chance of passage. More letters are needed and much more money, to help right the notion that Man no longer needs nature.

It's surprising how tall David Brower is. Sitting across the table, his delicate features, a trifle too small and a little too sharp, give the impression of a smallish, studious, more indoor oriented man.

But when he rises to his feet, he takes a surprisingly long time to stretch to his full height. It is then that it hits you. This is a tall man, a man who looks like the outdoorsman he is. Although he is 60, with an impressive thick shock of white hair, a smooth ruddy face, strong but unquestionably gentle, he looks in his 40s, more like a man who has just returned refreshed from a month backpacking his beloved Sierra Nevada.

But Brower doesn't get to do as much backpacking as he wants and needs. He is a naturalist/conservationist turned environmentalist, and the new word carries a much broader definition in terms of time and active commitment.

He is the controversial former executive director of the Sierra Club, a title he held during the 17 years he is credited with building that organization from a membership of 7,000 to a membership of 77,000. But philosophic differences changed that three and one half years ago when both the Sierra Club and Brower agreed that a split was necessary.

Long before that split, Brower had developed into the uncomfortable activist who restlessly knew that the environmental battles were in the political arenas where the tax exempt foundation money couldn't go.

So Brower, the elitists' naturalist who became a conservationist because he wanted to save wilderness joined the taxable Friends of the Earth and became a political lobbyist.

It was somehow fitting that he agreed to talk with EQM in his Washington, D.C. office, a cluttered, noisy refurbished townhouse about six blocks from the Capitol, where a six man staff headed by George Alderson directs the Friends of the Earth's legislative activities.

In an upstairs room, a little less noisy than the rest of the house,

---

Charles N. Conconi, "An Interview with David Brower: Founder of Friends of the Earth," *Environmental Quality Magazine* IV (April 1973), 19–26, 69.

Brower talked of the growing environmental movement that he is helping to carry to the global level.

With a gentle, often self-effacing sense of humor, Brower leaped enthusiastically from subject to subject, willing to talk to EQM for as long as necessary but anxious to be on with it. His responses were refreshingly candid and his motives obviously sincere in a town where hurrumping politicians consider candor, naivete and sincerity absurd.

But across the table, a man dressed in an old blue suit with ragged cuffs and wearing an indifferent blue tie was delivering a unique no-compromise message.

Brower the activist can probably best be described by the description of Russell Train—Chairman of the President's Council on Environmental Quality: "Thank God for Dave Brower. He makes it so easy for the rest of us to be reasonable. Somebody has to be a little extreme. Dave is a little hairy at times, but you do need somebody riding out there in front."

EQM: Since leaving the Sierra Club and forming Friends of the Earth about three years ago, do you think that the move accomplished what you had hoped?

Brower: I suppose it accomplished what the Sierra Club hoped to accomplish. They wanted me to walk the plank. We'd had a very major difference, primarily on the matter of atomic energy and the siting of atomic plants, and I lost that battle. I went to the Board and the electorate voted the other way so I really had no alternative but to leave. And leaving, I wanted to keep in the conservation business so I founded Friends of the Earth and the League of Conservation Voters, and also went into close cooperation with the John Muir Institute for Environmental Studies, a deductible group. We're trying to do things on several sides, all divided by the requirements of the tax law, and I think it has worked quite well.

The Sierra Club since I left has grown faster than when I was there. It is very good, a very powerful conservation influence, particularly in litigation, and Friends of the Earth has occupied its own niche quite well. It has become one of the organizations in those three and one half years that is listed among the big ones.

EQM: What is it that makes The Friends of the Earth so different from the Sierra Club or some of the other more well-known conservation organizations?

Brower: Our function is to put more emphasis into legislative and political activity right off the bat, also to be concerned with an international program and bring in other countries to cooperate with the United States so we can cooperate with them on a people-to-people basis, and to publish more vigorously than the Sierra Club has. I still think the printed word is one of the ways that you get your message across. The Friends of the Earth is political and legislative. We registered as lobbyists right away, and the Sierra Club still hasn't registered yet, I think. We wanted to be blatantly, effectively, substantially, legislatively active, which the IRS says makes you not tax deductible. So we took that course right at the beginning.

EQM: Do you feel you've been legislatively successful? Do you have any specific programs that you feel you've seen come to fruition?

Brower: Well, the one we like best is that we were fortunate to lead the coalition against the SST, and of course we blocked it in the previous Congress. We hope that Mr. Ehrlichman [Nixon's Domestic Affairs Advisor] and friends want to revive it that we can block it again.

EQM: Do you think you can block it again? There seems to be some movement in the direction of making another try for the SST.

Brower: I think we can block it just by getting some things out on the adverse effects of the SST above and beyond noise, which in itself is enough to condemn it, and its possible danger to the ozone barrier that will take two years at least to check out further. The absolutely inordinate and merciless use of fuel to get that extra speed—the statistic we've worked out is that if Mr. William M. Macgruder [former director, Federal SST Development] had had a chance to build his 500 SSTs, and they were flying at the anticipated rate, we would have to discover five or six new crude oil bays between now and the end of the century just to produce the extra speed. That's an absolutely immoral use of oil. There is no sense whatsoever in trying to keep people from being aloft a few hours extra by just extinguishing a resource that has to last a long time. It is absolutely ridiculous, and somebody really ought to see it that way.

EQM: The SST is politically and environmentally an international problem. Have you found much cooperation in working against the SST as you try to move the Friends of the Earth on to a more international basis?

Brower: Yes, we have. Friends of the Earth, Ltd. in England has put out a book attacking the Concorde, and Les Amies de La Terre in France has attacked the Concorde in French, and our other groups in other parts of the world, in Sweden and Switzerland, are working hard to prevent over-land flights. I think we have an international cooperation going on, including one of our new groups, Friends of the Earth, South Africa. I was in Kenya recently and the conservationists I talked to there, I guess I picked a skewed audience, had no interest in having an SST come.

EQM: That somewhat counters what we're told about emerging Africa and other developing nations who complain that the Western powers who have exploited the underdeveloped nations for so long, now want to clean up, without giving them a chance to industrialize and pollute on their own.

Brower: I don't know who is saying that in those countries. I think it is a few people who want to keep polluting on the old basis in this country and don't want their usurpation of the other country's resources interfered with. That's an elliptical statement. I could continue on that for a long, long time because one of the forthcoming major environmental battles will be, how do we accommodate the dreams of the Third World? But that's such a long subject, perhaps you want to get into that later.

EQM: Along that line, were you satisfied with the outcome of the first international environmental conference in Stockholm, Sweden last year?

Brower: I suppose anyone who was satisfied would be an idiot, and I'm only an idiot at times. I was not totally satisfied, but I was quite pleased that there was a conference and that so many people began to realize, the 120 countries or so attending, that there really is a problem and began to attack it and have been attacking it since. I was initially a little bit saddened that we wouldn't have the environmental capital of the Earth in Geneva or New York or some place to which we're accustomed to going. I ended up delighted, however, that it is Nairobi, that ninety Third World countries voted that they wanted it there and that the United Nations General Assembly unanimously agreed. There is a better chance now for Third World countries, and Kenya, I think, is going to be an awfully good one to start with feeling a responsibility toward the globe they have not felt before. They've generally felt 'where's our share?' And now I think they can get a better view than almost anyone else.

EQM: Coming back to this country and looking at it from a more general basis, would you give an opinion as to what is wrong or right with the environmental movement?

Brower: I think the thing that is wrong with the environmental movement is its failure to realize its own capability. There's been a sense of futility. It started strong, that is, the new intensive interest that began with Earth Day One. It was really quite a surprising thing to me. I never expected to see that much excitement built up, and I was not surprised to see it diminish in its superficial effects in subsequent Earth Days, and I suppose another one would be a little quieter still. Maybe not, maybe there was just a trough. But I never expected that much enthusiasm in the first place, and that kind of enthusiasm goes in spurts. I wasn't too worried to see it kind of steady down. The despondency some people have felt was absolutely reversed beautifully in the last elections, and the *New York Times* has commented editorially on the environmental successes. The League of Conservation Voters went into just under 60 campaigns and came out the way they wanted to in 43. Mr. [Representative Wayne] Aspinall was given a chance to stay in Colorado longer. This is all part of the great advantage I think that the organized environmental movements have been able to bring about, and they can do a great deal more. The question they need to ask themselves as they see something troublesome on the horizon is a question Garrett Hardin has put very well. He says, "Is it inevitable? Not if we say no." And we have to be patient enough to say no several times and in different languages, and it makes a difference.

EQM: What do you think then might be the major wrong? Is it that the older, more established conservation organizations prior to this time and prior to Friends of the Earth generally have stayed out of the political arena?

Brower: They did stay out too much. The organizations got into a tangle back in 1954 when the US Supreme Court came up with the US vs. Harris case on the anti-lobbying act and just about frightened every organization known to man. They all began to look for rugs to crawl under so the IRS wouldn't see them. The kinds of organizations that were then begun, the Council on Conservationists in New York, the Citizens Committee on Natural Resources, Trustees for Conservation, were all devices to try to get separately funded, legislatively active groups, but they could never raise enough money to stir up much dust. So the environment suffered a great deal while we were trying to figure out in the various organizations how to come back and fight the old fight. We're doing it in various ways now and one of the reasons that Friends of the Earth determined it would not try and be deductible was that we wanted to be one of the lobbying groups; now there are quite a few. We're finding that the best route is to have membership dues of organizations support the lobbying effort because no one cares whether $5, $10, or $15 dues are deductible, and let the clean, lily-white work—scientific, literary and educational—be funded by the foundations. This is happening elsewhere, but it isn't happening as fast as I would like to see it.

EQM: You're here in Washington and we have a new Congress, the 93rd. What efforts will the Friends of the Earth be making during this session?

Brower: We're going to have some meetings on that coming up. And I can't really say what our conclusions are going to be, but we want to meet with quite a few of the other organizations that are going to be particularly legislatively active, and submerge our personal jealousies or organizational rivalries to face what is a major threat to the United States—the breakdown of the balance of power in the three branches of government and the Executive branch's frightening and bullying of the Fourth Estate. We have specific environmental problems but this is destroying the environment of democracy itself, the over-reaching for power by the Executive branch. I think it is frightening and I think Friends of the Earth is going to do everything it possibly can to get Congress to come back to work full time.

EQM: How can you get Congress to do that?

Brower: I don't know. All we're going to do is to get people to say to their own congressmen, "We will support you, we will work for you here and we're expecting you to represent us." Congress too has a mandate to be an independent, bold, balanced part of the government and it has not been doing what it ought to do. We have probably not been supporting Congress well enough from where we were. We elect them, send them here and forget them. Now we want, really want to help. This is a movement that I think can be built, and I think there is enough concern around the country, reading the editorials from all over, and from what's happening on television, and from what's happening even to the mails. The slowing of information by the mails, and the Freedom of Information Act being trampled. It's something I don't think the President should be doing. I think he is extremely badly advised and I think we're going to have to try and persuade Congress to assert itself, and there are various ways it can. It can hold up appropriations for the White House. It can hold up on the confirmation of appointees. It can show its own muscle, until the President realizes that there are three branches of government. We need a strong President, we need a strong Congress, we need an independent court and we certainly need a press that is free from bullying.

EQM: One of the last great wilderness areas in the world, Alaska, has now been seriously threatened by the proposed Alaskan Pipeline. What chance do the environmentalists have in stopping the pipeline?

Brower: The Friends of the Earth have joined a three party suit against the Trans-Alaska Pipeline. They are seeking a sound environmental solution to the problem of getting oil out of Alaska when it finally is needed. I'm stating the bias in the case that it is only out of a rather unsupportable demand for doubling the use of oil every ten years or so that we feel we are so rushed to get the oil out now. The stress must be to use the oil we now have domestically far more efficiently than we do; to leave the oil in Alaska until we really need it, and make sure in the interim period that we have tested thoroughly the ways of getting it out. My own guess is that probably the best way will eventually be through a railroad, not a pipeline because railroad cars don't spill the way pipes do when they go. But here is an alternative that really hasn't been given any serious thought. The Department of the Interior in its environmental impact statement just tossed this possible alternative off with the most callous, most superficial reasoning. Former [Interior] Secretary [Walter] Hickel himself had said early in the game that if we were to accept bringing the oil out at only one quarter of the speed, that a railroad would be competitive. What he meant was the railroad could be built from the north slope down to Valdees, Alaska, which we think is an unacceptable destination in any event. But if it's only one route or another, and if you only want it one quarter as fast, then I say let's take it out one quarter as fast. Let's help the Alaskan economy for four times as long rather than going bust. It's an alternative in timing that has not really been given enough consideration.

EQM: Do you consider the Trans-Alaska Pipeline a serious defeat and do you think that this is an indication of how this Administration has been environmentally?

Brower: They certainly have not been responsive environmentally on anything that deals with oil. The President's energy policy, for example, where he talks of the necessity of getting into our oil reserves, going into the oil shale, going into the off-shore drilling, is just a mad dash for more oil. It shows that there is too much oil influence in his decision making. And I wish he would listen to some other people. But the oil pipeline case is not yet lost, and I think it is hard to predict what will happen as it goes to a higher court, or if the public begins to understand what is really at stake—which it doesn't yet. The public has been hearing the oil companies' side. It has not heard very much of the environmentalists' side because there isn't enough money to get that word out. And the executive agency, which should really be giving both sides, hasn't cared to. It just gives its advocate side. It wants the pipeline. It was persuaded that it needed it. It doesn't, but it's still telling the public we've got to have it.

EQM: Shortly after Richard Nixon came into office, he said the environment was the issue of the decade, and he was probably the first President to ever make such a statement. Do you think he has followed through on environmental awareness in the founding of the Environmental Protection Agency and other similar actions?

Brower: He has and he hasn't. He came through with a very good statement on population, and I think that some of the things that happened subsequent to that are the fault of the people and their failure to respond to that statement. That statement was zero at the box office. It brought in no supporting mail from the environmentalists who are concerned about the population problem. I've tried audiences all over the country on the question "how many wrote to the President?" Nobody wrote. And, "how many think there is a problem?" They all thought there was a problem. And I was one who didn't write, either. But this is part of the apathy and lethargy at work full time across the country.

The public, to a certain extent, when the President came through with the boldest statement any President ever made on population, has only itself to blame for not supporting it. Now, I will disagree from time to time about what William Ruckleshaus has done in the Environmental Protection Agency or what Russ Train has done on the Council on Environmental Quality, but taking the broad view, we are extremely fortunate to have those people and those agencies—with the support they are getting from the President—doing what they've done. This wasn't accomplished before. The Environmental Protection Act and the Council on Environmental Quality are two really good achievements. The achievements will go on from where they are if the public will express appreciation for some of the things that are done well. If the public will use the energy that it uses much too little, the energy and encouragement that comes from praise. When did you last write a letter to someone thanking them for something? Have we encouraged anybody? Russ Train has given me the nicest quote I know. He said: "Thank God for Dave Brower, because he makes it so much easier for the rest of us to appear reasonable." Well, I'm very grateful for what Russ Train has done.

EQM: What about Congress then? How responsive have they been?

Brower: They haven't been responsive enough. I think the people who have been calling for an invigoration of Congress are right. And the attack on the seniority system is right. The Congress has too much to do to allow people who are old to have so many positions of great power. I define old in my own private way, and I don't care what the calendar says. If a person has lost the ability to listen, if he has already made his decision, or if he is a thoroughly practical man in the Disraeli sense, "That he can be counted upon to perpetuate the errors of his ancestors," then he is old. And we have a lot of old Congressmen in positions of far too much authority. I don't object to age, because at 60 I can't object to it too much, but I think there needs to be a spectrum of ages in the legislative body, and I approve of that. I approve of what experience can do, but when it gets so overladen with tradition, the lack of the necessary spark, and the lack of the ability to think new, then it endangers the country. That's where Congress has been slipping rather badly lately, and I hope they can make a big shift.

EQM: But haven't they, environmentally, been more responsive than any other Congress, even though it was relatively safe politically for most of them?

Brower: It became a safer issue than it had been. Yet it is not exactly that safe, particularly when the people whose ox is being gored by strong environmental legislation are the people who are the big contributors. That is why it is hard to get good oil legislation when so many of the major contributions come from the oil executives. Congress got some good things started. I don't think the environmental organizations, our own included, were able to build as much support out in the field as we should have. One of the reasons is of course that we are always miserably underfinanced. I think it will always be that way so we have to learn to live without much money, but with a lot of devotion.

EQM: As the solutions become tougher, such as the enormous expense for water pollution clean up alone, can environmentalists expect Congress and the Administration to respond legislatively to protect the environment?

Brower: I think we can, and it's going to take quite a bit of money to restore what we've messed up. But it is not going to be money that is just poured into a hole and disappears. This means jobs, and it is jobs in doing what we want instead of jobs in doing what we don't want. We don't need people building SSTs and we don't need a government subsidy to make the SST go and pollute the upper atmosphere, pollute the soundwaves and diminish our oil supply. We do need that kind of money in making mass transportation work. We are, for example, constantly draining the land of its fertility to produce our crops. We're taking the whole spectrum of elements and organic materials away from the land. We're putting a few bits of synthetic substitutes back, but these don't nearly replace what we've taken. They possibly even expedite the drain. We're taking, then, this constant drain off the land, and then we're dumping it into the ocean where it creates another desert. We need to get the organic material back. To do that requires more technology, more jobs, new kinds of plants, and new kinds of marketing that will keep many, many people busy for a long time, and we will end up then with a country that is recycled and is likely to last a long time, instead of ending up as we are now with a country that is running downhill in its ability to produce.

EQM: What do you see as the major environmental problems facing this nation and the world?

Brower: The major environmental problem facing the world, I suppose, is the United States and its exorbitant appetite for resources. With 6 percent of the world's population, we want to use about half of everybody else's—everybody's. And we're looking for a larger share constantly, and that's a major environmental threat and I think it's a major threat to peace. In the course of doing this, we are also wiping out the diversity of organic things on the earth, and this is the diversity of the love of life that has been produced over the last three billion years.

In the course of a couple of centuries of industrial revolution with a lot of technology and a lot of energy, we have disrupted life frightfully, without really knowing what we have stamped out because we never had a chance to measure it before we crushed it. We've lost a great deal of diversity, especially the diversity of the soil that feeds us. We're losing key elements. We're running out of things that are necessary to keep the world working. The immediate manifestation of this is what the overuse of energy is allowing us to do. We've become addicted to electricity. We've become addicted to looking somewhere else and mining the resource capitals of the earth to take care of our everyday conveniences, instead of learning how to budget to live on the earth's environmental energy income, basically the sun.

Right now we are getting into the energy problem, where the crisis is not that we don't have enough energy, but that we're using too much. We reach too far for our oil and thus get into tangles with other countries. The oil in Southeast Asia is something we haven't looked at very hard.

EQM: Why is that?

Brower: The enormous reserves there are part of what I think this struggle has been about. There's oil in the last wilderness, such as Alaska, that we are reaching for at a frightful rate. I have a figure from a man in England who said that at the present rate of using oil, the world's going to need to discover three Middle Easts by the end of this decade. Well, we're not going to discover them. We're running out of oil, we're running frantically after coal and stripmining and permanently wrecking land that should not be wrecked. Knowing that, we start to look at the atom for an easy way out because the atom and the technology seem so promising, and we're running into the worst pollution of all—the pollution in this highly polluting atomic energy field is so great that we can't get the straight story, something like a $40–80 billion investment in the atom and growing. Many horrible mistakes are being made and covered up. We're finding out in a series of hearings that have been going on here with the Union of Concerned Scientists, the National Interveners, and others that from start to finish, from the mining of uranium to transporting it, to processing it, to running it through reactors, to reprocessing the fuel and to finally taking care of the waste, we have an unprecedented genetic peril to mankind and to other living things. We need to hear the stories, we need to hear the facts that they know in the national laboratories that aren't getting through. Fortunately, there are still some independent scientists who are helping break this news out.

I think that before the end of 1973, possibly by 1974, the atomic energy idea will have been shut down and put on a shelf until we've let the research catch up. The current immediate threat, as has been determined in the Bethesda hearings, the Atomic Energy Commission rule-making hearings on the safety of reactors, indicate that if a reactor of the present models we have—we have a good many in this country and that's all we're building is the light-water reactors—loses its cool, it could be an unprecedented disaster, catastrophic. The number of deaths can range from 10,000 to a million, depending on where the reactor is. Now you haven't been hearing this, but it is in the testimony. The press hasn't covered it, but it's there, and the basis of calculation has not been challenged. This, for example, is partly the threat of Indian Point. If that goes, if it loses its cool and the back-up system fails, look out New York. There'll be a million people or so dead from lethal radiation, not an explosion, but a lethal radioactive cloud that is deadly for 100 miles downwind. Now we've got to hear about this, instead of having it covered up. It's being covered up. That's the threat to all of us living anywhere near reactors. And Dr. Weinberg at Oak Ridge postulates 12,000 reactors eventually in the world to supply our supplemental power needs, and those reactors will be roughly five times the capacity of any we are now building.

EQM: Can't we build a safe one?

Brower: We can't build a safe one now. The Emergency Core Cooling System, the back-up system, has been shown in six tests to fail all six. They're theoretical—none has blown up yet. But the threat is really major. It's not getting through, and that's a threat to anyone now living anywhere near any reactor. The long-range threat, particularly with the still more dangerous liquid-metal fast breeder, that the Nixon Administration is now gung ho for is the ultimate disposition of the waste which must be segregated from living things for 500,000 years. There is no way to do that, and there is not ever going to be a way to do that. We have to realize some things are beyond technical efficiency—500,-

000 years takes us way back before Neanderthal man, and I don't think any of us remember any of the instructions they left for us.

EQM: What can be done to make this information public so environmentalists can combat this sort of thing, especially in the light of the power industry people saying, "You're seeing power shortages right now. If you don't let us go ahead with nuclear power, you're going to have increasing numbers of brown outs and black outs, with fossil fuel quickly running out!" There are places all over the country, throughout the Midwest this winter, and Northeast that have had crises because they did not have enough fuel oil, and the gasoline supply for the automobiles is going.

Brower: It's going because it's been oversold. They've addicted us to electricity, and I'm just using that as a short cut. They've addicted us to gasoline, they've addicted us to extravagant use. They have a major charge on their part to stop the advertising, to stop giving premiums away as you buy gasoline, to stop selling high energy-intensive paraphernalia in all stores and markets, and to say "Look, our responsibility to you now is to tell you that we are going to start guiding you now on how to use less." A few are beginning. They're just beginning, and I'm grateful for that.

EQM: But what about the profit motive?

Brower: You can still make a profit by doing something right as well as by doing something wrong. I think that some very good profit can be made building, if you've got to have an air conditioner at all, a more efficient air conditioner. If you've got to have a building, better insulation. If you've got to have agriculture, have agriculture that isn't energy intensive, but that spares the organic system better.

EQM: A more efficient engine?

Brower: A more efficient engine in a car. What is the matter with steam? Why can't we get a fair shake on that. There's plenty of evidence now showing that steam really can be adapted much more efficiently.

EQM: But you don't expect the oil industry to cooperate with something like that?

Brower: I certainly do. They will still be selling the oil that runs the machine. They can sell it for more.

EQM: Well, if you're running a steam engine, you're not going to be using gasoline.

Brower: No. but you'll be using oil. They can still make a profit with planning and with a transition period, and I certainly don't want this to happen overnight. I don't hesitate to predict that the oil company will maneuver itself into a profit making position, providing us with something that we need instead of something we don't. It sounds a little heretical, but it really isn't. This is the only sensible way to go. We cannot keep going the way we're going. We cannot keep using more and more energy. We're going to have to stop somewhere. Why don't we stop by using our heads instead of stopping by running right into the wall—off the brink.

EQM: How do you stop with electrical power, particularly when it is already running into problems and we're told that the only answer is nuclear power?

Brower: For one thing, you do what they did in Britain a year ago when they had their big coal strike. The Electrical Board was running full page ads in the *London Times* showing how people could use less. Yet if the energy utilities and the public utilities can't serve the public better, then possibly they should give up and let the government muddle away with it.

EQM: Barry Commoner and Paul Ehrlich are two of the best known environmentalists in this country, but generally they split on the emphasis of the impact of over industrialization versus over population as the primary factor affecting the environment and creating the environmental crisis. Do you take a side in that debate?

Brower: I may have read it wrong. I didn't think they split so much on over industrialization. I think they both feel over industrialization is harmful. But I'm completely with Paul Ehrlich and completely against Barry Commoner on his reliance on the demographic transition. Barry thinks the way to control population, and he's joined on this by Herman Kahn and the Hudson Institute, is to make everybody rich, so that people have better things to do than produce too many babies. And this fails on several scores. There is no way, as I see it, to bring the rest of the world up to the US standard. And I'm just saying the overall US standard, counting the Park Avenue people and averaging them out with the people in the ghettos and on the reservations. To bring the rest of the world up to that standard, the number I have is to multiply the drain upon resources by a factor of 20. The resources aren't there. We're running out—item after item. When we say we'll substitute something else—we're running out of the substitute. And the Club of Rome, for all the disagreements over some of the details, is still on the right track. We are running out. The resources aren't there to bring the other peoples up to this standard. It is cruel to let them think that they are. And that's where I believe Commoner's big error is.

The limits to growth strike at the limits to richness and the limits to have everybody get what the first people in the chainmail syndrome got in on. I have to tell my own children that they cannot see some of the wilderness I saw and enjoyed very much. I wish they could, but they can't. We spoiled it and can't go back. You can't unfry that egg. The Third World countries cannot use those resources we pre-empted for our convenience. They are gone, and we, of course, are still in the business of trying to pre-empt more, such as the presumed revival of the SST, where we are trying to pre-empt the output of five crude oil bays between now and the year 2000, while the rest of the people don't have anything—just so we can go faster. We have got to learn a new definition for equity, to share better and to cool our own demands, so that the people who are so much behind can catch up a little bit. And then hope to persuade them by our own cutback that we know something that they should profit from—that the mad dash to eat up the earth's environmental capital is over, that there are better things to do.

We will have a population crash then somewhere around 10 billion. Now that is not a rational route to go, and the best quote I know comes from a Welshman, Allen Reese, that when you are at the edge of an abyss, the only progressive step you can make is to move backward, and I think we're there. If we try to tell ourselves we're not, we're kidding ourselves and looking for a "giant step forward for mankind" that I would rather not take.

EQM: What direction will Friends of the Earth take in the coming years, especially in line with the significant emphasis you are placing on international cooperation?

Brower: The Friends of the Earth formula abroad is one where we try to find people in other countries who share our own ideas about the limits to growth, that we can't keep on this mad course, and who have a respect for biological diversity. Then these people become the Board of Directors for their country. They run their own show. We license the use of the name, or a reasonable translation, but we have no over-seeing group. We just meet together in set places like Stockholm, out-side of Paris, in Frankfurt, or maybe here from time to time, and see what we can help each other with for the next year or six months.

It is, as I said way back, a people-to-people approach. It's different from the non-governmental organizations affiliated with the UN be-cause they have got to work through governmental processes. It's dif-ferent from the International Union for Conservation which is pri-marily concerned with research. We're trying to work through the political and legislative process and courts of law and we are publish-ing around the world, trying to get an understanding as broad as we can of the limits of the planet—that it is only one Earth, as the Stock-holm Conference pointed out in its slogan. We think we have a pretty good mission in trying to help other people realize this, and also in helping them help us realize it, because we need to realize it more than anyone else.

EQM: As a final question, are you pessimistic or optimistic about the future?

Brower: I have been billing myself as an optimist up until the last two months, and I've become a little bit pessimistic, but I'll get over it. I think that by and large around the world and in this country, peo-ple are realizing the depth of the threat the lack of an adequate en-vironment will mean to our future. This word is getting around. It's not getting around nearly far enough and a lot of us have been talking to our own class. We have not been talking very well at all to what we could call Middle America. I don't think I could make a very good speech in a subway car in New York and get very much attention. We should try to find out how we get through to the people we haven't been getting through to because they all have only one pass at the planet. They all love life as much as anyone else does—all these other people from all these other colors and wage scales. And I think there is an extraordinary chance built of necessity to pull together to keep this planet working.

A Selected Bibliography

The following are the more important books, articles, and unpublished theses which treat the history of the American people's relation with the environment and, in particular, the development of the conservation movement.

COMPREHENSIVE ACCOUNTS

The number of general scholarly works is still small. George H. Williams and Clarence Glacken have given vital dimension to the American experience with nature in *Wilderness and Paradise in Christian Thought* (Harper, New York, 1962) and *Traces on the Rhodian Shore: Nature and Culture in Western Thought from Ancient Times to the End of the Eighteenth Century* (University of California Press, Berkeley, 1967). Roderick Nash's *Wilderness and the American Mind* (Yale University Press, New Haven, 1967) also surveys Old World opinion before delineating and interpreting the alterations in the American conception of and conduct toward wild country. In *Man in the Landscape* (Knopf, New York, 1967) Paul Shepard has written a history of the perception of nature in which American attitude has an important place. Hans Huth, *Nature and the American: Three Centuries of Changing Attitudes* (University of California Press, Berkeley, 1957) is strongest in analyzing the growth of popular appreciation of natural beauty in the nineteenth century. Particularly valuable for this period, but comprehensive in scope is Russel B. Nye's "The American View of Nature," a chapter in his *This Almost Chosen People: Essays in the History of American Ideas* (Michigan State University Press, East Lansing, Mich., 1966). Arthur A. Ekirch, Jr., *Man and Nature in America* (Columbia University Press, New York, 1963) reviews the way the growth of American civilization has disturbed natural harmonies while William Martin Smallwood, *Natural History and the American Mind* (Columbia University Press, New York, 1941) describes the impact of the early "naturalist" on the nation's cultural life. William R. Van Dersal's *The American Land, Its History and Its Uses* (Oxford University Press, New York, 1943) is an environmental history, albeit simplified.

Three studies that should not be missed in studying the human impact on the American environment and vice-versa are Richard G. Lillard's *The Great Forest* (Knopf, New York, 1947) Russell Lord's *The Care of the Earth* (Nelson, New York, 1962) and Rutherford Platt's *The Great American Forest* (Prentice Hall, Englewood Cliffs, N.J., 1965). Also relevant are Perry Miller, "Nature and the National Ego" in his *Errand into the Wilder-*

ness (Harvard University Press, Cambridge, Mass., 1956), 204–216, and Miller's "The Romantic Dilemma in American Nationalism and the Concept of Nature" most conveniently found in his *Nature's Nation* (Harvard University Press, Cambridge, Mass., 1967), 197–207. Ralph N. Miller, "American Nationalism as a Theory of Nature," *William and Mary Quarterly*, 12 (1955), 74–95, comments on some of the same themes. Of great importance for the present purposes are portions of Howard Mumford Jones, *O Strange New World* (Viking, New York, 1964); Charles L. Sanford, *The Quest for Paradise* (University of Illinois Press, Urbana, Ill., 1961); Neil Harris, *The Artist in American Society: The Formative Years, 1790–1860* (Braziller, New York, 1966); Morton White and Lucia White, *The Intellectual vs. the City* (Harvard University Press, Cambridge, Mass., 1962); James Thomas Flexner, *That Wilder Image: The Painting of America's Native School from Thomas Cole to Winslow Homer* (Little Brown, Boston, 1962); Arthur K. Moore, *The Frontier Mind: A Cultural Analysis of the Kentucky Frontiersman* (University of Kentucky Press, Lexington, Ky., 1957); Frederick A. Sweet, *The Hudson River School and the Early American Landscape Tradition* (Whitney Museum of American Art, New York, 1945); George Boas, ed., *Romanticism in America* (Russell and Russell, New York, 1961); Barbara H. Deutsch, "Cole and Durand: Criticism and Patronage, A Study of American Taste in Landscape, 1825–1865" (unpublished Ph.D. dissertation, Harvard University, 1957); and Roy Harvey Pearce, *The Savages of America: A Study of the Indian and the Idea of Civilization* (rev. ed., John Hopkins Press, Baltimore, 1965).

A geographer and intellectual historian, David Lowenthal, has almost completed a book on Americans' perception of their environment which promises to be a major study. Lowenthal has published "The American Image of Nature as Virtue," *Landscape*, 9 (1959–60), 16–26.

Literary historians have contributed to our understanding of the American attitude toward the natural world. Henry Nash Smith's *Virgin Land: The American West as Symbol and Myth* (Harvard University Press, Cambridge, Mass., 1950) is basic in pursuing the conception of the frontier environment while Leo Marx, *The Machine in the Garden: Technology and the Pastoral Ideal in America* (Oxford University Press, New York, 1964) illuminates a deeply-rooted conflict of values in American culture. Both volumes are available in paperback. Four early books led the way in discerning the impact of environment on American literature: Norman Foerster, *Nature in American Literature* (Macmillan, New York, 1927); Philip Marshall Hicks, *The Development of the Natural History Essay in American Literature* (Philadelphia, 1924); Lucy Lockwood Hazard, *The Frontier in American Literature* (Thomas Y. Crowell, New York, 1927); and Henry C. Tracy, *American Naturists* (Dutton, New York, 1930). Recently these have been supplemented by Wilson O. Clough, *The Necessary Earth: Nature and*

Solitude in American Literature (University of Texas Press, Austin, 1964) and Edwin Fussell, *Frontier: American Literature and the American West* (Princeton University Press, Princeton, 1965). Peter J. Schmitt, "The Virgin Land in the Twentieth Century: The Concept of Nature in an Urban Society, 1900–1925" (unpublished Ph.D. dissertation, University of Minnesota, 1967) is also useful.

As yet there is no comprehensive history of American conservation by a professional historian, but we have several excellent studies of limited periods. Ernest A. Engelbert, "American Policy for Natural Resources: A Historical Survey to 1862" (unpublished Ph.D. dissertation, Harvard University, 1950) and Ralph M. Van Brocklin, "The Movement for the Conservation of Natural Resources in the United States Before 1901" (unpublished Ph.D. dissertation, University of Michigan, 1952) document beginnings. Van Brocklin's work is available on microfilm from University Microfilms.

The first great surge of conservation during the Progressive period has received the most attention. Samuel P. Hays, *Conservation and the Gospel of Efficiency: The Progressive Conservation Movement, 1890–1920* (Harvard University Press, Cambridge, Mass., 1959) is a pathbreaking analysis. J. Leonard Bates, "Fulfilling American Democracy: The Conservation Movement, 1907–1921," *Mississippi Valley Historical Review,* **44** (1957), 29–57, Elmo R. Richardson, *The Politics of Conservation: Crusades and Controversies, 1897–1913* (University of California Press, Berkeley, 1962), and Roderick Nash, "The American Cult of the Primitive," *American Quarterly,* **18** (Fall, 1966), 517–537, extend our knowledge of this crucial era. While Harold T. Pinkett's "Gifford Pinchot and the Early Conservation Movement in the United States" (unpublished Ph.D. dissertation, American University, 1953) focuses on one man, its sensitivity to background and context, as well as Pinchot's central role in Progressive conservation, distinguishes it as a valuable general history.

Taking up where the Hays book ends, Donald C. Swain's *Federal Conservation Policy, 1921–1933* (University of California Press, Berkeley, 1963) is very thorough for national developments. Until we have Swain's promised book on conservation since 1933, Anna Lou Riesch's "Conservation Under Franklin D. Roosevelt" (unpublished Ph.D. dissertation, University of Wisconsin, 1952) remains the only general scholarly treatment of recent conservation history.

Histories of the public domain and federal land policy inevitably concern the environment and the conservation movement. The traditional work is Benjamin H. Hibbard, *A History of Public Land Policies* (Macmillan, New York, 1924), but it has been superseded by Roy M. Robbins, *Our Landed Heritage: The Public Domain, 1776–1936* (Princeton University Press, Princeton, 1942), E. Louise Peffer, *The Closing of the Public Domain: Disposal and Reservation Policies, 1900–1950* (Stanford University Press, Stanford, 1951), and Marion Clawson and Burnell Held, *The Federal Lands: Their Use and Management* (John Hopkins Press, Baltimore, 1957). In *Man and Land in the United States* (University of Nebraska Press, Lincoln, Neb., 1964), Clawson, a former director of the federal Bureau of Land Management and now a staff member of Resources for the Future, has written a simplified survey of the public's trusteeship of the environment. Vernon Carstensen, ed., *The Public Lands: Studies in the History of the Public Domain* (University of Wisconsin Press, Madison, Wis., 1963) is a collection of important essays. *Indian Forest and Range: A History of the Administration and Conservation of the Redman's Heritage* (Forestry Enterprises, Washington, D.C., 1951) by Jay P. Kinney describes federal concern for this portion of the environment.

There is an excellent chapter on conservation in A. Hunter Dupree, *Science in the Federal Government: A History of Policies and Activities to 1940* (Harvard University Press, Cambridge, Mass., 1957). Norman Wengert brings the insights of political science to his *Natural Resources and the Political Struggle* (Doubleday, Garden City, N.Y., 1955) as does Philip F. Beach to "Natural Resource Policy and 'The Public Interest' " (unpublished Ph.D. dissertation, Northwestern University, 1964). Another political scientist, Grant McConnell, has explored changing conservation ideology in "The Conservation Movement—Past and Present," *Western Political Quarterly*, 7 (1954), 463–478. H. Bowman Hawkes, "The Paradoxes of the Conservation Movement." *Bulletin of the University of Utah*, 51, No. 11 (1960), 1–35, is an insightful, historical survey. From the standpoint of a geographer Clarence J. Glacken has written "The Origins of the Conservation Philosophy," *Journal of Soil and Water Conservation*, 11 (1956), 63–66, which puts the American experience in the context of Western history. Two outdated but unique books are Ovid M. Butler, ed., *American Conservation in Picture and in Story* (rev. ed., American Forestry Association, Washington, D.C., 1941) and Robert Steele Funderburk, *History of Conservation Education in the United States* (George Peabody College for Teachers, Nashville, 1948).

Several scholars contributed to a 1958 Resources for the Future symposium on the history of conservation, the proceedings of which appeared as Henry Jarrett, ed., *Perspectives on Conservation: Essays on America's Natural Resources* (John Hopkins Press, Baltimore, 1958). Gordon B. Dodds, "The Historiography of American Conservation: Past and Present," *Pacific Northwest Quarterly*, 56 (1965), 75–81, is unique.

The leading textbooks in conservation and resource management, such as Shirley Walter Allen and Justin Wilkinson Leonard, *Conserving Natural Resources: Principles and Practices in a Democracy* (3d ed., McGraw-Hill, New York, 1966), Guy-Harold Smith, ed., *Conservation of Natural Resources* (3d ed., Wiley, New York, 1965), and Richard Highsmith, et al., *Conservation in the United States* (Rand McNally, Chicago, 1962), note historical developments briefly in the course of discussing current problems and policies. The bibliographies of these and similar volumes, moreover, will lead to additional literature.

Turning from scholars' accounts to those of participants in the conservation movement, we find a number of general surveys. The best is Stewart Udall's *The Quiet Crisis* (Holt, Rinehart & Winston, New York, 1963). Secretary of the Interior under John F. Kennedy and Lyndon B. Johnson, Udall reviews the conduct of Americans toward the environment since the arrival of the first settlers with an emphasis on the rise of conservation. The book is available in paperback. David Cushman Coyle, *Conservation: An American Story of Conflict and Accomplishment* (Rutgers University Press, New Brunswick, N.J., 1957) is an engineer's undocumented but reliable survey of the movement. More polemical in tone are two histories by former United States Congressmen. Robert S. Kerr, a Senator from Oklahoma, wrote *Land, Wood and Water* (Fleet, New York, 1960), an account that concentrates on irrigation, flood control, and hydropower production. Frank E. Smith, twelve years a Representative of Mississippi and, after 1962, director of the Tennessee Valley Authority, has compiled a useful history of conservation from the early national period to the 1960's in *The Politics of Conservation* (Panthern Books, New York, 1966). After a long career as a proponent of public control of water resources, Judson King completed *The Conservation Fight: From Theodore Roosevelt to the Tennessee Valley Authority* (Public Affairs Press, Washington, D.C., 1959) but the title promises a broader treatment than the book, which focuses on water, in fact contains.

An important recent contribution is Henry Clepper, ed., *Origins of American Conservation* (Ronald Press, New York, 1966) which brings together short, historical sketches by leaders in various fields of resource management. Charles H. Callison, ed., *America's Natural Resources* (rev. ed., Ronald Press, New York, 1957) is similar in format but concentrates on present needs. Ernest F. Swift's *A Conservation Saga* (National Wildlife Federation, Washington, D.C., 1967) is a reminiscence, partly historical, made by a central figure in recent wildlife conservation.

The federal government has taken a few steps toward preparing a history of American conservation. The following titles are self-explanatory: Ray Lyman Wilbur and William A. Du Puy, *Conservation in the Department of the Interior* (Government Printing Office, Washington, D.C., 1931); U.S. Department of the Interior, *A Century of Conservation, 1849–1949* (Government Printing Office, Washington, D.C., 1950) and *Highlights in the History of Forest and Related Natural Resource Conservation in the Department of Interior* (Government Printing Office, Washington, D.C., 1958); and Gladys L. Baker, Wayne D. Rasmussen, Vivian Wiser and Jane M. Porter, *Century of Science: The First 100 Years of the United States Department of Agriculture* (Government Printing Office, Washington, D.C., 1963).

PARTICULAR EVENTS, INSTITUTIONS, AND REGIONS

A number of studies within the general field of conservation and environmental history take as their subject a specific event, institution, or region.

The controversy between Secretary of the Interior Richard A. Ballinger and Chief Forester Gifford Pinchot over private claims to resources on public lands which came to a head in 1909 and 1910 has received extensive treatment. The initial studies, Rose M. Stahl, "The Ballinger-Pinchot Controversy," *Smith College Studies in History*, 11 (1926), John T. Ganoe, "Some Constitutional and Political Aspects of the Ballinger-Pinchot Controversy," *Pacific Historical Review*, 3 (1934), 323–333, and Alpheus T. Mason, *Bureaucracy Convicts Itself: The Ballinger-Pinchot Controversy of 1910* (Viking, New York, 1941) have not weathered well, particularly at the hands of Samuel P. Hays and Elmo R. Richardson (above). James L. Penick has recently reopened the issue in *Progressive Politics and Conservation: the Ballinger-Pinchot Affair* (Loyola University Press, Chicago, 1968).

The next great national scandal involving natural resources occurred in the early 1920's and concerned Wyoming oil deposits. No less than three books treat the Teapot Dome episode: Morris R. Werner and John Starr, *Teapot Dome* (Viking, New York, 1959), Burl Noggle, *Teapot Dome: Oil and Politics in the 1920's* (Louisiana State University Press, Baton Rouge, 1962), and J. Leonard Bates, *The Origins of Teapot Dome: Progressives, Parties, and Petroleum, 1909–1921* (University of Illinois Press, Urbana, 1963). There is also a dessertation, David H. Stratton, "Albert B. Fall and the Teapot Dome Affair" (unpublished Ph.D. dissertation, University of Colorado, 1955) and two articles, J. Leonard Bates, "The Teapot Dome Scandal and the Election of 1924," *American Historical Review*, 60 (1955), 303–322, and Burl Noggle, "The Origins of the Teapot Dome Investigation," *Mississippi Valley Historical Review*, 44 (1957), 237–266.

Although the Civilian Conservation Corps is a strong candidate for the most famous institution in American conservation history, only recently has it received book-length study in John A. Salmond's *The Civilian Conservation Corps, 1933–1942: A New Deal Case Study* (Duke University Press, Durham, N.C., 1967). Elmo R. Richardson has another investigation of the CCC underway and has already published "The Civilian Conservation Corps and the Origins of the New Mexico State Park System," *Natural Resources Journal*, 6 (1966), 248–267.

The difficult task of winning acceptance for the Tennessee Valley Authority's ambitious attempt at environmental engineering on a regional scale is described in Preston Hubbard, *Origins of the TVA: The Muscle Shoals Controversy, 1920–1932* (Vanderbilt University Press, Nashville, 1961). The history of TVA and its impact is the subject of C. Herman Pritchett, *The Tennessee Valley Authority: A Study in Public Administration* (University of North Carolina Press, Chapel Hill, N.C., 1943), Roscoe C. Martin, ed., *TVA: The First Twenty Years* (University of Alabama Press, University, Ala., 1956), Philip Selznick, *TVA and the Grass Roots: A Study in the Sociology of Formal Organization* (University of California Press, Berkeley, 1949), and Gordon R. Clapp, *The TVA: An Approach to the Development of a Region* (University of Chicago Press, Chicago, 1955). John H. Kyle, *The Building of TVA: An Illustrated History* (Louisiana State University Press, Baton Rouge, 1958) proceeds dam by dam. The second volume of Donald Davidson's *The Tennessee* (Rinehart, New York, 1946–1948) is also relevant.

Two key issues in American conservation history are the subjects of Lawrence Rakestraw's "The West, States Rights, and Conservation: A Study of Six Public Lands Conferences," *Pacific Historical Review*, 48 (1957), 89–99, and Roderick Nash's "John Muir, William Kent, and the Conservation Schism," *Pacific Historical Review*, 36 (1967), 423–433. Rakestraw's "Sheep Grazing in the Cascades: John Minto vs. John Muir," *Pacific Historical Review*, 27 (1958), 371–382, concerns another aspect of the conflict within conservation.

A number of works take a regional approach to the history of the American environment. For the East we have William F. Schulz, Jr., *Conservation Law and Administration: A Case Study of Law and Resource Use in Pennsylvania* (Ronald, New York, 1953), Gurth A. Whipple, *Fifty Years of Conservation in New York State, 1885–1935* (J. B. Lyon, Albany, 1935), and Marvin W. Kranz, "Pioneering in Conservation: A History of the Conservation Movement in New York State, 1816–1903" (unpublished Ph.D. dissertation, Syracuse University, 1961). Lawrence C. Durisch and Hershal L. Macon, *Upon Its Own Resources: Conservation and State Administration* (University of Alabama Press, Tuscaloosa, Ala., 1951) concerns the Southeast. The Midwest has received attention in Samuel T. Dana, ed., *History of Activities in the Field of Natural Resources at the University of Michigan* (University of Michigan Press, Ann Arbor, 1953), H. H. Michaud, "A Brief History of the Conservation of Natural Resources in Indiana," *Indiana Academy of Science Proceedings*, 58 (1948), 257–262, Vernon Carstensen, *Farms or Forests: Evolution of a State Land Policy for Northern Wisconsin* (University of Wisconsin, College of Agriculture, Madison, Wis., 1958) and Erling D. Solberg, *New Laws for New Forests: Wisconsin's Forest-Fire, Tax, Zoning, and County-Forest Laws in Operation* (University of Wisconsin Press, Madison, Wis., 1961). Two books that review the impact of civilization on the Western landscape are Raymond F. Dasmann, *The Destruction of California* (Macmillan, New York, 1965) and William O. Douglas, *Farewell to Texas: A Vanishing Wilderness* (McGraw-Hill, New York, 1967). Charles McKinley, *Uncle Sam in the Pacific Northwest: Federal Management of Natural Resources in the Columbia River Valley* (University of California Press, Berkeley, 1952) is a massive history. Richard A. Cooley's *Alaska: A Challenge in Conservation* (University of Wisconsin Press, Madison, Wis., 1966) is largely concerned with the present and future.

While many regional histories deal in part with the environment, several might be singled out as especially relevant for the present purposes: Richard G. Lillard, *Eden in Jeopardy* (Knopf, New York, 1966); James C. Malin, *The Grasslands of North America, Prolegomena to Its History, with Addenda* (privately published at Lawrence, Kan., 1961); Michael Frome, *Strangers in High Places: The Story of the Great Smoky Mountains* (Doubleday, New York, 1966); Francis P. Farquhar, *History of the Sierra Nevada* (University of California Press, Berkeley, 1965); Walter P. Webb, *The Great Plains* (Ginn, Boston, 1931); and William C. White, *Adirondack Country* (Duell, Sloan & Pearce, New York, 1954). In addition, many of the fifty volumes in the Rivers of America series are excellent environmental histories.

PARTICULAR RESOURCES

The history of forestry in the United States has received considerable attention. The pathbreaking studies were Jay P. Kinney, *The Development of Forest Law in America* (John Wiley & Sons, New York, 1917), John Ise, *The United States Forest Policy* (Yale University Press, New Haven, 1920), Jenks Cameron, *The Development of Governmental Forest Control in the United States* (John Hopkins Press, Baltimore, 1928), Herbert A. Smith, "The Early Forestry Movement in the United States," *Agricultural History*, 12 (1938), 326–346, and Gilbert Chinard, "The American Philosophical Society and the Early History of Forestry in America," *American Philosophical Society Proceedings*, 89 (1945), 444–488. Joseph J. Malone, *Pine Trees and Politics: The Naval Stores and Forest Policy in Colonial New England, 1691–1775* (University of Washington Press, Seattle, 1965) also concerns the early period.

The United States Forest Service and the National Forests it administers are the subject of Darrell H. Smith, *The Forest Service: Its History, Activities, and Organization* (The Brookings Institution, Washington, D.C., 1930), Michael Frome, *Whose Woods These Are: The Story of the National Forests* (Doubleday, Garden City, N.Y., 1962), Arthur H. Carhart, *The National Forests* (Knopf, New York, 1959), Bernard Frank, *Our National Forests* (University of Oklahoma Press, Norman, Okla., 1955), and Charles D. Smith, "The Movement for Eastern National Forests, 1899–1911" (unpublished Ph.D. dissertation, Harvard University, 1956). Ashley L. Schiff, *Fire and Water: Scientific Heresey in the Forest Service* (Harvard University Press, Cambridge, Mass., 1962) reviews an important controversy over the management of woodlands. William B. Greeley, Chief of the Forest Service from 1920 to 1928 and thereafter a leading figure in the lumber industry, has written *Forests and Men* (Doubleday, Garden City, N.Y., 1951) and *Forest Policy* (McGraw-Hill, New York, 1953), both of which contain substantial historical information. The Forest Service's *Highlights in the History of Forest Conservation*, Agricultural Informaton Bulletin 83 (U.S. Government Printing Office, Washington, D.C., 1948) is a useful chronology.

The most valuable recent accounts are Robert K. Winters, ed., *Fifty Years of Forestry in the United States of America* (Society of American Foresters, Washington, D.C., 1950), Samuel T. Dana, *Forest and Range Policy: Its Development in the United States* (McGraw-Hill, New York, 1956), and Henry Clepper and Arthur B. Meyer, eds., *American Forestry: Six Decades of Growth* (Society cf American Foresters, Washington, D.C., 1960). Clepper has underway a comprehensive history of North American forestry sponsored by Resources for the Future and the Forest History Society.

The development of private interest in forest conservation is discussed in Paul F. Sharp, "The Tree Farm Movement: Its Origins and Development," *Agricultural History*, 23 (1949), 41–45, Carl Alwin Schenck, *The Biltmore Story: Recollections of the Beginnings of Forestry in the United States*, ed. Ovid Butler (American Forest History Foundation, St. Paul, Minn., 1955), and Ralph W. Hidy, Frank Ernest Hill and Allan Nevins, *Timber and Men: The Weyerhauser Story* (Macmillan, New York, 1963). The Forest History Society's journal *Forest History* frequently contains articles on this subject.

Lawrence Rakestraw, "A History of Forest Conservation in the Pacific Northwest" (unpublished Ph.D. dissertation, University of Washington, 1955) is a model regional history. Agnes Larson, *The History of the White Pine Industry in Minnesota* (University of Minnesota Press, Minneapolis, 1949) also concerns a limited geographical area.

The pioneering study of water management is George Wharton James, *Reclaiming the Arid West: The Story of the United States Reclamation Service* (Dodd, Mead, New York, 1917). Jerome G. Kerwin's *Federal Water Power Legislation* (Columbia University Press, New York, 1926) is an amplification. Leahmae Brown, "The Development of National Policy with Respect to Water Resources" (unpublished Ph.D. dissertation, University of Illinois, 1937), Harold Kelso, "Inland Waterways Policy in the United States" (unpublished Ph.D. dissertation, University of Wisconsin, 1942), John T. Ganoe, "The Origin of a National Reclamation Policy," *Mississippi Valley Historical Review*, 18 (1931), 34–52, and Ganoe, "The Beginnings of Irrigation in the United States," *Mississippi Valley Historical Review*, 25 (1938), 59–78, are useful general histories. In addition, Bernard Frank and Anthony Netboy, *Water, Land, and People* (Knopf, New York, 1950) and Roy E. Huffman, *Irrigation Development and Public Water Policy* (Ronald Press, New York, 1953) contain some historical chapters.

The history of the management of the nation's major river system is told in Arthur DeWitt Frank, *The Development of the Federal Program of Flood Control on the Mississippi River* (Columbia University Press, New York, 1930) and Henry C. Hart, *The Dark Missouri* (University of Wisconsin Press, Madison, Wis., 1957). New England's interest in water conservation is partially documented in William E. Luechtenburg, *Flood Control Politics: The Connecticut River Valley Problem, 1927–1950* (Harvard University Press, Cambridge, Mass., 1953) while the California story is told in Sidney T. Harding, *Water in California* (N-P Publications, Palo Alto, 1960). Murray C. Morgan, *The Columbia: Powerhouse of the West* (Superior, Seattle, 1949) and George Sundborg, *Hail Columbia: The Thirty-Year Struggle for Grand Coulee Dam* (Macmillan, New York, 1954) discuss a key development in the Pacific Northwest.

Arthur Maass, *Muddy Waters: The Army Engineers and the Nation's Rivers* (Harvard University Press, Cambridge, Mass., 1951) deals with an organization that has exerted a major impact on parts of the American environment.

The history of soil conservation in the United States is ably presented in R. Burnell Held and Marion Clawson, *Soil Conservation in Perspective* (Johns Hopkins Press, Baltimore, 1965). Angus McDonald, *Early American Soil Conservationists* (Government Printing Office, Washington, D.C., 1941), portions of Graham V. Jacks and Robert O. Whyte, *Vanishing Lands: A World Survey of Soil Erosion* (Doubleday, Doran, New York, 1939), and Robert J. Morgan, *Governing Soil Conservation: Thirty Years of the New Decentralization* (Johns Hopkins Press, Baltimore, 1966) are supplemental. The related subject of range and grassland management is covered in Paul W. Gates, "American Land Policy and the Taylor Grazing Act," *Land Policy Circular*, n.v. (Oct., 1935), 15–37, and Phillip O. Foss, *Politics and Grass: The Administration of Grazing on the Public Domain* (University of Washington Press, Seattle, 1960). Dana's *Forest and Range Policy* (above) is also relevant here.

Mining has often had a profound effect on the appearance of the landscape. Thomas A. Rickard, *History of American Mining* (McGraw-Hill, New York, 1932) should be supplemented with A. B. Parsons, ed., *Seventy-Five Years Progress in the Mineral Industry, 1871–1946* (American Institute of Mining and Metallurgical Engineers, New York, 1947). Waste and conservation in the oil industry is the subject of John Ise, *The United States Oil Policy* (Yale University Press, New Haven, 1926), Stuart E. Buckley, ed., *Petroleum Conservation* (American Institute of Mining and Metallurgical Engineers, New York, 1951), J. Stanley Clark, *The Oil Century: From Drake Well to the Conservation Era* (University of Oklahoma Press, Norman, Okla., 1958), and Erich W. Zimmermann, *Conservation in the Production of Petroleum: A Study in Industrial Control* (Yale University Press, New Haven, 1957). Robert E. Hardwicke, "Anti-Trust Laws and the Conservation of Oil and Gas," *Tulane Law Review*, **23** (1957), 183–208, and J. Leonard Bates, "The Midwest Decision, 1915: A Landmark in Conservation History," *Pacific Northwest Quarterly*, **51** (1960), 26–34, concern two important aspects of oil conservation.

The best source of historical information on the wildlife conservation movement is James B. Trefethen, *Crusade for Wildlife: Highlights in Conservation Progress* (Stackpole, Harrisburg, Pa., 1961). T. S. Palmer, *Chronology and Index of the More Important Events in American Game Protection, 1776–1911*, Biological Survey Bulletin, 41 (Government Printing Office, Washington, D.C., 1912) is a useful listing. Edward H. Graham, *The Land and Wildlife* (Oxford University Press, New York, 1947) also pays some attention ot the history of game laws while Albert M. Day, *North American Waterfowl* (Stackpole, Harrisburg, Pa., 1949) focuses on an important wildlife resource. William S. Haskell, *The American Game Protective and Propagation Association: A History* (privately published, New York, 1937) and Carl D. Shoemaker, *The Stories Behind the Organization of the National Wildlife Federation* (National Wildlife Federation, Washington, D.C., 1960) describe the beginnings of two key organizations. Robert Henry Welker, *Birds and Men: American Birds in Science, Art, Literature and Conservation* (Harvard University Press, Cambridge, Mass., 1955) is unique and valuable.

Among American fishes, the salmon has received the bulk of scholarly attention: Richard A. Cooley, *Politics and Conservation: The Decline of the Alaska Salmon* (Harper and Row, New York, 1963), Anthony Netboy, *Salmon of the Pacific Northwest—Fish vs. Dams* (Binfords & Mort, Portland, Ore., 1958), and Gordon B. Dodds, "Artificial Propagation of Salmon in Oregon, 1875–1910: A Chapter in American Conservation," *Pacific Northwest Quarterly*, **50** (1959), 125–33, tell the story. Paul S. Galtsoff, *The Story of the Bureau of Commercial Fisheries* (U.S. Department of the Interior, Washington, D.C., 1962) takes a broader view.

The park movement in the United States has not been neglected by historians. John Ise's *Our National Park Policy: A Critical History* (Johns Hopkins Press, Baltimore, 1961) has replaced Jenks Cameron, *The National Park Service: Its History, Activities and Organization* (Appleton, New York, 1922) and Paul Herman Buck, "The Evolution of the National Park System in the United States" (unpublished M.A. thesis, Ohio State University, 1922). The study of national parks Noel D. Eichhorn has in progress under the auspices of the Conservation Foundation promises to be important. Donald C. Swain, "The Passage of the National Park Service Act of 1916," *Wisconsin Magazine of History*, **50** (1966), 4–17, is a detailed reconstruction of a significant event. There should be more studies of individual parks such as Douglas Hillman Strong's "A History of Sequoia National Park" (unpublished Ph.D. dissertation, Syracuse University, 1964), parts of which have been published as "The Sierra Forest Reserve: The Movement to Preserve the San Joaquin Valley Watershed," *California Historical Society Quarterly*, **46** (1967), 3–17. Arthur D. Martinson, "Mountain in the Sky: A History of Mount Ranier National Park" (unpublished Ph.D. dissertation, Washington State University, 1966), Roger C. Thompson, "The Doctrine of Wilderness: A Study of the Policy and Politics of the Adirondack

Preserve-Park" (unpublished Ph.D. dissertation, Syracuse University, 1961), and Charles Dennis Smith, "The Appalachian National Park Movement, 1885–1901," *North Carolina Historical Review,* 37 (1960), 38–65, also concern specific areas.

The important histories of Yosemite and Yellowstone National Parks are presented in Hans Huth, "Yosemite: The Story of an Idea," *Sierra Club Bulletin,* 33 (1948); 47–78, Holway R. Jones, *John Muir and the Sierra Club: The Battle for Yosemite* (Sierra Club, San Francisco, 1965); Carl P. Russell, *One Hundred Years in Yosemite: The Story of a Great Park and Its Friends* (University of California Press, Berkeley, 1947); Hiram M. Chittenden, *The Yellowstone National Park* (Stewart & Kidd, Cincinnati, 1915); Merrill D. Beal, *The Story of Man in Yellowstone* (Caxton, Caldwell, Idaho, 1946); W. Turrentine Jackson, "The Creation of Yellowstone National Park," *Mississippi Valley Historical Review,* 29 (1942), 188–189; and Louis C. Cramton, *Early History of Yellowstone National Park and Its Relation to National Park Policies* (Government Printing Office, Washington, D.C., 1932).

Freeman Tilden, *State Parks* (Knopf, New York, 1962) and C. Frank Brockman, *Recreational Use of Wild Lands* (McGraw-Hill, New York, 1959) contain some historical data.

Nash, *Wilderness and the American Mind* (above) places the wilderness preservation movement in the context of the history of ideas. His footnotes and bibliography lead to additional pertinent literature. The preservation of historical features of the environment is the subject of Charles B. Hosmer, *Presence of the Past: A History of the Preservation Movement in the United States Before Williamsburg* (Putnam, New York, 1965).

INDIVIDUALS

Biographies of Americans who figured prominently in the conservation movement offer still another approach to historical understanding. Excellent works exist on many of the men who first alerted the nation to its responsibilities with regard to the environment: Harold McCracken, *George Catlin and the Old Frontier* (Dial, New York, 1959); Lloyd Haberly, *Pursuit of the Horizon, A Life of George Catlin* (Macmillan, New York, 1948); Kenneth James LaBudde, "The Mind of Thomas Cole" (unpublished Ph.D. dissertation, University of Minnesota, 1954); David C. Huntington, *The Landscapes of Frederic Edwin Church* (Braziller, New York, 1966); Thurman Wilkins, *Thomas Moran: Artist of the Mountains* (University of Oklahoma Press, Norman, Okla., 1966); David Lowenthal, *George Perkins Marsh: Versatile Vermonter* (Columbia University Press, New York, 1958); Wallace Stegner, *Beyond the Hundredth Meridian: John Wesley Powell and the Second Opening of the West* (Houghton Mifflin, Boston, 1954); William Culp Darrah, *Powell of the Colorado* (Princeton University Press, Princeton, 1954); Linnie Marsh Wolfe, *Son of the Wilderness: The Life of John Muir*

(Knopf, New York, 1945); Edith Jane Hadley, "John Muir's Views of Nature and their Consequences" (unpublished Ph.D. dissertation, University of Wisconsin, 1956); Daniel Barr Weber, "John Muir: The Function of Wilderness in an Industrial Society" (unpublished Ph.D. dissertation, University of Minnesota, 1964); Andrew Denny Rodgers, *Bernhard Eduard Fernow: A Story of North American Forestry* (Princeton University Press, Princeton, 1951); Diane Kostial McGuire, "Frederick Law Olmsted in California: An Analysis of His Contributions to Landscape Architecture and City Planning" (unpublished M.A. thesis, University of California, Berkeley, 1956); Graham Hawks, "Increase A. Lapham, Wisconsin's First Scientist" (unpublished Ph.D. dissertation, University of Wisconsin, 1960). Sherman Paul, *The Shores of America: Thoreau's Inward Exploration* (University of Illinois Press, Urbana, Ill., 1959) is the best of many books on Thoreau for understanding his attitude toward nature.

The lives and thoughts of conservationists in the Progressive era have received attention in M. Nelson McGeary, *Gifford Pinchot: Forester-Politician* (Princeton University Press, Princeton, 1960); Martin L. Fausold, *Gifford Pinchot, Bull Moose Progressive* (Syracuse University Press, Syracuse, 1961); Harold T. Pinkett's dissertation (above); William Lilley, "The Early Career of Francis G. Newlands, 1893–1917" (unpublished Ph.D. dissertation, Yale University, 1966); Keith W. Olson, "Franklin K. Lane: A Biography" (unpublished Ph.D. dissertation, University of Wisconsin, 1964); Whitney R. Cross, "WJ McGee and the Idea of Conservation," *Historian*, 15 (1953), 148–162; Robert Woodbury, "William Kent: Progressive Gadfly, 1864–1928" (unpublished Ph.D. dissertation, Yale University, 1967); and Andrew Denny Rodgers, *Liberty Hyde Bailey: A Story of American Plant Sciences* (Princeton University Press, Princeton, 1949). The best discussion of Theodore Roosevelt's attitude toward the land is Paul Russell Cutright, *Theodore Roosevelt, the Naturalist* (Harper, New York, 1956). Also important is Whitney R. Cross, "Ideas in Politics: The Conservation Policies of the Two Roosevelts," *Journal of the History of Ideas*, 14 (1953), 421–438.

Of the conservationists active since the Progressive era, George W. Norris has been the subject of the most studies. Norman Zucker, *George W. Norris* (University of Illinois Press, Urbana, Ill., 1966) and Johnny Booth Smallwood, "George W. Norris and the Concept of a Planned Region" (unpublished Ph.D. dissertation, University of North Carolina, 1964) will soon be joined by the volumes of Richard Lowitt's biographical study which concern Norris' involvement in water management and regional planning. Also relevant for the recent period are George T. Morgan, Jr., *William B. Greeley, a Practical Forester, 1879–1955* (Forest History Society, St. Paul, Minn., 1961); Robert Shankland, *Steve Mather of the National Parks* (2nd rev. ed., Knopf, New York, 1954); Wellington Brink, *Big Hugh: The Father of Soil Conservation* (Macmillan, New York, 1951) concerning Hugh Hammond Bennett; Nancy Newhall, ed., *A Contribution to the Heritage of Every American: The Conservation Activities of John D. Rockefeller Jr.* (Knopf, New York, 1957); Roderick Nash, "The Strenuous Life of Bob Marshall," *Forest History*, **10** (1966), 18–25; and Nash's "The Wisdom of Aldo Leopold," *Wisconsin Academy Review*, **8** (1961), 161–167. In progress are biographies of Horace M. Albright by Donald C. Swain, Aldo Leopold by Susan Flader, and Hiram Martin Chittenden by Gordon B. Dodds.

ADDITIONS TO A SELECTED BIBLIOGRAPHY

The publications that follow have appeared since the first edition of the present work in 1968 or, in honesty, were unwisely omitted from the first edition.

There are several bibliographies of value to the historians of conservation. Gordon B. Dodds, "The Historiography of American Conservation: Past and Prospects," *Pacific Northwest Quarterly*, 56 (1965), 75–81, mentions many important works and points to omissions in the coverage of the field. Thomas Le Duc, "Historiography of Conservation," *Forest History*, 9 (1965), 23–28, is less comprehensive. A more recent review is Lawrence Rakestraw, "Conservation Historiography: An Assessment," *Pacific Historical Review*, 41 (1972), 271–288.

A number of excellent monographic works have recently come to the aid of the historian of the American environment. Paul Shepard has two titles. *Man in the Landscape: A Historic View of the Esthetics of Nature* (Knopf, New York, 1967) ranges far afield in its treatment but contains substantial American material. Shepard's *The Tender Carnivore and the Sacred Game* (Scribner's, New York, 1973) also transcends the American experience; its subject, however, is pertinent to any historical study of the human interface with the natural world.

Donald W. Whisenhunt, *The Environment and the American Experience: A Historian Looks at the Ecological Crisis* (Kennikat, Port Washington, N.Y., 1974) is cursory but as much in this bibliography's mainstream of concern as any other title. Whisenhunt treats ideas, religion, economics, politics, and demography with a view to showing how "revolutions" in each field led to the questionings of the environmental movement of the 1960s. Also comprehensive and oriented toward contemporary concerns is Roderick Nash's *The American Conservation Movement* (Forum, Press, St. Charles, Mo., 1974). Other wide-ranging treatments may be found in Nicholas Roosevelt, *Conservation: Now or Never* (Dodd, Mead, New York, 1970) and Frank Graham, Jr., *Man's Dominion: The Story of Conservation in America* (Lippincott, New York, 1971).

More focused, in this case on early Americans, is Peter N. Carroll, *Puritanism and the Wilderness: The Intellectual Significance of the New*

England Frontier, 1629–1700 (Columbia, New York, 1969). In *Back to Nature: The Arcadian Myth in Urban America* (Oxford, New York, 1969) Peter J. Schmitt analyzes the environmental attitudes of Americans from the 1890s to the 1920s. Schmitt's use of unusual source material from popular culture lends exceptional value to his account. In the tradition of works previously listed by Samuel P. Hays (for the Progressive period), Donald Swain (for the 1920s) and Anna Lou Riesch (for the Franklin Roosevelt years) is Elmo Richardson, *Dams, Parks, and Politics: Resource Development and Preservation in the Truman-Eisenhower Era* (University of Kentucky, Lexington, Ky., 1973). The advent of the United States Forest Service's interest in wilderness preservation is well treated in Donald N. Baldwin, *The Quiet Revolution: Grass Roots of Today's Wilderness Movement* (Pruett, Boulder, Col., 1972). Michael Frome's *Battle for the Wilderness* (Praeger, New York, 1974) is concerned with recent statements of the meaning of wilderness and with wilderness policy. Frome has a new account of an important bureau, *The Forest Service* (Praeger, New York, 1971), while William C. Everhart has written *The National Park Service* (Praeger, New York, 1972).

Among the important recent biographical studies several stand out. Douglas H. Strong, *The Conservationists* (Addison-Wesley, Menlo Park, Calif., 1971) contains short sketches of leading figures from George Perkins Marsh to Stewart Udall. Mention should also be made of Strong's article "The Rise of American Esthetic Conservation: Muir, Mather, and Udall," *National Parks Magazine*, 44 (1970), 5–9. Donald C. Swain's *Wilderness Defender: Horace M. Albright and Conservation* (Univ. of Chicago, Chicago, 1970) goes far beyond the man to an interpretation of major trends of the times. Along with Robert Shankland's study of Stephen T. Mather, previously cited, Swain's *Albright* is mandatory for an understanding of early national park history. Susan L. Flader has published a volume on the origins of Aldo Leopold's ecological ideas entitled *Thinking Like a Mountain: Aldo Leopold and the Evolution of an Ecological Attitude Toward Deer, Wolves, and Forests* (University of Missouri, Columbia, 1974). The book is narrower in scope than the full life-and-times that Leopold deserves and that Flader promises.

Good secondary treatments are understandably rarer for the recent period. Donald Fleming's book-length article "Roots of the New Conservation Movement," *Perspectives in American History*, 6 (1972), 7–91, is a seminal study. The best of several accounts of the 1969 oil spill off Santa Barbara, California is Robert Easton, *Black Tide* (Delacorte, New York, 1972). An interesting sociological approach to the environmental movement of the 1960s may be found in James McEvoy III, "The American Concern with Environment" in William R. Burch, Jr., Neil H. Cheek, Jr., and Lee Taylor, eds., *Social Behavior, Natural Resources, and the Environment* (Harper & Row, New York, 1972), pp. 214–236. Roderick Nash's revised edition of *Wilderness and the American Mind* (Yale University Press, New Haven, Conn., 1973) extends coverage from 1966. The pesticides controversy, which Rachael Carson's book launched in 1962, is traced to the end of the decade in Frank Graham, Jr., *Since Silent Spring* (Houghton Mifflin, Boston, 1970). Richard A. Cooley and Geoffrey Wandesforde-Smith, eds., *Congress and the Environment* (University of Washington, Seattle, 1970) is a collection of essays on many of the important environmental issues of the 1960s.

Collections of documents, with an interpretive framework provided by the editor, are valuable to the environmental historian. John Opie, ed., *Americans and Environment: The Controversy over Ecology* (D.C. Heath, Lexington, Ky., 1971) is a good example of this kind of work. Another is Roderick Nash, ed., *Environment and Americans: The Problem of Priorities* (Holt, Rinehart and Winston, New York, 1972). The collection of essays entitled *Environmental Decay in Its Historical Context* (Scott Foresman, Glenview, Ill., 1973) edited by Robert Detweiler, Jon N. Sutherland, and Michael S. Werthman has a world perspective but includes American material. Duke Frederick, William L. Howenstine, and June Sochen, eds., *Destroy to Create: Interaction with the Natural Environment in the Building of America* (Dryden, Hinsdale, Ill., 1972) is focused on the United States. The heavy stream of "environment" and "ecology" readings books issuing from presses in recent years is not of direct concern in this historically oriented listing. But among the many titles Carroll Pursell, ed., *From Conservation to Ecology* (Crowell, New York, 1973) deserves attention for its historical approach.

Donald Worster has brought the readings book approach to bear on a limited time span in *American Environmentalism: The Formative Period, 1860–1915* (Wiley, New York, 1973). The volume collects crucial but comparatively little-known statements by philosophers of man-nature relationships. Still more unusual in the kind of little-known documents it presents is Barbara Gutmann Rosenkrantz and William A. Koelsch, eds., *American Habitat: A Historical Perspective* (Free Press, New York, 1973). Chapter-length introductions interpret the primary and secondary statements. Ian G. Barbour, ed., *Western Man and Environmental Ethics* (Addison-Wesley, Reading, Mass., 1973) brings together secondary statements of great value in understanding American attitudes.

Two new massive collections of documents concern American environmental history: Robert McHenry, ed., *A Documentary History of Conservation in America* (Praeger, New York, 1972) and Frank Smith, ed., *Conservation in the United States: A Documentary History* (5 vols., Chelsea House, New York, 1971). Most of the selections in these volumes are primary sources, some of them quite rare. Their collection by the editors is fortunate for scholars in the field who will, however, have to supply most of their own interpretations.